THE NEURO-IMAGE

Cultural Memory
in
the
Present

Mieke Bal and Hent de Vries, Editors

THE NEURO-IMAGE

*A Deleuzian Film-Philosophy
of Digital Screen Culture*

Patricia Pisters

STANFORD UNIVERSITY PRESS

STANFORD, CALIFORNIA

Stanford University Press
Stanford, California

This publication was supported by the Internationales Kolleg für Kulturtechnikforschung und Medienphilosophie of the Bauhaus-Universität Weimar with funds from the German Federal Ministry of Education and Research. IKKM BOOKS. Volume 9. An overview of the whole series can be found at www.ikkm-weimar.de/schriften.

Printed in the United States of America on acid-free, archival-quality paper

Library of Congress Cataloging-in-Publication Data

Pisters, Patricia, author.
  The neuro-image : a Deleuzian film-philosophy of digital screen culture / Patricia Pisters.
  pages cm. — (Cultural memory in the present)
  Includes bibliographical references and index.
  ISBN 978-0-8047-8135-0 (cloth : alk. paper)
  ISBN 978-0-8047-8136-7 (pbk : alk. paper)
    1. Motion pictures—Psychological aspects. 2. Motion pictures—Philosophy
  3. Motion pictures—History—21st century. 4. Digital media—Psychological aspects. 5. Digital media—Philosophy. 6. Neurosciences and motion pictures.
  7. Deleuze, Gilles, 1925–1995. I. Title. II. Series: Cultural memory in the present.
  PN1995.P534 2012
  791.4301—dc23

                                                              2011045585

Contents

Acknowledgments

Without the invitation of the Internationales Kolleg für Kulturtech-nikforschung und Medienphilosophie (IKKM) to come to Germany for a research fellowship, I would not have been able to write this book. I would like to express my deep gratitude to Lorenz Engell and Bernhard Siegert for having given me the opportunity to work in the calm and inspiring surroundings of Weimar and the Bauhaus University. The generosity and academic trust on the basis of which IKKM operates was invaluable. My thanks go also to IKKM's staff members, who always assisted whenever necessary. In presenting parts of the work during lectures and seminars, I have benefited greatly from the questions of and conversations with my cofellows David Rodowick, Erich Hörl, Tom Gunning, and especially Eric Alliez. It goes without saying that the shortcomings in this book are entirely mine, but the critical and engaged readings of others have helped me shape and sharpen my thoughts. Therefore, I sincerely thank James Williams, who had the generosity to read and comment on early versions of the chapters. I'm also much obliged to Stephen Zepke, John Protevi, Aluizio Cruz, Quelita Moreno, Julia Noordegraaf, Gregg Lambert, Paul Patton, and Steven Shaviro, who gave valuable advice on (parts of) the manuscript. Rachel O'Reilly and Tim Yaczo have offered much-appreci-ated editorial assistance. The preparation of this book is also connected to the organization of the International Deleuze Studies Conference in Amsterdam during the summer of 2010. This conference could not have been realized without the tremendous commitment of Maryn Wilkinson, Daisy van de Zande, Flora Lysen, Amir Vodka, Eloe Kingma, and many students and volunteers. Working with Rosi Braidotti was and is a continuing pleasure. In connection to the summer camp that preceded the conference, I would also like to thank Ian Buchanan, Gregory Flaxman, Elena del Rio, Eleanor Kaufman, Joshua Ramey, and all participants who made it an inspiring event. Others have helped this book with feedback and friendship over the years. Many thanks to Laura Marks, Felicity Colman, Nir Kedem, Patricia MacCormack, Amy Herzog, Wanda Strauven, Sudeep Dasupta, Kaouthar Darmoni, and David Martin-Jones. I am also grateful to Emily-Jane Cohen at Stanford University Press for her patience with my persistence, to Tim Roberts and Joe Abbott for their editorial advice, and to Mieke Bal for her support at crucial moments. I would like to acknowledge my colleagues at the Department of Media Studies at the University of Amsterdam for fostering a creative and stimulating environment. The continuing growth of the department presents many challenges, but to be part of such a dynamic and inspiring group of scholars in a rapidly changing and evolving field remains a true pleasure. Jobien Kuiper, Doetsje de Groot, and Jaap Kooijman make managing in turbulent times much easier. José van Dijck and Frank van Vree are always supportive, with wise and insightful advice. It is impossible to mention all staff members, but I feel privileged to work with each and every one, as well as with my students, PhD students and the members of the film-philosophy seminar I co-organize with Josef Früchtl and Christoph Lindner. When I first ventured into the field of neuroscience, the positive responses of Raymond van Ee and Frans Verstraten were of great importance. I want to thank my friends and family for their companionship and sharing of both tough and cheerful times. Without my mother, who always helps whenever needed, this book would have taken much longer to write. Last, but not least, I am greatly thankful to Gertjan for his enduring love and support, and to Rocco for having had the courage to come to Weimar with me, learn English, and begin his own international adventure. Although "the neuro-image" is based on a concept of the future, I have written this book in memory of my father and his great love for science fiction.

Introduction

SCHIZOANALYSIS, DIGITAL SCREENS, AND NEW
BRAIN CIRCUITS

The film *Michael Clayton* (Tony Gilroy, 2007) opens with a delirious monologue.[1] We see first the lights, windows, and screens of New
York City by night; then the camera moves slowly to an inside view of
one of many office buildings, as a voice, later identified as Arthur Edens
(Tom Wilkinson), speaks of a moment of clarity he experienced while ex-
iting the "vast and powerful law firm" for which he works. "The time is
now," he stutters, signaling his having "been reborn" away from his career at the firm, which "excrete[s] poison" into humanity. He has been de-
fending a company called U/North from a three billion dollar class action
lawsuit for biopollution. During a meeting with the victims of U/North,
Edens snaps. His encounter with one particular young female victim,
Anna (Merritt Wever), who lost her parents to U/North soil pollution,
flicks a kind of synaptic switch in his mind. His ordinary way of thinking—in support of the multinationals he is supposed to defend—abruptly
changes, and he begins to see things anew. He stops taking his medication
for manic depression, and his own mad revolution against his habituated
behavior is finally enabled to foment. As a protest on behalf of the victims
whose claims he is supposed to ignore, he undresses in the middle of a U/
North hearing, embarrassing both his own firm and U/North. His friend
Michael Clayton (George Clooney), who is the law firm's fixer, is called in

to talk Edens back into medication and normative professional behavior. Edens refuses. In a key scene in the middle of the film we see Edens in the center of a New York City street, traffic assaulting him from all sides and, more important, hundreds of city screens surrounding him, with ads for "TV on your phone" and food technology for U/North. While the camera circles Edens, showing the vortical stream of images, lights, and sounds that surround him, he remains frozen. In the midst of all this insanity we watch as Edens realizes something in this moment (flagged by the opening monologue): that the time (to change) is now.

Arthur Edens, delirious and intelligent, caught up in the vortex of the contemporary urban cityscape full of networked electronic and digital screens—screens that are themselves always already connected to assemblages of power, capital, and transnational movements of peoples, goods, and information—is a typical character in a new type of cinema belonging to twenty-first-century globalized screen culture that I want to explore in this book and that I will describe as "the neuro-image." For several reasons the film *Michael Clayton* brings us to the heart of what this book is about. Edens's insanity points to the first aspect of the neuro-image that I want to take into account: it carries inside it some form of schizoanalysis or collective analytics and is therefore particularly indebted to the work of Gilles Deleuze and Félix Guattari on capitalism and schizophrenia.[2] Many of the questions that I address in this book pertain to the schizo-analytic nature of the neuro-image: What does this image type entail? How does schizoanalysis, as defined by Deleuze and Guattari, relate to pathological schizophrenia and screen culture? What are its (cultural) symptoms? What are its philosophical dimensions and its political and ethical implications?

A second important aspect of the neuro-image we find in *Michael Clayton* is the omnipresence of media screens. Not only is this scene showing Edens in the streets of New York quite typical for contemporary screen culture, but throughout the film, small and large screens appear everywhere: navigation displays, computer screens, cell phones, television sets, urban screens, and surveillance technology; they are the markers of both a typical twenty-first-century media city and the practices of everyday media use.[3] The neuro-image is part of this networked media practice, related to digital technology's ubiquity, and engages with these technologies in "an internal struggle with informatics."[4] This struggle, according to Deleuze, is fundamental to cinema's very survival as a "will to art": "An original will to art has already been defined by us in the change affecting the intelligible content of cinema itself: the substitution of the time-image for the movement-image. So that electronic images will have to be based on still another will to art, or on as yet unknown aspects of the time-image."[5] This book will make sense of the neuro-image's relation to the digital, through reference to current debates and research in contemporary screen culture. Indeed, (how) does the neuro-image relate to a "will to art" in the context of this electronic image culture, especially of contemporary information overload? Might it lead us to discover as-yet-unknown aspects of the time-image? If so, is the neuro-image a special type of time-image, or should we speak of a third image type? A return to Deleuze's cinema books but also to *Difference and Repetition* will be necessary to propose some answers to these questions.[6]

In *Michael Clayton* Arthur Edens's madness is repeatedly (but partially) referred to in terms of a chemical unbalance in his neurological system. "Part of it is chemical, part of it is insanity, but for part of it you are also right," Clayton tells him. This insistence on brain processes introduces a third important aspect of the neuro-image. Deleuze has famously argued with regard to the ongoing development of cinema that "the brain is the screen":

The brain is unity. The brain is the screen. I don't believe that linguistics and psychoanalysis offer a great deal to the cinema. On the contrary, the biology of the brain—molecular biology—does. Thought is molecular. Molecular speeds make up the slow beings that we are. . . . The circuits and linkages of the brain don't pre-exist the stimuli, corpuscles and particles that trace them. . . . Cinema, precisely because it puts the image in motion, or rather endows the image with self-motion, never stops tracing the circuits of the brain.[7]

If the movement-image and the time-image are related to certain circuits in the brain, is it then possible to distinguish yet other aspects of the brain-screen that are typical for the neuro-image? To answer this question, I will consider biological aspects and principles of the brain alongside recent findings in neuroscience and relate these to the emerged features of the neuro-image. Deleuzian (schizoanalytic) philosophy, cinema in digital networked screen culture, and neuroscientific findings are thus the three domains this book brings together to comprehend this new image type, its form, and significance.

Schizoanalysis: Delirious Insights, Illusionary Realities, Affective Truths

As Arthur Edens insists in *Michael Clayton*, it is important to see his delirium not as "just madness." Rather, Edens's symptoms, and schizophrenia more generally, can be considered as a sign of time. In his introduction to Deleuze's *Essays Critical and Clinical*, Daniel Smith explains: "Authors and artists, like doctors and clinicians, can themselves be seen as profound symptomatologists, . . . 'physicians of culture' for whom phenomena are signs or symptoms that reflect a certain state of forces."[8] Smith articulates several themes in Deleuze's writings on literature that are important for understanding the ways in which schizoanalysis relates the "clinical" and the "critical"[9]—through the destruction of the world (singularities and events), the dissolution of the subject (affects and percepts), the disintegration of the body (intensities and becomings), the "minoritization" of politics (speech acts and fabulation), and the stuttering of language (syntax and style). Without going into Smith's brilliant level of detail on each, I would like to consider these "themes" as accordant with schizoanalytical powers. Insofar as they relate to general contours of the neuro-image,[10] they mark out a Deleuzian symptomatology that I will develop in detail in each chapter, in relation to contemporary media culture and neurobiology. At this point I will return to *Michael Clayton* and Arthur Edens's monologue to briefly introduce certain characteristics of these powers of schizoanalysis.

First of all, the fundamental delirious character of Edens's opening monologue is most powerfully expressed in his intense description of becoming-other: from reborn, to near-dead, to emerging from the "asshole of a powerful organism," he creates a body without organs that resists and refuses the normal organization of his corporate body, and all of the institutionalized power structures that it involves. It is as if inorganic life traverses his body, turning the architecture of his corporation into a body and his own body into something inorganic. Smith explains that "according to Deleuze and Guattari, what we call a 'delirium' is the general matrix by which the intensities and becomings of the body without organs directly invest the sociopolitical field."[11] So this power of the delirium is not just the product of the mad but also a particular form of resistance (to ways of life) in reality, as well as in art. Arthur Edens, in his delirious perception, all of a sudden sees the "madness" of contemporary capitalist culture and refuses to continue playing this infernal game that relies on the cynical abuse of human and natural resources. The film quite literally asks us to consider Deleuze's rhetorical question regarding cinema's situation: "Surely a true cinema can contribute to giving us back reasons to believe in the world and in vanished bodies. The price to be paid, in cinema as elsewhere, was always a confrontation with madness."[12]

So the first power of schizoanalysis inherent to the neuro-image is the power of the delirium, a dangerous, intense, and resisting force of schizoflows and overabundance. It must be noted, too, that the devilish difficulty we have with these schizoforms of resistance is to see that they are an immanent form of resistance, which means that the system against which such forms struggle functions according to the same schizophrenic logic. Capitalism and schizophrenia, as Deleuze and Guattari have shown so powerfully, belong together. Capitalism follows a schizophrenic logic that at the same time calls forth its own resistance. The delirium of the schizo gives us insight into this double logic of contemporary culture: Edens is part of the maddening system; only in confronting his madness can he resist the inhuman madness of the system. In his schizoid delirium he gains sense of a minority position—in this case that of the victims of U/North—and in this way tries to tell a different story, one that potentially shatters the majoritarian forces of capitalism. More generally put, the neuro-image acknowledges that there is no safe or morally transcendental position from which we can resist. Instead, we discover the need to develop multiple forms of resistance from within the system, while always running the risk of being even more fully captured or overwhelmed by its logic.

The schizophrenic confrontation with madness can be related to two important "schizophrenic symptoms" that contemporary culture must confront more than ever before: the powers of the false and the powers of affect. These are the second and third powers of schizoanalysis at stake in the neuro-image. In the cinema books Deleuze discusses the powers of the false with respect to the Nietzschean cinema of Orson Welles. As Welles's characters show, the false can be "base" and deadly, but it can also be "noble" and creative.[13] In *Michael Clayton* the powers of the false play out in different ways. Clayton's job is to "adjust the truth" (one of the taglines of the film). He has to make sure that rich clients who run into trouble, such as U/North, get away with the damage they have done in the least disabling way. Clayton has to put the manipulating powers of the false to work in favor of the capitalist machine. The powers of the false play quite a different role when Edens apparently hallucinates in his delirium, but these hallucinations, the film suggests, are more real than what Edens formerly took for reality. Through them, Edens is able to really see how the corporate system works against humanity. Here, then, the powers of the false (as hallucinations on Edens's brain-screen) work against the system. I will argue that contemporary culture has moved from considering images as "illusions of reality" to considering them as "realities of illusions" that operate directly on our brains and therefore as real agents in the world. While recognizing the truth of his corporate life in his hallucinations, Edens also very strongly believes in the affirmative powers of this apparent fiction. Differently again, the powers of the false play out in Michael Clayton's son Henry's (Austin Williams) obsession with the multiplayer game *Realm and Conquest*. As a contemporary transmedial narrative (a characteristic form of digital screen culture, as we will see), this game appears in the film itself on computer screens, in Henry's stories, and in a book that Edens reads avidly—underlining, highlighting, and taking important clues from it as he attempts to prove that his hallucinatory visions are real. Here, the powers of the false become more generally defined as a belief in fiction, an aspect of the neuro-image that I will explore in greater detail in Chapter 2.

The power of affect is equally important, relating to a radical rephrasing of the question of the subject in Deleuze and in contemporary culture. Edens is engulfed with overwhelming sensations and suddenly sees with stunning clarity the affective truth of his actual situation. His office building becomes a filthy body, and he becomes the excrement of this body, covered by the dirt of what is going on inside the building. These feelings and visions go beyond his own individual affections and perceptions. As sensations of becoming-other, they can only be felt. This is a confrontation with the virtual where individual identities are lost. Smith recalls Deleuze's reframing of the question of the subject—"How can the individual transcend its form and its syntactical link with a world in order to attain the universal communication with events?"—and explains Deleuze's contribution toward an answer in this way:

What he calls "schizophrenization" is a limit-process in which the identity of the individual is dissolved and passes entirely into the virtual chaosmos of included disjunctions. . . . The self is a threshold, a door, a becoming between two multiplicities, as in Rimbaud's "I is another." . . . In a becoming, one term does not become the other; rather, each term encounters the other, and the becoming is something between the two, outside the two. This "something" is what Deleuze calls a pure affect or percept, which is irreducible to the affections or perceptions of a subject.[14]

The autonomous power of affects and percepts (and their principles of relation to feelings and perceptions) is thus the third great schizoanalytic power that I will investigate in relation to a possible definition of the neuro-image.

If schizophrenia and schizoanalysis are part of an immanent system, one of the key questions that keeps imposing itself is this: Where in the immanent system can "schizoresistance" occur? Although it is possible to argue that only art can create these forms of resistance (as Deleuze seems to argue in his preference for European art cinema in *The Time-Image*), I would like to propose that it is much more logical that resistance (perhaps only moments of resistance), and also the "will to art" that Deleuze emphasizes, can be found in many different places in contemporary audiovisual culture, including dominant and popular art forms. (This is not to say, of course, that all forms of screen or media culture are artistic.) I will show, accordingly, that the delirious powers of the false and powers of affect are related to a "becoming-minoritarian" of (cinematographic) language that indicates its political dimensions. As Smith explains, actual conditions of immigration, for instance, create minoritizations of languages that affect both minority and hegemonic languages:

For the more a language acquires the characteristics of a major language, the more it tends to be affected by internal variations that transpose it into a "minor" language. English, because of its very hegemony, is constantly being worked on from within by the minorities of the world, who nibble away at that hegemony and create the possibility of new mythic functions, new cultural references, new vernacular languages with their own uses.[15]

In cinematographic language the language of Hollywood is the hegemonic language. Yet it is possible still to consider *Michael Clayton* as a minoritarian Hollywood film, even if it uses big stars. Produced by a small company, Samuels Media, it was not exactly a blockbuster; at the same time, however, its thrilling form, political content, and the presence of George Clooney, known for his political commitments, and Sydney Pollack (who plays his boss), recall the powerful political thrillers of the 1970s such as *The Parallax View* (Alan J. Pakula, 1974), *Three Days of the Condor* (Sydney Pollack, 1975), and *All the President's Men* (Alan J. Pakula, 1976). If we can consider that in *Anti-Oedipus* Deleuze and Guattari refer to schizophrenization as a process for understanding the ways in which capitalism produces its own immanent "antiproduction,"[16] then we can understand the contemporary media culture in which this film plays a part as a schizoid system full of abstract and experimenting machines that produce both art (creation of the new) and its opposites (manipulation, control, mediocrity). The neuro-image is part and parcel of these variegating media machines. How to define art and resistance in the contemporary media culture, and indeed decipher boundaries for the neuro-image, remains an important question that will return in this book. But let me first introduce in more detail some aspects of contemporary media culture that are important as the "natural" milieu for the neuro-image.

Digital Screens: Networked Software Cultures, Deep Remixability, and Database Logic

The digital turn in culture at large, and in media culture specifically, is the context in which the development of the neuro-image must be situated. Much has been written about this turn. Therefore, without proposing an exhaustive description of the complexity and heterogeneity of digital culture, I simply want to mention three elements that are most important for the framing of my analyses of the neuro-image: networked software cultures, deep remixability, and database logic. Contemporary culture is increasingly generated by software. According to new media theorist, practitioner, and historian Lev Manovich, software permeates all areas of contemporary societies: "The school and the hospital, the military base and the scientific laboratory, the airport and the city—all social, economic, and cultural systems of modern society—run on software."[17] Particularly in media theory, extensive recognition is now given to both "the role of software in forming contemporary culture, and cultural, social and economic forces that are shaping development of software itself."[18] Software, as Manovich has argued most prominently, enables creation, publishing, accessing, sharing, and remixing images, moving image sequences, 3D designs, texts, maps, and other interactive elements—as well as various combinations of these elements—in websites, motion graphics, video games, commercial and artistic installations, and virtually every niche of our increasingly technocratic culture. Software also provides tools for social communications and the sharing of information, experience, and knowledge, such as web browsers, email, wikis, virtual worlds, and other Web 2.0 platforms such as Facebook, MySpace, Flickr, and YouTube.[19]

The ubiquity and diversity of cameras and screens is a particularly prominent aspect of this networked, "softwarized," digital culture. Film cameras have long since entertained or rallied against the contributions of many other camera types, including television cameras and surveillance cameras and more recent proliferating consumer cameras on mobile phones and other portable devices. Screens have multiplied everywhere, are more and more linked to all kinds of software, and, despite retaining their media-specific differences, are connected in vast distributed networks. As Alexander Galloway points out in his book *Protocol*, such networks are not limitless but work increasingly as complex diagrammatics. And as these more elaborate kinds of systems (of relations), networked systems are neither open nor closed. A network, according to Galloway, is "a set of nodes and edges, dots and lines. The dots may be computers (server, client, or both), human users, communities, LANs, corporations, even countries. The lines can be any practice, action, or event effectuated by the dots (downloading, emailing, connecting, encrypting, buying, logging on, port scanning)."[20] To comprehend difference or change within networks, you can do a number of things with such a diagram, Galloway indicates. You can connect the dots, disconnect them, or even delete them. You can filter out which dots are connected or create portals for the creation of future dots. "In short, a network-as-diagram offers all sorts of possibilities for organization, regulation and management," he suggests. "The Internet is not simply 'open' or 'closed' but above all a form that is modulated," which means "information does flow, but it does so in a highly regulated manner" more accurately described as "regulated flow."[21] Many others have commented on the network paradigms of contemporary culture. The specific inherencies of the neuro-image to network culture will return in some of the case studies in this book.

Another characteristic of digital software culture is that social software—software that has enabled the emergence of Web 2.0—has transformed the cultural logics of the Internet itself from a hypertext environment of interactive applications into a "participatory culture" populated by so-called prosumers (active content-producing consumers). Citizen journalism, YouTube (and other online file-sharing cultures), blogging, and transmedial storytelling all incorporate audiences across different media forms while gathering them in closer interrelation. These combinations of (digital) cultural shifts are what Henry Jenkins has characterized as "convergence cultures."[22] How does the neuro-image relate to the spirit of Web 2.0? And in what specific ways? Connected to participatory culture is the fact that software has made culture "deeply remixable." This means that, as Manovich explains in *Software Takes Command*, not only can content be remixed and recombined, but also different technologies (such as design, animation, and live action) can be recombined.[23] Mash-ups, remakes, samplings: contemporary culture is profoundly fragmented and constantly recreated. What were once avant-garde strategies have now become everyday practices. Professional filmmakers increasingly use cheap digital cameras and are interested in creating low-tech DIY-aesthetics, as exemplified par excellence in the Dogme 95 movement initiated by Lars von Trier and Thomas Vinterberg.[24] At the complete other end of such digitally shifted aesthetics are the ever more sophisticated "high-tech" special effects and the latest generation of 3D cinema. So how do we define a will to art in this context, when we can observe a democratization of low-cost artistic strategies on the one hand and a high-cost form of new artisanal computer work on the other?

The deep remixabilty of contemporary digital culture is also a result of the database becoming a basic unit of organization, creation, and control. In *The Language of New Media* Lev Manovich has called this the database logic of contemporary culture. After the arrival of the World Wide Web, Manovich argues, "the world appears to us as an endless and unstructured collection of images, texts, and other data records," so "it is only appropriate that we will be moved to model it as a database. But it is also appropriate that we would want to develop a poetics, aesthetics, and ethics of this database."[25] This prominence of database form impacts contemporary culture to perpetuate "archival intensity," a term introduced by Jacques Derrida in his seminal book *Archive Fever*.[26] We have moved into an era where so much material previously hidden in closed archives is becoming increasingly available, often through online databases, which, because of their organization and coding, are able to give fragments or snippets of historical data and images that can be recalled in nonchronological order. This abundance of historical audiovisual material, available in new but quite specifically ordered ways, affects our prior understanding of history and memory. Combined with the fact that the traditional (and scholarly) notion of media objects as "texts" seem to be replaced by the notion of media operating as "dynamic software performances," memory and history are consequently (and increasingly) seen as dynamic, as well, and are continually transforming in an open archive.[27] Although the (media) text in itself has certainly not disappeared, it could be argued that contemporary media in general is more fluid than the more or less stable text of the book and the classical film. So what does this mean in relation to our definitions of a new image type? Does the neuro-image testify to this contemporary database logic? And is it possible that this open and dynamic logic can trickle back to previous more stable image forms, destabilizing older media objects or allowing different readings of them in a database logical perspective?

Several art and media historians have analyzed changes to cinema in the digital age along these lines. Anne Friedberg demonstrates how the screen has multiplied in computer culture, yet the figure of the window as frame has remained prominent in today's screen culture "from Alberti to Microsoft," albeit with different characteristics, such as simultaneity and the multiplication of perspectives.[28] Nicholas Rombes has written about the aesthetic changes of cinema and cinematic experience in terms of mobile, remixed, fragmented, and nonlinear viewing in his book *Cinema in the Digital Age*.[29] Lev Manovich has ventured into a practice of "database filmmaking," which he calls "soft cinema," characterized by multiple screens, automated selection parameters, and combinations of different media (animation, motion picture, graphics), the result of which is a work of unlimited possible combinations and never the exact same film.[30] Matthew Fuller suggests that we see media culture in terms of ecologies of dynamic systems "in which any one part is always multiply connected, acting by the virtue of those connections, and always variable, such that it can be regarded as a pattern rather than simply as an object."[31] David Rodowick similarly recognizes that the new virtual life of cinema is driven by software but emphasizes that "concepts of image, screen, time, space, and movement are as relevant to contemporary moving image theory as they were to classical film theory."[32] According to Rodowick, the virtual life of film will continue in two forms: as information and as art. Film as film, Rodowick suggests, is dead. I will argue differently, proposing that the neuro-image is a continuation of film as film, even if, or indeed precisely because, it can be encountered transmedially. Rodowick's insistence, however, on the importance of film theory's ability to offer up critically relevant tools for understanding the digital turn in contemporary culture will be supported at several instances in this book, with special emphasis on the film-philosophy of Gilles Deleuze. These general aspects and theoretical positions on digital culture serve as my main references and will return in the subsequent chapters. However, the core premise of this book is that in order to really come to terms with what is happening in contemporary audiovisual culture, it is not only film and media theory and (Deleuzian) philosophy that can provide useful insights, but the contemporary neurosciences as well.

Principles of the Brain: Disciplinary Interferences, Rhizomes, and Fractal Patterns

Deleuze proposes extremely rich and fundamental relationships in culture between (continental) philosophy, neurology, and the (film) screen: "There is a special relation between philosophy and neurology. . . . Something that's interested me in cinema is the way in which the screen can work as a brain."[33] I will take Deleuze's suggestion literally and will depart on a transdisciplinary adventure of encounter with recent neuroscience. But before I address specific neuroscientific practices and findings, some general remarks are in order. In *What Is Philosophy?* Deleuze and Guattari foster necessary enthusiasm for disciplinary encounters when they argue that philosophy, art, and science are fundamentally related, since they are the three large domains of thinking: thinking in concepts, thinking in percepts and affects, and thinking in functions. Philosophy, art, and science further share a struggle against opinion and against chaos, but each does so in specific ways:

What defines thought in its three great forms—art, science, and philosophy—is always confronting chaos, laying out a plane, throwing a plane over chaos. But philosophy wants to save the infinite by giving it consistency: it lays out a plane of immanence that, through the action of conceptual personae, takes events or consistent concepts to infinity. Science on the other hand, relinquishes the infinite in order to gain reference: it lays out a plane of simply undefined coordinates that each time, through the action of partial observers, defines states of affairs, functions, or referential propositions. Art wants to create the finite that restores the infinite: it lays out a plane of composition that, in turn, through the action of aesthetic figures, bears monuments of composite sensations.[34]

Deleuze and Guattari reflect on encounters among these great domains of thinking, which begin "when one discipline realizes that it has to resolve, for itself and by its own means, a problem similar to one confronted by the other."[35] In *Negotiations* Deleuze explains how the biology of the brain discovers a material likeness to philosophical thought: "New connections, new pathways, new synapses, that's what philosophy calls into play as it creates concepts, but this whole image is something of which the biology of the brain, in its own way, is discovering an objective material likeness, or the material working."[36] Although this book is not focused on exploring exact correlates between the material brain and its immaterial effects, it does explore neurology and philosophy as productive partners in an important dialogue that is capable of generating great insight. I will return to this point shortly after some general remarks about interdisciplinarity.

Deleuze and Guattari distinguish different ways in which disciplines can meet and interfere with each other. Extrinsic interference occurs when each discipline remains on its own plane and utilizes its own methodological elements—for instance when philosophy creates concepts of sensation (think of Deleuze's own cinema books), science creates functions of sensations or of concepts (such as scientific theories of color or of beauty), and art creates sensations of concepts or of functions (such as art based on scientific models like DNA or brain images). Intrinsic interference happens when concepts or conceptual personae, affects or aesthetic figures, functions or partial observers leave their own plane and slip (most subtly) onto other planes.[37] Deleuze and Guattari give the example of Zarathustra, who, as a conceptual persona, is almost an aesthetic figure in Nietzsche's work. We can also think of Hume's Philo, Cleanthes, and Demea discussing the question of belief in *Dialogues Concerning Natural Religion*. But perhaps we can also think of an aesthetic figure that behaves philosophically, such as the strange Visitor in Pasolini's *Teorema* (1968), who confronts the other characters in the film with the ungroundedness of their being (albeit in a very sensual way). More general inferences have to do with the unavoidable relation of each field to its own negative: "Philosophy needs a nonphilosophy that comprehends it; just as art needs nonart and science needs nonscience."[38] As Eric Alliez has shown in his book *The Signature of the World*, to understand the contemporary world, we need to set a "solidarity" in motion between the different fields of thinking.[39] In *The Neuro-Image* all three forms of disciplinary interferences will alternate in various degrees. I will return to specific methodological implications of this approach at the end of this introduction.

In *What Is Philosophy?* the brain plays an important role, as it is presented as the junction of the three domains of thinking. Since Deleuze argues that the brain is also the screen, and the screen can work as a brain, it is useful to first establish how exactly the brain and the (film) screen can work as a meeting place for art, science, and philosophy. The opening sequence of *Fight Club* (David Fincher, 1998) is a relevant and interesting metaplace at which we can begin looking for connections. The sequence presents literally a ride through the brain. In this, the film exemplifies the fact that with the neuro-image we quite literally have moved into characters' brain spaces. We no longer see through characters' eyes, as in the movement-image and the time-image; we are most often instead in their mental worlds. On the DVD of Fincher's film two audio-track commentaries explain how this sequence was made: by synergizing the visual effects of a cinematographic immersive ride and a neuroscientific brain mapping process.[40] The idea for the shot was that it would start in the amygdala and then backtrack to the frontal lobes and to the outside of the forehead. The artists of the visual effects department and the neuroscientists consulted for the sequence discovered they had actually quite similar (digital) visualization techniques and were able to work together very well. Using Deleuze and Guattari's typology of interdisciplinary interferences, we could say that they worked together extrinsically. The visual artists wanted to create a sensation of a function, the feel of a ride from the amygdala to the frontal lobes as "dark, scary, wet and very visceral," while the neuroscientists focused on the function of a sensation, in which different parts and chambers of the ride are correct in their neurological detail. The sequence is thus also emblematic for the neuro-image, given how it invites further investigations into the various implications of such encounters at the same junctions this book also hopes to contribute to.

Additionally, the rhizomatic and fractal qualities of these opening-sequence images from *Fight Club*, produced with a digital technique called "nested instancing," are also important. In "nested instancing," a technique used to simulate the complexity of actual brain dynamics, model neurons are loaded into digital software one at a time, repeatedly, into different chambers of the (model) brain. It is well known that Deleuze and Guattari give such rhizomatic form incredible attention and prominence across their writings. In *A Thousand Plateaus* they indicate that "rhizomatics" is another name for their entire philosophy, which operates by following the heterogeneous and multiple connections that are also characteristic of brain processes; and as they indicate, too, it is interchangeable with the concept of schizoanalysis. When they introduce rhizomatic thinking, they refer very specifically to neuroscientific studies of the brain:

Thought is not arborescent, and the brain is not a rooted or ramified matter. What are wrongly called "dentrites" do not assure the connection of neurons in a continuous fabric. The discontinuity between cells, the role of the axons, the functioning of the synapses, the existence of synaptic microfissures, the leap each message makes across these fissures, make the brain a multiplicity immersed in its place of consistency or neuroglia, a whole uncertain probabilistic system ("the uncertain nervous system"). Many people have a tree growing in their heads, but the brain itself is much more a grass than a tree. "The axon and the dentrite twist around each other like bindweed around brambles, with synapses at each of the thorns."[41]

In this same outline of rhizomatic thinking, or schizoanalysis, Deleuze and Guattari also make important conceptual distinctions between short-term memory and long-term memory. Rhizomatic thinking is led by short-term memory and works under the conditions of the multiple, the collective, the discontinuous process that includes forgetting. Tree thinking operates in long-term memory (family, race, society, civilization). Deleuze and Guattari clearly prefer the strategies of rhizomatic short-term memory, but they acknowledge that long-term and short-term, rhizome and tree, can never be seen in strict opposition. Rhizomes and trees can be both good and bad, "for there is no dualism, no ontological dualism between here and there, no axiological dualism between good and bad, no blend or American synthesis. There are knots of arborescence in rhizomes, and rhizomatic offshoots in roots. Moreover, there are despotic formations of immanence and channelization specific to rhizomes, just as there are anarchic deformations in transcendent systems of trees, aerial roots, and subterranean systems."[42] Furthermore, they indicate that they do not wish to present two different and opposed models but that relations between the tree and the rhizome are continuously forming, breaking, and reconnecting. Because of its complexity and probabilistic character as an uncertain system, the brain similarly functions in dynamic processes that can never be entirely fixed. This is why it can never function as a deterministic model (even if it can be taken up in all kinds of deterministic discourses). The brain is instead a continuously changing process and therefore fundamentally connected to movement and time. For Deleuze this is also the basic connection between the brain and cinema; and insofar as the contemporary neuro-image also asks questions about the future of cinema, this continuous transforming nature of the brain will be a rich recurring reference. When we finally come to assess the neuro-image's dynamic and multifaceted political dimensions, we will see how rhizomatic structures are involved in the neuro-image's paradoxical status: able to be incorporated by "capturing machines" and controlling powers (any brain, film, movement, device), it can also offer powerful possibilities for resistance.

As I have pointed out, Deleuze and Guattari take the rhizomatic structure of the brain as the guiding principle of their entire philosophy, the composure of which is itself demonstrated in a fractal way. In this sense the brain's dynamic structure operates as a fractal figure in their thought, much like the "nested instancing" technology used to create the brain ride of *Fight Club*'s title sequence.[43] It is amazing to see how, from one book to the next, Deleuze (on his own or with Guattari) develops a vast network of complex, multiple, and heterogeneous topics through which consistent and similar patterns and concerns reemerge like fractal thoughts. In his article "Schizoanalysis and the Phenomenology of Cinema" Joe Hughes has demonstrated, for instance, how the concept of "passive syntheses" (defined as operations that occur in the mind, as unconscious sensorimotor neurological actions) reemerges with variation in *Anti-Oedipus, The Logic of Sense*, and *The Movement-Image*: "In all three books subjectivity is founded on a material field which is described in the same way: material fragments communicate with one another independent of any subject."[44] The concept of passive synthesis developed in *Difference and Repetition* in relation to time is also important for the neuro-image, as will become clear in the middle part of this book. At this point, however, it is necessary to acknowledge how my bringing together of these three domains— schizoanalysis, neuroscience, and contemporary cinema practice—raises some serious methodological questions.

Methodological Challenges

Because the work of Deleuze and Guattari draws on a multitude of disciplinary sources, many intelligent and far-ranging commentaries and analyses have been written on the relationships between Deleuze and science and between Deleuze and different forms of art. Bringing all three domains of thought together, however, as I intend to do in this book, poses many challenges and risks. Therefore, from the beginning I want to explicitly indicate some of the positions and limits I am assuming when taking on this work. It is important to note that I do not imply any hierarchical order between the different domains of thought. I am not claiming, for instance, that philosophy or cinema is now (or increasingly) determined by discoveries in neuroscience or that software is now really taking command and controlling actions and thoughts. Rather, I want to bring recent developments in these different fields together to see how they resonate with each other to perhaps give us a more complete understanding of the complexities and political realities of life in the twenty-first century. My home discipline is media theory and film-philosophy, and this discipline forms my (pragmatic) grounding. I very much sympathize with

Daniel Frampton's filmosophical approach, in which he considers films as thinking entities, or so called "filminds."[45] Frampton does not suggest a perfect analogy between the human mind and the filmind, but he does point out that we could speak of the filmgoer's experience in terms of a (Deleuzian-sounding) "becoming with" the film characters, film idea, or film style: "The filmgoer experiences film more intuitively, not via technology or external authorship, but directly, as a thinking thing. . . . Film form is always there, and thus necessarily part of the actions and events, and filmosophy simply, holistically, bonds film's actions to dramatically thoughtful motives and intentions. Film style is now seen to be the dramatic intention of the film itself."[46]

In each chapter of this book a case study of a film, or a specific set of films, provides either the starting point or focal point of my elaborations and reflections. Rather than working as illustrations, films are instead acknowledged as actual seeds of thought: important encounters that create new brain circuits (new perceptions, new feelings, new thoughts) and that connect to or resonate with philosophical reflections and scientific findings. My speaking position is therefore not as a neuroscientist or a philosopher pur sang but as a film scholar, or rather film philosopher, extrinsically related to the fields of neuroscience and cinema practice. Additionally, I will take note of intrinsic slippages of aesthetic figures, conceptual personae, and partial observers.

I will introduce neuroscientific findings into the analysis of specific films to see what they can bring to the other fields of thought. Since modern neuroscience is by and large cognitive neuroscience, this has led me to a reconsideration of the difficult relationship between Deleuze and the cognitive sciences. Questions of the mind have traditionally been studied in the cognitive sciences and in analytical philosophy. Deleuzian thought seems far removed from these two already connected fields. However, as John Protevi has argued, recent shifts in cognitive science toward more ecologically embedded and bodily affective models makes the potential connection of Deleuze's work to the cognitive sciences less odd (in an epistemological sense) and more accessible for further development.[47] In the chapters that follow, my analyses will shift among a "holistic" approach to filmosophical thoughts, general resonances between the three domains of thought, and more small-scale analyses that draw from a neurocognitivist approach. In other words, methodologically, my analyses will shift and slip between the conceptual level of infinity, the finite level of referentiality, and the compositional level of sensations. This approach is in accordance with that distinguished by Deleuze and Guattari in *What Is Philosophy?*

Interdisciplinary encounters between neuroscience and other disciplines and domains of thought are, of course, not new. Recently, neuroscientist Antonio Damasio has argued in *Looking for Spinoza* for the profound connections between Spinozan philosophy and affective neuroscience. Considering Spinoza as a "protobiologist" ("the biological thinker concealed behind countless propositions, axioms, proofs, lemmas, and scholia"),[48] he establishes Spinoza as a relevant thinker to neurobiologists. Spinoza's notion of the correspondence between body and mind (specifically in the direction of body *to* mind) matches modern neurobiological findings. Still, Damasio's open-minded search for an encounter with a philosopher is relatively rare within neuroscientific publications.

Jonah Lehrer's *Proust Was a Neuroscientist* provides another exception to singular-disciplined models of scholarship. In the introduction to his book Lehrer recalls the starting point of his interdisciplinary reflections. While waiting for the results of scientific experiments in a neuroscience lab, Lehrer began to read Proust's *Remembrance of Things Past*. Expecting to be perhaps merely entertained by a fictional story, in opposition to all the scientific facts involved in his work, he slowly began to discover a surprising convergence: the novelist had predicted many of the experiments neuroscientists have been conducting over the last two decades! Lehrer discusses the work of several writers, painters, and composers (Proust, Woolf, Cézanne, Stravinsky, and others) who seem to predict many scientific discoveries. He notices the deep schism between scientists and artists that perpetuate their description(s) of the world in incommensurable languages: "Thus, in our current culture, we have two epistemological extremes reflexively attacking the other. Postmodernists have ignorantly written off science as nothing but another text, and many scientists have written off the humanities as hopelessly false."[49] Lehrer calls for a constructive dialogue through which the mutual suspicion between scientists on the one hand and artists and philosophers on the other might be overcome. Referring to Ian McEwan's novel *Saturday*, which presents a single day in the life of a neurosurgeon, Lehrer argues that this novel shows how even "on intimate terms with the cortex's material workings," we are confronted with "the only reality we will ever know: our experience. The feeling of consciousness. The feeling of feeling."[50] Lehrer sees McEwan's novel as a potent demonstration that even in this age of dizzying scientific detail, the artist remains a necessary voice.

Here I hope to contribute to the building of a bridge, called for by Lehrer and others, between the hard sciences and the humanities. Filmic fictions (art) and philosophical reflections aim to provide us with powerful truths about the experiences and metaphysical depths of contemporary media culture, while findings in neuroscience seek to describe and illuminate material aspects and functions of these experiences and depths. Although each discipline is replete with its own insights, it is only when film (or art), philosophy, and science are taken up together that we can truly comprehend the richness, layeredness, and immense complexity of human experience in contemporary digital media culture.

Neuroscreens—Neurophilosophy—Neuropolitics

This book is divided into three parts, representing three dimensions of exploration for the neuro-image: neuroscreens, neurophilosophy, and neuropolitics, with three chapters dedicated to each part. Although the aspects of the neuro-image that I have laid out above (schizo powers of delirious overflow, powers of illusion, and powers of affect) play a role in each part and every chapter (another case of nested instances perhaps), they unfold with different emphases throughout the book. In Part 1, Neuroscreens: Principles of the Brain (Chapters 1–3), I present an initial investigation of contemporary neuroscreens. Modern film theory in the 1960s and 1970s, as it developed as Apparatus Theory, considered cinema as a "machine of the visible" that gave us illusions of reality. In contrast, contemporary media culture and its brain-screens present us with the reality of illusions and in this sense might be better considered as machines of the invisible. It is not so much the redeeming representation of reality that cinema presents us today. Rather, as we have just seen in my discussion of the opening sequence of *Fight Club*, we have moved literally into the minds of our characters, into the realm of the chaotic virtual, in which we are shown often directly and without warning the inner world of our brains. Deleuze cites Paul Klee when he says that art is not meant to re-produce the visible but to present the invisible.[51] The invisible can be described as the virtual; the time-image makes the virtual visible; the neuro-image does this, too, but in a somewhat different way.[52] Taking "the brain as screen" in a nonmetaphorical sense, I hope to demonstrate how the neuro-image presents its own versions of the invisible as a "brain ride."[53] In the three chapters of this first part the screen is thus read in accordance with principles of the brain, in an attempt to ground our contemporary screens in the physical materiality of the brain.

Chapter 1, "Schizoid Minds, Delirium Cinema, and Powers of the Machines of the Invisible," investigates the clinical and critical aspects of schizophrenia by looking at schizophrenia as a neurological disease alongside contemporary cinema that explicitly deals with schizophrenia. I treat these as equally important sources of information and observation: the clinical symptoms of schizophrenia as neurological disease (including positive and negative symptoms and gendered differences) are instructive and resonate with cinematographic expressions and truths of "delirium cinema." An analysis of *The Butterfly Effect* will, moreover, point out another important "schizo" dimension of such cinema: our changed relation to time. This chapter will return to the 1970s' cinema of Fassbinder and Cassavetes to contrast and connect their versions of deliria to the more recent work of Lars von Trier and David Lynch, whose films demonstrate how the image has explicitly become a brain-screen in the delirium of the "digital turn." The final part of this chapter will map contemporary digital culture as a schizoid culture full of hallucinating realities and increasing affective qualities and will attempt to position and characterize the neuro-image within this culture.

Chapter 2, "Illusionary Perception and Powers of the False," focuses on the hallucinatory schizoanalytic "symptom" of the powers of the false. First I map the possible connections between film theory and cognitive neuroscience that can assess the turn to considering the screen as "illusions of reality." Moving from this holistic perspective to a more detailed approach, I draw connections between recent findings in perceptual neurosciences that address visual illusions and two recent films that deal with visual illusions and magic, namely *The Prestige* and *The Illusionist*. These films that appeared in the same year both go back to the threshold of the twentieth century to investigate the beginnings of cinema (and the media age) to reinvent media history itself and give the digital age an appropriate past. The end of Chapter 2 zooms out again to look at another film by Christopher Nolan, *The Dark Knight,* and investigate the conceptual implications of the powers of the false that correspond with the neurological necessity for "fictional selves" as described by cognitive neuroscientist Michael Gazzaniga.

Chapter 3, "Surveillance Screens and Powers of Affect," considers another important aspect of contemporary screen culture, namely, the omnipresence of surveillance cameras. The discourse on surveillance is most often considered in terms of control and paranoiac affects. However, alternative theoretical engagements are possible as well, which I will argue by looking at the aesthetic figures in *Red Road* and the art project *Evidence Locker.* In this chapter I investigate the schizoanalytical powers of affect via findings in affective neurosciences most famously elaborated by Antonio Damasio and Joseph LeDoux. The film analysis on a neurological level allows us to acknowledge a tension between "emotion" and "feeling" that relates to a particular form of suspense film in contemporary cinema that could best be described as "affective neurothrillers."

After this first mapping of aspects of the neuro-image as brain-screens, and in relation to schizoanalysis, digital culture, and neuroscience, Part 2, Neurophilosophy: Turning Madness into Metaphysics (Chapters 4–6), investigates the philosophical groundings and implications of the neuro-image. While returning to schizoid symptoms of overflow and temporal confusion, the powers of the false and the powers of affect, the chapters of Part 2 pay less attention to their neuroscientific bases and more to the ontological, epistemological, and aesthetic dimensions of the neuro-image.

Chapter 4, "Signs of Time: Metaphysics of the Brain-Screen," will develop the specific problem of time that was introduced in Chapter 1 as one of the confusing aspects of the schizoid mind (and of overabundant media culture). Henri Bergson's *Introduction to Metaphysics* and his essays in *Mind-Energy* allow a general reconsideration of the relationship between physics and metaphysics, and his concerns with neurology serve as a general investigation of the temporal ontological implications of neuroscience. In this chapter I will revisit the cinema of Alain Resnais, analyzing

Resnais's films as cerebral membranes that are marked by a schizophrenic database ontology avant la lettre. Cross-reading Deleuze's cinema books with his conception of time in *Difference and Repetition*, this chapter will develop the neuro-image as a new dimension of time. Suggesting that the movement-image is based in the first synthesis of time of the present, and the time-image in the second synthesis of time of the past, I demonstrate how the neuro-image is based in the third synthesis of time, the future. This type of image has its incipience in *The Time-Image* but has developed to become central to the digital age.

Chapter 5, "Degrees of Belief: Epistemology of Probabilities," returns to the powers of the false and the reality of illusions. It proposes that in a world where the powers of the false render everything uncertain, Hume's skeptical epistemology, based on degrees of belief, seems to regain contemporary importance. Hume's thought will be related to the transmedial storytelling of the television series *Lost* and James Cameron's 3D spectacle *Avatar* and to these moving images' deliberative travels between knowledge and faith. Both of these popular media forms are concerned with the powerful mythical desire to rebegin, described by Deleuze as a fundamental myth of desert islands. Here the question of major and minoritarian languages in the neuro-image will be addressed explicitly. Hume's epistemology and the question of belief also leads us to consider the problems of providence and free will that haunt contemporary media culture as well. This is one of neuroscience's acknowledged "hard questions," addressed in this chapter through the philosophical problems raised by the case studies.

Chapter 6, "Powers of Creation: Aesthetics of Material-Forces," takes up the question of affective powers in an aesthetic sense. This chapter refers to Deleuze's work on Leibniz and the baroque "fold." I will argue that in contemporary cinema, often referred to as neobaroque or digital baroque, the neuro-image has particular aesthetic aspects that directly express material-force relations of the affective brain-screen. Following my investigation of how cinema in the movement-image and the time-image has proposed its relations to the brain, often through the figure of a mad (neuro)scientist, I will analyze two films by Darren Aronofsky, *Pi* and *The Fountain*, to show the aesthetic implications of the neuro-image in relation to the affective powers of creation in the brain.

Part 3, Neuropolitics: Transnational Screen Connections (Chapters 7–9), considers the political and ethical aspects of the neuro-image. Here I address the more explicit micropolitical implications of schizoanalysis. The schizoanalytic elements of changed temporal relations, the powers of the false, and powers of affect will return in the chapters forming this part but are here discussed in their specific political dimensions.

Chapter 7, "The Open Archive: Cinema as World-Memory," returns to the question of time within the schizoid database ontologies of contemporary culture and looks at the ways in which historical images sometimes behave as "strange attractors" of history. I will look in particular at Gillo Pontecorvo's *The Battle of Algiers* and its redistributions and digital remixes to analyze how this film becomes a slippery memory of historical reality. Grappling with the similar insights of Eyal Weisman, I will address how the strategies of *The Battle of Algiers* and of Deleuzian rhizomatic philosophy become slippery tools in the hands of majoritarian forces, such as (most prominently) the Israeli army. In this chapter the schizophrenic production and antiproduction of cultural memory and political strategy is related to the ever-growing and transnationally spreading viral archive of digital culture, revealing a growing tension between "hyperhistoricity" on the one hand and "posthistoricity" on the other that perhaps, I will argue, could better be described as "prehistoricity" in contemporary media culture.

Chapter 8, "Divine In(ter)vention: Micropolitics and Resistance," investigates, through the minoritarian cinema of Palestinian filmmaker Elia Suleiman, the political aspects of the fabulating powers of the false. This chapter quite necessarily works through the renowned theoretical objections to Deleuze's work voiced by postcolonial scholars and political philosophers by reinvestigating Deleuze's key, yet largely misunderstood, concepts, such as nomadic thinking and becoming-minoritarian. Elia Suleiman's trilogy—*Chronicle of a Disappearance, Divine Intervention*, and *The Time That Remains*—shows how art can contribute to politics via the creation of a people. Here, "violence" and "laughter" are discussed conceptually, as forms of resistance that "gain time" for the future in a neuro-image based in the third synthesis of time.

Chapter 9, "Logistics of Perception 2.0: Multiple Screens as Affective Weapons," finally investigates the ways in which the Iraq War has seemingly multiplied on many different screens. While on the one hand this explosion of war images has led to what Nicholas Mirzoeff has called a "banality of images," I want to consider the affective aspects of multiple war screens in terms of an infernal baroque *Gesamtkunstwerk*. Several Iraq War films, including Brian De Palma's *Redacted*, Kathryn Bigelow's *The Hurt Locker*, and Paul Haggis's *In the Valley of Elah*, show in a reflective way how these multiple screens have quite literally entered our minds to present a "logistics of perception" completely different from the kind that Paul Virilio and Jean Baudrillard theorized in relation to the first Gulf War, when they implored the disappearance of reality behind extensive technological mediation. Here I will argue that in contemporary screen culture, understood through a Deleuzian schizoanalytic lens, reality returns with an affective vengeance—with positive and negative effects.

The films I chose for this book as my doorways of (mad, illusionary, affective) perception all share certain elements that shape (or prefigure) the neuro-image as a "genre," in the sense of Rick Altman's definition of syntactic and semantic elements of film genres.[54] Their characters are schizos, forgers, magicians, con artists, tricksters, (mad) scientists, affected surveillance operators, traumatized or paralyzed soldiers, and other persons evidencing "abnormal" behavior. Their preferred locations are psychiatric wards, desert islands, laboratories, cosmic space, surveillance rooms, battlefields, and crowded screen-covered cities. Their narrations are complex, extended or transmedial, and free indirect.[55] Stylistically they follow the abstract patterns of networks, mosaics, fractals, and other complex geometric (con)figurations. They may be part of mainstream Hollywood (majoritarian) but in one way or another relate to the powers of schizoanalysis. In almost every case these artistic expressions are the finite composite sensations that "restore the infinite." As such they mediate between the philosophical concepts that reach out "to infinity" and the scientific state of affairs that give us "referential propositions."[56]

At this point I should state my position in relation to certain debates that tend to arise in proximity to the territory that I traverse throughout the book. First, in taking schizophrenic pathological symptoms as the starting point for further investigation into salient aspects of digital screen culture, I mean to imply that contemporary culture is "schizophrenic" in its changed relation to time, in its powers of the false, and in its powers of affect. I certainly do not want to romanticize schizophrenia as a disease; it is quite frightening and tremendously difficult to live in a state of engulfment, hallucination, paranoia, and fear. But these pathological symptoms do shed light on the processes of our own brains (or changed conception of the brain itself) and collective culture. As neuroscientist Marta Kutas has argued, we all have schizophrenic characteristics in our neurological system, but only in an intensified or multiplied form do they become a disease.[57] I also imply that schizophrenia is both a symptom of contemporary culture and a form resistance. This is in line with Deleuze and Guattari's rich conceptualizations of schizophrenia and capitalism in *Anti-Oedipus* and *A Thousand Plateaus*.

In respect to the possible future developments or death of cinema, a question so strongly conjured by the presence of the neuro-image itself, I suggest that cinema is not dead, is perhaps more undead, but could even be considered more alive than ever. Film as film is indeed profoundly marked by digital culture, but the internal changes in film aesthetics (from database logic, to changed relations to time, to the cinema's more illusionary and affective powers) were already present before the digital age and are thus not dependent on digital technology per se. In my engagement with neuroscience I have to emphasize that I am not suggesting any hierarchy between disciplines but look instead for productive encounters. Therefore I will not argue that neuroscience can dictate our inquiries in a deterministic way (the brain remains too probabilistic in any case, and the "experience of our brains" is difficult if not impossible to translate in purely neurological terms). Nor will I argue that the humanities disciplines should be called in to "tame" the wild and flexible materiality of our neural networks or the neuroscientific discourse about this. But neither does politics disappear; on the contrary, the micropolitics of our brains and the macropolitics of our institutions or political systems, economies, and ideologies have to be thought together.

If the brain is the screen, screens and brains have to be studied together. Calling this new type of image the "neuro-image" is to acknowledge the fact that images now quite literally show us the illusionary and affective realities of the brain. Obviously the movement-image and time-image also have a relation to the brain, albeit a different one, as I will show more elaborately in the later chapters of this book. However, the fact that we now literally enter brain-worlds in cinema (the earlier mentioned *Fight Club*, James Cameron's *Avatar*, Christopher Nolan's *Inception*, and Duncan Jones's *Source Code* are just some of the most recent films of this type) means that a transdisciplinary encounter between film, philosophy, and neuroscience is not only important but also necessary to pursue. Perhaps other names could be given to this type of image too (the future-image, perhaps—numerous suggestions are possible), but any name has its own limitations.

The larger issue—one that has tended to drive disciplinary allegiances and standoffs throughout the history of (film) theory itself—is in fact where we should be situating the *screen* (in relation to the neuro-image). Should it be quite literally inside the brain or situated externally? In his article "Where Is the Screen?" Robert Pepperell takes up this question by referring to two dominant traditions: internalism, which locates the screen entirely in the mind (referring to neurological studies that see, for instance, vision as entirely depending on operations of the mind), and externalism, which sees the screen completely in the world (referring to equally important neurological studies that show, for instance, that perception depends completely on our continuing interactions with the world).[58] Pepperell proposes to look at the screen in a third way, as a "dialethic" relationship, acknowledging the simultaneous truths of both models. He explains:

Were the mind and world distinct we could more justifiably defend the internalist view that the screen is perceived somewhere inside the perceptual apparatus of the brain. Were the mind and the world unified we would tend towards the externalist position that the perception of the screen occurs as much in the world as it does inside the mind, since the two are continuous. But on the third count, that of simultaneous distinction and unity, we encounter a dialethic state—the screen is perceived "in here" and "out there" at the same time.[59]

This is exactly the position that Deleuze gives to the brain and the screen when he argues that "the brain's precisely this boundary of a continuous two-way movement between Inside and Outside, this membrane between them."[60] This is also the position of the screen that I will defend in this book.

The Power of Images, Mirror Neurons, and Creation of New Brain Circuits

In *L'Abécédaire de Gilles Deleuze* (*The ABC of Gilles Deleuze*) Claire Parnet proposes *zigzag* as the final corresponding term of a Deleuzian alphabet.[61] Deleuze loves ending with this word. "There is no word after zigzag," Deleuze says to Parnet. "Zed is a great letter that establishes a return to A." Zed as the movement of the fly, the movement of lightning, is perhaps the elementary movement that presides at the creation of the world. Deleuze even proposes half-jokingly to replace the Big Bang with "Le Zigzag." For the creation of a universe, for any universe, for everything there is, he argues that the most elementary question is, How can a connection between singular points, between different fields of forces be created? It is possible to imagine a chaos of potential, but how is it that we can bring elements into real relation? According to Deleuze everything consists of connection, and these connections are rarely made in a linear or predictable fashion. Each connection is prepared, however, by a "somber precursor"—a kind of experience with a trajectory that is barely noticed but brings about a reaction between different points or forces. And then we have the lightning, *le zigzag*, that creates an insight ("l'éclair qui fait voir"), a flash-forward perhaps, a glimpse from (a speculative) future that imposes an affective thought.

In *Michael Clayton* Arthur Edens's moment standing frozen in the middle of the traffic and urban screens of New York City could be considered his somber precursor. His encounter with Anna, one of the victims of U/North, is the moment the lightning hits. But Michael Clayton, too, has an insight provoked by a special encounter. At the beginning of the film all we know of Clayton is that he probably works as a fixer (a "truth adjuster") for his law firm and may be in financial trouble himself (just before seeing a client who was the cause of an accident and needs access to Clayton's truth-"fixing" skills, Clayton himself is shown in some underground gambling venue). However, in the scene that actually frames the film's intro (intercut with these limited other scenes), Clayton is shown driving along a country road. It is very early in the morning. The winter landscape is covered in mist. The music has a slightly threatening undertone and Clayton's expression is somber, and then he stops the car. The music stops too. He looks through the car window and the branching structures of leafless trees are reflected in the glass screen. He opens the window to see more clearly and then gets out. The camera is behind him, and for a few seconds his body blocks the view of what he is actually looking at. The branches of the trees seem to grow out of his head, and a moment later, branches reflect on his car like neural patterns. The mise-en-scène here seems to emphasize the brain-screen. Then we see what attracted Clayton's attention: in the distance atop a hill, next to a few trees, three horses seem to summon him. Clayton walks toward them, uncertain, in doubt, questioning. The horses don't run away. In several close-ups we see how they look at Clayton, who can almost touch them now. The horses seem magical, as if they come from another temporal dimension and want to tell him something. In a long shot we see his car in the distance, the engine obviously still running, as steam escapes from the muffler. Then there is a sudden explosion . . . and the car goes up in flames. The horses run away. Clayton runs back to the car and realizes he has been saved by this strange encounter. After this glimpse at the future of the story line, the narrative moves four days back in time.

The scene in itself is breathtaking. Without exactly explaining these events, the affective qualities of the images, the cold early morning mist, the trees, the horses, the expression on Clayton's face, and the explosion tell us that this is a decisive moment, a moment of insight. The subsequent narrative of the film will show us the events that led to this moment. Toward the end of the film this scene is repeated, like a feedback loop with slight variations. As spectators we now know how all of the characters are painted in moral gray tones, how inhuman decisions get made by people under extreme pressures (Tilda Swinton is brilliant in her role as top manager Karen Crowder of U/North), how Arthur Edens is murdered for his delirious and endangering transgressions, and how Clayton has realized that he has no choice (the choice of no choice) but to accept a check from his boss in order to pay his debts instead of pursuing the crimes of U/North (and the implication of his own firm) that he discovered through Edens. The horse scene is picked up for the second time when Clayton drives his car in the misty countryside. But now we also see that the contract killers who also murdered Edens are following Clayton. The same music now sounds hastier, more threatening. We have seen, too, that Clayton found the book of his son's multiplayer fantasy game, *Realm and Conquest*, in Edens's apartment—one of the drawings in the book depicted horses standing next to a leafless tree. On the level of the narrative this sign could be seen as a superfluous explanation for Clayton's stopping of the car. It could also be considered a dark (opaque) precursor that leads to Clayton's flash of insight, or even an acknowledgment of the *question* of belief as being just that. We see how in the subsequent events Clayton finally acts upon his friend's summons for schizoid resistance and change.

At the same time, the affective qualities of this scene also work without narrative explanation. This has to do with the immanent power of images, described by Deleuze in his cinema books. When Deleuze argues that images are not representations and that they affect us directly, this has to be seen in terms of his cogent understanding of the brain. The fairly recent discovery of mirror neurons gives further material referentiality to Deleuze's conception of the power of cinematographic images. Mirror neurons are neurons that fire when we actually do something but that also fire when we see (or hear) somebody else doing something. For some parts of the cerebral mechanism, then, seeing is doing (the phenomenon is sometimes referred to as "Monkey see is monkey do"). Thus for these parts of the brain there is no difference between seeing someone or something in reality or seeing someone on film. Damasio describes this phenomenon, discovered by neuroscientist Vittorio Gallese and his team, in *Looking for Spinoza*.[62] Something we see literally touches areas in the brain that imitate the perceived actions or feelings. This means that in neurological terms images cannot (just) be considered representations of an objective reality but instead have an internal power that creates certain effects in the brain—which means images create new brain circuits in the spectator who receives and processes them. As Antonio Damasio argues, neural patterns and corresponding mental projections of objects and events outside the brain are creations of the brain that are related to the reality that causes these creations, not a passive reflection of this reality. Each brain will have a slightly different perception of reality (of images). Even the same brain, changing over time, will see the same image differently at a different moment. Moving between outside and inside, this is a dynamic and dialethic conception of the brain-screen.

Mirror neurons, and the way in which the brain is affected by images, can give insights into the implications of Deleuze's brain as screen. There is also specific compatibility between our knowledge of mirror neurons and Deleuze's taxonomy of images in his cinema books. In *The Movement-Image* Deleuze classifies image categories such as the action-image, the affection-image, the impulse-image, and the relation-image: they cause action, affection, impulses, or thoughts in the brain. They touch the brain directly, and they also modify our subjectivities; they are what Deleuze calls "material aspects" of our subjectivity in which the brain and the mind are one. So spectatorship, in terms of Deleuzian film-philosophy, can best be seen in terms of being affected by "signaletic material" that changes and forms our subjectivities in an ongoing process. Seeing *Michael Clayton* is, in fact, a neurological experience of becoming Michael Clayton (if only momentarily). And horses in the winter mist, we might consider, become potentially forever connected to Clayton's story of insight and change. In *Difference and Repetition* Deleuze discusses signs as our most important way of learning (which is nothing other than creating or enforcing new brain circuits): "Learning takes place not in the relation between a representation and an action (reproduction of the Same) but in the relation between a sign and a response (encounter with the Other). . . . To learn is indeed to constitute this space of an encounter with signs. . . . They testify to the spiritual and natural powers which act beneath the words, gestures, characters and objects represented."[63]

The film *Michael Clayton* makes clear that to take signs seriously is a matter of belief and choice and not of certain knowledge. Choice in Deleuzian terms is related to the vitalism that signs testify to, and it is usually provoked on an affective level; it can be sensed more than known. So how is sensation a kind of choice experience, or experience of choice, in the brain and in what ways does it relate to spirituality? In *What Is Philosophy?* Deleuze and Guattari discuss how sensation in art (cinema) responds to chaos by contracting "the vibrations of the stimulant on a nervous surface or in a cerebral volume: sensation itself vibrates because it contracts vibrations. It preserves itself because it preserves vibrations. Sensation is the contracted vibration that has become quality, variety. That is why the brain-subject is here called soul or force, since only the soul preserves by contracting that which matter dissipates, or radiates, furthers, reflects, refracts, or converts."[64]

A sensation is therefore a contraction, a passive synthesis, a contemplation of elements of matter that preserves the before in the after. Deleuze and Guattari relate this aspect of sensation not just to humans but to all kinds of organisms. Plants and rocks do not possess a nervous system, but they seem to share chemical affinities and physical causalities that constitute "microbrains" or an "inorganic life of things," as they put it.[65] Further, this vitalistic conception of spirituality has nothing to do with dreams or fantasy, but it is rather "the domain of cold decision, of absolute obstinacy, of the choice of existence."[66] The cold decision is somewhat how it sounds, seeming to contradict the sensations that go with it, but in fact it is completely logical from a vitalistic perspective that sees the universe full of microbrains that are constantly moving, acting and reacting, but that in sensations find a moment of pause, where all options are still open, and a decision has to be made. When in *The Movement-Image* Deleuze discusses the affection-image, the image category that creates sensations par excellence, he explains this idea of spiritual choice further: the alternatives are not between terms (such as *good* or *bad*) but between modes of existence of the one who chooses.[67] The true spiritual choice is choosing choice (choosing that you have a choice) or choosing that you have no choice. While Michael Clayton first assumed that he had no choice (but to accept the money from his boss), his spiritual choice, enforced by the encounter with a sign (the horses), is to choose choice. The question of the spiritual choice is of great importance, says Deleuze, because "choosing to choose is supposed to restore everything to us."[68] What is regained is a belief in this world, because the modern fact is that the link between man and world is broken. Deleuze argues:

This link must become an object of belief: it is the impossible which can only be restored with a faith. . . . Only belief in the world can reconnect man to what he sees and hears. The cinema must film, not the world, but belief in this world, our only link. . . . Whether we are Christians or atheists, in our universal schizophrenia, we need reasons to believe in this world.[69]

So perhaps, against all odds, the multiple and heterogeneous screens that surround us with schizoid franticness, instead of removing us always further from reality, may come to our salvation. By investigating the conditions, limits, and potential flashes of insight of neuro-images, this book endeavors to see how art, science, and philosophy can come together to turn our contemporary madness into metaphysics and into micropolitical forms of resistance that are at the basis of any change. The neuro-image testifies to how the brain has become our world and how the world has become a brain-city, a brain-world.

PART I

NEUROSCREENS
Principles of the Brain

Schizoid Minds, Delirium Cinema, and Powers of the Machines of the Invisible

If the cerebral model is an important reference to assess images, and all images are fundamentally related to the brain in the sense that brains are screens and screens operate like brains, then changes in the image are also connected to changed conceptions of the brain.[1] In *The Time-Image* Deleuze frequently refers to modern neuroscience to suggest a strong link between the ambiguous and unresolved narratives of the time-image (exemplified by Antonioni, Resnais, and Godard) and the discovery of synapses and electronic or discontinuous chemical communication between neurons. This discovery, he argues, was "enough in itself to shatter the idea of a continuous cerebral system" and "to introduce half-uncertainty in the neural transmission."[2] In his references to neuroscience Deleuze emphasizes the intimate connections between experience, scientific knowledge, and artistic expression:

Scientific knowledge of the brain has evolved, and carried out a general rearrangement. The situation is so complicated that we should not speak of a break, but rather of new orientations. . . . The process of association increasingly came up against cuts in the continuous network of the brain; everywhere there were micro-fissures which were not simply voids to be crossed, but random mechanisms introducing themselves at each moment between the sending and receiving of an associate message: this was the discovery of a probabilistic or semi-fortuitous cerebral space, "an uncertain system." . . . It is obviously not through the influence of science that our relationship with the brain changed: perhaps it was the opposite, our relationship with the brain having changed first, obscurely guiding science. . . . Our lived relationship with the brain becomes increasingly fragile, less and less "Euclidean" and goes through little cerebral deaths. The brain becomes our problem or our illness, our passion, rather than our mastery, our solution or decision. We are not copying Artaud, but Artaud lived and said something about the brain that concerns all of us: that "its antennae turned towards the invisible," that it has a capacity to "resume a resurrection from the death."[3]

In this chapter I want to present an investigation of "the brain as our illness and passion" by referring explicitly to schizophrenia as a contemporary brain disease.[4] Coined as a disease a hundred years ago by Eugene Bleuler, schizophrenia seems increasingly connected to the modern world and contemporary globalized screen culture. As a neurological disease, schizophrenia differs from neurosis, which is the mental disorder emphasized in psychoanalysis.[5] As Freud defined it, neurosis is based on a repression complex related to a reality principle that remains intact. In schizophrenic psychosis the reality principle no longer holds and is replaced by the internal reality of the brain (the reality of illusions, the reality of the "invisible").[6] Deleuze argues that neurosis is not an adequate model to understand the contemporary world, as opposed to the (schizophrenic) brain, which is significantly related to electronic (digital) images:

Neurosis is thus not the consequence of the modern world, but rather of our separation from this world, of our lack of adaptation to this world. The brain, in contrast, is adequate to the modern world, including its possibilities of the expansion of electronic or chemical brains: an encounter occurs between the brain and color, not that it is enough to paint the world, but because the treatment of color is an important element in the awareness of the "new world" (the color-corrector, the electronic image . . .).[7]

By posing the brain in opposition to neurosis, Deleuze implies that all brains are potentially schizophrenic or, in any case, that madness has become its default value. Here it is important to note that the encounter between a brain and a color (and color-corrector) implies a fundamental link between the brain and the screen. In the twenty-first century both our knowledge of the brain and the situation of the audiovisually mediated world seem to invite new thoughts about "schizoid minds" and "schizoid screens."

We should bear in mind that Deleuze and Guattari use the term *schizophrenia* in a particular way. As Eugene Holland has explained, schizophrenia indicates a

specific mode of psychic and social functioning that is characteristically both produced and repressed by capitalist economy. In the worst case—when capitalism is unable to countenance the process of schizophrenia it has itself produced—the result is "madness": schizophrenia as a process succumbs to a repression that generates "the schizophrenic" as entity and the miseries of the psychiatric patient. But in the best cases the processes of schizophrenia take the form of viable social practices and the joys of unbridled, free-form human interaction.[8]

In *Anti-Oedipus* Deleuze and Guattari describe schizophrenia as the immanent system of production and antiproduction, related to "capitalism's awesome schizophrenic production of energy and charge, against which it brings all its vast powers of repression to bear, but which nonetheless continues to act as capitalism's limit."[9] The fundamental problem that defines the borderline between schizophrenia as a process and schizophrenia as a disease, Deleuze and Guattari argue, is how to negotiate the fact that an empowering and liberating breakthrough turns just as easily into a disempowering or deadly breakdown.[10] To understand these powers and dangers of schizophrenia, Deleuze and Guattari propose a schizoanalysis of the modern world.

Schizoanalysis was first developed by Guattari in his work with patients in the innovative psychiatric clinic La Borde. He proposed schizoanalysis as a mode of thinking with or alongside schizophrenia, responding and connecting to patients' specific assemblages of desires. Schizoanalysis "brings forth solutions—modifying behaviours, opening vistas, renewing fields of reference, building confidence: respond(s) to the event [e.g., a patient mentions in passing 'I feel like learning word processing'] as the potential bearer of new constellations of universes of reference."[11] So, in contrast to psychoanalysis, schizoanalysis does not so much return to the past, even if "understanding how it is that you got where you are" and according to which (non)functional model you got there is a fundamental part of the method.[12] Rather, it is directed toward the future, to experimenting with producing new models, new subjectivities, with uncertain outcomes not based on preestablished diagnoses. In principle, therefore, schizoanalysis as an analytic practice is related to schizophrenia as a disease. But from this psychiatric practice schizoanalysis proposes a much more general method to evaluate the contemporary world, a method that Deleuze and Guattari have developed extensively in *A Thousand Plateaus* and Guattari has developed in his own writings even further. As noted by Gary Genosko in his insightful introduction to the work of Guattari, Guattari constructs schizoanalysis as "a complex semiotic assemblage," consisting of a new type or system of signs, a "squared sign with four equal parts":

On the bottom left side one finds material-energetic fluxes and on the top left side, the machinic phyla and their diverse technological strands, on the bottom right side, there are the existential territories of subjectivities (human and inhuman and inorganic) and on the top right side, incorporeal universes containing values, points of reference, relations with others, aesthetic experiences, utopias, imaginings, etc. On the left hand side of the square (flux and phylum) are techno-materialist functions expressed discursively, whereas on the right hand side (territories and universes) are ethico-aesthetic concerns and a myriad of qualitative issues organized non-discursively.[13]

I will stay close to the clinical conditions of schizophrenia and the psychiatric basis of schizoanalysis by looking at the technomaterialist and ethicoaesthetic sides of the neuro-image in its explicitly pathological dimensions in contemporary delirium cinema. Guattari was particularly interested in the cinema of madness, such as Marco Bellocchio's *Fists in the Pocket* (1965), Peter Robinson's *Asylum* (1972), and David Lynch's *Eraserhead* (1977), that gave artistic expression to the conditions of schizophrenia as a disease. In outlining the schizoid aspects of contemporary neuro-images, I will approach the technomaterialist dimension by way of recent neuroscientific definitions of schizophrenia. Contemporary delirium cinema will provide indications for the ethicoaesthetic dimension. The underlying assumption is that these pathological aspects tell us something about more general, salient characteristics of the neuro-image and that the schizoid mind enables the sharpest focus on contemporary culture. The final part of this chapter will make an argument for a schizoanalysis of contemporary media culture at large and discuss the different dimensions and limits of the neuro-image within this media culture.

Clinical Schizophrenia: The Disconnection
Hypothesis, Neuroplasticity, Split Brains

A clinical diagnosis of schizophrenia is based on behavioral observations and self-reported abnormal mental experiences. Symptoms of schizophrenia are conventionally divided into "positive" and "negative" types. Positive symptoms include (paranoid) delusions, hallucinations (often auditory), thought disorder and incoherent verbal expression, and bizarre behavior (all related to a feeling of experiencing "too much" of everything, seeming hyperenergetic, and frantic). Negative symptoms include emotional flattening, social withdrawal, apathy, impaired judgment, difficulties in problem solving and abstract reasoning, poor initiative and motivation, difficulty in planning, and self-neglect (all related to a lack of energy, to the point of catatonic collapse). Most forms of schizophrenia show a combination (in various degrees) of several of these symptoms.[14] Furthermore, it should be noted that the borders of clinical schizophrenia are not fixed: "Schizophrenia shares a familial predisposition with several clinical syndromes, including schizoaffective disorder, schizotypical personality disorder, and probably psychotic affective illness. This suggests the possibility of clinical and perhaps genetic overlap between certain forms of affective illness and schizophrenia."[15]

When referring to schizophrenia throughout this book, I will propose an inclusive definition of mental illnesses as "delusional or affective illnesses" that are defined as brain disorders by contemporary neuroscience, including neurological diseases such as epilepsy, autism, and (manic) depression. Some other clinical facts about schizophrenia are important as well. Research has shown that schizophrenia is generally more common in urban populations, which, considering the increasing urbanization of the contemporary world, makes it all the more a symptom of today's culture of capitalist oversaturation of people, goods, and (screen) technology.[16] Schizophrenia affects both genders in equal measures, but there are also noticeable gender differences, such as generally a later onset in women (probably due to hormonal differences) and a different balance between negative and positive symptoms (men tend to suffer more negative symptoms, women relatively more positive ones).[17] I will investigate this in the films I will discuss. In addition, although schizophrenia is part of all cultures, there are cultural differences (for instance in the content of the delirium that can be culturally determined, or the way the disorder is conceived—as illness, as sorcery, as spiritual medium) and differences related to specific cultural conditions, such as the effects of migration.[18] In the Netherlands, for instance, scientific research has indicated that male adolescents or young adults of Moroccan descent are seven times more likely to develop schizophrenia than their indigenous Dutch peers. This is explained in terms of Batesonian "double binds" between the demands of two different societies and as an effect of long-term frustrations that lead to changes in the brain. Environmental factors thus seem to be important as potential triggers of schizophrenia, which is confirmed by recent neuroscientific findings.[19]

Modern neuro-imaging techniques have given us new insights into what happens in a schizophrenic brain. Of course, the interpretations of these visualizations of (now) observable cerebral structures and processes are not undisputed. An important hypothesis is that the problem of schizophrenia has to do with the workings of neurotransmitters and the failure of certain specific areas of the brain to fully connect. Rather than delineating regional anatomical abnormalities of specialized areas of the brain ("impaired functional specialization"), the key assumption in this "disconnection hypothesis," proposed by Karl Friston, among others, is that the pathophysiology of schizophrenia is expressed as involving abnormal connections or dysfunctional integration of cortical areas. The problem, in other words, is in the synaptic connections more than in the brain areas themselves (in any case the latter seem secondary).[20] That synaptic connections are in a continual state of flux further implies time-dependent changes in connectivity or abnormal plasticity.[21] Changes in brain circuits that occur in the development of schizophrenia can be either due to specific "patterns of connectivity and neural activity intrinsic to the developing nervous system" (schizophrenia usually manifests itself in early adulthood) or are related to "use-dependent changes in synaptic efficacy that are elicited by interactions with the environment."[22] The latter form of schizophrenic connections, as experience-dependent plasticity, seems to be more important. The fact that the brain is a dynamic plastic system that can change and modulate long-term and short-term synaptic connections is a strong indication for the neurological disconnection hypothesis.

Friston refers to different types of neurological findings that provide arguments for his hypothesis, such as the identification of neurochemical disconnections and functional disconnections in functional magnetic resonance imaging (fMRI) brain scans, which suggest "that schizophrenics have an abnormal pattern of functional connectivity involving both an absence of correlations between prefrontal and superior temporal regions and the presence of abnormal positive correlations between prefrontal and more posterior middle temporal cortex."[23] In sum, modern neuroscientific studies consider schizophrenia a brain disorder that can be related to abnormal synaptic connections and plasticity.

Another hypothesis in neuroscientific discourse that is important in connection to schizophrenia is the research conducted with split-brain patients, which suggests the potential of different balances of left and right hemisphere functions in schizophrenic brains. I will return to this area of neuroscience more specifically in the next chapter. Here I want to refer to a 2008 lecture by neuroanatomist Jill Bolte Taylor, who presented her personal experience of a stroke in her left hemisphere to TED-TV.[24] At the beginning of her talk Bolte Taylor explains that her professional interest in neuroscience developed because she has a schizophrenic brother and wanted to understand why he was not able to connect to reality in the way neurotypical persons can. Her stroke made it very clear that the two brain halves process information in very different ways, which seems to give them different "personalities":

Our right hemisphere is about right here, right now. It thinks in pictures and it learns kinesthetically through the movement of our bodies. Information in the form of energy streams in simultaneously through all of our sensory systems. Then it explodes into this enormous collage of what this present moment looks like. What this present moment smells like and tastes like, what it feels like, and what it sounds like. I am an energy being connected to the energy all around me through the consciousness of my right hemisphere.

The left hemisphere thinks linearly and methodologically. The left hemisphere is all about the past and all about the future. It picks details from the present, and details from those details and categorizes them, associates them with everything we learned in the past and projects into the future all of our possibilities. The left hemisphere thinks in language. It's that ongoing brain chatter that connects me and my internal world to my external world. It's that little voice that says "I am, I am." This is the part of my brain that I lost on the morning of my stroke.

Bolte Taylor's story is incredibly moving and insightful. She recalls how on the morning of her stroke she tried to take a shower, but her hands seemed like primitive claws, and she could no longer define the boundaries of her body and the wall: the molecules and atoms of the wall and her arm coincided. At some moments when her left-brain gave a wave of clarity, she realized she had to call for help. Locating what she thought was her business card, containing her work phone number, all she could see were pixels: "pixels of words" blended with pixels of the card's background and the pixels of the symbols. Her brain hemorrhage became bigger, and by the time she was brought in to hospital, she felt "enormous and expansive, like a genie just liberated from her bottle," expanding into the universe. How could she ever squeeze the enormousness of herself inside that tiny little bottle (body) again? When she woke up in the hospital, she was "like a baby in a woman's body" and had to learn everything from scratch. With the help of her mother, it took her eight years to recover. Some neuroscientists argue the distinction Bolte Taylor makes between the two hemispheres is outdated. Indeed, it is by now common knowledge that the two brain halves may have specific functions but that to function well, these hemispheres need to communicate and connect.[25] However, Bolte Taylor's view is that she had an unusually unrestricted experience of the right hemisphere; this insight in differences between the hemispheres can still be quite illuminating for our understandings of schizophrenia, some forms of which (and this is confirmed by recent experiments) involve imbalanced hemispherical functions.[26]

It is interesting to see how neuroscientific findings on schizophrenia, alongside Bolte Taylor's personal insights into hemispherical dysfunction, dialogue with Deleuze and Guattari's considerations of the pathological characteristics of the disorder. In *Anti-Oedipus* (and in the posthumously published collection of articles by Deleuze, *Two Regimes of Madness*) they distinguish two poles of schizophrenia, two poles in the delirium. One is the machinic pole or the pole of the machine-organ. Here Deleuze and Guattari seem to anticipate the neurological disconnection hypothesis when they argue that the schizophrenic presents what the unconscious really is, namely a factory full of "machinic connections." They recall Bruno Bettelheim's story of little Joey, who "can live, eat, defecate and sleep only if he is plugged into machines provided with motors, wires, lights, carburetors, propellers and steering wheels: an electric feeding-machine, a car-machine that enables him to breathe."[27] "Connecticut, Connect-I-Cut!" . . . Deleuze and Guattari explain Joey's machinic desire:

Every machine functions as a break in the flow of relations to the machine to which it is connected, but at the same time it is also a flow itself, or the production of a flow, in relation to the machine connected to it. . . . Everywhere there are break-flows out of which desire wells up, thereby constituting its productivity and continually grafting the process of production onto the product.[28]

Deleuze and Guattari give a very positive, almost Dadaist, reading of little Joey's disorder, one that results in all kinds of unexpected and creative connections. Their point, however, is clear: machinic and unexpected connections are key aspects of schizophrenia. Wild synaptic connections function like little machines that produce new desires. Especially emphasized by Deleuze and Guattari are those break-flows that destabilize and escape from the psychoanalytic family triangle. The delirium is not so much related to the Oedipal theater of the Freudian unconscious but instead is connected to the feeling of "too much of history." The delirium concocts "races, civilizations, cultures, continents, kingdoms, powers, wars, classes and revolutions"; all delirium is sociopolitical and economic or world-historical, they argue.[29] Here Deleuze and Guattari stay close to the experiences of real schizophrenics but turn the condition into something positive, mostly defining it as a way out of the psychoanalytic familial matrix. It is not difficult to recognize in this that the machine-organ pole translates the positive symptoms of clinical schizophrenia into a process capable of investigating the libidinal economy of the social field. The other pole of the delirium is the pole of the Body without Organs. The Body without Organs (BwO) relates to a rupture of the normal organization of the organs: "Why not walk on your head, sing with your sinuses, see through your skin, breathe with your belly," Deleuze and Guattari propose most famously in *A Thousand Plateaus*.[30] At the same time, the BwO is also the zero-degree model of death: "It is catatonic schizophrenia that gives its model to death. Zero intensity. The death model appears when the body without organs repels the organs and lays them aside: no mouth, no tongue, no teeth—to the point of self-mutilation, to the point of suicide."[31] This pole can be related to the negative symptoms of clinical schizophrenia, recognized by Deleuze and Guattari as such when they refer to the BwO as catatonic schizophrenia.

Whether involving machine-organ connections or creations of (deadly) BwOs, the most important characteristic of the experience of schizophrenia that Deleuze and Guattari emphasize is the sensation of intensity, of a becoming. The delirium can only be grasped at the level of sensations: "I feel that I'm becoming-woman, I feel that I'm becoming-God, I feel that I'm becoming a clairvoyant, I feel that I'm becoming pure matter."[32] These "delusional" and "affective" dimensions of schizophrenia are part of an "a-signifying semiotics" that Guattari and Deleuze develop as a counter to the purely linguistic dominance of semiology. A-signifying semiotics "is reticent, hesitant, working only with parts and their intensities, without imposing on them further form: signification never culminates."[33] Recalling Jill Bolte Taylor's story, which concludes with an explicit call for more acceptance of the affective and connecting openness of the right hemisphere, we could argue that Deleuze and Guattari's concern for schizophrenia relates to a similar desire to create more awareness for the "world of the right hemisphere" in a dominantly left-hemispheric culture. I will now turn to some films that deal explicitly with schizophrenia, to see how this ethicoaesthetic comprehension of clinical conditions is rendered in different penetrating ways and to consider further problems relating to the schizophrenic aspects of the neuro-image.

Schizophrenia's World-Historical and Familial Disconnections

Malek Bensmail's documentary *Alienations* (2003), in which the filmmaker follows the doctors and patients of one of the few mental hospitals in Algeria, presents viewers with a privileged, respectful, and telling picture of clinical schizophrenia. Bensmail, an Algerian documentary filmmaker working in France and Algeria, spent long periods filming in the mental hospital in Constantine, where his father used to work as a doctor. In the filmed patients, we recognize both the positive and negative poles of schizophrenia: connecting machine-bodies especially in their speech link everything in seemingly wild ways, and catatonic BwOs, completely blunted or suicidal. The film opens with the scene of a girl who is having an intense conversation in French with a man who, we later learn, is a doctor. Explaining that she has degrees in biology, medicine, law, and veterinary medicine and speaks seven languages, the girl concludes by saying that she feels she has supernatural and metaphysical powers. The longer she talks, the more we realize the fantasmatic and paranoid nature of her discourse. But the intensity of her feelings and the abundance of energy to her hallucinations, which Deleuze and Guattari describe as the positive symptoms of schizophrenia (usually stronger in female patients), are remarkable. As mentioned, while schizophrenia can affect both genders and most schizophrenics show a mixture of (or alternate between) negative and positive symptoms, there are noticeable differences in the condition between genders as well. Male patients tend to display more negative symptoms, such as social withdrawal, self-neglect, and illogical thinking and sometimes more susceptibility to alcohol, drug abuse, or violent outbursts.[34]

In another scene male patients, whom the filmmaker follows more closely, have a group conversation. One of the patients starts a discourse about America, which he ends by singing Michael Jackson's "We are the world, we are the children . . ." He speaks a mixture of French, Arabic, and English. The effect of his intermixing of languages is somewhat lost in translation, but in terms of the content he states:

Now, you have to remember this: you were told, "we are the world—we are the children." Don't cut me off when I'm speaking. . . . Yes! But I want to say something else. Why is America bombing Iraq, bombing Iraq, bombing Iraq. Iraq has never asked anything of them. They want everything from the whole world because they sing, "we are the world we are the children." We are all brothers. Even the pacific Jews, I'm with them.

Several things are noticeable in this scene. First, the confusion of language is striking. No language is spoken very well. This is a well-known symptom of schizophrenia, but it is also very much a general (schizophrenic) problem in Algeria, which, since independence, has only partially and quite unsystematically replaced the previous French educational system with Arabic, creating disorder symptomatic of the colonial past. Second, the world-historical dimensions of the discourse are striking. World politics, the war in Iraq, the Israel-Palestine conflict, and many more elements are all connected (Connect-I-Cut) in one discourse. However, just as the confusion of language can be made to make sense, this confusion and mixture of political references is actually not so very strange, because world politics is also what overwhelms "sane" people, causing feelings of despair and anxiety. Third, the impression of mutual respect between doctors and patients is significant. There appears to be a bond between doctors and patients that is only separated by a small degree of sanity (or perhaps a white coat). Apart from the world political situations mentioned here, it is very clear that many patients have deep wounds from the civil war in Algeria during the 1990s, when life there was insecure for everybody. Victims and perpetrators are equally afflicted and brought together in this reality. Fourth, the role of the camera itself cannot be ignored. The camera is not a "fly on the wall" but is clearly addressed. Sometimes the patients speak to the filmmaker directly and are very conscious of what is being filmed. (During the shooting of the film they saw the recordings regularly.) The filmmaker is implicated in the process of filming, what Deleuze has called the "mutual-becoming" of filmmaker and characters in the modern political film.[35] Further, doctors, patients, and the filmmaker are all implicated in the same world, which is very touching and implies that the spectator is implicated as well—it is also our world. We can recognize here Deleuze and Guattari's arguments: that the delirium moves between connecting machinic and deadly catatonic poles, that it is world-historical and sociopolitical, and that many elements of the schizo are actually also part of our daily experiences—especially the feeling of being overwhelmed by world politics (which is enhanced by increasing amounts of audiovisual data). The film, however, also seems to indicate something else.

When we look at the film from a perspective of cultural specificity, it is the socius, the political, that seems to be always the prime target and source of the deliriums of the patients in this Algerian clinic. Algeria is a collective culture where there is little consideration for individual problems or traumas in the first place. This factor, according to Bensmail, is the most fundamental problem for these patients: they blame the government (Bouteflika and older presidents are frequently mentioned). Problems are not considered at the level of the individual or near home in the family context. In collective cultures thinking on an individual level could be an important level of micropolitical movement (which does not automatically mean forgetting about the world-political). In this respect something remarkable happens in the film. The patient just quoted for his discourse on Iraq later confesses to Bensmail's camera a personal childhood trauma of sexual abuse, an experience that he never told the doctors. Such stories are infrequently told in collective cultures because these are taboo subjects—one could argue that the camera in this case helps to individualize this patient productively.[36]

For Deleuze and Guattari the enemy is psychoanalysis's insistence on the individual, Oedipus, and the family. Everything they positively argue for in *Anti-Oedipus* as aspects of schizoanalysis is negatively assumed by the concepts of psychoanalysis. For instance, they argue that the first reason for a "breakthrough" to turn into a clinical "breakdown" is neuroticization and oedipalization: "First the process is arrested, the limit of desiring-production is displaced, travestied, and now passes into the Oedipal subaggregate. So the schizo is effectively neuroticised, and it is this neuroticisation that constitutes his illness."[37] In certain contexts, however, it might be argued that a return to the family could sometimes be a necessary step. Although Deleuze and Guattari certainly acknowledge the existence of Oedipus and the influence of the family, they perhaps create too strong a binary opposition between psychoanalysis and schizoanalysis or, more generally, between the family and the socius. In *Alienations* the patient's personal confession about a childhood trauma of sexual abuse might just as well be a breakthrough (and not automatically a neuroticization). At other moments of the film the longing for a family, for a mother and a father, is so overwhelmingly part of almost all the patient's desiring machines that it cannot be ignored. This is not to argue that we should go back to Oedipal psychoanalysis per se—the shortcomings of the Oedipal model as a fixed matrix are obvious and well demonstrated by Deleuze and Guattari (and others). I also do not want to deny the imprisoning family structures that take form in a collective society. However, the principle of the family as part of the whole network of connections, desires, and love should not be overlooked. In a contemporary intercultural, transnational world it is clear that the notion of the family itself has changed through emancipation and migration.[38] The schizoid mind is world-historical, without a doubt, but it is also still closely associated with the (problem of the) family. Family and society are both important elements in the brain's influencing environments, and this importance resonates in many films that deal with schizophrenia.[39]

The Temporal Architecture of Schizophrenia

The Butterfly Effect (Eric Bress and J. Mackye Gruber, 2004) is another film in which the family is important, not as an Oedipal matrix but in connection to the main character's paternally inherited brain disease and to a traumatic childhood experience. The film also goes beyond these hereditary and childhood problems to ask questions about our relationship to the brain's temporal architecture and the desire to change our destinies. *The Butterfly Effect*'s tagline is "Change one thing, change everything," referring to chaos theory and how chaos relates to the quite ordinary state of the human brain.[40] The film's emblematic title image is a brain scan that very subtly suggests the flapping wings of a butterfly. On the DVD extras scientists explain how chaos theory in physics describes how a very tiny difference (such as a slightly different position in space) can create enormous differences in resulting movements and outcomes that are unpredictable. *The Butterfly Effect* takes these insights of modern science and grounds them with knowledge of psychiatric disorders and the real traumatic influence human beings can have on each other. It then gives this experimental grounding a more fantastic spin, allowing its main character, who suffers from epileptic seizures and blackouts, to travel through time, change one little thing in the past, and thus change the future present.[41] As Deleuze has shown in his cinema books, the problem of time is intrinsically related to the medium of film and has metaphysical dimensions.[42] In the second part of this book I will return to the philosophical questions of time and the brain in respect to the neuro-image. (In fact, a new relation to time will be a crucial argument in the conception of the neuro-image, as I will argue in Chapter 4.) Here, however, I want to remain close to the film, its specific temporal experiments and its clinical and scientific references to the brain, to consider it as just one possible experiment (among many possible others) in connecting a different conception of time to the delirious schizobrain. In this sense *The Butterfly Effect* offers not only an imaginative spin on a contemporary neurological condition but could also be read in a more allegorical way about our "times."[43]

In *The Butterfly Effect* the madness of the film's main character, Evan Treborn (Ashton Kutcher), is portrayed as a neurological disease: he suffers from blackouts and epileptic seizures. The story of the film is told from three moments in Evan's life: Evan at the age of seven (played by Logan Lerman), when he and his friends Lenny (Elden Henson), Tommy (William Lee Scott), and Kayleigh (Amy Smart) have a traumatic (incestual) experience orchestrated by Mr. Miller (Eric Stolz), who is Kayleigh's and Tommy's father; Evan at the age of thirteen (played by John Patrick Amedori), when the four friends cause an accident; and Evan at the age of twenty, when he is in a mental institution in severe states of delusion, where the film starts. The plot moves back and forth between these different moments. However, the time layers are interwoven with other possible pasts and their respective futures through which Evan wakes up in changed presents. In his blackouts Evan seems to be able to change the past. Wanting to save Kayleigh from a known future in which she is a traumatized, depressed, and lonely diner waitress, he goes back to the moments of their childhood, makes different choices, and returns to a present where Kayleigh has changed—differently—into a sorority girl, then a heroin junkie prostitute, and also an earthy type of hippie girl, depending on the impact of the different changed pasts. However, the destinies of all the other characters, including Evan's own, change in each temporal alteration as well, in some cases very dramatically. (In one version Evan saves Kayleigh but kills Tommy; in another he causes Lenny's institutionalization; in yet another he prevents the accident when they are teenagers but is wounded himself and wakes up in a present where he has no arms and his mother dies of lung cancer because she starts chain-smoking after Evan's accident).

Aesthetically, the images of the time travel and memory flashes also have different color saturations and densities, which create patterns of recognition. A very special shade of red, called "Miller Red" in the director's commentary, indicates the presence of danger. "Institutional green" is connected to Evan's father's insanity and thus the hereditary legacy of his seizures and frightening abilities. We see here quite literally what Deleuze has called "an encounter occur[ring] between the brain and color," that is "an important element in the awareness of the 'new world.'" The brain and film aesthetics are interconnected, indicating that the combination creates new worlds. In *The Butterfly Effect* it is even suggested quite literally that the brain should be seen as a film: think of your life as a film, rewind, go back, reedit. The problem is that the complexity of the brain itself (and chaos) does not allow us to foresee all the consequences, in spite of our desire for control.

Evan Treborn is put in an fMRI scanner several times throughout the film, and the unusually excessive plasticity of his brain is discovered mostly in the outer layers of the cerebral cortex, where hemorrhaging and massive neural reconstruction can be noticed. "Forty years of memory in one year; it's an overloaded city, like a reprogrammed brain," Evan comments on his own brain scans, referring in these sequences to general scientific insights about the abnormal plasticity and synaptic connectivity of schizophrenic and epileptic brains. Epilepsy can be considered a modern affective brain disorder that is an important reference in elaborating schizoanalysis. Gary Genosko has demonstrated that Guattari was especially interested in Marco Bellocchio's film *Fists in the Pocket* (1965) because of its treatment of epilepsy. Genosko compares this film to Anton Corbijn's *Control* (2007), about Joy Division's lead singer, Ian Curtis, who suffered from severe epileptic attacks and finally committed suicide. Genosko points out that the affective intensities of epileptic seizures have the potential to create new visions, new aesthetics.[44] I would like to emphasize here this understanding of epilepsy as a form of schizophrenia in which neural connections are made much too quickly and its relationship to contemporary screen culture as an overloaded "brain-city."[45] In *The Aesthetics of Disappearance* Virilio refers to "pyknolepsy," a mild form of epilepsy in which a person is disconnected from reality and misses parts of the ongoing, oversaturated present. In pyknolepsy, and even more in epilepsy, the brain operates too quickly, makes too many connections at the same time, causing literal overload and seizure.[46] Similarly, we can say that our screen and media overload produces epilepsy and therefore calls for a schizoanalysis. I will return to schizoanalysis by way of media culture more generally at the end of this chapter (and to Virilio's "aesthetics of disappearance" in connection to our contemporary screens in the last chapter).

For now I want to conclude my remarks on *The Butterfly Effect* by referring to three scenes that were deleted in the theatrical release but reinserted into the director's cut ("Thank God for DVD," the directors exclaim with relief). In the first deleted scene Evan finds documents in an old shoe box that indicate he inherited his disease from the male side of his family. Not only his father but also his grandfather had been hospitalized for the same mental illness. In another scene he learns from his mother that he was actually her third baby; two others were stillborn before him. This leads to the ending that the directors originally planned, where Evan, after so many variations of the past and its futures in the present all go wrong, decides to go back to the moment before his birth and strangle himself with the umbilical cord, preventing his own birth. His mother, this cut suggests, will then have a daughter from another husband (breaking the male insanity heritage), and Kayleigh will marry somebody else. The studio did not want this ending, considering it too dark.[47] It is a dark ending indeed. But apart from being dark, it is also a mysteriously powerful narrative option that, in fact, can only be explained as an "insane" solution to the question of (im)possible futures. *The Butterfly Effect* is told from the perspective of the future, an important dimension of the neuroimage that I will develop later in this book.

What is striking at this point is the fact that so many films that deal with contemporary insanity and mental illness refer to the family, to birth, death, and the longing for parents and for parenting. It seems that schizoanalysis will have to reconsider the family, but, next to genetic components that influence the disease, to recognize family structures as important (dis)connecting machines and influential environments. At the same time, *The Butterfly Effect* makes clear that there is never a linear and direct cause (such as the Oedipus triangle) and especially that schizophrenia is a temporal phenomenon. This insight seems to be shared by neuroscientific perspectives, according to which "the temporal architecture of schizophrenia is characterized by bursts of complex, nonlinear phenomena alternating with truly random events."[48] I will return to the metaphysical aspects of this "temporal architecture" in Chapter 4. I will also return to the nonlinear dynamics of schizophrenia when I discuss more explicitly the nonlinear temporality, database logic, and archival intensities of contemporary digital culture (in Chapter 7).

From Eye to Brain: Delirium in the Digital Age

I have emphasized the world-historical, familial, and temporal dimensions of schizophrenia; I now want to focus on changed portrayals of the realities of delirium and its affective dimensions in cinema in the digital age. To do so, I propose to read earlier films that show female delirium, Fassbinder's *Fear of Fear* (1975) and John Cassavetes's *Love Streams* (1984) in (asymmetric) parallel to two contemporary delirious films, *Antichrist* (Lars von Trier, 2009) and *Inland Empire* (David Lynch, 2007). As I have mentioned, schizophrenia in women is generally expressed in more "positive symptoms" than it is in men. Women are said to show "more signs of situational and free-floating anxiety, depersonalisation and derealisation."[49] Here, then, I will look at some key filmic expressions of "female" schizophrenia and the complex interplay between individual, familial, and societal components that connect to madness. My hypothesis is that although Fassbinder and Cassavetes present mental matters in a powerful and deeply moving way, the aesthetics of their films leave the "reality principle" intact. This is not the case in the later films by Von Trier and Lynch, which illustrate a change that seems to be symptomatic for the neuro-image. I will first discuss Fassbinder and Von Trier and then Cassavetes and Lynch to develop this argument.

Fassbinder's depiction of characters on the verge of mental breakdowns is well known and has been discussed extensively. Therefore, I will focus only on his film made for German television (WDR), *Fear of Fear*, which explicitly delves into insanity. Margot Staudte (Margit Carstensen) is a middle-class homemaker who is pregnant with her second child. While Margot seems happy with her daughter Bibi (Constanze Haas) and husband, Kurt (Ulrich Faulhaber), from the beginning Fassbinder's mise-en-scène and camera work tells us that this is not actually the case. The apartment they live in is comfortable but cramped; Margot always seems stuck between the frames of her kitchen door, or between the couch and the table in the living room. An online review of the film suggests one of the salient features in the mise-en-scène:

Fassbinder's motif of fragmented people, show[s] them literally and metaphorically, cut off. The narrow hallways and doors block characters from each other and, by implication, themselves. Fassbinder is especially deft at using this device to develop, through purely visually means, the enigmatic character of Bibi, Margot's young, often silent daughter. Her fragmentation does not bode well for the future, but of course it adds to the poignancy of this sweet-natured but profoundly unfulfilled child.[50]

At several other instances Fassbinder emphasizes the bond between mother and daughter and suggests that Bibi, who completely identifies with her mother, could very well follow the same path as she. Contrary to *Petra von Kant*, in which Margit Carstensen plays a distant mother who is too involved with her own despair, Margot in *Fear of Fear* appears to love her daughter too much, this suggested by a parallelism in framing. Another stylistic feature that emphasizes that Margot is "framed" is the recurrent surveilling point-of-view shot, implicating the perspectives of Kurt's mother (Brigitte Mira) and sister (Irm Hermann) living in the apartment above them. The disapproving look from family and society is similarly employed in other Fassbinder films, especially *Ali: Fear Eats the Soul* (1974), in which an elderly woman, Emmi, falls in love with a Moroccan guest worker (El Hedi Ben Salem). Emmi is movingly performed by the same Brigitte Mira who in *Fear Eats the Soul* is on the receiving end of the surveilling eyes of her neighbors. However, while the fear in *Fear Eats the Soul* refers to the anxieties of normative society to accept any kind of unusual love affair, more often the fear in *Fear of Fear* refers to Margot's inner relation to a fear that foments in relation to itself, alongside the oppressive demands of normative behavior.[51]

Margot's fear is expressed on the one hand by the frequent use of mirrors that show her disintegration and loss of her sense of self. Looking in the mirror, she says, "This is me. Me. Me? What is that? What is that, me? Uhh." At other moments she just stares, repeats words, as if in a trance, or collapses in bed or on the couch. Her field of vision becomes unstable. When panic attacks kick in, her point of view is rendered in "wavy" images. Margot tries to fight her fears by occupying herself with baking cakes or playing with her child and listening to Leonard Cohen records, but she feels she cannot stop her fear, which seems to be a "free-floating" anxiety and not directly related to one particular cause. Although (as I have suggested) the film's style indicates some societal causes, Margot herself does not know why she feels so scared. Her husband is absent-minded and too preoccupied with his work and studies to notice what his wife is going through. ("I want you to love me Kurt, to desire me, to wrench me from my despair," she whispers at a certain moment without him hearing it.) She finds relief in cognac and tranquilizers, provided to her in large quantities by the local pharmacist in exchange for sex. She cuts herself ("to take my mind off the fear") and is then diagnosed with schizophrenia. At the end of the film she is rediagnosed as severely depressed: "but we can treat that with drugs," the female doctor in the clinic states. The doctor additionally gives Margot advice to "read, go to school or look for a job, earn your own money." In the final scene of the film Margot is home again, typing, and she is sedately calm. Her brother-in-law Karli (Armin Meir), who has always sympathized with her, passes by to tell her that on the other side of the street Mr. Bauer (Kurt Raaben), the insane man who always stared at Margot (another recurrent, frightening mirror image throughout the film), has hanged himself. Margot gets up and looks out of the window. As the end credits begin over her point of view, the images start to wave again. Since the credits are another frame of the film, one can wonder if it is really Margot's point of view (indicating there is no "progress" for Margot) or if this is a general reference to the central theme of the film. The film's conclusion remains ambiguous.

Fear of Fear is related to the clinical symptoms of schizophrenia that express a free-floating fear and to the depersonalization typical in feminine schizophrenia that has a highly affective dimension. "The most terrifying fear is the fear that has no discernible cause. It simply exists; like an air plant, it requires no soil to flourish and grow, only a host," a reviewer suggested when the film came out in New York in 1976.[52] Although for Margot this is indeed what she experiences, Fassbinder suggests some kind of "soil" in oppressive societal norms and a certain lack of communication. It could also be argued that Margot simply does not know how to deal with her strong feelings of love and vitality that just don't fit into the narrow space in which her life must play out. In a free indirect way the film stays with Margot by directly presenting her subjective (wavy and "straight") points of view, as well as more objective shots that frame her. It is always clear that we look with Margot, that her reality is distorted, and that she knows that what she sees does not align with others' realities. Furthermore, however subjectively the film presents Margot's experiences on Fassbinder's screen, we remain on the outside of her mental space or, more accurately, retain a critical relation to it.

It is interesting to compare Fassbinder's perspective on female insanity with that of Lars von Trier in his film *Antichrist*. Previously, in *The Idiots* (1998), Von Trier explicitly dealt with madness, confronting borderline experience through simulation. *Antichrist* was Von Trier's own therapeutic project that he used to work himself out of a deep depression that had prevented him from working for a long time. Out of the pitch-blackness of his deepest fears and anxieties this film addresses a "grief deeper than grief."[53] The cause of the grief in *Antichrist* is not "free-floating" but instead very specific: a couple simply indicated as She and He (Charlotte Gainsbourg and Willem Dafoe) lose their child, a quintessential experience of devastation. Through this story, however, Von Trier connects to deep layers of an asubjective collective unconscious that penetrates the images, the characters, and the narrative. Von Trier, first through his own madness, and subsequently through his film, connects with these "feminine" aspects of schizophrenia in ways that are illuminating for our larger comprehension of schizoanalytics.

Like other Von Trier films, such as *Breaking the Waves* (1996) and *Dogville* (2003), *Antichrist* is structured in chapters. After a black-and-white prologue (where we see in slow motion how a child falls from a window while his parents are making love), chapters entitled "Grief," "Pain (Chaos Reigns)," "Despair (Genocide)," and "The Three Beggars" show the film's events in somber colors, followed by an epilogue, also in black and white. After the death of the child "She" is so grief stricken that she collapses into a catatonic state. "He" is a therapist and decides to take it on himself to help her through her mourning and beyond it. "You've always been distant to me, now that I come to think of it," She remarks. "I never interested you until now that I'm your patient." She throws away all the medication she is supposed to swallow, and the grief she experiences from her loss washes over her completely (in this sense she takes the opposite direction of Margot, who is heavily medicated at the end of Fassbinder's film). He observes her, analyzes the steps in her mourning process (catatonia, grief, panic attacks), and gives her exposure therapy, asking her to make a list of what she is afraid of. In spite of the obvious "cause" in this film, like Margot in *Fear of Fear* She answers, "I don't know what I'm afraid of. Can't I just be afraid without a definite object?" The couple decides to go to the woods, an archetypical place for frightening experiences, and often the location of horror films (and the genre that Von Trier most closely aligns this film with). Moreover, the woods are called Eden, which brings in another set of archetypical and biblical associations.

In Eden, where the couple has a cottage and where She spent last summer with their son working on a thesis, the therapy continues. In the woods He encounters a deer with a dead fawn hanging from her rear. Later, He also sees a fox disemboweling itself, who speaks to tell him "Chaos reigns." He finds her thesis work, a study on witch hunts in the sixteenth century and other misogynist practices (in the film chapter titled "Genocide"). It becomes evident that She has started to believe that women are indeed as evil as such misogyny contested and that they are controlled by Nature. The much-discussed and -debated horror scenes of genital mutilation (She crushes his testicles and, when in a flashback we see that She thinks that she saw her son falling but did nothing to prevent it, severs her clitoris with a rusty pair of scissors) leads to a final confrontation. While hiding from his maniacal wife in a fox nest He encounters a third symbolic animal, a crow buried alive that manages to survive, just as He does when She pulls him out from the ground. He finally burns her at the stake. In the epilogue He walks in the woods, eating berries, while hundreds of anonymous women with digitally blurred faces walk toward him. The Jungian archetypical references to the collective unconscious (analyzed most convincingly by Christian Kerslake in connection to the Deleuzian unconscious) are not difficult to decipher.[54] The forces of Nature strongly connect to motherhood and femininity, and the forces of inner nature are all bundled into a transhistorical fear.

What is interesting in the context of the neuro-image is that we encounter here a form of schizophrenia that is related to a Jungian hypothesis, "according to which in schizophrenia there is an *abaissement du niveau mental* to a fatal level, at the moment in which the individual enters into contact with the archetypes or the symbols of the collective unconscious, whose tide washes over him."[55] This is why the strong performances of the sole two actors in the film are infused with a collective crowdedness that gives the horror an affective power that cuts so deeply. Moreover, like in Kubrick's *The Shining* and Tarkovsky's *The Mirror* (both films are acknowledged sources of inspiration for Von Trier), we have entered a mental world. *The Shining* and *The Mirror* are time-images, described by Deleuze as crystals through which the actual and the virtual rotate, sometimes even in indistinguishable ways. Yet in these films there is always a movement back and forth between the actual and the virtual, the mental and reality. In *Antichrist* there is no way of telling at what point we have slipped into Her and/or His mental space, and we certainly don't escape either psychotic reality. Compared to Margot's insanity and fear in Fassbinder's film that we see through Margot's eyes, here we have entered the chaotic reality of the brain-world that is normally invisible to the eyes, but brought to the screen with digital technology as a machine of the invisible.

While Von Trier's Dogme films used digital technology to obtain a certain freedom and at the same time impose rules that organize the possibility of creative work in a world of unlimited possibilities, in *Antichrist* digital technology is used to create special effects.[56] The film was shot on digital video, and in postproduction an additional eighty shots were generated with digital effects, such as the talking-fox scene. Other effects, such as the moment where She fuses with the green nature that surrounds her, and the scenes of enigmatic slow motion in the woods that have a painterly quality, were also created digitally. These digital aesthetics are part of the seamless slippage into the mental world of the neuro-image. If the comparison between *Fear of Fear* and *Antichrist* has shown how our conception of the screen has shifted "from eye to brain," a comparison between another couple of delirious filmmakers indicates other aspects of this shift into a different type of image culture: John Cassavetes's portrayal of madness and David Lynch's strange worlds show a transition from body to brain (albeit a sensual and affective brain tightly related to the body).

Between Body and Brain: DIY
Spectacles of Madness

At this point I should explicitly mention the contexts and frameworks through which we reencounter previous types of cinema (a point that I will develop in different directions in Chapters 5, 7, and 9). One of the great things about contemporary digital culture is that not only do old masterpieces of cinema become replayable (often with interesting commentaries, background material and insightful stories, and uncut or alternative versions) but also that much material from televisual archives and other previously invisible material (because of safe storage in more or less closed archives) can be re-viewed. For my preparation of a symposium on Cassavetes at the EYE Dutch Film Institute, where I watched again on beautiful celluloid prints classics like *Opening Night* (1977), *Gloria* (1980), *Faces* (1968), and *A Woman Under the Influence* (1974), I searched for Cassavetes material online. I was able to directly access via YouTube the bewilderment and embarrassment of TV show host Dick Cavett and his audience when John Cassavetes, Peter Falk, and Ben Gazzara appeared on the famous show on the occasion of the release of *Husbands* in 1970, where the three actors behaved like fools: Cassavetes throwing himself on the floor every three minutes, Gazzara taking off his socks and shoes to show his hairy legs, and Falk ignoring the host of the show to address only the audience.[57] In another YouTube clip, a 1965 episode of the French television program *Cinemas Cinemas*, Cassavetes gives a guided tour of his house (his film set), while he and his team are working on *Faces*.[58] Similarly, I can be affected by the revelations of the documentary *I'm Almost Not Crazy* (available online in fragments of ten minutes) and its insights about Cassavetes's philosophy of love.[59] In *Cassavetes in 60 Seconds* and other clips, Cassavetes repeatedly expresses that he thinks the "world is very chicken," too tight, too afraid.[60] However, while navigating these specific sequences, I noted that slowly but surely other images started to impose themselves on me—images not from the wonderful Cassavetes retrospective or the DVD box, not from YouTube's open and viral archive, but from my own memories of another film, namely David Lynch's *Inland Empire*. Lynch's often surreal and dark enigmatic images do not seem to connect easily with the earthly world of Cassavetes. Nevertheless, I suggest that by "going digital" with *Inland Empire*, Lynch's work reveals more explicitly than ever before its connections to the concerns of Cassavetes's films, especially regarding the role of spectacle and madness in contemporary media culture, then and now.

Cassavetes's films seem a no-budget celluloid precursor to the DIY/Dogme digital aesthetics that are currently common practice in independent cinema, in European cinema, and on YouTube ("John saw the dawn two hours earlier than anybody else," Peter Falk says in several documentaries on Cassavetes). Lynch, on the other hand, is much more known as a "celluloid fetishist" who pushes the aesthetic potential of high production values and, arguably, has even set the standards for the current production values of contemporary quality television series[61] since his acclaimed 1990s *Twin Peaks*, shot on 35 mm film and with budgets exceeding $1 million per episode.[62] However, as a fast adaptor, with *Inland Empire* Lynch made a huge embracing leap toward the digital: "Film is like a dinosaur in a tar pit," he declared in an interview.[63] *Inland Empire* was shot on a relatively primitive Sony PD-150, a consumer-grade model that was introduced in 2001 at a retail price of less than $4,000. Most commonly used in the production of home movies and viral video, it is a DIY medium indeed. As one reviewer has already argued, this movie is great on the big screen but its natural home is the small screen:

Watch *Inland Empire* on DVD and you sense that this lurid, grubby fantasy springs from deep within the bowels of YouTube as much as from inside its heroine's muddy unconscious. . . . And not only does *Inland Empire* often look like it belongs on the Internet, it also progresses with the darting, associative logic of hyperlinks. Indeed part of the movie originated on David Lynch's Website, davidlynch.com, itself a labyrinth of wormholes and worlds within worlds.[64]

Others have described the film as "random access cinema," typical for the digital age, characterized by a database logic and a digital poetics.[65] We see here that all of a sudden, this switch to the digital has brought Lynch's work closer to Cassavetes, if only in terms of a shared frayed aesthetics. In terms of production costs Lynch has also discovered the kind of freedom the camcorder grants in allowing for a smaller crew and the cessation of accountability to financiers; these freedoms and this independence was always already dear to Cassavetes.

One layer below the surface of these films (which are beginning to show more aesthetic similarities), there is a basic difference in the source from which they derive their power, namely through the body or the brain. If Cassavetes was a very physical director of a cinema of the body, Lynch is a cerebral director, creating a cinema of the brain. As Deleuze has argued in *The Time-Image*, "body or brain is what cinema demands to be given to it, what it gives to itself, what it invents itself, to construct its work according to two directions, each one of which is simultaneously abstract and concrete,"[66] each one being equally emotional and thoughtful. These regimes, moreover, constitute two different types of cinema: "The brain gives orders to the body, which is just an outgrowth of it, but the body also gives orders to the brain, which is just a part of it: in both cases, these will not be the same bodily attitudes nor the same cerebral gest. Hence the specificity of a cinema of the brain, in relation to that of the cinema of the bodies."[67] Cassavetes works very much from the bodies of the actors, theatricalizes or "spectacularizes" them—not in the sense of glamorizing them but in the sense that the characters are brought back to their bodily attitudes that become expressive of a feeling (tiredness, boredom, despair, depression, love) and that constitute the truth of their character. As Deleuze has argued in *Faces*, bodily attitudes are expressed in the face; in *A Woman Under the Influence* Gena Rowlands expresses and constitutes a housewife "under the influence" of social norms and boredom through her bodily attitudes and gestures; in *Gloria* the abandoned child sticks (literally) to the body of the woman who first pushes him away, which constitutes a powerful bond between the two when they are on the run in New York.[68] Cinema of the body: full of intense feelings, full of unconscious thoughts. Lynch on the other hand has always been intrigued by matters of the mind. His main inspiration is surrealism, which insists on the mental distortions of dreams, visions, and delirium. His films have always been explorations of characters' emotions through a presentation of their inner life. In *Blue Velvet* (1986) the passage into the dark, inner fantasies of the main character is marked very clearly and quite literally when the camera zooms into a cut ear and zooms out of a mind at the end of the adventure. Later films *Lost Highway* (1997) and *Mulholland Drive* (2001) are much more ambiguous about the status of images. The title of *Inland Empire* should be taken as inner or mental empire, where, quite differently, the virtual and the actual are indistinguishable. Cinema of the brain: full of intense thoughts, full of unconscious feelings.

So if the source of their filmmaking is so different, where or how do Cassavetes and Lynch meet? Here we have to dive another level deeper into the worlds of Cassavetes and Lynch to see how they specifically do two things: direct their actors, and conceive the role of "the spectacle" or "mediation." In the documentary *A Constant Forge* (Charles Kiselyak, 2000), lead actor Peter Falk explains how he did not understand at all what he was doing or saying in *A Woman Under the Influence* (for instance, at the dinner table when he starts talking about seeing babies everywhere); or at least he never knew what his character's motivation was. This ambiguity meant that the actors had to rely more on their bodily performance to deliver the actual sensibility of the film. Very often, it was only onscreen that they saw what these performances revealed. Laura Dern, the main character in *Inland Empire*, has expressed a similar experience of confusion as an actress working with Lynch, having no idea what she was doing, why and in what kind of world she was operating (real, imaginary, Hollywood, Poland).[69] In 2007 the Foundation Cartier in Paris hosted *The Air Is on Fire*, an exhibition of Lynch's paintings, one of which is titled "Bob Finds Himself in a World for Which He Has No Understanding." This, Lynch comments in the DVD extras, is a common condition for human beings.[70] We can say, then, that although they construct their films from different starting points, the two directors share a basic sense of ambiguity about the nature of behavior, about the nature of reality, about the possibilities of knowing where exactly we are in the world. Nothing is crystal clear in either Cassavetes's or Lynch's worlds. In both worlds characters are quite lost, in identity crises. Nothing is familiar, so the only reliable way to "understand" is by intuitive performance or unconscious acting.[71]

Here we see how Cassavetes and Lynch can be brought closer together in terms of an uncertainty of knowing, and an ambiguity of reality, that calls for "a constant forge" into the unknown territories of life, hidden in either the body or the brain. In comparison to the temporal confusion of Treborn in *The Butterfly Effect*, we can recognize a more spatial schizoid confusion. Moreover, the filmmakers quite obviously engage a notion of "the spectacle" as a means of exploring these territories. For both, only in "the spectacle" can true creativeness emerge and some truth about (emotional) life be acknowledged. We must understand that this is a very different conception of the spectacle than Guy Debord's critical understanding of "the society of the spectacle."[72] In the society of the spectacle, mediation (film, television, other media) absorbs life and returns it only as a shallow simulation. (This is Baudrillard's understanding of the spectacle as well: reality, real life, disappears in the copy of the copy of the copy in audiovisual culture. I will return to Baudrillard's spectacularization in Chapter 9.) The spectacle numbs and dumbs people in this version of its conception. However, in the way Cassavetes and Lynch look for dramatization, theatricalization, performance, mediation, and spectacle, life is actually constituted or reconstituted in front of the camera. This I think becomes more relevant when we look at contemporary mediated culture and view it in relation to the different conception of spectacle that both Cassavetes and Lynch show us in their delirious films.

For Cassavetes life and film are completely intertwined. In *Opening Night* he and Gena Rowlands are/play a couple on three planes or dimensions: in real life (they are married), in the film, and in the theater play within the film. Similarly, in order for the husbands in *Husbands* to become friends, Cassavetes, Falk, and Gazzara actually spent time together to become real friends. Out of that intimacy and friendship, out of playing together as performance, something true emerges. And of course it is well known that Cassavetes's own house served as a location for most of his films. Lynch is much less privately involved in his films (although parts of *Inland Empire* were shot in his own house); on several occasions he has investigated this concept of spectacle in quite opposite ways from Cassavetes. Where for Cassavetes actual bodies, actual friendships, actual relationships create something genuine in a spectacle that makes us forget that we are looking at a technologically mediated form, Lynch shows precisely the opposite—namely, that technology and mediation can create real experiences and emotions. Think of the famous scene in *Mulholland Drive* in Club Silencio, where the host of the show announces it is all a show, all playback, yet the performance of the singer Rebekah del Rio of Roy Orbison's "Crying" is so genuinely moving that it is one of the most intense and dramatic moments of the film.[73] In *Inland Empire* also, the most realistic moment in the film, where Nikki/Sarah dies among the homeless on Hollywood Boulevard, is revealed as spectacle when a widening frame discloses the film camera and we hear the word *cut*.

Both Cassavetes and Lynch have themselves indicated that their approach to spectacle is not a common one. Cassavetes expressed his contempt for Hollywood as an industry and repeatedly argued that "television sucks."[74] In *Mulholland Drive* Lynch, too, comments on Hollywood and the shallow illusions of stardom, wealth, and happiness it creates, where the protagonist's dream career as an actress turns out to be the delirium of a junkie. Laura Dern's character, Nikki, in *Inland Empire* (or Sue in the film within *Inland Empire*) ends up "stabbed in the gut and staggering along Hollywood's Walk of Fame, leaving a trail of blood."[75] It is not so difficult to read this image as a commentary on the Hollywood industry and dominant media machines (which I will discuss momentarily). Their different approaches reveal the reality in and of performance, making them such interesting interrogators of the truth of the spectacle—and thus exemplary for a shift in thinking about the type of spectacle that contemporary culture demands (but certainly does not always give).

Another aspect of Cassavetes's and Lynch's late works that relates to contemporary culture has to do with "collecting" and "connecting." *Love Streams* (1984) is about a brother and sister, Robert Harmon (played by Cassavetes) and Sarah Lawson/Harmon (played by Rowlands). Sarah has just been divorced from her husband and has lost custody of her child to him, while her brother, Robert, is a famous writer and womanizer. As Deleuze observes, they are both collectors: Sarah collects luggage and animals that she offers to her brother; Robert collects women. Deleuze explains this collecting as a desire for connecting: "How can one exist, personally, if one cannot do so alone? How can something be made to pass through these packets of body, which are at once obstacles and means? Every time, space is made up from these excrescences of body, girls, luggage, animals, in search of a 'current' which would pass from one body to the next."[76] Here we have another image—a metaphor almost for contemporary database culture, where within the quantity of data, we look for the quality of relations and connections.

In *Inland Empire* Laura Dern does not collect things, neither objects nor persons. Rather, we are presented with a journey through the seemingly wild and random collection of worlds and images in her mind. As in Cassavetes's films, it is very hard to give a plot summary, or in any case, a plot summary does absolutely no justice to the experience of the film. But it is clear that the heroine is thrown into emotional turmoil by what she experiences when she tries to make sense of the different type of mental images, among which figure Eastern European women, prostitutes, an animated bunny family, and an otherwise schizophrenic shifting of times and places. How do these collections of mental images connect? Note that Nikki/Sarah regularly sees the word *axxonn* written on walls. *Axxonn* is not only the title of an online drama series by Lynch but, of course, "axons" are also the presynaptic neurons in our brain that send out signals to other neurons, dentrites—the postsynaptic neurons.[77] In other words *axxonn* in the film refers also to the notion of neurons looking for connections. As in *Love Streams*, the connections fail for large parts of the film, yet something passes through. Something of a current, a connection, a stream passes through the body, passes through the brain.

Similarly in *Opening Night*, both in the film and the play, Cassavetes brings forth the image of a woman who lives in such a state of suspended identity, not knowing where to place her continuing intense sense of love ("Love is a continuous flow; it never stops," she says in the film). Yet it is this same love that forces itself on the spectator, affects the spectator directly. In this way Cassavetes's films restore "a belief in the world" even though this belief is broken by personal disappointments, traumas, and the incapacities to connect (because of jealousies, pettiness, ignorance, or whatever reason). As Deleuze has indicated, the price to be paid for such powerful restoration is a confrontation with madness, a confrontation Cassavetes never avoided. Nor did Lynch. Interestingly, when asked about *Inland Empire*, Lynch responded that it is "about a woman in love and in trouble, and it's a mystery, and that's all I want to say about it." Laura Dern/Nikki/Sarah does not know where or when she is (she has trouble recognizing the order of things), and the film suggests further that even in her three identities, she could be the dream of yet another woman. In fact, all women are in trouble in *Inland Empire*, and the emotions are often panic or despair—a confrontation with madness indeed. Nevertheless, there is also room for more affirmative motions. The lyrics of one of the songs in the film (which is also the theme song of the DVD menu) are "Strange what love does, so strange what love does." At the end of the film Lynch, with all his dark emotions and frightening mindscapes, stages a strange family reunion. Was it Nikki/Sarah's alter ego? Was this film, in spite of all appearances, about the frightening forces of (motherly) love after all, just like all other films about women in distress discussed here?

It is clear that neither Cassavetes nor Lynch is afraid to torture his audience by presenting emotionally disturbing images or by annoying us with ambiguities in characters' behavior and confusions of spatial (and temporal) references. Both directors undermine all our habitual forms of recognition—of place, time, and fixed identities. Their unconventional attitudes toward the centrality of the spectacle, their filming in a free and independent way, and their search for connections and intensities to escape from the spectacle, make their work very relevant for digital screen culture. When asked about his digital cinema, Lynch frequently compares filmic relations to a spider's web: "We are like the spider. We weave our life and then move along in it. We are like the dreamer who dreams and then lives in the dream. This is true for the entire universe."[78] In the documentary *I'm Almost Not Crazy* Cassavetes points toward the importance of the spectacle without the metaphor of the spiderweb. Indicating first that philosophy means "to know how to love," he then says, "You start thinking about life, and you realize everything is a movie." The spectacle brings love and life. Life itself is not enough. However different they may be, in digital culture (of which Cassavetes was ahead in spirit, and which Lynch with high speed catches up), both "body" and "brain" need to connect to others. With their emphasis on the search for love and the confrontation with our emotions, especially (but not exclusively) embodied in the spectacle of the "woman in trouble," both directors show that love streams (in bodies and brains) and data streams (in our contemporary machines) are looking for connections in seemingly random, unpredictable delirious ways.

As is clear from all the films I have discussed in connection to clinical and critical schizophrenia, unconnected or lost feelings of love (motherly love, fatherly love, or love as a vitalistic force) translate into terrible feelings of disorganized thought, hallucinations, free-floating fear, panic attacks, and feelings of depersonalization. There is nothing romantic about this. What all delirious characters show is "the latent fragility of everyone's experience, its reliance on assumptions that are uncorroborated, unanalyzed or simply forgotten. . . . Delirium is disturbing and feared precisely because it threatens and puts shockingly into question the world of each and every one of us in all its supposed obviousness."[79] What the filmmakers discussed in this chapter show us, however, is that this onscreen confrontation with madness touches us directly and changes our perception of reality, allowing us to see and feel new things breaking through, without breaking down. Perhaps most remarkable is the fact that in all of these films, the characters seem to struggle with something called "love" or "life forces"; or perhaps it could be argued that the reality of the right hemisphere is breaking through the dominance of the left. As Bolte Taylor experienced after her stroke:

What a bizarre living being I am. Life! I am life! I am a sea of water bound inside this membranous pouch. Here, in this form, I am a conscious mind and this body is the vehicle through which I am ALIVE! I am trillions of cells sharing a common mind. I am here, now, thriving as life. Wow! What an unfathomable concept! I am cellular life, no—I am molecular life with manual dexterity and a cognitive mind![80]

Here, then, I will define the neuro-image both as symptom of and antidote to the madness of contemporary media culture. The neuro-image is part of this culture but also a form of resistance. It "goes with the (schizo) flow" and yet potentially produces something new, something creative, a new world with which to connect.

Powers of Machines of the Invisible: The Neuro-Image and the Abstract Media Machine

Laptops, mobile phones, webcams, iPods, satellite television, and Web 2.0: new forms of media grow like wild plants without deep roots (rhizomes) between older forms of mass media (newspapers, film, radio, and television). Undeniably, old mass media have also been changed by this digital revolution, but this does not mean that they have disappeared completely in the rhizomatic media network. The national television news is no longer the only source of most current information; CNN competes with Arab satellite channels, bloggers, and citizen journalism; hypes emerge online; YouTube and Twitter allow everybody to become a media producer. However, deeply rooted trees are not easily overgrown. The media have become individualized and fragmented and specialized and opened up, and they are still medial. This is not an either/or logic but an ever-growing process. Contemporary media culture can only be thought in the stammering stream of an and . . . and . . . and . . . logic: a schizophrenic logic of intensity and multiplicity that begs for a schizoanalysis. "We're tired of the tree. . . . Thought is not arborescent," Deleuze and Guattari argue by referring to the brain when they introduce nonhierarchical rhizomatic thinking in *A Thousand Plateaus*.[81] At the same time, they indicate that out of every rhizome a tree can grow, and that trees can behave rhizomatically. Therefore, it is not a matter of saying that old media are tools of capitalist ideology, while new media free us from ideological interpellation. "Old" and "new" media are two different ways of thinking and behaving that can have both positive and negative effects, produce the most beautiful creations and the most horrible suffocations.

The media are complex and interwoven networks of grass roots and tree structures.

Like zombies or vampires, old mass media have strong regenerative powers, as indicated by the fact that transnational television formats such as *Big Brother, Idol, X-Factor,* and other popular competition shows are still able to keep a mass audience on a Saturday night in front of the television set. Mass media are indeed no longer the most important makers or distributors of the news, but they still have a huge filtering function. Only when an Internet hype is reported by the seven o'clock news (or on the "old media" conglomerates' Internet portals) does it become massively popular. In any case there is always interaction between old and new media. Mass media take on new forms as well: podcasting reproduces radio; the seven o'clock news on demand retains its status as the seven o'clock news, and if you missed a program, it is usually available online. In this way new media do not weaken the power of the traditional media but reinforce it. Alongside extreme fragmentation and multiplication, the Internet becomes a huge store, a database, and an audiovisual archive of the mass media.

So where does this leave cinema? Is cinema dead, undead, or still alive? In their book *L'écran global*, Gilles Lipovetsky and Jean Serroy argue that cinema is alive and well and that we have entered a fourth phase of cinema, which they call the age of hypermodern cinema.[82] The maxim of their book is a quote from Elia Kazan: "Films are the dialogue of the contemporary world." Specifically, they argue that cinema has given the world its most radically modern apparatus: the screen. The hypermodern screen age (*écranosphère*) is characterized by what they call image-excess, image-multiplex, and image-distance. The excessiveness of images is understood in terms of length, baroque aesthetics, speeds of editing, violence, and sexuality. The multiplex aspect they consider in respect to the hybridization of genres, multicultural and transnational exchanges in style and content, complex narration, and the multiplication of perspective and story lines. By distance-image, they refer to new combinations of immediate sensation and cognitive distance, as well as various types of self-reflexive references. They also refer to the proliferation and rising status of historical, memorial, and minority cinema that offers polemical views.

Most important, they argue that cinema has extended its "dispositive" by spreading into culture at large. After the cine-idolatry of early and classical cinema, and the cinephilia of the modern age of cinema, we have now entered a culture of cinemania. A cinema spirit turns every event into a cinematic spectacle (the Olympic Games of Beijing's opening ceremony directed by Zhang Yimou is a case in point); media culture at large has become star-driven because stars best catch attention amidst overabundant information; and history is translated into images. Moreover, everybody films and is on film; cameras and screens are everywhere. In *Hypermodern Times* Lipovetsky further argues that the human being in this age has more freedom to choose than ever but is all the more fragile.[83] He does not mention schizophrenia in any way, but the inference seems plausible: how to choose, how to connect if so many options are open and the consequences are not predictable? In any case, according to Lipovetsky and Serroy, cinema is stronger than ever in our age. I take these descriptions of our global screen culture as an important background for my discussions of the neuro-image throughout this book.

In *The Virtual Life of Film* David Rodowick has argued the relation of cinema to global contemporary media culture quite differently, proposing that film will only survive the contemporary moment "virtually," as a reminiscence of the cinema it once was. According to Rodowick there are only "two futures for electronic images" that allow cinema's virtual survival: either as information (Rodowick gives the dissemination and appropriation of the shocking Abu Ghraib pictures as an important example—I will return to these pictures in my last chapter); or as art (Sam Taylor-Wood's beautiful photographs, installations, and videos are Rodowick's main reference for this virtual afterlife of film).[84] According to Rodowick cinema as cinema, as the experience of film, is dead. While I agree with Rodowick's in-depth theoretical approach toward the changes to the filmic image in the digital age, as well as with his assertion that film theory still has much to contribute to theories of contemporary image culture, I would like to propose the survival of cinema as film. Perhaps it is the case that the movement-image is (more or less) dead and survives (only) as information. Perhaps the time-image has deceased while continuing to live in contemporary art practice in a different form. However, cinema is still alive and well in the neuro-image (which reprises aspects of the movement-image and the time-image in many instances).

The neuro-image also has a strong relationship to the virtual, of course, but in connection to our brains rather than in connection to the virtuality of the filmic image itself, as information and art. Here I want to return to Deleuze's comments on the continuing importance of Artaud, who "said something about the brain that concerns all of us: that 'its antennae turned towards the invisible,' that it has a capacity to 'resume a resurrection from the death.'"[85] The neuro-image is not cinema's first return from the dead; it now reaches toward the invisible of the brain-screen. This is in contrast to Apparatus Theory, which addressed the psychoanalytic turn of the 1970s and 1980s and considered cinema a "machine of the visible." As Jean-Louis Comolli argued, cinema as a "machine of the visible" produces an "impression of reality": "Directly and totally programmed by the ideology of resemblance, of the 'objective' duplication of the 'real' itself conceived as a specular reflection, cinema technology occupied itself in improving and refining the initial imperfect dispositif, always imperfect by the ideological delusion produced by the film as 'impression of reality.'"[86]

Cinema in Comolli's theoretical approach belongs to the "regime of the visible," which enhances our perception of the material world.[87] Hereafter, however, by entering into our brain/mind, cinema has become a machine of the *invisible*. This paradigm shift also demands that we no longer consider cinema an "illusion of reality" but rather in terms of the "reality of illusion." It also involves a shift from considering cinema and the spectator as a "disembodied eye" defined by the look and the gaze, desire and identification, to considering cinema and the spectator as an "embodied brain," defined by perceptions (even illusory ones), selections (even random ones), memories (even fake ones), imaginations, suggestions, and above all emotions as pure affect. This embodied nature of the brain and the physical aspect or quality of the brain is crucial. It is related also to a final characteristic of our paradigm shift, which is the shift from considering the spectator in front of a spectacle (screen) to a spectator embedded or immersed in an audiovisual environment in which filmmaker and camera, characters and spectators, world and screens are all circling and questioning each other and in which we have to ask ourselves constantly: Where is the screen? How do I relate to it? What does it make me see, feel, grasp, do?

A schizoanalysis of media culture takes into account at least three immanent (autonomous and connected) powers of the image: the power of the virtual (related to the problem of time), the power of the false (related to the power of images to operate directly on our brains and in the world), and the power of affect (related to the asubjective dimensions of emotions and feelings). These powers do not provide an unequivocal model of analysis. They present themselves in all kinds of forms and on different levels. They metamorphose into good and bad, noble and base, and become everything in between. The media constitute an immanent networked system that feeds itself—an abstract machine that always grows, expands, produces from the most cruel and horrific to the most beautiful and sublime. Production and antiproduction, interdisciplinary schizoanalysis is therefore a method to understand the immanent powers of the image. The brain and the screen maintain an intimate and complex relationship. The camera has penetrated our mind, for better and for worse, but the brain also determines for a large part what we see onscreen, for better and for worse. The new cinematic regime of digital culture points to the fact that the screen is that thin membrane between world and brain and that the mediated image produces all kinds of invisible powers, exceeding the classic regime of the representable visible world. The schizophrenic minds presented in the delirium cinema of this chapter point toward these invisible powers that were already present in the time-image but seem to have entered into a new zone of intensification with the neuro-image. Although all screens work on our brains, and all brains are screens, I will reserve the term *neuro-image* for those cinematic experiences (in cinema or elsewhere in the media landscape) that have creative power or present some force of resistance in the abstract media machines while equally operating according to a schizophrenic logic. I turn now from the strictly clinical dimensions of the neuro-image to look at "the powers of the false" or "illusionary perception" in neuroscience, Deleuzian philosophy, film theory, and contemporary cinema.

Illusionary Perception and Powers
of the False

In the late nineteenth century and the early twentieth, cinema was often connected to stage illusionism, to the mysteries of technological inventions, and to intuitions about the workings of the human mind.[1] Two twenty-first-century films, each set in this earlier period, *The Illusionist* (Neil Burger, 2006) and *The Prestige* (Christopher Nolan, 2006), elaborate on this renewed contemporary interest in cinema's relation to perceptual illusions through the stories of professional conjurers. The simultaneous appearance of these films can also be related to a renewed theoretical interest in the luring powers of the screen and the tricks it can play with the brain. Early theoretical visions regarding cinema's connection to the operations of the mind, such as those in Hugo Münsterberg's *The Photoplay*, were not considered an integral part of modern film theory's history as it developed into an academic discipline from the 1950s onward. Münsterberg's visionary take on film from 1916 has only recently been rediscovered by way of Allan Langdale's new edition of Münsterberg's book.[2]

In 1956, when Edgar Morin, one of the last of the "early film theorists" outside of the shift to institutionalization, published his untimely book *The Cinema, or, The Imaginary Man*, film theory was about to enter its ideological phase. Film scholars, drawing on structural linguistics and psychoanalysis, started to seek academic legitimacy by beginning to "treat the radically debiologised [*sic*] subject/spectator as an effect of the film text,

all (unconscious) mind, stripped of flesh, poetry, skepticism and imagination."[3] Morin's ambitious project to question cinema in all its complexity
and in relation to the mysteries of the human mind did not receive great
recognition; his fascination with popular genres was even scorned as a
mystification of popular cinema's alienating power in service of capitalist
ideology. Yet his propositions, that human reality is semi-imaginary and
that cinema is the technology that allows us to see how human beings and
the world are interpenetrated, are incredibly sophisticated. The cinema,
according to Morin, is the world half-assimilated by the human mind:

All the things that it projects are already selected, impregnated, blended, semi-
assimilated in a mental fluid where time and space are no longer obstacles but are
mixed up in one plasma. All the diastases of the mind are already in action in the
world on the screen. They are projected into the universe and bring back identifiable substances from it. The cinema reflects the mental commerce of man with
the world. This commerce is a psychological-practical assimilation of knowledge or of consciousness. The genetic study of the cinema, in revealing to us that
magic and, more broadly magical participation inaugurate this active commerce
with the world, at the same time teaches us that the penetration of the human
mind in the world is inseparable from an imaginary efflorescence.[4]

Münsterberg's and Morin's sensitivity to the ambiguous relationships
between cinema, reality, and the mind seems to be much better understood in the early twenty-first century. Relating film theory to recent developments in neuroscience, especially, it is possible to appreciate anew
the magical qualities of cinema and the reality of the illusionary quality of perception. This chapter points out some experimental transdisciplinary connections that occur in such movements between neurobiology and film-philosophy when we focus particularly on the phenomenon
of visual illusions or illusionary perception.[5] The Deleuzian-Nietzschean
concept of the powers of the false will also allow for a new evaluation of
illusions, magic, and the possibilities of fraud and trickery. Throughout
my discussions I will refer closely to *The Illusionist* and *The Prestige* to indicate how these films, set circa 1900 in Vienna and London respectively,
relate to contemporary questions in neuroscience and film-philosophy in
which the powers of the false articulate a more general schizoanalytical
power of the image. I will also show how Nolan's subsequent film, *The
Dark Knight* (2008), is in interesting ways related to the powers of the false

and the reality of illusions in our brain. At chapter's end I will address the philosophical and ethical implications of these proposed illusionary principles of the brain-as-screen. First, however, it is necessary to present some preliminary reflections on the relationship between Deleuze, cognitive (neuro)science, and film theory.

Deleuze, Cognitivism, and Film Theory

To consider cinema's relationship to the brain and the mind today, we might be expected to turn to cognitive approaches. In fact, investigating this question of the relation between film and mind as a pertinent field of inquiry in itself, a new journal, *Projections: The Journal for Movies and Mind*, has been launched. *Projections* is the first specialist film journal addressing cinema's relationships to cognitive neurosciences. Now that modern brain-scanning technologies enable penetrative observations of brain processes during the viewing experience, film and film spectatorship offer excellent test cases for neuroscientific experimentation, mainly because film is so complexly concerned with natural perception: "Viewing a film is an intensely emotional perceptual experience. Isolated from the distractions of normal every-day life, the viewing experience also encompasses the psychological paraphernalia we use in coping with the world outside the theatre. For these reasons, film spectatorship is an ideal context for examining the workings of the mind in general."[6] Of course, most streams of contemporary neuroscience fall under the umbrella of cognitivism, and as a continental philosopher Deleuze is not connected to cognitivist or analytical schools of thought.[7] Deleuze and cognitivism therefore seem, in a traditional sense, at odds. Yet the richness of Deleuze's film theory, in particular his profound insights into undertheorized neurobiological aspects of screen theory, make this encounter seem unavoidable if we are to take seriously both Deleuze's thought in this area alongside more "disciplined" recent discoveries into the biology of the brain in our assessment of contemporary screen culture. Here, then, let us briefly consider the plausibility and means by which this connection between Deleuze and the contemporary cognitive sciences can take place.

John Protevi has identified important developments in cognitive science that enable possible encounters with Deleuze and makes specific reference to Mike Wheeler's *Reconstructing the Cognitive World: The Next Step* and Bruce Wexler's *The Brain and Culture*, both of which draw on the work of a specific group of cognitive scientists, labeled 4EA cognition scientists.[8] The initialism 4EA refers to embodied, embedded, enactive, extended, affective cognition. Protevi demonstrates that this type of neurodynamic cognitive science resonates with Deleuzian concepts. Both approaches are organized in opposition to notions of self-identical subjects, the representationalist subject, the isolated or world-transcendental subject, and the nonnatural (debiologized) subject. As Protevi summarizes: "The 4EA schools resonate with Deleuze in seeing cognition as immanent to extended/distributed/differential bio-environmental systems in which 'real experience' is the non-representational direction of action via the integration/resolution of differential fields."[9] In transdisciplinary terms we can speak here of general resonances; neurodynamic cognitive processes, patterns, and transformations resonate with Deleuzian impersonal intensities, preindividual virtualities, and processes of individuation. Furthermore, for Protevi, an encounter between the cognitivists and Deleuze is not only possible but also fruitful because Deleuze can help to conceptualize the sociopolitical and affective implications of the 4EA school's findings.

Alva Noë's notable revision of John Searle's internalist approach of the brain in *Action in Perception* indicates another important development within the cognitivist neurosciences that more strongly dialogues with a Deleuzian approach. Noë proposes an externalist approach to perception that takes into account the sensorimotor (bodily) skills necessary to perceive anything at all:

The enactive approach seeks to explain the quality of perceptual consciousness not as a neural function caused by and realized in the brain (as Searl [*sic*] would have it), but rather in terms of patterns and structures of skillful activity. In the enactive approach, brain, body, and world work together to make consciousness happen. Indeed, from an enactive standpoint, this is precisely what is required for an approach to count as genuinely neurobiological. Experience is not caused by and realized in the brain, although it depends causally on the brain. Experience is realized in the active life of the skillful animal. A neuroscience of perceptual consciousness must be an enactive neuroscience—that is, a neuroscience of embodied activity, rather than a neuroscience of brain activity.[10]

The way neural activity here is embedded in a sensorimotor dynamic is an example of a 4EA position compatible with a Deleuzian framework. Earlier I referred to Robert Pepperell's proposition of a dialethic model of viewer-screen relationships that hopes to reconcile internalism with externalism.[11] If externalism means (as the quote above suggests) that neurological processes are fundamentally connected to the brain, incorporate bodily and external processes, and thus maintain a relation between the inside and the outside, then the "strange encounter" between Deleuze and cognitivism becomes quite plausible. Their meeting is in fact an exploration of the implications of the brain as screen, halfway between the external world and internal brain processes.

Cognitive neuroscience consists of heterogeneous fields of study, and the discipline itself is already fundamentally transdisciplinary (biology, psychology, medicine, and physics all now share some investigative territories with cognitive neurosciences). As is clear from my first chapter, one of the subfields of neuroscientific research investigates clinical diseases such as schizophrenia, epilepsy, depression, and autism. Neuroscience is further divided into several specialized areas of interest and includes perception studies focused around visual illusions and questions of attention and awareness, linguistic neurosciences, questions of left and right hemispheres and their delineation and interaction, research into memory (short term, long term, amnesia), and affective neuroscience that studies emotions and feelings.[12] Interestingly, the areas of neuroscientific study (perception, attention awareness, memory, emotion) correspond largely to the way in which Hugo Münsterberg, professor of Experimental Psychology at Harvard in the 1910s, organized his treatise *The Photoplay*, which aimed at describing the film experience. Arguably, Münsterberg was the first film theorist to seriously argue for the film medium as a model for the workings of the human mind.[13] In the chapter "Depth and Movement" Münsterberg describes the impression of dimensionality and the illusion of movement that is of fundamental importance to watching a film. "Attention" is the following mental attribute essential to the art of film he discusses, where certain elements of the screen become more salient than others. In "Memory and Imagination" he analyzes the ways in which film can show us memory (flashbacks and suggestions are discussed). "Emotion" is proposed as the highest of the mind's and film's operations. As

Allan Langdale summarizes Münsterberg's conception of film as mind: "Light sensations come into our eyes and our minds sort out basic perceptual cues like depth and movement, then process stimuli through attention, and the associations of memory and imaginations, resulting in an emotional response."[14]

The specialized areas into which cognitive neuroscience is subdivided tend both to confirm Münsterberg's insights and to outline more concrete propositions through which we can consider Deleuze's idea of the brain as the screen. Of course, cognitive neuroscientists tend to study only a very small part of any field in which they are specialized to investigate (e.g., what happens in the brain when we see one particular visual illusion, or what happens when we remember our own life in episodic memory). Similarly, one of the characteristics of current cognitive film theory is that its wholesale uptake of scientific methods—which achieve mainly increments of insight into subsectioned aspects of the film experience—potentially marginalizes more "holistic" approaches that might tackle larger philosophical implications for the field itself.[15] To read Münsterberg's early "study" in contrast is to observe an attempt to present a holistic approach toward all elements involved in viewing a film: Münsterberg describes the complete aesthetic experience using his insights as an experimental psychologist. The significance of the extrapolations he achieved tends to indicate that his approach itself remains quite prescient. Today, while the 4EA developments in cognitive science bring Deleuze and cognitive neuroscience closer on fundamental issues—in terms of the connections between brain, body, and world—many of the same methodological challenges that Münsterberg confronted remain. How to combine a more holistic conceptual Deleuzian approach with more detailed cognitivist elements? Put differently, how might we cogently and productively move between and connect the three Chaoids: the "referenced chaos" of science, the "composed chaos" of art, and the "chaos rendered consistent, become thought" of philosophy?"[16] In this chapter I deal with these methodological challenges, while explicating the schizoanalytic power of the false through a neuroscientific and filmic lens.

Visual Illusions in Neuroscience and Cinema

The powers of the false potentially begin at the most basic level of our perceptions; perceptions can always mislead and remain open to deception. Filmmakers and magicians alike are often drawn toward close considerations of these manipulative and creative potentialities of perception. Neil Burger and Christopher Nolan have both indicated that as filmmakers they are attracted to the cultures of magic of the late nineteenth century because cinema is so closely related to conjuring: playing with the mind and creating visual illusions. In *The Illusionist* and *The Prestige* some of the tricks of the famous magician Robert-Houdin, such as the Orange Tree (an orange tree that seems to grow swiftly onstage in *The Illusionist*) and the Bullet Catch (the magician catches a bullet fired at him with his hand in *The Prestige*) are restaged.[17] Robert-Houdin also experimented with electricity. This early modern connection between technological inventions and magic is introduced in *The Prestige* through the character of the great and mysterious inventor Nikola Tesla (played by David Bowie in the film), who invents in the film a machine for teleportation by electricity.[18] In *The Illusionist* phantasmagoric projections of images on smoke screens create very realistic apparitions of the dead. We are reminded that magic and cinema technology have been connected since the nineteenth century and continue to connect and surprise today.

Visual illusions thus play a key role in this relationship between magic and cinema.[19] Visual illusions are like magic in that they indicate that the brain can see the same image in two different ways (for instance the famous Duck or Rabbit Drawing) or can be fooled by visual data, seeing, for instance, motion where there is none (as with the Rotating Snake Illusion). For this reason visual illusions have fascinated not only magicians and filmmakers but also philosophers, psychologists, and, more recently, neuroscientists. Some visual illusions are very old, such as the Waterfall Illusion of Motion aftereffects mentioned by Aristotle.[20] Many geometric illusions (such as the Müller Illusion or the Zöllner Illusion) were discovered in the nineteenth century. In recent decades computer technology has developed many additional kinds of illusions (for instance Hybrid Images, which are images seen differently at different spatial distances). Because they seem to indicate truths about our perceptual system and the functioning of the brain, visual illusions have also provided rich material for neurobiological experiments.[21]

Visual neuroscientists see three broad reasons for studying visual illusions. First, visual illusions can be caused by the brain itself, involving limited to no (or very distorted) connections to perceptual reality, such as in schizophrenic (and other) mental disorders, including psychoses, epilepsy, and migraine, and may include visual hallucinations as forms of illusion. (Here we could say that the study of these illusions relates to the ultimate inner pole of the brain and its impact on what we perceive, the internalist position par excellence). Second, visual illusions are interesting to neuroscientists because they reveal how standard viewings "are 'hardwired' into our brains, and thus can cause inappropriate interpretations of the visual scene. Hence illusions reveal mechanisms of normal perception to such an extent that they challenge our default notion that what we see is real."[22] Third, our brain is constantly looking for known patterns in random structures with low information content, called *pareidolia*, which makes phenomena like visual illusions an interesting area of investigation.[23]

There are many different types of visual illusions and different ways in which our perception can be illusory, all of these having different implications for the ways in which our perceptual system functions in relation to our cognitive skills and consciousness.[24] As Richard Gregory outlines, different kinds of illusions can be separated into those with a physical cause (such as light distortion or shadows, or ambiguous images) and those with a cognitive cause of misapplied knowledge (such as the hollow face that is seen as convex because faces are rarely hollow).[25] With the exception of pure hallucinations, it seems that any consideration of the perception of visual illusions requires us to recognize the brain-screen as situated both inside and outside the brain in a dialethic relationship.[26] Gregory returns to the work of von Helmholtz (1866), who early signaled this fundamental relationship between perception and (knowledge of) the world in a way that seems consistent with a 4EA cognitive approach:

Following from Helmholtz's lead we may say that knowledge is necessary for vision because retinal images are inherently ambiguous (for example for size, shape and distance of objects) and because many properties that are vital for behavior cannot be signaled by the eyes, such as hardness and weight, hot or cold, edible or poisonous. For Helmholtz, ambiguities are usually resolved, and non-visual object properties inferred, from knowledge by unconscious inductive inference from what is signaled and from knowledge of the object world. It is a small step to say that perceptions are hypotheses, predicting unsensed characteristics of objects, and predicting in time, to compensate neural signaling delay.[27]

In film theory, too, one of the fundamental disciplinary questions concerns the relation between reality and the illusory characteristics of the film image. This problem is increasingly discussed in a dialethic way that acknowledges the relationship between the brain and the world. In *The Reality of Illusion*, for instance, Joseph Anderson gives an ecological (4EA) approach to cognitive film theory and addresses this question of the relationship of the screen and the world anew, referring to visual illusions. Traditionally there are two opposing schools of thought negotiating this problem. On the one hand film is seen as the ultimate realistic form of art (we can consider Bazin's and Kracauer's contributions to film theory here as cinematographic versions of externalism). On the other hand film is considered the perfect illusory or artificial form of art (Metz and Eisenstein's "internalist" conceptions of the screen are representative of this latter stream of thinking). Anderson's position is constructed through studies of visual illusion and draws on the example of the Necker cube in particular to see whether this can shed new light on the problem. The Necker cube is a visual illusion: when you stare at the wire frame model of a Necker cube for some time, the cube seems to flip its orientation between two possible visual interpretations of the same picture. Anderson compares the ambiguities of the Necker cube to film viewing:

It is not a matter of being in a semi-hypnotic state in a darkened theatre. It is not a matter of suspending disbelief. It is not a matter of being "positioned" as a spectator or "sutured" into a text, and it has nothing to do with dreaming. It is instead our perceptual system alternating between two incompatible sets of information (a three dimensional world or a flat screen with shadows on it).[28]

Visual illusions (such as the Necker cube, and the spectacle on a film screen) demonstrate that perception in itself can be ambiguous, alternating between different interpretations of illusions that are both real on our brain-screen. Film viewing is such an illusion, which nevertheless triggers the activation of information within the neocortex, allowing us not only to see but also to understand, learn from, and interpret visual information.

The workings of perception of reality and illusory perceptions of reality (like cinema) are quite similar. Or, as Ira Konigsberg argues, "If we cannot come to any conclusions about reality, if reality must always remain an illusion, then those unreal images on the screen (and the sound filling the auditorium) are even more pertinent."[29] They can tell us something about the manipulating and creative powers of the false of visual culture in general and of contemporary screen culture in particular.

A Free Indirect Relationship Between World and Brain

In *The Photoplay* Münsterberg himself referred to visual illusions, comparing them to the (new) film medium as a way of attaining further understanding of what film does to the brain. Münsterberg studied visual illusions closely and even discovered new ones, such as the Münsterberg Checkerboard Illusion. He takes an internalist position on the workings of perception; however, his views on the tricks of perception and their value for study remain quite open to a dialethic approach: "Since we cannot be sure that movement really takes place in objective reality, the perception of movement may well be mental, an operation of the mind. . . . Optical illusions throw perception into question, they prove that perception, at least in some cases, is a mental act and has only a partial relation to 'reality.'"[30]

In a similar way cinema is a mental act with a partial—or open and dynamic—relation to reality. In his cinema books Deleuze elaborates these ideas more systematically. He emphasizes that cinema, through its particular audiovisual quality, gives us subjective perceptions (a character's spatial or mental point of view) rendered as objective observations (the camera's point of view, presumably giving a picture of reality). In this way cinema catches us in "a correlation between a perception-image and a camera-consciousness which transforms it."[31] Subjective (internal) and objective (external) images become like "communicating vessels" such that in many cases it is difficult to distinguish objective reality from subjective imagination. Before turning to the next section, where I focus on specific visual neuroscientific findings, here I would like to address this more general question concerning the ways in which cinema is related to the mind in its presentation of stories in a "semisubjective" ("semi-imaginary" or "free indirect") way, allowing for visual illusions to play an important role.[32]

Set in late nineteenth-century Vienna, *The Illusionist* is the story of a professional conjurer, Eisenheim (Edward Norton), and his love for a woman, Sophie (Jessica Biel). The story is actually told through the eyes of Chief Inspector Uhl (Paul Giamatti), who arrests Eisenheim on the orders of Prince Leopold (Rufus Sewell),[33] who thinks Eisenheim is a fraud and charlatan. The film begins with Inspector Uhl speaking in voice-over about his investigations into Eisenheim's youth, while the film images turn into flashbacks. Throughout the film Uhl is shown participating in or witnessing the film's story (such as the scenes where he visits Eisenheim's stage performances or investigates the murder of Sophie, the crown prince's fiancée who loves Eisenheim). In other scenes, however, the camera wanders off on its own and gives us images that Uhl certainly cannot see or access, or have any possible awareness of (such as the conversations between Sophie and Eisenheim during their childhood friendship, or the love scene between them when they are adults). The status of these images is unclear. Perhaps Uhl only imagines these scenes, yet the camera renders all images objectively. In this way *The Illusionist* shows very clearly how cinema has this "specific, diffuse and supple status" between subjective and objective.[34] Neil Burger admits to a specific interest in this confused status of the image, between subjective and objective, between imaginary and real, internal and external. As the film ends, we can think (with Inspector Uhl) we have "figured out" how Eisenheim has played tricks on everybody's minds in order to get Sophie back. However, we cannot be sure. As Burger explains:

It may be exactly how he [Uhl] is imagining or it may be just that, his imaginings. The movie is told from Uhl's point of view and he does not know everything. He thinks he has it but does he really? Or is it just something he chooses to believe? The whole movie is about perception, how we see the world, how we see in general. What we believe, what we won't believe, what we take on faith. For Uhl this is what he chooses to believe or what the audience chooses to believe, and maybe it's true, maybe it isn't.[35]

In a different way *The Prestige* also presents its events semisubjectively, when telling a story of rivalry between two magicians in Victorian

London, Robert Angier (Hugh Jackman) and Alfred Borden (Christian Bale).[36] The narrative is more complicated than *The Illusionist*'s since there are two crisscrossed points of view: Angier's, who is reading Borden's notebook in the past, and Borden's, who reads Angier's diary in the diegetic present. The story also addresses other layers in time, and these interwoven temporal perspectives add further complications to the narrative. (This temporal complexity, as I indicated in the previous chapter, is an essential characteristic of the neuro-image, but this argument will be developed more systematically in the second and third parts of this book. Here I focus only on the perceptual dimensions.) In *The Prestige*, also, subjective and objective images are heterogeneously combined. Here, too, many questions of distinguishing between tricks and truth remain unresolved. Although the end of the film reveals the ultimate secret of the power behind Borden's magic disappearances and reappearances, other mysteries— including the scientific powers of electricity in the machine designed by Nikola Tesla, and Angier's double appearance at the end of the film—remain utterly unresolved. In an interview on the DVD extras Christopher Nolan admits that these mind games are his main motivation for making films: "I would hope people would walk away having been entertained by the story but that there would also be all kinds of resonances and, I don't know, interesting thoughts banging around their brains." Here Nolan acknowledges that vision is a mental operation, with a partial (in any case open and dynamic) relationship to the external world, and that illusionist filmmakers, as neuroscientists with different means, show us how the nature of the brain and the nature of the filmic image call perception's relation to reality into question.

Watch More Closely: Attention and Awareness

Illusionists and filmmakers also play with aspects of perceptual illusion in other ways. It is a well-known fact that many conjurer tricks (be these of illusionists, con men, or filmmakers) are based on a play between attention and awareness that guides what we actually and consciously see (and don't). In *The Prestige* Angier creates a stage act called "The Transported Man" in which he leaves the stage by one door and immediately enters again through another door at the other end of the stage. The film shows how Angier achieves the trick by using a look-alike. It works because the audience does not pay attention to the differences between the two men who are dressed identically, have the same haircut and make the same gestures of catching Angier's top hat (it is the hat that captures the audience's attention, more than the person catching it). The trick is revealed to the audience slowly as the look-alike becomes increasingly drunk, starts behaving unpredictably, and moves his body differently than Angier does. Borden finally intrudes into the show, taking the place of Angier's stand-in and making the audience aware of all of the tricks in the act. In another scene Borden, who is in prison because he is accused of the murder of Angier, distracts the attention of a guard by pretending he is too clumsy to perform a trick with a red ball and drops it, so that the guard does not notice that Borden has chained him to a table. Magicians and filmmakers alike play with the spectator's attention and awareness.

Münsterberg emphasized the central function of attention in film viewing. Beyond the first-sense impressions of perception (which, as we have seen, can be already illusionary), attention plays a key role in creating meaning out of what we see on the screen. As Münsterberg argues:

The mere perception of the men and women and of the background, with all their depth and their motion, furnishes only the material. The scene which keeps our interest alive certainly involves much more than the simple impression of moving and distant objects. We must accompany those sights with a wealth of ideas. They must have a meaning for us, they must be enriched by our own imagination, they must awaken the remnants of earlier experiences, they must stir up our feelings and emotions, they must play on the suggestibility, they must start ideas and thoughts, they must link in our mind with the continuous chain of the play, and they must draw attention constantly to the important and essential element of the action. An abundance of such inner processes must meet the world of impressions and the psychological analysis has only started when perception of depth and movement alone are considered. . . . The chaos of the surrounding impressions is organised into a real cosmos of experience by our selection of that which is significant and of consequence. . . . Our attention must be drawn now here, now there, if we want to bind together that which is scattered in the space before us. Everything must be shaded by attention and inattention.[37]

Münsterberg outlines several characteristics of attention: it is something that comes into the center of consciousness; it makes other impressions fade away to the point that we don't see them; it adjusts the body of the perceiver to the perception; it groups ideas, feelings, and impulses around the object of attention.[38] He gives a range of filmic effects (such as lighting, speed, or repetition) that steer our attention. The filmic close-up, which eclipses literally all other objects from the scene, is the technique that emphasizes most clearly the effects of attention: "the close-up has objectified in our world of perception our mental act of attention and by it has furnished art with a means which far transcends the power of any theatre stage."[39] Münsterberg gives the example of a locket hung on the neck of a stolen or exchanged infant and shown in close-up, which guides our attention and tells us that everything will hinge on this locket twenty years later, when the child is grown up. While Münsterberg's observations are rather impressionistic, the issues he raises about perception as partly illusory and directed by attention are pertinent. For Münsterberg attention equals conscious perception that makes us unaware of other objects in the perceptive field. In this way he expresses the classic psychological insight "that even though we think we see everything that is in front of us, we actually have a very limited conscious representation of the outside world."[40] The question, now, is whether contemporary neuroscience can offer refined insight into how perception is colored or limited by what catches our conscious attention.

Neuroscientists today have very sophisticated technology at their disposal, which makes it possible to observe and measure processes that take place in the brain when we perform all kinds of tasks (including watching and seeing). With respect to the question of attention, recent experiments have indicated that it is useful to reevaluate the classic distinction between the conscious (attention/awareness) and the unconscious (inattention/unawareness) in order to consider a new distinction between attention and awareness instead.[41] Traditionally, consciousness has been considered in terms of attention but specifically in relation to reportability (being able to *tell* what it is that catches our attention and respond to what we are aware of). However, recent neuroscientific observations of the brain tell us that even objects that are not consciously reported, remembered, or compared to other objects can still be registered in a conscious mode, only at a more restricted level of consciousness. Neuroscientists Victor Lamme and Pieter Roelfsema have made a distinction between different modes of vision to understand the divide between conscious and unconscious modes in a more differentiated way: "An analysis of response latencies shows that when an image is presented to the visual system, neuronal activity is rapidly routed to a large number of visual areas. However, activity of cortical neurons is not determined by this feed forward sweep alone. Horizontal connections within areas, and higher areas providing feedback, result in dynamic changes in tuning."[42]

The brain activity called "feed-forward sweep" enables us to immediately distinguish form, color, shape, movement, and other large visual categories like faces, animals, and so on. This process of the brain (which makes it possible to jump away from a falling object for example) is largely unconscious. Feedback processing refers to the processes that take place one-tenth of a second after the feed-forward sweep, and are called recurrent interactions or resonances. At this point more conscious processes commence, and we can relate what we see to other experiences, memories, emotions, and so forth. Furthermore, the circuit of recurrent consciousness can be restricted (P-conscious) or elaborate (A-conscious).[43] If something does not catch our attention (in the sense that we cannot report on it), this can be because something becomes stuck in or limited to (unconscious) feed-forward processing, or because recurrent (conscious) processing is not elaborate enough. The implication is that not everything that we cannot report on is unconscious, that there is conscious experience that exists independently from reportability.[44] To deal with this insight, Lamme proposes that we might better distinguish between attention and awareness (rather than the notion of conscious and unconscious modes):

Instructing to focus attention (either in man or monkey) almost invariably leads to enhanced neural responses through the brain. . . . Typically, the neural responses are enhanced right from the outset, which indicates that the attention works on the feed forward sweep. . . . From the combined neural and psychological perspective, attention thus is a rather different phenomenon than awareness. It is best described as a set of mechanisms that enable the better routing of sensory inputs towards the executive systems of the brain. Attention is selection. . . . The way in which we have defined awareness at the neural level is rather different. As soon as visual input undergoes recurrent processing of some (as yet not precisely defined) critical mass, awareness arises. This could work for attended as well as unattended stimuli.[45]

This definition of attention, as belonging to immediate feed-forward processing, challenges the idea that attention would be part of consciousness

(Münsterberg's classic psychological insight). Attention, according to this definition, belongs more to unconscious processes. Objects that we do not attentively see (or are able to report on), however, are not automatically relegated to the unconscious but can be part of conscious experiences while remaining stuck somewhere in the network of resonances. The implications of this insight are yet to be analyzed more fully, but perhaps a return to film theory and the two "magic" films of this chapter can provide some preliminary thoughts for further reflection.

Let us return to the example of the locket mentioned by Münsterberg. In fact, the whole narration of *The Illusionist* is entirely constructed around a locket. At the beginning of the film Eisenheim as a young boy fabricates a locket for Sophie. When he gives her the locket, we see in close-up that the locket can be opened with a secret mechanism (and how). At several key moments in the narrative the locket turns up, until finally, at the very end of the film, it is shown in close-up in Sophie's hand; this is a repetition of the image of the locket from the film's beginning, but at this point, with the whole story imbued in it, it carries even more signification. On one level the locket is thus indeed a visual narrative device that steers our attention in the classic psychological way described by Münsterberg. On another level, when we take into account both the ways in which cinema presents a semisubjective reality and the neuroscientific distinction between attention and awareness, we can develop this analysis further.

As I have already mentioned, *The Illusionist* is told from inspector Uhl's perspective, while the images are presented more objectively and give us sometimes more information than he can possibly know. Many of the scenes with the locket are presented in this ambiguous way between objective and subjective vision. During the course of the film Uhl slowly discovers what the spectators already have seen before him. For instance, the spectator knows from the film's beginning that the locket can be moved into a heart shape to reveal a picture of a young Eisenheim. The spectator has also seen that Sophie secretly still wears the locket after fifteen years. These scenes are revealed in close-up, but with an objective camera, without any eyewitness or report from Uhl. We can see here how this one visual object, a locket, is presented in a semisubjective way that indicates the ambiguous relation of perception to reality. We cannot know if all of these scenes occurred as we have seen them occur, or if some, or all, have been a projection of Uhl's mind.

If we consider all these close-ups of the locket not in terms of conscious attention, as Münsterberg proposed, but as objects of automatic (unconscious) feed-forward recognition, we might then investigate whether the film also distinguishes moments of restricted and elaborate resonance. On an aesthetic cinematographic level, the locket in close-up has indeed become part of habitual recognition, a cliché that does not necessarily resonate with deeper levels of our imagination, memory, or emotions. Yet the locket in *The Illusionist* does not give us the pure and automatic cliché either. How does the film then trace resonating circuits in the brain? We must watch closely to answer such questions.

Toward the end of the film a narrative perspective on the locket scenes is more clearly subjectively restricted to inspector Uhl's actual observations. When Sophie is conjured as an apparition onstage, she mentions the locket, saying that she was wearing it at the time of her death. This is not a particularly emphasized remark, given the mesmerizing nature of the event of her apparition on the stage. A moment later in the film Inspector Uhl searches Eisenheim's workplace and finds a notebook entitled "Orange Tree." When he opens it, he finds only a drawing of a locket. Disappointed that the notebook is not about the secrets of the trick of the growing orange tree, as he had hoped, Uhl puts it back on the desk. But then he has second thoughts: the drawing of the locket starts resonating with aspects of events that previously occurred, aspects that begin moving into his field of awareness (we have to remember that Uhl, because of the semisubjective narration, has actually not yet seen the locket in the way the spectators have). He suddenly recalls Sophie's words onstage, and then he remembers something that vaguely caught his attention when he first began the investigation of Sophie's murder . . . something that he saw from the corner of his eyes in the stable where Sophie could have been murdered . . . something, indeed, "caught up in the back of his mind," as Burger comments on the DVD. His insight is rewarded when he returns to the stable to find the locket in the hay next to a gemstone that came from the crown prince's sword, providing enough evidence to arrest the crown prince for murder. We could thus conclude that the cliché of the locket in close-up that catches our immediate attention surpasses the status of habitual recognition and becomes an object of awareness when it enters resonant circuits of the brain (of the character in the film and of the spectator alike, at this moment).

Münsterberg's observations about attention are still valuable but can be considered more precisely by referring to neurobiological findings. Questions of stereotypical representation and complex narration in cinema might benefit from the application of such neuroscientific principles, as we have just seen. Concerning Deleuze's cinema concepts, the difference between attention and awareness could also provide new insights into the relation between movement-images (which are sensorimotor images) and time-images (which relate to various levels of the virtual, time, and imagination). How do filmmakers in the contemporary neuro-image play with our immediate and habitual attention, alongside the layers of resonances necessary for awareness? What are the philosophical and ethical or political implications of such powers of the false? I will return to these questions momentarily (and at several other instances in this book, especially in Chapters 5 and 8). For the moment, continuing with the problem of attention and awareness, several aspects are worth further reflection. According to Münsterberg, film can be seen as a manipulative art form that steers the attention of the viewer, enabling the creation of the most powerful emotions but also causing potentially dangerous effects. In 1917, in a posthumous publication, he asked, "How can we make sure that this eagerly sought entertainment is a help and not a harm to young minds?"[46] To refine this insight using neuroscientific knowledge of how the brain actually processes visual information, we might say the power of the false can potentially arise at three different levels: at the unconscious level of automatic processing of habitual sensorimotor images, as nonreportable but yet (restricted) conscious resonances (perhaps it is here that intuition or premonitions are situated?), and/or within elaborate feedback circuits. The powers of the false probably have a different impact at each point—much of this remains to be investigated. It is possible, however, to consider at least some interesting aspects of such powers (and brain dynamics) of the false through the work of neuroscientist Michael Gazzaniga on memory feedback circuits.

Split Brains, Fictional Selves, and False
Heroes of the Neuro-Image

In *The Mind's Past* Gazzaniga refers to the tricks magicians play on our minds, hilariously recounting the conjurer Harry Blackstone Senior, who in his stage performance "magically" conjured a full-sized donkey out of his hat by shifting audience attention to himself and a beautiful assistant, while a second assistant simply walked onstage unnoticed with a donkey.[47] Gazzaniga recounts this trick in the context of his research into the behaviors of split-brain patients, which reveal "schizoid" truths about our brains. One of these truths is that it is not just perception (be it internally or externally distorted) that can fool us, but our memories (which are influenced by many manipulating factors) may as well. Put differently, Gazzaniga deals with the illusions that can be produced in the elaborate feedback circuits involved in conscious seizure awareness. Gazzaniga has engaged in more than forty years of research with split-brain patients, research that began with the treatment of epileptic patients. For some forms of epilepsy, splitting the brain is the best treatment. As Gazzaniga explains, "Disconnecting the two hemispheres localizes a seizure to the hemisphere in which it begins. During the seizure the other half-brain remains in control of the body. The patient stays conscious and in charge during the attack."[48] These patients, in effect, have two minds that operate independently. Just like the experience of Jill Bolte Taylor, who had a complete breakdown of her left hemisphere that shut down her "little brain shatter that tells you 'I am,'" split-brain patients confirm the separate "personalities" of the two half-brains. Gazzaniga is particularly fascinated by a specialized mechanism in the left hemisphere that not only tells a person who he or she is (in an ongoing way) but does so by continuously interpreting actions and feelings generated by systems located throughout the brain. Gazzaniga calls this neural mechanism "the interpreter":

Reenter the interpreter, the means of analyzing things such as why a feeling changes and what a certain behaviour means. For example, give a command to the silent, speechless right hemisphere: "Take a walk." Then see how a subject typically pushes back her chair from the testing table and starts to walk away. You ask, "Why are you doing that?" The subject replies, "Oh, I need to get a drink." The left brain really doesn't know why it finds the body leaving the room.

When asked, it cooks up an explanation. There it was. The half-brain, which asks how A relates to B and constantly does that when solving problems, is also the hemisphere that provides our personal narrative for why we feel and do the things we feel and do. Even though, as in the split brain patient, feelings and actions are precipitated by a brain system operating outside the left brain's realm of knowledge, the left brain provides the string that ties events together and makes actions or moods appear to be directed, meaningful, and purposeful.[49]

The consequences of this specialization of the left hemisphere is that by keeping our personal story together, the reconstruction of our past is "deleterious," and we are constantly learning to lie to ourselves.[50] The self is fictional, Gazzaniga concludes. But that doesn't mean we do not need that fiction. As Jill Bolte Taylor's story confirms, we need that little voice telling us who we are and why we do things. It might be (shockingly) beautiful to dissolve into the chaotic pixels of the universe of the right hemisphere; and the left hemisphere may indeed play too dominant a role for many asignifying forces to be contained, but we certainly need our left brain to (at least) recognize this and to be able to find a sustainable balance in life. "Sure, life is a fiction, but it's our fiction and it feels good and we are in charge of it. That is the sentiment we all feel as we listen to tales of the automatic brain. We don't feel like zombies; we feel like in-charge, conscious entities—period," Gazzaniga tells us.[51] Nevertheless, it is just as important to acknowledge that the illusionary and fictitious character of the stories we tell ourselves, and each other, is actually the default process in our constructions of our selves. This acknowledgement has further implications for evaluating our ethical behavior and the constructive and deconstructive powers of the false.

The dramatic fictions of contemporary audiovisual culture point out that this interpreter role (of the left brain) not only works in personal and interpersonal stories but might occur on a cultural level as well. At least many contemporary stories show an awareness of this particular aspect of the (collective) brain. A case in point is Christopher Nolan's film *The Dark Knight* (2008), the sequel to his *Batman Begins* (Christopher Nolan, 2005) and the film that also immediately followed his work on *The Prestige*.[52] Nolan renews the popular Batman story in interesting ways. Batman, or in daily life Bruce Wayne (Christian Bale), is fighting organized crime in Gotham City with the help of Lt. James Gordon (Gary Oldman) and district attorney Harvey Dent (Aaron Eckhart). The criminal mastermind The Joker (Heath Ledger) is no longer the insane-but-comical evil opponent that Jack Nicholson portrayed in Tim Burton's *Batman* (1989) but a darker and more uncontrollable force of madness. Several aspects of *The Dark Knight* seem compelling in the context of the issues discussed in this chapter and of the neuro-image more generally. First, it is remarkable that Gotham City in Nolan's mise-en-scène, unlike in previous versions, is much less fantastic and more like any modern metropolis, a city full of skyscrapers, communication technology, and audiovisual screens. This realistic setting renders the madness that reigns in the city all the more close and affecting. Bruce Wayne owns a media firm and is extremely rich. His office and his secret hiding place, of which only his butler, Alfred (Michael Caine), knows, are full of high-tech screens and media applications. It is suggested that Wayne delivers all cell phone technology to the government and the army. At the end of the film Wayne gives his confidant in the office, Lucius Fox (Morgan Freeman), the power to control a multiscreen wall that is connected to every cell phone in Gotham City. Lucius in return protests: "You've turned every cell phone of Gotham City into a microphone and a high frequency generator-receiver. With half the city feeding you sonar, you can image all of Gotham." He refuses this surveilling power offered to him (as "too much for one man") and decides only to help Batman in order to get back at The Joker ("Consider this as my resignation," he tells Batman). In the next chapter I will engage more directly with the surveillance aspect of digital culture. Here let us focus on *The Dark Knight*'s mise-en-scène as a typical networked brain-city of the neuro-image.

Another important element in the mise-en-scène is obviously The Joker. Heath Ledger, who tragically died shortly after the production of *The Dark Knight*, is in several ways connected here to forces of madness and contemporary fears.[53] The Joker announces himself as an "agent of chaos." His behavior is uncontrollable and unpredictable. He also associates himself with contemporary discourses about terrorism: "See what I did with a couple of guns and some tons of gasoline?" Without tanks, bombs, or a high-tech army The Joker resembles a dark "nomadic war machine," as described by Deleuze and Guattari in *A Thousand Plateaus*. His (only) "army" is a disordered assembly of paranoid schizophrenics that he has released into the city. A madman explains this machinic collaboration with The Joker when the police discover a cell phone embedded in the poor man's stomach that will set off explosives in the city ("The Boss said he'd make the voices go away"). Seemingly, this is all very dark indeed. However, The Joker does have a political message. He is not interested in the piles of money that the heavily organized crime factions in the city are after—he just burns it, ridiculing criminal forms of capitalist greediness. He similarly derides the false forms of safety that come from obeying rules and upsets the established order to show the chaos underneath it. "You know the thing about chaos?" he asks. "It's fair!" Although nobody in his or her right (or should we say left?) mind would argue that The Joker's chaotic reign is desirable, the schizoanalytical message is not to be missed.

The Dark Knight's schizoanalytic message is much more subtly embodied in Batman's relationship to the other hero of the film, Harvey Dent. While Batman has always helped Gotham City undercover (few people know the secret of his true identity), Harvey Dent is the legal face of the city's fight against crime—a knightlike figure and a symbol for the causes of honesty and justice. However, when The Joker attacks him and burns one side of his face, his dark side reveals itself. Dent kidnaps Lt. Gordon's wife and children and becomes a revenge-seeking dark force: Harvey Two-Face (symbolized by his "coin of chance" that he always carries to let fate make his decisions). Batman saves Lt. Gordon, who has confronted Dent, but decides to take the blame for having killed Dent, perpetuating the myth that as a "White Knight" Dent remained committed to saving Lt. Gordon. Knowing the powers of the false and the necessity of "fictional selves," Batman in this gesture accepts being despised by the people of Gotham, instead of assuming his traditional heroic role, so that Harvey Dent can be remembered as a hero. "I am whatever Gotham needs me to be," Batman says to Gordon and his son. In voice-over he continues: "Sometimes the truth isn't good enough. . . . Sometimes people deserve to have their faith rewarded." Batman drives away into the night, to be hunted as a villain, and Dent receives a heroic memorial service. Lucius Fox types his name into the sonar surveillance system as Wayne requested him to do, and the system autodestructs. It is not difficult to see how the forces of Gazzaniga's left hemisphere interpreter (conjuring necessary fictional stories) are here consciously recognized on a cultural level. In this way *The Dark Knight* is a typical neuro-image that plays with the real effects of illusions.

Powers of the False and Stories We Need

We can bring these analyses of *The Illusionist*, *The Prestige*, and *The Dark Knight* back to Deleuze's concept of the powers of the false to consider their ethical implications. In *The Time-Image* Deleuze relates this power to the cinema of Orson Welles, arguing that *F for Fake* is the manifesto of Welles's work and his reflection on cinema. Not surprisingly, Welles presents himself in this film as a magician. Deleuze relates Welles's fascination for conjuring to a fundamental aspect of modern cinema of the time-image, in which truthful narration has been replaced by falsifying narration. The forger becomes the character of the cinema, Deleuze argues, "not the criminal, the cowboy, the psycho-social man, the historical hero, the holder of power, and so on as in the action-image, but the forger pure and simple, to the detriment of all action."[54] What the forgers in Welles show us is that the truth always refers to a system of judgment—a system that is shattered in a regime of falsifying narration. Welles's cinema shows that the "truthful man" does nothing other than judge life on the basis of preconceived principles. In his films the prevailing system of judgment falls apart and is replaced by a certain power of the false. In *F for Fake* the famous art forger Elmyr de Hory demonstrates that he can forge a Picasso in ten minutes, which no expert can distinguish from the original. In all his films Welles proposes a whole range of forgers, among whom the artist holds the most generous powers of creating the truth; but other types of forgers, less generous, less creative, more deadly even, exist as well. Deleuze mentions Nietzsche's truthful man (the frog) and the sick man (the scorpion) who embody the spirit of revenge in different ways. According to Deleuze the image relations of the powers of the false (in normal perception, as well as in cinema) indicate that "it is not a matter of judging life in the name of a higher authority which would be the good, the true; it's a matter, on the contrary, of evaluating every being, every action and passion, even every value, in relation to the life which they involve. Affect as immanent evaluation, instead of judgment as transcendent value."[55]

If cinema is a semisubjective way of storytelling that has an inherently ambiguous relation to reality and truth, and if perception itself is a mental operation that only partly relates to reality, obviously the false is not inherently bad or wrong. Illusion or falsity is no longer an error if reality is in fact quite ambiguous or if our mental inferences produce real but incorrect perceptions. Instead, the false truly becomes a power. Falsifying narrations and visual illusions, whether in phenomenal reality or screen reality, are all operating in the world and at the same time creating new circuits in the brain. The power of the false, therefore, becomes a power of the will—or in Nietzschean terms, a will to power: "Neither true nor false, an undecidable alternative, but power of the false, decisive will."[56] If the screen is a manipulative force that has the power to create (new) circuits in the brain, then the brain itself has certain controlling powers as well. Neuroscientists have conducted experiments with visual illusions to investigate whether the brain has voluntary control in choosing between different ways of seeing. In the Wagon Wheel Illusion, for instance, the brain can decide to rotate the wheel to the left or to the right. Raymond van Ee and others have shown how in watching rivaling stimuli, such as that of the Necker cube, subjects have "to a considerable extent independent control over the reversal rate of either of the two competing Necker cube percepts."[57] When we cannot know with certainty which properties of the image are true, our brain has to decide and make a choice, based on an affective evaluation, and believe. In Chapter 5 I will return to the larger epistemological questions that the powers of the false carry with them. It is important that we find here again a dialethic conception of the brain-screen. If the forger (artist or idiot, creator or destroyer) can create new circuits in the brain by creating new images with a partial relation to reality, it is also true that on the reception side of the screen not everything is decided or predictable beforehand—a decisive will is involved in processing the images in different ways.

Returning to *The Illusionist* and *The Prestige*, we can draw two possible conclusions. Although both films deal with visual illusions, magic, and the powers of the false, each seems to have chosen a different attitude toward the art of conjuring. Neil Burger at the end of his commentary (spoken over images of the film), asks, "How do you make your way in a world where you are unable to pin down what really is true whether that be on a political level or on a spiritual one? Are there powers that can't be explained? Does the universe make moral sense? We probably will never know. That's the story of *The Illusionist*." Burger poses these questions exactly when Uhl decides he has figured out how Eisenheim performed his magic and knows what really happened. At this moment it is no longer important whether it actually was true or whether it was a trick, because Eisenheim loves Sophie, and "he did it all to be with her." *The Illusionist* here subscribes to the affective dimension of the evaluation that Deleuze relates to the powers of the false. In *The Prestige* the stakes are rather different. There the emphasis is not so much on the fact that we have to decide what is true (based on alternative principles of affective or ethical evaluation). Instead, the film enhances the idea that we, the spectators, want to be fooled. When Angier comes up with a performance that is not a trick but actually quite mysterious (Tesla's electric transportation machine), the theater owner advises him: "It's very rare to see real magic. Dress it up, disguise it. Give them enough reason to doubt it!" The audience, in other words, knows it is being fooled, but that is precisely what it wants. "The world is solid," Angier says. Producing wonder is the highest ambition a magician and filmmaker can have. Nolan's *The Dark Knight* argues even more strongly in the same direction: people not only want to be fooled but even need to be fooled. We conjure up the stories that we need, both in our individual brains and collectively in cultural stories.[58]

Contemporary neuro-images show a striking consciousness of these affective and ethical powers of the false. But whether visual illusions suggest to our brain that we really can't determine the truth (and thus have to decide for ourselves what we believe to be real), or whether we accept that we really want and even need to be fooled because reality is actually too solid (or quite awful), it almost doesn't matter. The dynamic mysteries of the world, the brain, and the magic of the screen ask us to watch more closely and evaluate anew what we see and experience each time we look, again and again. Contemporary neuro-images testify to a growing consciousness of these realities and truths of illusions and to the powers of the false. They invite an affective evaluation and an epistemology based on belief. In the next chapter I will investigate the affective dimensions of the neuro-image by referring to affective neuroscience, laying the groundwork for the epistemological questions that will concern us in Part 2.

3

Surveillance Screens and Powers
of Affect

Affect is another major schizoanalytic force of the neuro-image, alongside the powers of the false and the illusionary principles of the brain-screen. In this chapter I focus on affects related to surveillance within contemporary screen culture. Arguably, one of the most salient characteristics of media culture today is its multiplication of screens and cameras in a network of surveillance cameras and other surveilling tools. CCTV screens, satellite tracking grids, GPS positioning on mobile displays, webcams, Internet polling, and other networked surveillance data (from governments, companies, or peer-to-peer data) constitute a new kind of apparatus, a complete surveillance apparatus. Most literature on contemporary surveillance is considered in terms of its controlling power, and via questions of security and freedom, referring frequently to both Foucault's panopticon and Deleuze's postdisciplinary update on Foucault's perspective in "Postscript on Control Societies."[1] What is striking about the discourses surrounding surveillance is that they are usually connected to oppositional affects: a desire for security on the one hand and the (paranoid) feeling of being persecuted on the other. In general, surveillance is connected to feelings of panic related to issues of control and freedom.[2]

In a conversation with Antonio Negri, Deleuze points out that in a control-based system, cybernetic machines and computers control societies. However, Deleuze argues, "the machines don't explain anything, you have to analyze the collective arrangements of which the machines are just one component."[3] In the same conversation, when asked about the political dimensions of the control society, Deleuze refers to artworks as "war-machines" that can operate like "circuit breakers." Here he also refers again to the brain: "I think subjectification, events, and brains are more or less the same thing. . . . If you believe in the world you precipitate events, however inconspicuous, that elude control, you engender new space-times, however small their surface or volume. It's what you call pietas. Our ability to resist control, or our submission to it, has to be assessed at the level of our every move."[4]

In this chapter I will assess in closer detail some of these levels of our "resistance or submission to control" in multiple-screen culture by looking at expressions of surveillance affects in recent cinema and contemporary art. Given that surveillance is now developing into an entire apparatus, I argue that its affects take on greater dimensions, beyond the usual affects of panic and of being followed and watched; it also potentially offers other forms of "resistance," beyond the now familiar critiques of control. As I will show, some contemporary neuro-images investigate quite new or different feelings toward the watchful camera eye.

In 2004 the artist Jill Magid spent thirty-one days in Liverpool for the project *Evidence Locker*. As the project's website indicates, during that time she developed a close relationship with City Watch, the surveillance office of the Liverpool Police and City Council.[5] The project concept was to use the 242 public surveillance cameras of the city as her film crew. Wearing a bright red trench coat, she would call the officer on duty with details of where she was and ask them to film her in particular poses and even guide her through the city with her eyes closed. The CCTV images were then selected, manipulated, and edited by Magid herself. For access to this footage she had to submit thirty-one Subject Access Request Forms, which she composed as though they were letters to a lover (addressed as "You," indicating both the surveillance camera and the officer on duty). The letters give an "intimate" portrait of the relationship between herself, the police, and the city. As a "third party witness," any visitor to the project's website can receive these letters one-by-one through a private email address, together with a daily clip of surveillance footage. Over the course of one month, one can develop a "personal" relationship with the artist and the surveillance eyes of Liverpool, reading letters such as this one, dating from the beginning of the project:

Sunday, February 1, 2004

Day 4

Dear Observer,

I met you today. I came to your office. You had been informed of my arrival. . . .

You marked a path on my map. I followed it. I got tea at Café Nero and wrote a postcard. You watched me, from two angles, when I did this.

You followed me through the center of town, on the streets without cars. I walked circles around your feet and your neck got stuck. It was funny to see you following me. You constantly moved to meet me.[6]

The intimate, aesthetic, and affective dimensions of the surveillance apparatus—usually seen as a much more impersonal and controlling power—are striking here. In a similar way the film *Red Road* (Andrea Arnold, 2007), about a surveillance officer working for Glasgow's City Eye control room, provides a different take on the surveillance gaze and on the affective dimensions of this aspect of contemporary screen culture. I will investigate the wider spectrum of the affective dimensions of the neuro-image by first sketching the dominant context of the paranoid (though often real and justified) affects of surveillance discourses before moving to *Red Road*'s perspective on surveillance. Principles from affective neuroscience will then be integrated to enable an assessment of the affective dimensions of Arnold's film. In this way I hope to develop some more general notions about the schizoanalytic powers of the neuro-image where affect operates as a parallel or even primary force on our brain-screens.[7]

Conspiracy Cinema, Paranoid Affects, and "Dimensions of Relationality" of Surveillance

Since the early 1970s, and especially in the wake of the Watergate scandal, themes of surveillance, conspiracy, and paranoia have permeated Hollywood cinema. Political thrillers, such as *The Anderson Tapes* (Sydney Lumet, 1971), *The Parallax View* (Alan J. Pakula, 1974), *The Conversation* (Francis Ford Coppola, 1974), *Three Days of the Condor* (Sydney Pollack,

1975), and *All the President's Men* (Alan J. Pakula, 1976), are particularly worthy of mention. According to Deleuze the themes of surveillance are characteristic for the new type of Hollywood cinema he announces at the end of *The Movement-Image*; thus, they have been part of the cinematographic image for some time.[8] Surveillance is often related to Foucault's analysis of Bentham's panopticon and its disciplinary and self-disciplinary effects. Orwell's *1984*, filmed by Michael Redford in 1984, is a clear example of the panoptic Big Brother discourse, frequently displayed in cinema. *Fortress* (Stuart Gordon, 1993), for instance, presents a futuristic panoptic prison. *Demolition Man* (Marco Brambilla, 1993), *The End of Violence* (Wim Wenders, 1997), *The Truman Show* (Peter Weir, 1998), and *Snake Eyes* (Brain De Palma, 1998) are other well-known Hollywood films that address the panoptic powers of surveillance cameras in more or less serious ways. In the 1990s, CCTV cameras as panoptic instruments of surveillance par excellence became increasingly imbricated with networked computers, satellite tracking systems, and all kinds of biometric identification technologies. Films such as *The Net* (Irwin Winkler, 1995), *Gattaca* (Andrew Niccol, 1997), *Enemy of the State* (Tony Scott, 1998), and, more recently, *Minority Report* (Steven Spielberg, 2002), *Children of Men* (Alfonso Cuarón, 2006), *A Scanner Darkly* (Richard Linklater, 2007), the *Bourne* trilogy, the television series *24* (FOX, 2001–10), and *The Last Enemy* (BBC, 2008) all subscribe in various ways to the paranoid logics of terrorism and crime prevention on the one hand, conspiracy and totalitarian control on the other.[9]

In his essay "Video Surveillance in Hollywood Movies" Dietmar Kammerer argues that although the relationship between surveillance and the media is complementary, the incorporation of CCTV formats and other surveillance screens and technologies in popular culture, including television drama and Hollywood cinema, is not one of simple representation or cause-and-effect: "We cannot simply ask: 'Does TV promote surveillance, because it exploits it in its formats like Big Brother?' or 'Is *Enemy of the State* a critique of surveillance society?' Maybe, maybe not—but what is important to recognize is that CCTV and media have much more in common than simple subject matters. It is not a question of 'conspiracy' or 'complicity' but rather of 'complications' and 'complexity.'"[10] Many of the films I have just mentioned relate to Foucault's panopticon model, or to Deleuze's elaboration of Foucault's disciplinary society into a control society, where individuals are no longer confined to particular spaces that discipline them (prisons, schools, hospitals) but can move freely while nevertheless being constantly watched and controlled. All that an individual caught in the controlling powers of the panoptic or networked gaze can do is move and think faster: run and outsmart the system, which protagonists in many surveillance films do either more or less successfully. Such films are full of highly adrenalized affects; fear, paranoia, and a desire to fight or take flight (both at the same time) run through them. However, as the scope of surveillance increases and develops into a whole ubiquitous apparatus, its effects and affects must be investigated in a larger cultural context as well. As I will argue in this chapter, one way of attending to the complicity and complexity of "surveillance (and) cinema" is by looking at the ways in which contemporary films engage affectively on different scales with the multiple screens of the surveillance apparatus. First, however, it is necessary to return to some of the current surveillance discourses to understand these dominant affects of fear, flight, and fight on the one hand and indifference toward its controlling affects in the name of security on the other.

On the website of the BBC series *The Last Enemy*, a high-tech surveillance conspiracy thriller set in the very near future, a section called "The Truth Behind *The Last Enemy*" presents current facts on surveillance: "Britain has about five million CCTV cameras"; "ID cards link your basic personal information to something uniquely yours—like the pattern of your iris, your face shape or your fingerprint"; "millions of children as young as 11 are to have their fingerprints taken and stored on a Government database"; and "the report of the Royal Academy of Engineering said that travel passes, supermarket loyalty cards and mobile phones could be used to track individuals' every move."[11] *The Last Enemy* zooms in on aspects of this unfolding issue of securitization and in doing so dialogues closely with contemporary surveillance discourses. In addition to series details and statistical reportage, the BBC site also includes video-recorded discussions with Benedict Cumberbatch (the actor who plays mathematical genius Stephen Ezard in the series, whose suspicions about a government surveillance conspiracy are discovered to be true) discussing his character and arguing that in the call for more security and control there is

laziness in the belief it's only the guilty who have something to lose; the innocent have nothing to hide. Too many of the perils of a surveillance society seem
abstract, a load of "what ifs" that will never have much bearing on most of our
lives. Yet the innocent do have something to hide—their privacy, and it is linked
with dignity. The innocent will have to prove every day that they are innocent
by what is on their card.[12]

One of the readers (Nick, London) comments:

That's it? I care more about stopping people being robbed and attacked on the
streets than about whether some anonymous bureaucrat can check my driver's
license record or my health records. In fact I feel no sense of a loss of dignity at
all those kind of checks, it's when I'm a victim of crime that I feel a loss of dignity. The dilution of habeas corpus/freedom of speech etc. is an entirely different matter of course.[13]

Where exactly this dilution begins, however, is difficult to establish, and
The Last Enemy is precisely a visionary and cautionary tale about this
dilemma of freedom and control and the prices paid for security and
protection.

In her extended discussion of these dilemmas of contemporary media, giving special attention to the racial and sexual dimensions of webcam culture and other surveillance fiber optics, Wendy Chun addresses
the possible relation between the two dominant positions of freedom and
control:

We still play a role in the creation of our machines and their languages, and
through our technologies—through our always compromised using—we can
imagine and move toward a different future. . . . To face this future and seize
the democratic potential of fiber optic networks, we must reject current understandings of freedom that make it into a gated community writ large. We must
explore the democratic potential of communication technologies—a potential
that stems from our vulnerabilities rather than our control. And we must face
and seize freedom with determination rather than fear and alibis.[14]

Chun calls for a break from the dominant affects of a surveillance culture
that move only between protecting freedom by a controlling gaze and es-
caping the unfreedom this controlling gaze imposes. Both positions can
only lead to paranoid affects of distrust and fear. Chun proposes we take
into account our vulnerabilities and potential, which is the approach of Jill
Magid's and Andrea Arnold's artistic explorations of surveillance screens,

as I will try to show. First, it is useful to open up these new perspectives a little further at a media theoretical level, which is possible with the work of Matthew Fuller.

In *Media Ecologies* Matthew Fuller calls for new approaches to surveillance culture. Influenced by the work of Guattari (and to a lesser extent, Deleuze), Fuller develops a media-ecological approach toward the collective arrangements our surveillance screens connect to—a methodology tailored to comprehend the more slippery and dynamic aspects of control society. Fuller proposes to consider webcams and CCTV circuits not as single media apparatuses for study but as "elements" involved in "dimensions of relationality," wherein it is the combinatorial arrangement of relations that "provide a means toward describing, actuating, or multiplying the powers of an element within a composition." Any media elements (cameras, screens, software), furthermore, are part of a "potentially infinite set of axes, or more accurately, axiometric forces, that compose the element."[15] Here, the notion of movable scale, something akin to a temporary, selected view from an infinite camera zoom, provides for the purpose of analysis "a certain perspectival optic by which dimensions of relationality and other scales may be 'read'" (132). Fuller's ecological approach allows for literally *shifting* insight into different involved elements, which may be "as diverse as practices, institutions, atomical structures, weather patterns, linguistic formations, protocols, transport infrastructures, a glance" (132). Fuller mentions three dimensions of relationality that correspond with different modes of surveillance: notorious abuse, generalized chilling, and surveillance as production. In the first kind abusive forms of surveillance, command, control, communication, and intelligence are all considered different scales of totalitarianism. Fuller's second notion, generalized chilling, relates to ongoing, networked, modes of inhabiting surveillance, scaled to the level of the individual's operations "of norms, affordances, and expectations" (147) in the awareness of constant surveillance. Surveillance as production is differently seen, in a Foucauldian sense, in that it produces "disciplined" or molded subjects. Surveillance technologies can be disobeyed or rebelled against, as is expressed in many of the panoptic discourses described above. They can also be seen in a Deleuzian way as a series of modulations: "Life, activity, becomes a flowing force that is gated, transducted, filtered, recombined, rendered positive as if it were a stream of data" (148). These forms of surveillance as production involve the possibility of invention and fabulation: artistic "war machines" that can break the circuit (as explored by *Evidence Locker* and *Red Road*).

As Fuller shows, in such diverse scaled dimensions of relationalities, it is possible to describe the "bit parts" of surveilled communities, as well as the primary compositional elements within surveillance systems, in terms of "flecks of identity":

This is what at its scalar levels control sees, an informational token of conformity or infraction. An element, cluster or concatenation of data, flecks of identity—a number, a sample, a document, a racial categorization—are features that identify the bearer as belonging to particular scalar positions and relations. Such flecks are processed in ways that make them resolvable, contradictory, that make them bear—given certain forms of interpretation—certain values, deprecations or openings, and are made useable. The citizen has a place, a speed, a set of functions as a variable within a social, bodily and technical algorithm. (148)

Contrary to the all-seeing panoptic eye, the controlling eye does not depend so much on seeing (after all, CCTV images are fuzzy, often flecks indeed) but on socioalgorithmic processes: "date, time, location, status, speed, choice, amount, accomplices" can all form a pattern that allows perspectival mobilization of data as evidence (149). All this is in part, Fuller argues, a consequence of digitization and the particular forms of seamless connections and transfer it affords.

Chun and Fuller provide important insights that enable us to move beyond the usual discussions of conspiracy and paranoia in addressing discourses of surveillance. Although these discourses and the films that express them in one way or another are important—addressing timely questions of power and control—it is also clear that we need alternative circuits of perception to be able to locate additional and alternative forms of complicity and resistance. *Evidence Locker* and *Red Road* can be considered particularly scaled dimensions of relationalities that address our surveillance brain-screens on an affective level and change our perspectives on power and control. This is in line with the conceptual strength and nuance of more recent affect theory, which indicates that "power" should be seen as a multilayered concept. In her book *Deleuze and the Cinemas of Performance*, for instance, Elena del Rio points to the difference between two kinds of power: a controlling power (*pouvoir*, usually associated with

the paranoid affects of surveillance as indicated above) and a more molecular power (*puissance*, which allows a variety of forces and affects).[16]
When we talk about surveillance, both these powers have to be taken into
account as the relationship between "surveiller" and "surveilled" becomes
more complex and engages in different dimensions of relationality. In the
next section I will focus on dimensions of affect to investigate its powers
as *puissance*.

Affective Aesthetics of Surveillance Screens in *Red Road*

Red Road is the first film of a more recent Dogme project initiated by
Lars von Trier's Zentropa films entitled *The Advance Party*. For the project three filmmakers were invited to make their first feature based on the
same set of characters, played by the same actors. Additional conditions
required that all three films must be set in Scotland and shot on digital
video. From these common conditions the directors would take the films
into three entirely different narratives, styles, and universes. *Red Road* is
a typical film of the digital age, both in terms of its Dogme-conditioned
production and in its transnational character.[17] The film also explicitly addresses contemporary surveillance culture. As Andrea Arnold explains in
an interview:

I've been looking at doing something about CCTV because in Britain we have
20% of the world's cameras on our tiny island—that's a lot of cameras, and
they've been increasing gradually over the years. I often looked at the cameras
and wondered who's behind them, who's watching, what does it mean. Is it Big
Brother, are our daily lives constantly going to be watched? And I've also been
wondering why Britain has so many cameras. When I was given this project and
the character description of Jackie—because it was an unusual way of starting—
it was described that she was cool and aloof and that she had this terrible thing
happen to her in the past, and I had this idea that she was separated from life, she
was watching life, but not taking part. And I thought she could be a CCTV op-
erator. I started from the character and the emotional place, so I'd say the story
is about Jackie and her journey. I decided at one point to be ambivalent about
what I say about CCTV, I feel it was enough to show it, and to show what it
can do. . . . If you live in London or Glasgow or any big city in the UK, you're

caught on camera 300 times a day. Those details aren't in the film, but I thought it would be interesting for people to have their own ideas about this.[18]

Here in the background of the film is Arnold's questioning of the scale of "generalized chilling," the individual awareness of the surveillance apparatus. In the film we often see Jackie behind her multiple-screen video wall with images of the city of Glasgow. Although Arnold did use one real CCTV camera across the city during production, most images on the wall are shot by handheld digital video cameras and precisely choreographed, distributed, and edited across the multiple screens to give them their typical real-time aesthetics of continuity and simultaneity, characteristic for surveillance aesthetics.[19] Another important characteristic of the aesthetics of these surveillance images in the film is that they are rather fuzzy and grainy. As indicated by Fuller, in contrast to the suggestions of panoptic discourse, the eye is not the most important or even most useful tool for distinguishing, deciphering, and assessing the "flecks of identities" caught up in surveillance media. On a scale of visuality these images, because of their diffused and blurry quality, are better described as affection-images. They have, as paradoxical as this may seem for panoptic surveillance technology, mostly haptic or tactile qualities, in which the eye is less engaged with mastering the image and more often searching, questioning, "touching" the surface of it, with less certainty than has been usually associated with the controlling gaze and the omnipotent Eye.[20] Here the affectionate qualities of both the surveillance images in *Red Road*'s surveillance screens, and the style of the film as a whole (in which affection-images dominate) indicate that we have to read the surveillance discourse perhaps along this different, affective scale.

The first images of *Red Road* emphasize the tactile qualities of surveillance images. We see several blurred CCTV images on TV monitors in close-up (accompanied by an equally blurry soundtrack), then a medium shot that reveals the multiple screens from a distance. Then we see a close-up of a pair of rubbing hands and another close-up of eyes looking at the screens. Before we see the main character, Jackie (Kate Dickie), and associate these hands and eyes as belonging to her, we watch just those hands, rubbing, touching a display, and wrestling a joystick to zoom in on particular images. A smile is thrown into the mix of this screens-hand-eye assemblage when on one of the screens Jackie sees a man taking his old dog for a walk and on another screen a cleaning lady dancing to her iPod music. This is a haptic kind of voyeurism. We also can see this is habitual recognition, the daily routine of a police officer observing the city to protect its people. Jackie's smile indicates that she feels somehow connected to these people on the screens, a friendly though aloof engagement that connotes a different kind of affective dimension to the surveillance apparatus than we are used to imagining.[21]

Soon Jackie's routine is interrupted: a quite different scene screens on the video wall. We have previously seen Jackie going to a wedding, meeting her family-in-law that apparently she had not seen for a long time. Her confrontation with her father-in-law is especially painful and seems to recall an unresolved conflict. She leaves the party early and returns to work, passing through the street she normally sees on her screens. She encounters the man with the old sick dog and starts a conversation with him as if they know each other. Of course, to him she is just a passerby, and he moves on quickly. Back at her surveillance workstation, she reports a lone girl in the streets that might need protection. On another screen she sees a woman running away, chased by a man. She makes another phone call, performing her standard protocols for interpreting the "flecks of identity" on her screens. However, just when she moves to report the incident, she realizes that she was falsely alarmed: it was just a game; the man and woman make out against a wall. At this point Jackie's body language becomes pronounced. As she leans backward in her chair, her left hand is tensely stretched on her desk, while her right hand caresses the joystick that operates the cameras. When the man throws his head backward at his climactic moment, she catches a glimpse of his face. Jackie's eyes dilate; her body freezes. She zooms in on his face. Overwhelmed, she leaves her station, asks one of her colleagues for a smoke ("I thought you'd quit," he says in surprise), and runs outside to light up.

From this moment onward the film explores an extremely rich array of affects that range from the most basic emotions to the most complex and ethical ones. Jackie's habitual work of tracking the screens and taking action when necessary is broken. This man's appearance on one of her screens overwhelms her with emotions that seem to be sexually charged but are clearly also mixed with other feelings, possibly a traumatic memory. Jackie is first and foremost intensely affected by the image of this one man on her multiple screens, while the narrative level of the film seems to leave quite open any possible qualification or explanation of the affects at stake. Both the performance and body language of the actor in close-ups and the haptic quality of the blurry CCTV images evoke this intense level of affect. Soon after, a first cycle of resonances and circuitous feedback begins to unfold in the narrative. Jackie starts to look for the dimensions of relationality of this man's image, trying to connect him to other patterns, cues, information. First, she looks through her cameras and screens, selecting only images that relate to him (neglecting her role of attending to so many others). She zooms in, follows the man, and discovers what he does, where he lives. In her own apartment she looks for an old newspaper article that identifies the man as the murderer Clyde Henderson, and by making calls in her function as a CCTV officer, she finds out he was released from prison earlier for good behavior. She then abandons her safe position in the control room to follow him in his neighborhood and visit him in his flat on Red Road.

To consider the cinema of surveillance in terms of this primacy of the affective, I turn to Brian Massumi's seminal essay "The Autonomy of Affect," which outlines the distinction between affect and emotion, or between the effect or intensity of the image (its strengths as unqualified affect) and the content or quality of the image (relating to conventional meanings in an intersubjective context as emotions).[22] These two levels indicate that image reception on the brain-screen is at least bilevel, where unconscious (intensive) processes and conscious qualities are parallel but not exactly symmetric: "The relationship between the levels of intensity and qualification is not one of conformity or correspondence but rather of resonance or interference, amplification or dampening."[23] Emotion is qualified intensity—it is owned and recognized, Massumi argues, whereas affect is unqualified and not ownable:

The autonomy of affect is its participation in the virtual. Its autonomy is its openness. Affect is autonomous to the degree to which it escapes confinement in a particular body whose vitality, or potential for interaction, it is. Formed, qualified, situated perceptions and cognitions fulfilling functions of actual connection or blockage are the capture and closure of affect. Emotion is the most intense (most contracted) expression of that capture—and of the fact that something has always and again escaped. (35)

Red Road delivers manifold encounters between unqualified affects and their gradual qualifications in Jackie's story. However, as Massumi indicated, "both levels, intensification and qualification, are immediately embodied" (25). Here it is necessary to make a move into affective neuroscience to see how specific neuroscientific principles offer further insights into the powers of affect.[24]

Principles of Affective Neuroscience: *Red Road* as "Neurothriller"

The neurological research of emotions has developed into an important subfield of cognitive neuroscience: "affective neuroscience." Affective neuroscientists study not only which regions of the brain are involved in emotional experiences (such as the prefrontal cortex and amygdala, or the difference between left- or right-hemisphere activity) but also the relations between emotions and learning, memory, social responses, vigilance, decision making, emotional communication (prosody), and affective styles.[25] Affective neuroscientists usually make a distinction between emotion (which takes place within the immediate materiality of body and brain) and feeling (which is related to memories and other resonating feedback systems in the brain). Antonio Damasio, for instance, shows how emotion precedes feeling:

The first device, emotion, enabled organisms to respond effectively but not creatively to a number of circumstances conducive or threatening to life. . . . The second device, feeling, introduced a mental alert for the good or bad circumstances and prolonged the impact of emotions by affecting attention and memory lastingly. This happens in both animals and humans. Eventually, in a fruitful combination with past memories, imagination, and reasoning, feelings led to the emergence of foresight and the possibility of creating novel, non-stereotypical responses.[26]

In light of Massumi's distinction between affect and emotion, terminology might become slightly confusing here. It seems that what neuroscientists call emotion is closer to what Massumi calls affect: "something that happens too quickly to have happened, actually, is virtual. . . . The virtual, the pressing crowd of incipiencies and tendencies, is a realm of potential," and seems to correspond to the immediate and unconscious emotional responses indicated by neuroscientific experiments.[27] What neuroscientists call resonating feelings is in fact more comparable to what Massumi describes as the conscious narrativization and capturing of affects in qualified emotions. For clarity's sake, I will stay with the neuroscientific distinction between emotion and feeling, while bearing in mind Massumi's recognition of the possibility of a dual-level analysis of affective powers. What is especially important is the irreducibility of the connection between the virtual and the actual, between affects and emotions (or emotions and feelings in neuroscientific terms), and that these connections are manifold, dynamic, and parallel but asymmetric: "In our description of nature the purpose is not to disclose the real essence of the phenomena but only to track down, so far as possible, relations between the manifold aspects of our experience."[28] The asymmetric parallel between emotion and feeling will be an important principle for understanding the paradoxical affective "phase space" that *Red Road* presents.

What is also important here is to recognize that there is a time lapse between unconscious emotion and conscious feeling. The embodied brain knows before we are conscious of its knowing. Damasio has demonstrated specifically that the bodily skin responses and corresponding brain activity of experimental subjects to stimuli is registered before subjects process this stimuli at a conscious level. Damasio has called this and similar mechanisms the "somatic markers" of our emotions, which he has measured through skin conductance response (SCR) experiments.[29] Damasio also discusses the neurological materiality of the brain in relation to unconscious emotions and conscious feelings. He refers to a range of research studies that were used to create forms of neurological disease treatments (including for Parkinson's Disease) that involve placing electrodes in the patient's brain. It is worth quoting one of the illuminating cases he describes:

The doctors found one electrode contact that greatly relieved the woman's symptoms. But the unexpected happened when the electric current passed through one of the four contact sites of the patient's left side, precisely two millimeters below the contact that improved her condition. The patient stopped her ongoing conversation quite abruptly, cast her eyes down and to her right side, then leaned slightly to the right and her emotional expression became one of sadness.

After a few seconds she suddenly began to cry. Tears flowed and her entire de-meanour became one of profound sadness. . . . Asked about what was happen-ing, her words were quite telling: . . . *I'm falling down in my head, I no longer wish to live, to see anything, hear anything, feel anything. . . . I'm fed up with life, I've had enough. . . . I'm scared in this world. I want to hide in a corner. . . . I'm hope-less, why am I bothering you?* The physician in charge of the treatment realised that this unusual event was due to the current and aborted the procedure. About ninety seconds after the current was interrupted the patient's behaviour returned to normal. The sobbing stopped as abruptly as it had begun. The sadness van-ished from the patient's face. The verbal reports of sadness also terminated. Very rapidly, she smiled, appeared relaxed, and for the next five minutes she was quite playful, even jocular. "What was that all about?" she asked. She was as puzzled as her observers were.[30]

Damasio explains that the scientific explanation for this woman's unprec-edented, switched emotions was that the electrical current had passed into one of the brain stem nuclei that control actions that produce the emotion of sadness, the production (and elimination) of tears, including the facial musculature and the movements of the mouth, pharynx, larynx, and dia-phragm necessary for crying and sobbing. The most remarkable finding here, Damasio argues, was that emotion-laden thoughts only came af-ter the emotion itself was activated. What is important for the discussion of the emotions in *Red Road* is that in affect-related forces, unconscious bodily responses seem to arrive before conscious feelings or thoughts. Like Massumi, Damasio refers to Spinoza, who had proposed this insight al-ready in *The Ethics*, arguing at several instances that "the human mind is the very idea or knowledge of the human body" and "the mind does not have the capacity to perceive . . . except in so far as it perceives the ideas of the modifications (affections) of the body."[31] In the scene from *Red Road* that upsets Jackie, it is equally noticeable how Jackie's body seems to "know something" before she appears conscious of the powerful emotions she is about to experience. Her hands are particularly strong indicators of the force and ambiguity of her triggered emotions—one seems tense and anxious, the other caressing and sexually aroused. Quite viscerally, there is incredible sexual tension announced in her body between her and this man who simultaneously arouses fear, disgust, and anger. This tension of ambiguous emotions (indicating mixed feelings) is intensely expressed and spread over the images without yet making sense. It will return at several other key moments in the film.

Sexual arousal, fear, disgust, and anger—all the emotions that we can see running through Jackie's body in this film—are what neuroscientists call the basic emotions that are related to our most basic (and universal) biological "striving to persist" (and it is not coincidental that Spinoza's *conatus* resonates here as well).[32] What makes this film so powerful is that it plays on these parallel but paradoxically resonating affective levels: between emotion and feeling, between virtual and actual. Furthermore, the film's mechanisms of suspense work precisely through the asymmetrical and potentially manifold levels of activation and connection, between emotions and feelings. We can therefore consider *Red Road* an "affective neurothriller," which, just like delirium cinema (populated by schizos and other mentally disordered characters, discussed in Chapter 1), and the films that thematize the powers of the false and illusionary perception (discussed in Chapter 2), can be considered a subtype of the neuro-image. Suspense in an affective neurothriller is not so much situated on a narrative level, where the audience knows more than the character does (conventional theories of filmic perception analyze suspense in this way). Hitchcock, for instance, played with narrative information and the knowledge of the audience ("Let them play God") to create many of his suspense thrillers.[33] Other classic suspenseful scenarios include those in which characters find themselves in dangerous situations, perhaps threatened by a murderous persecutor, or under the pressure of a (literal) deadline. Obviously, this does not mean that in movement-images and time-images emotions do not play an important role or that narrative development is of no importance in the neuro-image. But it is important to observe that in the neuro-image, in (asymmetric and largely unconscious, or perhaps intuitive) correspondence with scientific developments about the brain, the neural bases of our emotions and feelings can be addressed more precisely and directly, allowing images to operate on a neural level, playing out the tensions between emotions and feelings. The intensity we experience in *Red Road* is a tension we grasp at its incipience in the embodiment of Jackie's reactions to what she sees on her screens. When the narrative progresses, we find out that Jackie has lost her child and husband and that the man who so affects her, Clyde Henderson (Tony Curran), must have been the murderer. At this point suspense clearly associates itself with the (narrative) fact that Jackie is involving herself with a murderer—she could endanger herself. Yet this alone does not explain the paradoxically mixed emotions of sexuality, fear, disgust, and anger.

Two scenes are particularly revealing with respect to Jackie's mixed emotions. At the beginning of her search for Clyde Henderson, Jackie is in the Red Road neighborhood, where she follows some of Clyde's friends into the flat and enters Clyde's shabby apartment where a party is going on. The lighting in the small and crowded living room is hazy, dark, and red. She is standing against a wall when Clyde sees her and, clearly interested in this unknown guest, walks toward her. Approaching her closely, he tells her that he has the feeling he has seen her before. He moves closer, touches her face. The fear in her eyes is unmistakable, and the soundtrack indicates her heart is pounding, but at the same time, an erotic desire is spreading in every grain of the haptic images, in every fiber of Jackie's body. In an incredibly intense way the mise-en-scène, soundscape, and cinematography express here how Jackie is aroused in two opposite ways, torn between her emotions and feelings. She and Henderson almost kiss; she escapes into the elevator, literally throwing up: fear, desire, anger, and disgust. We still have no frame or explanations for these events at this stage, but the affective suspense means that we hold our breath, tracking her emotionality ourselves as spectators, when Jackie continues her investigations. She visits Clyde's apartment again (which he shares with a friend and his girlfriend) when he is not home. She follows him on her surveillance screens to discover more about his (quite suspicious) whereabouts. She eventually enters a bar at midnight to encounter him in a second scene that is also very strong in its ambiguous mix of emotions and feelings. Before she enters this bar, we observe Jackie pick up a sharp stone, for reasons unknown. At the bar Clyde tells Jackie how much he desires her, and after some conversation and a few drinks, he carries her to his sleazy apartment. Jackie finds out Clyde has a daughter who does not know him. The bedroom is again shrouded in dark colors, and the sex scene that follows is once more intensely erotically charged, suspenseful, and suggestive of danger—permeated with ambiguous emotions and mixed feelings. This time, however, when Jackie runs away, she has a much more conscious plan: revenge. She abuses herself with the rock that she picked up earlier, runs outside, and makes sure she is seen on the surveillance cameras so that the police will be informed. She files a complaint resulting in the capture of Clyde, who is sent back to prison. On her surveillance screens Jackie watches him taken into custody. From this moment onward, she experiences increasingly intense cognitive emotions and feelings.

Before discussing briefly these higher affective or cognitive levels, it is worthwhile engaging a neuroscientific finding that could explain Jackie's confusing mixture of emotions, including why she seems to be attracted to a potentially dangerous man. Nothing in the story indicates that Jackie is merely naively attracted to an incompatible (i.e., "the wrong") man. Affective neuroscientists Andreas Bartels and Semir Zeki have done some interesting research correlating neural aspects of maternal love and romantic love (related to sexual desire) that brings a useful perspective to Jackie's seemingly paradoxical behavior. Bartels and Zeki have concluded that maternal and romantic love share not only "a common and crucial evolutionary purpose, namely the maintenance and perpetuation of the species, . . . [but] they also share a core of common neural mechanisms."[34] As the narrative of *Red Road* unfolds, Jackie's sexual arousal, as precisely a force of life, is quite literally a "complicated" unconscious bodily response toward this man that took away her offspring. This attraction could (still) be explained as ultimately perverse behavior, relating maternity and sexuality in ways that modern cultural discourses have often tried to separate. But if we consider that it is possible that her maternal and sexual neurons unconsciously start firing together and become confusingly intertwined in such scenes, particularly given the memories that Jackie has of past events, the admixture here of feelings of fear, disgust, arousal, and anger brings to the film a rather accurate sense of the very neural confusions informing its suspense, in all its intense affective dimensions.[35]

In the final part of the film, Jackie discovers her own interest in redemption after traversing a whole range of complex emotions and feelings. As affective neuroscientific research indicates, basic emotions can develop into more complex social and ethical emotions, like shame, guilt, and other more cognitive evaluations that help us in decision making, learning, and value judgments or ethical behavior.[36] Although emotion and cognition have independent neural systems, it is generally acknowledged that these systems are also interdependent.[37] As I have indicated, Spinoza already pointed to this biological dimension of the body's conatus, which he developed into a philosophy of basic and complex emotions in *The Ethics*. Damasio, in *Looking for Spinoza*, acknowledges this common ground between affective neuroscience and philosophy and calls for an integrated field of study on emotion. From Spinoza we can also consider that an ethics of affects might have at its basis the transformation of passive sad affects into active joyful affects. In *Red Road* we see that Jackie's agency in revenge may feel like poetic justice, but it does not lead to more active affects, let alone any element of redemption. After a confrontation with Clyde's roommate, who is furious with her because her false complaint will send Clyde to prison for life, she finally acknowledges her own deep sorrow over losing her husband and child, and in the end she drops the charges. When Clyde is released, he and Jackie have one more encounter in the streets of Red Road. It becomes clear at this point that he was driving drunk and hit Jackie's husband and little girl while they were waiting for a bus (Jackie having stayed home after a quarrel with them). Guilt, a cry for empathy, forgiveness, and redemption are the complex emotions that play through the last scenes of *Red Road*. These cognitive and social feelings are more highly constructed in the film's late narrative developments and through coalescing explanations that the end of the film wraps up.

Mirror Neurons: Empathy and "As-If-Loops" in Spectators' Brain-Screens

A last development in affective neuroscience I would like to raise in the context of the powers of affect is the question of empathy related to the discovery of mirror neurons. This discovery seems to be relevant in rethinking spectatorship and the relationship between the viewer's brain and the screen. Here I want to move away from the analysis of the emotions and feelings in *Red Road*, to the question of how these (and other) images relate to the viewer's brain-screen—how they can affect us. In my introduction I briefly discussed mirror neurons, their possible connection to a Deleuzian conception of cinematographic images, and the general power of images to create new brain circuits. In the context of the powers of affect, it is worthwhile to look closely again at this neurological phenomenon. In his article "The Shared Manifold Hypothesis" Vittorio

Gallese, one of the discoverers of mirror neurons, explains how these neurons, first observed in monkey brains but soon after in the human brain as well, function: "In a series of single neuron recording experiments we discovered in a sector of the monkey ventral premotor cortex, area F5, that a particular set of neurons, activated during the execution of purposeful, goal-related hand actions, such as grasping, holding or manipulating objects, discharge also when the monkey observes similar hand actions performed by another individual."[38]

Other experiments with both monkeys and humans have indicated that not only actions but also more minute or incremental goal-oriented movements are neurologically triggered in the same area of mirror neurons. Fundamentally, to understand the intended goal of an observed action, and to eventually reenact it, Gallese argues that a link must be established between the observed agent and the observer:

This link is constituted by the *embodiment* of the intended goal, shared by the agent and the observer. . . . The observed action produces in the observer's premotor cortex an activation pattern resembling that occurring when the observer actively executes the same action. . . . Although we do not overtly reproduce the observed action, nevertheless our motor system becomes active *as if* we were executing that very same action that we are observing. To spell it out in different words, action observation implies *action simulation*.[39]

Action simulation and action observation thus (partly) rely on the same cortical network. This simulation is useful for predicting and controlling action. A similar structure seems to be at work in the far more complex domain of intersubjective relationships, as Gallese proposes:

It is clear that the discovery of mirror neurons provides a strong neurobiological basis for a subpersonal account of inter-subjective representational content. . . . This implicit, automatic, and unconscious process of motor simulation enables the observer to use his/her own resources to penetrate the world of the other without the need for theorizing about it, without the need to necessarily use propositional attitudes. A process of action simulation automatically establishes a direct implicit link between agent and observer. Action is the "a priori" principle enabling social bonds to be initially established.[40]

Mirror neurons thus form the basis of our bond with others; empathy is grounded in the embodied similarity and simulation of the other on a neurological level. Mirroring resonance mechanisms in this way form the basis of our empathy with others, but are also at the basis of our learning and social skills. Damasio has called this mechanism the "as-if-loop" that gives the brain a "playground where variations on the body-state theme can be played," which is important for our empathic (affective) and social bond with others.[41]

Since their discovery in 1995, mirror neurons and their functionality have been subjected to much research. It has even been argued that mirror neurons are the unique basis of our entire psychological and sociopolitical structures and organizations.[42] But what might mirror neurons contribute to theories of our relationship to the screen? In film theory this relationship is classically conceived in terms of identification. Christian Metz distinguished primary cinematographic identification (with the point of view of the camera) and secondary cinematographic identification (with the characters onscreen).[43] Theories of identification have been elaborately discussed in the context of the psychoanalytic mirror stage and the representation of (unobtainable) Ideal Egos, voyeurism, and ideological subject positioning.[44] The Lacanian mirror stage, most famously elaborated in the context of cinema by Slavoj Žižek, always involves the "detour" of an alienating spectral image, a representation that covers up the fact that it is actually an illusion, evading the fundamental reality of the hole or lack in the individual's psychic makeup, who is forever alienated from a true self.[45]

Classic cognitivists (as opposed to the 4EA cognitivists discussed in the previous chapter and the affective neuroscientists in this chapter), however, have argued against the psychoanalytic conception of identification based on an alienating desire for illusionary images (of the "other") and have proposed concepts of sympathy and forms of narrative engagement such as alliance and allegiance.[46] All these theories are much more developed than I am indicating here, and they have all made important contributions to our understanding of film spectatorship. What I want to suggest is simply that in both the psychoanalytic accounts of identification and in classic cognitivist film-screen relationships, there is an implicit idea of the screen as an external representation at a distance, as an illusion of reality. In spite of the great emphasis on sexual drives in psychoanalysis, it also shares with classic cognitivism the notion that the body does not play an important role in understanding the viewer-screen relationship. The screen itself is conceived as a "protective screen" to keep real reality (located prior to or underneath illusions, and considered too ugly or frightening to watch directly) at a distance. It supposedly functions as a shield, as the protagonist Matthew (Michael Pitt) in Bertolucci's film *The Dreamers* (2003) says when he enters a film theater and takes a front seat in the dark auditorium: "The screen really was a screen; it shielded us from the world."

In contrast, mirror neurons (alongside so many other recent findings in neuroscience) indicate that the screen is not situated as a protection between our minds and the outside world but that there is a direct and embodied screen effect in our brains.[47] Neuroscientists conducting research on mirror neurons have also experimented with showing test subjects human actions displayed on video screens. Mirror neurons were shown to work the same way whether viewing others in real life or viewing them on screens.[48] Here the "protective" function of the screen seems much weaker than classic theories of film spectatorship have theorized. It is not that manipulations like framing, montage, mise-en-scène, and cinematography or other aspects of selection and mediation do not have an effect—they most certainly do. Nevertheless, such studies tell us that the power of images is more direct than we have ever conceived before. This finding can be positive for learning, opening our minds and creating a collectively shared consciousness. Of course, it can obviously also indicate negative effects, as Münsterberg foresaw when he wrote about the "perils to childhood in the movies."[49]

With the discovery of mirror neurons we can grasp also the literal conception of Deleuze's dictum "the brain is the screen" in a dialethic way: we have simulation mechanisms inside our brain, "as if body loops" are "not only internally driven, but also triggered by the observation of other individuals."[50] It is now conceivable to speak of spectatorship in terms of becoming: we quite literally become what we see, at least on a neurological level. Something in our brain circuit resonates in (asymmetric) resonance with what we see and changes immediately, without "protection." We are truly affected, touched by what we see. We do not need to identify with a character (or his or her ideological subject position) to be affected by a character's experiences. Even though identification with characters may occur, affective encounters can take place on many different levels. The brain-screen relationship becomes very complex because of all the variations and levels of neurological engagement and empathy possible.[51] We can "co-sense" in many variations and in relations both the emotions and feelings (or affects and emotions in Massumi's terms) of the characters, in addition to the aesthetic intensities and qualities of the images on our screens.

How, then, given the phenomenon of mirror neurons, can we still make distinctions between ourselves and others and between ourselves and the world? My first chapter makes clear that schizophrenia, as a pathological disease in which too much illusionary or affective power takes over on the brain-screen, can be quite disastrous. In regard to mirror neurons, Gallese reports on patients that suffer from "echopraxia," a compulsion to imitate everything they see at the speed of a reflex action.[52] Less-disturbing forms of contagion in watching other people are part of normal behavior. (This contagion is most obvious, for example, in laughing or yawning, or in the smiling waiter who is tipped more generously because he or she makes customers smile and feel more positive.) What this indicates is that although mirror neurons ensure our brain moves imitatively when we watch others moving or going through emotions, there must also be mechanisms that prevent us at some point in the feedback loops from completely performing the same action. On an affective level, however, this inhibition mechanism is less strong. We might not engage in a fistfight in front of the monitor when we see a battle onscreen, but depending on the level of intensity, our skin does crawl, our heart does pound, and our tears do flow when we see a horror movie, a chase scene, or a melodramatic moment.

In "The Neuroscience of Metafilm" Norman Holland gives an interesting explanation for why we usually do not imitate completely what we see.[53] He discusses patients with prefrontal damage who—much like the "echopraxia" patients mentioned by Gallese—lack the inhibitory control to refrain from acting in response to a story or to other people's behavior.[54] Holland uses this phenomenon to explain why many "metafilms" (films about the process of filming, or in which "fiction" and "reality" become intermingled) make us feel such palpable confusion, even anxiety. They invoke a sort of confusing "echopraxia":

I suddenly feel a contradiction in my perceptions. Is what I am perceiving just a story or is it something real? I will begin to feel a vague sense of having to do something, but at the same time I know that part of what I am perceiving is fiction. . . . My brain is getting two inconsistent signals. One says, Be ready to act. The other says, Don't act. In effect, I am asking the dorsolateral prefrontal cortex to set my brain both for non-action and action. (71)

Holland's observations are interesting, and inhibition controllers in the prefrontal cortex probably play an important role in evaluating and processing the as-if-loops in our brains. However, when Holland discusses the uncanny effects of the metafilm *Adaptation* (Spike Jonze, 2002), it is clear he has not taken the existence of mirror neurons into account: "Suddenly the film about writer Charlie Kaufman isn't just a story—it is a physical fact happening on the screen in front of me. In my experience of it, it has acquired a different kind of reality from the narrative I was temporarily believing" (70). But isn't any film, even every perception, a "physical fact happening on a screen?" Not (just) the screen in front of me but the screen inside my brain? It seems that Holland is, on a "metalevel" so to speak, caught between two conceptions of the screen: a classical "protective" screen and a direct "brain-screen." Indeed, fiction and reality intermingle in strange ways in the neuro-image; however, this intermingling occurs not only in metafilms but also in the whole of contemporary image culture. All images in contemporary screen culture have to be seen through particular scales and dimensions of relationalities that play with reality and fiction and the different "powers of the false."

Both Sides of the Camera: From Peeping Toms to Sensing Alices

It may seem I have moved a long way from the issue of contemporary surveillance screens, their ubiquity and critical negotiation, through which I started to unpack the schizoanalytic powers of affect in contemporary screen culture. To complete the analyses of this chapter by way of return to those beginnings, we can recall Deleuze's insistence on the possibility of resisting the power (as *pouvoir*) of the panoptic gaze with "war machines" such as artistic practices. Matthew Fuller also calls for strategies that can break the interpretative control over "flecks of identity":

Irises, fingerprints, postal codes, number plates, age, spending power, magazine subscriptions, criminal record, drug use, gender assignment, dates, location, racial category, medical records, credit rating, telephone use patterns, energy use, salary, insurance status, shampoo preference, local crime level and type, employment history, citation records. Control has no need of individuals per se, only as referents: as scalar nodes in the flows of cash, commodity and behavior. . . . Instead of, or at the very least alongside of, demanding that surveillance conform to the conditions of a previous state it is time to extend operations within, against, and outside such systems and to explore the disruptive advantage of its particular qualities.[55]

Fuller proposes three concrete strategies of resistance: evasion, overload, and noncompressibility. While evading or dropping out of the webcam spectrum might not be so easy (Fuller mentions projects like *Spot the Cam*, which maps surveillance cameras, as exemplary of the attempt), overloading the system can be quite an effective tool of resistance that tests the thresholds of surveillance systems. Elaborating on the last strategy of resistance, noncompressibility, Fuller draws on Deleuze and Guattari's rhizome structures that resist the reduction of complexity into simple characteristics and misplaced concreteness in a controlling surveillance system. My suggestion in this chapter has been that both *Evidence Locker* and *Red Road* are war machines that "explore the disruptive advantage" of surveillance systems by showing their incompressibility on an affective level. In *Evidence Locker* Jill Magid does not evade or overload the surveillance apparatus (by "breaking out"), but she "breaks in" through overexposure and through the creation of personal links to an impersonal mechanism. In *Red Road*, director Andrea Arnold follows a rhizomatic strategy by showing the emotional and complex relations and dimensions of one of the "flecks of identity" on the main character's surveillance screen, emphasizing the "controlling gaze" as an affective human being. Both Arnold and Magid point out the power (as *puissance*) of the tactile and affective qualities of surveillance images, which goes against the grain of the all-seeing omnipotent *pouvoir* ascribed to contemporary surveillance screens. Both address the manifold relations between individual emotions and feelings, protocol-governed behavior and social demands, and the multiple screens that mediate directly but asymmetrically between those dimensions, to show certain forms of "affective resistance" that art can offer us.

Another element that *Red Road* and *Evidence Locker* share is that they present perspectives from both sides of the camera. Both Arnold and Magid show that the "flecks on the screen" and the "invisible eyes behind the screen," when taken on an affective dimension of relationality and on different scales, are more complex nodes in the surveillance apparatus than the abstract agents of crime or of control found in dominant conceptions of power and control. Jackie leaves her place behind the camera and enters the space in front of it, where the affective qualities of Arnold's camera take over (and, as I have detailed above, she even plays to the cameras as a performer, to attain her revenge). Magid, in turn, sometimes leaves the streets and visits the police officers on duty in their office, looks at the images from their perspective, and addresses them intimately in her letters. In one letter she describes a small incident on her way back from a visit to the control rooms. Three young boys walk toward her and pull her bag. She calls the CCTV officer to ask if he saw it, not because she felt scared or threatened but to see if they got it as a picture for her project. The officer did not notice it initially, but when reviewing the images of five minutes prior, he does, and promises to find them. Magid's plea, "Please don't worry about it, they were just being bratty," has no effect. She is asked to fill out a witness report. The boys are identified. Magid's heart sinks; she is reluctant to fill out the report. Then the CCTV officer offers to show what happened to her. She writes to (the power of) the camera:

So I went down to your building with him and I saw it myself. I saw what you saw, and I could see what you meant. It did look obvious from your window. Like they had planned the whole thing. I could not recall anymore what happened, not even which arm the bag had been on; it all got muddled. I filled out your forms and you drove me home, in that yellow van you film the city with. (*Evidence Locker*, Letter 15)

Red Road and *Evidence Locker* show that cinematic artistic war machines are not entirely clear, simple, or ideal counterforces. Occupying both sides of the camera, changing positions between observing and being observed, they problematize the complex and confusing affects of surveillance, and arguably of contemporary images of culture at large. In one of her last letters Magid confesses her affective relation to City Watch to one of her observers:

Friday, February 27, 2004

Day 30

Dear Observer,

Then you—the most powerful you—surprised me: So about this artwork of yours . . . I thought you had not remembered. I realized then, that before I had arrived, you simply had approved me. You let me come here blankly, with an ambiguous identity, and I got to make one myself.

And You, You with capital Y. You who walks for me. You who I trust completely . . .

Things come out to you slowly, not all at once, and still not everything.

About the red coat, about the letters, about the spaces I am in when you are not around.

You wanted to ask a million things.

You are nervous, scared for those above you. This city is unique and you want it protected.

. . . And I tell you, hurting the city's reputation is not my intention. Neither is it to judge what you do. Let others do that. I tell you: I did not critique your system; I made love to it.

You blushed. (*Evidence Locker*, Letter 30)

Making the surveillance camera blush by admitting our affective relationship to it is what Jill and Jackie, as new aesthetic figures, pursue. They are no longer purely voyeuristic Peeping Toms, exploiting (or being exploited by) the panoptic power of the gaze.[56] Occupying both sides of the camera, embodying and expressing the ambiguous neurothrills and affective powers of the surveillance apparatus, we might instead call them "Sensing Alices" who can guide us through the surveillance adventures of contemporary multiple-screen culture. They will not overturn the whole system, but they may give us the (micropolitical) urge to confront a surveillance camera with a smile or to (literally) re-view simplistic interpretations of flecks of identity, simply because they have offered us alternative experiences, touching our brain-screens imperceptibly, directly.

PART 2

NEUROPHILOSOPHY

Turning Madness into Metaphysics

Signs of Time

METAPHYSICS OF THE BRAIN-SCREEN

I have drawn connections between digital screens, neuroscience, and Deleuzian philosophy in order to investigate and elaborate on the brain-screens of contemporary neuro-images. In accordance with Deleuze and Guattari's definitions of transdisciplinarity in *What Is Philosophy?* I have moved between intrinsic and extrinsic forms of interferences and proposed to connect the delirious and schizoanalytic characteristics of contemporary culture, its powers of the false and its powers of affect, to recent findings in pathological, visual, and affective neuroscience—connections that show that cognitive neuroscience, Deleuzian philosophy, and digital screen culture share an affectively embodied "manipulating" brain. In the second part of this book I will discuss contemporary image culture with more emphasis on its philosophical dimensions. As such, I will no longer rely explicitly on neuroscientific findings but investigate how contemporary cinema can be defined as neuro-images metaphysically, epistemologically, and aesthetically. In this way I will demonstrate that the discussed developments in cinema do not rest exclusively on scientific views (which by their nature could be falsified). There is, in other words, a strong philosophical basis to this work, which resonates with contemporary science, without being dependent upon it. In the following chapters transdisciplinary connections will be more of the third kind of interferences distinguished by Deleuze and Guattari as general resonances and correspondences between the three domains of thinking that "need each other." In the present chapter I focus on metaphysical questions of the neuro-image.[1] In Chapter 5 I will discuss epistemological problems raised by contemporary image culture. In Chapter 6 I will emphasize its aesthetic characteristics and the importance of (artistic) creation.

With respect to screen culture I will take up more explicitly the recurrent question of cinema's death (or its possible survival) after the digital turn. As is well known, cinema's death certificate has been issued several times before the digital age as well. The arrival of the television set in the 1950s and the introduction of the home videotape in the 1980s are just the most obvious moments in the past in which its funeral was announced. In 1961, when the small screen started to become a common object in the living room, Alain Resnais was interviewed for television in coincidence with the premiere of *Last Year in Marienbad* (this interview is now available on YouTube). The interviewer concluded by asking whether cinema is dead, alive, or about to be (re)born.[2] "It will continue to flow, like a river," Resnais answered, assuming in this way the development of cinema to be a continuation with the past and a movement toward the future. Deleuze, at the end of his cinema books, written during the 1980s when the electronic video image was massively introduced and cybernetics started to raise questions about the future of the image, similarly demonstrates a belief in the survival of cinema, stating that "the life or afterlife of cinema depends on its internal struggle with informatics."[3] He argues in the same chapter that this struggle does not necessarily rely on computing skills or cybernetic machines but on a will to art: "An original will to art has already been defined by us in the change affecting the intelligible content of cinema itself: the substitution of the time-image for the movement-image. So that electronic images will have to be based on still another will to art, or on as yet unknown aspects of the time-image."[4] The question of time remains very important in the transformation into a new image type. What is particular about creative audiovisual images is that, in contrast to ordinary perception, they can "render time relations sensible and visible."[5]

In Deleuze's cinema books the temporal dimensions of the movement-image and the time-image are investigated through the work of Henri Bergson. Therefore, it is useful to return to Bergson's temporal metaphysics to see if and how the temporal relations of the neuro-image might differ from those of the movement-image and the time-image as Bergson himself elaborated. Not coincidentally, Bergson's metaphysics is developed in (intuitive) partnership with sciences of the brain, as is very clear from his essays in *Mind-Energy*.[6] His attention to the "neurological" and even "pathological" metaphysics of time (Bergson refers to psycho-pathological disorders such as amnesia, aphasia, hallucinations, and delirium to develop his philosophy of time [151–56]) will specifically come to resonate in this chapter with the temporal architecture of schizophrenia, discussed in Chapter 1 (on delirium cinema).[7] Deleuze extends Bergson's metaphysics by adding the film screen into the equation (time = brain = screen). In *The Time-Image* Deleuze indicated that the movement-image has not at all disappeared but "now exists only as the first dimension of an image that never stops growing in dimensions."[8] If the time-image is its second dimension, then I suggest it is possible to consider the neuro-image as a third dimension of the image. To explain and justify this, however, I will first look at Deleuze's three syntheses of time as he developed them in *Difference and Repetition*.[9] In the second part of this chapter I will return to the cinema of Alain Resnais to argue that his films, conceived by Deleuze as the ultimate example of brain-screens of the time-image, can be considered a neuro-image avant la lettre, or as digital cinema without digits. Resnais's films are fascinating in the context of the neuro-image because they already inherently comprehend the fact that not only are the differences between image types not clear-cut, but also such differences are better thought in terms of "nested instancing," partial overlap, and continuous growth. In this way Resnais's work further demonstrates how the neuro-image can be sensed at its incipience as a will to art and can anticipate aspects of digital culture, such as a participatory aesthetics and database logics. The final part of this chapter looks at the more recent film *Earth* (Julio Medem, 1996) to consider the "cosmological perspective," still absent in Resnais but now prominent in the third dimension of the image as neuro-image.

Bergson's Metaphysics of Mind-Energy and Time

To determine how the movement-image and time-image might be elaborated in relation to the neuro-image, it is necessary to recall Bergson's temporal conception of metaphysics and its unfolding through and beyond cerebral physicality. In "The Very Life of Things," his insightful introduction to Bergson's *Introduction to Metaphysics*, John Mullarkey summarizes the three remarkable aspects that characterize Bergsonian metaphysics. First is Bergson's intuitive method, which goes from things to concepts in order to capture "the effort to bend thought backwards towards its object."[10] It is thought that installs itself in the very life of things. It is not thought of the thing, or consciousness of something, but thought as thought, consciousness as consciousness. Second, there is the primacy of becoming and process, things in the making. We find ourselves in a mobile and manifold reality, and this "process metaphysics designates the continual change and transformation of phusika. . . . Physics in process is metaphysics" (xiii). Third, Bergson's is a nonsymbolic (nonrepresentational, nonlinguistic) way of thinking: "Not fanciful projection by us but pathetic introjection of us and the object in our 'being made'—our own and its own co-becoming. That is why the true 'empiricism' is the true 'metaphysics'" (xvii).

Throughout *An Introduction to Metaphysics* Bergson insists that science and metaphysics come together in intuition, and he stresses the necessity of this movement: putting more science into metaphysics and more metaphysics into science.[11] Adding that this does not mean that science and metaphysics are the same, Bergson indicates that integral experience is the aim of intuitive metaphysics: "Metaphysical intuition, although it can only be obtained through material knowledge, is quite other than the mere summary or synthesis of that knowledge. It is distinct from these . . . as the motor impulse is distinct from the path traversed by the moving body, as the tension of the spring is distinct from the visible movements of the pendulum. In this sense metaphysics has nothing in common with a generalization of facts; and nevertheless it might be defined as integral experience."[12] Keeping this distinction in mind, it is now important to bring the domains together.

The most intimate way of entering into the very life of things, of grasping by intuition from within, is "our own personality in its flowing through time, our self which endures."[13] In quite beautiful passages Bergson describes how we can observe our own inner life, our own consciousness in duration, by moving from perceptions and motor habits to memories, passing through emotions and feelings that move as continuous fluxes beneath these surfaces.[14] (Münsterberg's descriptions of the film experience come to mind here, and Deleuze's dictum "the screen is the brain" resonates quite literally. I will return to Deleuze's cinema books momentarily.) Bergson insists on the dynamic complexity of this inner life that shows a continuing variety of qualities and progress. Furthermore, he warns that no single symbolic representation, but also no single image, nor even any abstract concept, can replace the intuition of duration:

> Here the single aim of the philosopher should be to promote a certain effort, which in most men is usually fettered by habits of mind useful for life. Now, the image has at least this advantage that it keeps us in the concrete. No image can replace the intuition of duration, but many diverse images, borrowed from very different orders of things, may, by the convergence of their action, direct consciousness to the precise point where there is an intuition to be seized. By choosing images as dissimilar as possible, we shall prevent any one of them from usurping the place of the intuition it is intended to call up, since it would then be driven away at once by its rivals. By providing that, in spite of their differences of aspect, they all require from the mind the same kind of attention, and in some sort the same degree of tension, we shall gradually accustom consciousness to a particular and clearly defined disposition—precisely that which it must adopt in order to appear itself as it really is, without any veil.[15]

Bergson adds in a note that by "images" he means here those images that a philosopher may need to make his thought known to others. These images might also be seen as the actual images on our (digital) screens; and the diversity of images that Bergson calls for may be provided by contemporary audiovisual culture. I will argue these points more explicitly and politically in the last part of this book. For now, I want to emphasize Bergson's notion of consciousness "without a veil." This indicates that Bergson sees the brain-screen without the "protection" of an exterior representation, but "dialethically," as an ongoing process of cobecomings of world and brain, matter and memory/consciousness.[16] It is also important to add that, for Bergson, our perceptions, our conscious experiences, are always opened up to the larger whole of the universe. Matter is as much shaped by consciousness as consciousness is formed upon matter.[17]

Placing consciousness as the most important tool to understand this metaphysics of time as duration, and insisting on the cocreation of physics and metaphysics, it is not surprising that Bergson makes frequent references to the biology of the brain. In *Mind-Energy* he describes the fantasy of looking into the skull:

Could we look through the skull and observe the inner working of the brain with instruments magnifying some billion times more than our most powerful microscopes, if we then should witness the dance of the molecules, atoms and electrons of which the cerebral cortex is composed, and if in addition we possessed the rule for transposing the cerebral into the mental—a dictionary so to speak which would enable us to translate each figure of the dance into the language of thought and feeling—we should know, quite as well as the supposed soul, what it was thinking, feeling and wishing, what it would be believing itself doing freely, though it would only be acting mechanically.[18]

Just as contemporary neuroscience makes a distinction between the Easy Problem (the mapping of material correlates for specific functions of the brain, which is now possible with all kinds of brain-scanning instruments of Bergsonian fantasy) and the Hard Problem (how does consciousness arise? how does the brain enable the mind?), Bergson makes clear that even if we could understand and map the brain perfectly, this would never be enough to explain the experience of consciousness nor to grasp intuitions of the changes and improbabilities of human consciousness that are more than its cerebrality.[19] The relation of the brain to thought is complex and subtle, Bergson insists: "Mental life overflows cerebral life. But the brain—precisely because it extracts from the mental life whatever it has that may be played in movement, whatever is materializable—precisely because it constitutes thus the point of insertion of mind in matter—secures at every moment the adaptation of the mind to circumstances, continually keeping the mind in touch with realities." The brain is therefore in fact an organ that keeps consciousness, feeling, and thought connected to life, an "organ of attention to life."[20]

In correspondence with insights from cognitive neuroscience, Bergson argues that the brain is an organ for action and choice: "The brain is a crossway, where the nervous impulse arriving by any sensory path can be directed into a motor path. . . . The brain is an organ of [action and] choice."[21] However, the fact that the brain has to choose and act is directly related to consciousness that retains the past and can anticipate the future. To choose, we must remember and foresee: "Life is employed from the start in conserving the past and anticipating the future in a duration in which past, present and future tread one on another, forming an indivisible continuity. Such memory, such anticipation, are consciousness itself."[22] Here then we come full circle. Bergson's metaphysics is based on an intuitive grasping of duration in consciousness, which makes it a temporal metaphysics: metaphysics as universal consciousness of the coexistence of past, present, and future in an indivisible duration. A large part of *Mind-Energy* is devoted to problems of time and memory, taking up the problems already developed in *Matter and Memory*, the latter informing the basis of Deleuze's film books, to which I will turn now.

Deleuze's Bergsonian Cinema Project and the Three Syntheses of Time

Many important commentaries have explored the nature of Deleuze's Bergsonianism in his cinema books. It is not my intention to discuss these commentaries extensively here.[23] However, for the sake of developing an argument about the possibility of a third image type (with yet a different dimension of time, though one not unrelated to those of the previous image types), I will briefly summarize Deleuze's four commentaries on Bergson. One of the most problematic issues is that, in spite of Bergson's specific objections to cinema as a mechanism that resembles the tendency of human intellect toward spatializing time in immobilized sections to which movement is added, Deleuze considers Bergson's philosophy of perception (matter) and memory (time) as duration, as nevertheless essentially cinematographic. Deleuze's contrariness in identifying a cinematic Bergson in spite of Bergson, which Deleuze explains only by stating that Bergson could not yet grasp the essence of the cinematographic apparatus, is considered by many as too easy or historicist a solution to the problem of contradiction. Nevertheless, Deleuze's Bergsonian view of cinema itself has generally been welcomed as a new way to think filmically without taking language or linguistics as a model.[24] Another way of looking at Deleuze's remarkable move of reading Bergson against Bergson is to recognize this as Deleuze's first (key) shift into his "brain is screen" argument. Consider that Deleuze does not spend any thought on the technical conditions of the projection of twenty-four frames per second that give the illusion of movement. Instead, he perceives the "realities of illusion" on the brain-screen.

In his first commentary on Bergson Deleuze proposes that Bergson thinks of time not as "clock time" (which Bergson also calls "cinematographic illusionary time"), that is, not as a succession of divisible immobile sections, but instead as indivisible mobile sections, as movement-images. Deleuze argues that cinema immediately gives us movement-images: "The cinema would rediscover that very movement-image of the first chapter of *Matter and Memory*."[25] The second thesis of the first commentary is that Bergson (in accordance with modern scientific developments) considers time no longer a succession of special poses, privileged moments, but a succession of "any-instances-whatever," and cinema reproduces movement by relating to these "any-instances-whatever": "Bergson forcefully demonstrates that the cinema fully belongs to this modern conception of movement."[26] The final thesis in the first commentary considers movements as mobile sections of duration in relation to a whole that also keeps changing. This means that movement is always open to change, never given, nor givable: "Movement always relates to change. . . . If we think of pure atoms, their movements, which testify to a reciprocal action of all the parts of the substance, necessarily express modifications, disturbances, changes of energy in the whole. What Bergson discovers beyond translation is vibration, radiation."[27] In the chapters that follow this, Deleuze maps the different ways in which framing and montage open the whole to transform it.

In his second commentary on Bergson Deleuze indicates how Bergson identifies the images with movement, with a world of universal variations, undulations, rippling:

This infinite set of all images constitutes a kind of plane of immanence. The image exists in itself, on this plane. This in-itself of the image is matter: not something hidden behind the image, but on the contrary the absolute identity of the image and movement leads us to conclude that the movement-image and matter are identical. . . . The material universe, the plane of immanence, is the machinic assemblage of movement-images. Here Bergson is startlingly ahead of his time: it is the universe as cinema in itself, a metacinema.[28]

The following part of Deleuze's commentary on Bergson consists of distinguishing the varieties of movement-images as perception-images, action-images, affection-images. They constitute three "material aspects of subjectivity," related to the brain as a "center of indetermination." Deleuze concludes this part of his commentary by posing the screen immediately as a screen: "And each of us, the special image or the contingent center, is nothing but an assemblage of three images, a consolidate of perception-images, action-images and affection-images."[29] The remaining chapters of *The Movement-Image* discuss in detail the different image types and the different signs they emit.

The third and fourth commentaries are developed in *The Time-Image*. Here Deleuze moves to take images as "immaterial aspects of subjectivity." By referring to the distinction Bergson makes between habitual recognition of sensorimotor activities (necessary for moving in the world and developed in the movement-image) and attentive recognition (that does not extend in movement but connects to a recollection-image), Deleuze develops the idea of the exchange between the actual and the virtual. Again, the correspondence of Bergson here with more contemporary research into the neural processing of images is striking: "A zone of recollections, dreams, or thoughts corresponds to a particular aspect of the thing: each time it is a plane or a circuit, so that the thing passes through an infinite number of planes or circuits which corresponds to its own 'layers' or its aspects."[30] In this way Deleuze distinguishes recollection-images, dream-images, and crystal-images. And while the recollection-image (usually flashbacks) and dream-images are considered as the memories and dreams of the movement-image, where it is still possible to distinguish between the actual and the virtual (in classical cinema there are often markers, such as a zoom into a character's head or a dissolve after a pensive face that transports us into another dimension), in the crystal-image the actual and virtual are no longer distinguishable. Here we move to Deleuze's fourth commentary on Bergson: "What the crystal reveals is the hidden ground of time, that is, its differentiation into two flows, that of presents which pass and of pasts which are preserved."[31] Deleuze refers to Fellini's statement that "we are constructed in memory, we are simultaneously childhood, adolescence, old age and maturity" as a fundamentally Bergsonian conception of nonchronological time, the coexistence of all sheets of the past, and the existence of its most contracted degree.[32]

It is quite possible to argue that *The Movement-Image* and *The Time-Image* together already successfully address the whole range of the actual and the virtual, the indivisible plane of immanence of Deleuzian philosophy. As Deleuze in one of his last texts asserts, "the plane of immanence includes both the virtual and its actualizations simultaneously, without there being any assignable limit between the two. . . . The virtual image absorbs all of the character's actuality, at the same time as the actual character is no more than a virtuality."[33] Recall that movement-images and time-images both relate to the actual and the virtual but in different ways. Moreover, they also exist in close exchange and interconnection with one another (the division between the two image types is not absolute). In this sense there is perhaps no need for a third type of image, a "neuro-image" as I propose in this book. Indeed, there are many instances that justify a view of the neuro-image as simply an extension or intensification of the time-image, given that many of its schizoanalytical implications (discussed in depth in the first three chapters) are already present there. In Alain Resnais's work in particular, to which I will return soon, the screen as a cerebral membrane is proposed already very explicitly in the time-image (and also perhaps implying Deleuze's brain-screen argument for the whole of cinema).

A return to *Difference and Repetition* might allow us to distinguish yet other metaphysical dimensions of time and to make a distinct case for the conception of the neuro-image as a third type of image, or in any case a third dimension of the image. *Difference and Repetition* is a book that poses the problem of the virtual and the actual specifically in terms of difference and repetition, addressing the complex problems of the conditions of appearances, things, life forms as they differ and are repeated. As James Williams has indicated, a consciousness of repetition is proposed by Deleuze in terms of certain variegated syntheses of time, which offer a "complex but deeply rewarding and important philosophy of time [that] will, no doubt, come to be viewed as one of the most important developments of that philosophy."[34] In chapter 2 of *Difference and Repetition* Deleuze develops the passive synthesis of time. Here, too, Bergson is the main reference, although the starting point of his reflections is Hume's thesis that "repetition changes nothing in the object repeated, but does change something in the mind which contemplates it."[35] Repetition has no in-itself, but it does change something in the mind of the observer of repetitions: on the basis of what we perceive repeatedly in the present, we recall, anticipate, or adapt our expectations in a synthesis of time. This synthesis is a passive synthesis, since "it is not carried out by the mind, but occurs in the mind."[36] The active (conscious) synthesis of understanding and memory is grounded upon this passive synthesis, which Deleuze, referring to Bergson, calls duration and which occurs on an unconscious level.[37] Note also that although Bergson refers to the observation of our inner life in duration as consciousness, the temporal contractions that generate it are largely unconscious. Deleuze distinguishes different levels of passive syntheses that have to be seen in combinations with one another and in combination with active (conscious) syntheses:

All of this forms a rich domain of signs which always envelop heterogeneous elements and animate behavior. Each contraction, each passive synthesis, constitutes a sign which is interpreted or deployed in active syntheses. The signs by which an animal "senses" the presence of water do not resemble the elements which the thirsty animal lacks. The manner in which sensation and perception—along with need and heredity, learning and instinct, intelligence and memory—participate in repetition is measured in each case by the combinations of forms of repetition, by the levels on which these combinations take place, by the relationships operating between these levels and by the interferences of active syntheses with passive syntheses.[38]

The first synthesis Deleuze distinguishes is that of habit, the true foundation of time, occupied by the passing present. However, this passing present is grounded by a second synthesis of memory: "Habit is the originary synthesis of time, which constitutes the life of the passing present. Memory is the fundamental synthesis of time which constitutes the being of the past (that which causes the present to pass)."[39] As James Williams explains, the first synthesis of time occurs because habits (repetitions) form our expectancies based on what we have experienced before, "as in the passive assumption that something will occur."[40] The second synthesis Williams calls archiving, "as in the passive sense of the present passing away into the past as a stock of passing presents."[41] The second synthesis of time is equivalent to Proust's involuntary memory.[42] In the description of these two syntheses of time Deleuze refers explicitly to Bergson. The first and second syntheses relate, such as in the alliance of the soil (foundation) and the sky (ground), but they also have their own characteristics.[43]

The conception of the syntheses of time is incredibly sophisticated and complicated, and I cannot do justice to the richness of Deleuze's arguments here (Williams and others have done this powerfully and convincingly). Nevertheless, I take that it is possible to argue that the first synthesis of time, habitual contraction, can be recognized in terms of movement-images linked to (as Deleuze also states) the sensorimotor aspects of the brain-screen. Similarly, I consider that the second synthesis of time can be related to the dominant form of time in the time-image, where the past becomes more important and manifests itself more directly. Importantly, each synthesis of time has its own relation to other times. The first synthesis of time as "the living present" relates to the past and the future as dimensions of the present.[44] In this way the flashback (and flash-forward) in cinema can be seen as the past and future of the movement-image. In the second synthesis of time the past becomes the actual ground, as the synthesis of all time and thus the present and the future become dimensions of the past.[45] The time-image's dynamics—the past as the coexistence of all its layers (as Bergson proposed)—are further elaborated by Deleuze in his commentaries on Bergson, in which different time-images are distinguished based on their reliance on the past. Time-images are established here as dimensions of the "pure past," of the second synthesis of time: the present and the future become dimensions of the past; the virtual becomes more indistinguishable from the actual at certain crystallizing points, in comparison to movement-images, which have the present as its main dimension.

In *Difference and Repetition*, however, Deleuze distinguishes a third synthesis of time: the future. Deleuze writes, "The third repetition, this time by excess, [is] the repetition of the future as eternal return."[46] In this third synthesis, the foundation of habit and the ground of the past are "superseded by a groundlessness, a universal ungrounding which turns upon itself and causes only the yet-to-come to return."[47] In this third synthesis the present and the past are dimensions of the future: "In the work of the third passive synthesis," Williams explains, "there is the sense of the openness of the future with respect to expectancy and archiving."[48] Williams refers to this openness and its risks as the possibility of change (making the future different from the past and the present). It is the condition for the new. This third synthesis is complex, since it does not simply repeat the past and the present but instead cuts, assembles, and orders from them, to select the eternal return of difference: "Identities, or the same, from the past and the present, pass away forever, transformed by the return of that which makes them differ—Deleuze's pure difference of difference in itself."[49] The three syntheses of time together account for the importance, originality, and wider significance of Deleuze's philosophy of time.

In elaborating the third synthesis of time, Deleuze breaks from Bergson, and Nietzsche becomes the main point of reference. In *The Time-Image*, too, Bergson disappears in favor of Nietzsche, although Nietzsche is not explicitly connected to the question of time in the cinema books. Chapter 6 of *The Time-Image*, for example, discusses Orson Welles and the powers of the false, and Nietzsche is an important reference for understanding the manipulation of such powers (as we saw in Chapter 2). The powers of the false are discussed first as a consequence of the direct appearance of time (the pure past of the second synthesis of time), then, at the end of the discussion of Welles, are connected to the creative powers of the artist and the production of the new (though not explicitly to the eternal return and the future). Deleuze's notion of a "series of time" thereafter emerges in *The Time-Image*, especially in the chapter on bodies, brains, and thoughts (Chapter 8); Antonioni's and Godard's films of bodies particularly announce this time as series. Deleuze, however, leaves his explanation of this chronosign of time as series for the conclusion of the book: "the before and after are no longer themselves a matter of external empirical succession but of the intrinsic quality of that which becomes in time. Becoming can in fact be defined as that which transforms an empirical sequence into series: a burst of series."[50] We can observe that after all the insistence on elaborating the Bergsonian temporal dimensions of the movement-image and the time-image, this form of time (series of time) remains rather underdeveloped on a theoretical level in the cinema books. Looking back to *Difference and Repetition*, it is not difficult to connect Deleuze's own logic to suggest that the powers of the false and the series of time that can be sensed in some time-images might belong to this third synthesis of time. Taking this logic one step further, I suggest that this third synthesis of time that already appears in *The Time-Image* (in a more or less disguised form) is the dominant sign of time under which neuro-images are formed.

The neuro-image belongs to the third synthesis of time, the time of the future (though this certainly does not exclude the other times, as the past and the present now become dimensions of the future).[51] I will explore the appearance of this future "time that is now" in recent films in the last section of this chapter and in the following two chapters. First, I want to revisit more of the works of Alain Resnais in order to underscore the fact that Deleuze has already mapped out the contours of the neuro-image in his cinema books. Another look at Resnais will also allow us to see how his cerebral screens actually anticipate the digital logic of our contemporary screens as a will to art (and thus to indicate a resonating link between the neuro-image's brain-screen and the digital age, in a non-techno-deterministic way).

Appearance of the Future: Emergence of the Neuro-Image in Resnais's Time-Images

"Thunderbolts explode between different intensities, but they are preceded by an invisible, imperceptible dark precursor," Deleuze says in *Difference and Repetition*.[52] Perhaps Resnais's films, while ultimate expressions of time-images, could at the same time be considered dark precursors of the neuro-image. Many of his films have been recognized as masterpieces, especially the puzzling *Last Year in Marienbad* (1961). "This film is an enigma," says the French interviewer to Resnais in the interview mentioned at the beginning of this chapter, expressing a broader public feeling about the film at the time. But following Deleuze's discussions of the problem of time and the ways in which cinema can make time perceptible, and considering the changes to screen culture in the digital age, it is perhaps possible to see Resnais's films anew, as the avant-garde of a new type of image that we can now understand more fully.

Deleuze mentions Resnais's *Je t'aime, Je t'aime* (1968) as one of the few films that shows how we inhabit time.[53] For decades this film has been literally invisible, but a recent DVD edition has rendered it viewable again.[54] *Je t'aime, Je t'aime* is the strange "science fiction" of Claude Ridder (Claude Riche), who has tried to commit suicide after the death of his girlfriend, Catrine (Olga Georges-Picot). He survives, collapses into a catatonic depression, and following his release from a mental hospital is recruited as a guinea pig for a scientific experiment at a remote research center, Centre de Crespel, in the Belgian countryside. "Our only subject of research is time," the scientists explain to him in the laboratory. They have built a machine, which looks like a giant brain, referred to as *la citrouille* ("the pumpkin"). The experiment involves the scientists sending Claude back in time exactly one year (to 5 September 1966, at 4:00 p.m.) for the duration of one minute. Prior experiments on mice have shown that it is possible to disappear back in time and return safely. However, a mouse cannot report on this experience, which seems crucial for understanding more of what happens when we travel back in time.

The test is therefore ready for a human, which of course involves significant risks. This is why Claude was chosen for the experiment: having wanted to die once already, he is assumed to care less about the possibility of losing his life again. The ethical implications of this suggestion and Claude's consent are not addressed in the film, but the philosophical concept of multiple deaths is relevant, as will become clear later. Before Claude enters the brain-machine, he is heavily sedated with drugs that, it is explained to him, make him "completely passive though still capable of receiving memories." As if the scientists had read *Difference and Repetition*, they seem to have created a machine for literally traveling into the second passive synthesis of time. The inside of *la citrouille* is soft and lobelike, although another image evoked is that of a giant womb, though without the usual abject associations as in many horror films.[55] Claude lies down, sinking into the soft folds of the brain machine, and waits for the memories to come to him.

The scene to which Claude returns is a scene at the seaside during a holiday in the south of France with Catrine. He is snorkeling and gets out of the water. Catrine, who is sunbathing on the rocks near the water, asks him, "Was it good?" This scene is repeated several times but always with slight differences and subtle variations—in the order of the shots within the sequence, its variable beginnings and endings, and with slightly different camera angles and shot lengths. It is as if his memory is looking through a kaleidoscope at all the possible combinations of the mosaic snippets of memory. Soon, however, this mosaic memory of his loved one ("Catrine, Je t'aime, Je t'aime," Claude whispers half-conscious back in the citrouille) starts to transport him to other fragments of memory. In a nonchronological way pieces of his life present themselves: other moments with Catrine, scenes at work, *temps-morts* while waiting casually for a tram in Brussels, sexual encounters with other women. More surreal oneiric scenes also return: a girl in a bathtub in the office, a nonsense letter, bosses that have gathered around his desk to watch him writing, a woman who tells him in a tram "J'ai terreur" (instead of "J'ai peur," meaning, "I'm terrored," instead of "I'm frightened"). These dream scenes are filmed differently; Claude is always seen from the back, but they do have the same status as the recollections (the recollection-images are always filmed in one take, while the scenes in the present with the scientist are filmed in movement-image continuity style, making the dispersed snippets more recognizable in their returning and variable combinations).

Another important scene repeated with variations is a scene in a hotel room in Glasgow, where Claude and Catrine are on vacation. This is the moment where Catrine will die because of a leaking gas heater. Was it an accident or not? The memory is not clear and changes slightly each time. As writer Jacques Sternberg explains in the DVD extras, Claude did not leave his girlfriend purposively behind with a leaking gas heater—the girl herself in fact chooses to die. It is eventually revealed in the film that she takes sleeping pills and smiles when performing this action, which, importantly, is the first time in the entire film she smiles. The first time we see this memory of the hotel room scene, the flame of the heater burns. It is only in retrospect, at the film's end, that we understand that Claude's memory is here transformed by his feelings of guilt; at the last return of the "same" scene, we see the flame is actually extinguished, compared to earlier versions of the memory where it was not. On the DVD commentary Sternberg explicitly mentions the fact that *Je t'aime, Je t'aime* corresponds to our mental life: we remember in snippets of nonchronological fragments; our memories change each time we go back to them; our memories change us. The film presents quite literally a meeting between physics (the scientists in the film) and metaphysics (the larger questions raised by the experiment of time traveling and the functions of memory) that Bergson called for, expressed in an artistic and imaginative way.[56]

My American Uncle (1980) is another Resnais film that mixes fiction with scientific findings about the brain. Here the genre is less "science fiction," where scientists invent strange experiments to reveal truths about the nature of time and memory as in *Je t'aime, Je t'aime*, but instead more "docu-fiction." Voice-overs by the French neurobiologist Henri Laborit, author of countless neuroscientific studies and one of the first to experiment with antipsychotics to treat schizophrenia, as well as scenes where he speaks in direct address to the camera, organize the film conceptually. Laborit delivers the latest findings about the workings of the human brain from a modern evolutionary perspective (his contributions, it should be noted, mostly align closely with current cognitive neuroscientific principles). It is possible, he explains, to distinguish three brains: a "primitive, reptile" brain for survival, a second "affective and memory brain," and a third brain, the outer layer or neocortex, which allows associations, imagination, and conscious thoughts. Throughout the film he explains how these three layers, in constant exchange with one another, and ever-influenced by engagements with others and our environment, can explain human behavior. These scientific intermezzos are seamlessly connected to the stories of three different characters, Jean (Roger Pierre), Janine (Nicole Garcia), and Leon (Gerard Depardieu), who tell their life stories and whose own lives meet at certain moments. The fictional stories translate the scientific discourse of the neurobiologist quite literally (sometimes too literally for contemporary audiences, who tend to distance themselves from overemphasized comparisons between humans and laboratory rats). Nevertheless, *My American Uncle* also gives moving insight into what ultimately motivates the filmmaker, the philosopher, and the scientist: to understand more profoundly why we do what we do and to find ways to improve not only individual destinies but also the fate and future of humanity.

To see how the future emerges in Resnais, it is useful to recall first Deleuze's analysis of his work as a typical time-image, a cinema based in the past, as cinema that plunges us "into a memory which overflows the conditions of psychology, memory for two, memory for several, memory-world, memory ages of the world."[57] In *Je t'aime, Je t'aime* we dive into the memory of one person; *Last Year in Marienbad* gives us the memory of two characters. In *Hiroshima mon amour* (Alain Resnais, 1959) the memory of the lovers coincides with the memory of Hiroshima and Nevers in France; similarly, in *Muriel, a Time of Return* (Alain Resnais, 1962) the characters relate to the memories of Boulogne and Algeria; and in *The War Is Over* the Spanish civil war mixes with a new age of young terrorists. *My American Uncle* explores the ages (and biographies) of several characters and adds an evolutionary perspective; *Life Is a Bed of Roses* also presents "three ages of the world." Deleuze ends his discussion of the "data sheets" of Resnais's memories with a more general conclusion: "This is what happens when the image becomes time-image. The world has become memory, brain, superimposition of ages and lobes, but the brain itself has become consciousness, continuation of ages, creation or growth of ever new lobes, re-creation of matter."[58]

For the most part, then, Resnais's screens as cerebral membranes are based in the second synthesis of time, the pure past. But we often also encounter the future from within the second synthesis of time. For instance, in the impossible love affair between the French woman and the Japanese man of *Hiroshima mon amour*, the future is raised in relation to memory and forgetting, as the man says: "In a few years when I have forgotten you, I will remember you as the symbol of love's forgetfulness. I will think of you as the horror of forgetting." And the woman, too, when she recalls her first love, trembles at the fact that the intensity of such shattering love can be forgotten, a new love can be encountered again. The same goes for the world-memory and its futures addressed in *Hiroshima mon amour*. At several instances it is repeated that the traumas of war and other disasters will be repeated in the future: based on the idea that we have seen nothing, that we will forget, everything will start all over: "Two thousand dead bodies, eighty thousand wounded, within nine seconds. The numbers are official. It will happen again," the woman says in voice-over as images of a reconstructed Hiroshima fill the screen.[59]

Also in *Je t'aime, Je t'aime* the future emerges as a dimension of the past. In the film Claude returns to the brain machine and travels from the past to the present regularly, but he stays increasingly longer, until he can (literally) no longer escape from time. When Claude's memory has changed into a version in which he is guilty of his girlfriend's death, he commits suicide once more in the past: the scientists discover his body outside the brain machine in the park of the research center with a gunshot wound:

this time he will die. And here we start to see that the second synthesis of time, when it speaks of the future, opens up to the third synthesis: underneath the layers of memory is always this even more fundamental problem of death, the problem of the third synthesis of time, the problem of the future as such. Or as Deleuze argues: "Between the two sides of the absolute, between the two deaths—death from the Inside or past, death from the Outside or future—the internal sheets of memory and the external layers of reality will be mixed up, extended, short-circuited and form a whole moving life."[60] The third synthesis of time is related to death, both the shattering of the subject in its groundlessness, and the "final end of time."[61] So when the future appears in the second synthesis of time of the past, there is an opening to the third synthesis of time where the future is conceived not only from the past but also from the future as such, the future of the eternal return of death and rebeginning.[62]

The third synthesis of time as the future as such becomes even more evident at the end of *My American Uncle*. The last images of the film present a particular political coda to the expositions and dramatizations that went before. This last scene follows directly after we have heard Laborit in voice-over declaring in a future conditional tense that as long as we do not understand how our brains work, and understand that until now it has always been used to dominate the other, there is little chance that anything will change. What follows are images of a traveling camera through a ruined cityscape, and because the words that just preceded these images still resonate in the sequence, we understand that this war-ruined landscape might be understood as an image from the future: the eternal return of the series of war and disaster. The images are, in fact, from riots in the Bronx in the 1970s, when Resnais filmed them. But the empty streets and destroyed buildings also immediately remind us of a desolate bombarded Sarajevo and Grozny (still future urban war zones at the time of filming) and Boulogne (the setting of *Muriel*, a city that suffered heavily during the Second World War, the past at the time of filming). So the past, the present, and the future are now a dimension of the future: the eternal return and series of death and war.

But this dimension is also one of creation and rebeginnings: the camera finally holds on the only colorful image that it detects. On one of the somber walls a forest is painted. It is a mural by Alan Sonfist; a city screen avant la lettre as a hopeful sign of a possible new future. While the camera zooms in, the forest turns into a purer green and then nothing more than grainy pixels, mosaic snippets in our brain that must search for new connections, new variations and series. In the last three chapters of this book I will investigate more elaborately the political dimensions of cinema based in the third synthesis of time already so prominent in Resnais's cerebral screens. Here it is important to see how the future emerges in Resnais's time-images and how the future, as the third synthesis of time, at certain moments transforms the time-image into a neuro-image. In the neuro-image the future becomes the speculative moment from which the eternal return bursts time into serially remixed repetitions.

The Digital Logic of the Neuro-Image

Resnais's neuro-images avant la lettre also show that these brain-screens behave in ways now quite characteristic for digital culture, as I described in my introduction (perhaps a will to art has preceded these cultural developments as much as technological inventions). It may seem like a stretch to think of Resnais as a Web 2.0 filmmaker. However, the volatile and ever-changing characteristics (and matter) of time in Resnais—in which memories are constantly transformed each time we go back to them—is not unlike Manovich's conception of software performances, in which images play out as a set of possible variations and transformations (to create 2.0's cinema).[63] In this sense the memories that keep on presenting themselves in new variations in *Last Year in Marienbad*, *Je t'aime, Je t'aime*, or *Muriel* could be compared to the always slightly different versions of "soft cinema," or to navigation patterns on websites that change only subtly from a previous visit.

Software performances are closely related to a database logic, also described by Manovich.[64] Contemporary culture is driven by databases from which, time and again, new and different selections are made. In traditional structuralist terms, concepts of the database seem dominated more by paradigmatic relations of options in depth rather than by surface narrative strings, although several narratives can be constructed out of the database selections.[65] We can see how in Resnais's films the future—mostly as a dimension of the past, sometimes as dimension of the "future as such" of the third synthesis of time—forms ("informs" perhaps) its aesthetics. In *The War Is Over,* for instance, the main character, Diego Mora (Yves Montand), imagines in a sort of "database flash-forward" the unknown girl that has helped him to escape from the police at the Spanish border (he only heard her voice on the phone): a montage of flash-forwards featuring female faces gives various possible options of what the girl could look like. These kinds of database options of various futures return at other moments in the film as well. In *Je t'aime, Je t'aime* Catrine and Claude are in bed when the doorbell rings; in one version they open the door, but in another they don't. These possible variations are also the basis of a later film of Resnais's, *Smoking/No Smoking* (1993), where the same story is told twice in different versions according to the choice of the heroine (played by Sabine Azéma), at the beginning of the film, to quit or to continue smoking. *My American Uncle* is also database-like when at the beginning of the film several objects are shown without any clear meaning or connections between them. Later, some of the objects are suggestively linked to different stories and characters and obtain (symbolic) meaning, only to return in a mosaic of many different objects and persons at the end of the film. Here Resnais's screen resembles a typical web page that offers many entrances at the same time, while each chosen object or pathway hides another version of a story.[66]

A final characteristic of Resnais's work—its seeming "digital without digits"—becomes evident when we watch the original trailer of *Last Year in Marienbad* on the DVD redistribution of the film. While we see a compilation of images from the film itself, a voice-over speaks to us:

For the first time in the history of cinema, you will be the co-author of a film. Seeing the images you will create your own story, according to your sensibilities, your character, your mood, your past life. And it is up to you to decide, if it is this image, or this, that presents the truth or a lie, which image is real or imaginary, which one in the present or in the past. All the elements are given, you will have to decide.

Come play the real game of truth. Come taste this new sensation. Better than 3-D cinema, better than the giant screen. You will be yourself the center of this love story that you have never seen before but perhaps have lived.

Similarly, in a television interview about the film on YouTube, Resnais emphasizes the fact that individual spectators must select their own

interpretations and that his interpretation as film director is not more important than any explanation assumed by anyone else. "I request the help
of the spectator, because that is the best way to respect him," Resnais
explains.[67] Placing himself firmly within cinema traditions, Resnais here
also anticipates the Web 2.0 logic of participatory culture. Certainly not
all images in digital participatory culture are high art, nor do the various "machines of capture" (be they used for capitalist, fundamentalist, or
other purposes) operate according to the same logic; in fact, the creative
potential, collective intelligence, and democratic (though not unlimited)
access to the expressions and constructions of culture have expanded exponentially. But Resnais's cerebral screens anticipate the temporal metaphysics of digital culture and therefore can be considered as an early
neuro-image. More than any other director, Resnais also shows that the
neuro-image is not a break with the modernist concerns of the time-image
but a continuation of these "avant-garde" artistic concerns that return in
a "democratized" (or hypermodern) form in media culture today. In more
general terms it is possible to conclude that the third synthesis of time, the
dominant temporal dimension of the neuro-image, connects to the logic
of digital screen culture. Where the movement-image follows the motor-
sensory logic of continuity editing, and the time-image relates to a logic
of the irrational cut and the incomprehensibility of the crystals of time,
the neuro-image mixes and reorders from all the previous image regimes,
ungrounding and serializing according to a digital logic. The cinema of
Resnais, as a digital cinema without the digits, demonstrates that it is first
and foremost a "will to art" that allows cinema's survival in and adaptation to the digital world.

Thinking from a Nonhuman
Cosmological Perspective

A final aspect of the temporal metaphysics of the neuro-image, also
already pointed out by Deleuze in *The Time-Image*, appears in his discussion of Robbe-Grillet's "peaks of the present." The Augustinian conception of time in Robbe-Grillet is one of the other few moments where
Deleuze in *The Time-Image* explicitly addresses the future, in this case as
"the present of the future." Another way of understanding such a strange

conception of time, Deleuze indicates, is to take a nonhuman cosmological perspective:

The essential point rather appears if we think of an earthly event which is assumed to be transmitted to different planets, one of which would receive it at the same time (at the speed of light), but the second more quickly, and the third less quickly, hence before it happened and after. The latter would not yet have received it, the second would already have received it, the first would be receiving it, in three simultaneous presents bound to the same universe. This would be a sidereal time, a system of relativity, where characters would not be so much human as planetary, and the accents not so much subjective as astronomical, in a plurality of worlds constituting the universe. It would be a pluralist cosmology, where there are not only different worlds, but where one and the same event is played out in these different worlds, in incompatible versions.[68]

Here again in the cinema books we see a glimpse of the third synthesis of time that Deleuze in *Difference and Repetition* connects to the explosion of the sun, the nebulae, and nebulous circles of dissolved selves, in which difference can be reformed in an eternal return.[69] Rather than metaphoric this cosmic perspective has to be taken literally. In *A Thousand Plateaus* Deleuze and Guattari discuss the "Ages of the World" in relation to music and the concept of the refrain.[70] After the classical and romantic ages the modern age (for lack of a better word, Deleuze and Guattari say) is the age of the cosmic. This does not mean that in previous times there was no connection to the cosmic (like the three brains and the three image types, they always already belong to each other, and each time has its own relationship to the future), but again, it is a matter of shifting the balance between the different layers, ages, images. Referring to Paul Klee, Deleuze and Guattari discuss how modern artistic practice and philosophy (and science we would have to add) open onto the forces of the cosmos more directly: "The essential relation is no longer matters-forms (or substances-attributes), neither is it the continuous development of form and the continuous variation of matter. It is now a direct relation of material-forces. A material is a molecularized matter, which must accordingly 'harness' forces, these forces are necessarily forces of the Cosmos."[71] To understand the cosmic temporal aspects of the neuro-image more concretely, I will now turn to a more recent expression of a neuro-image. Bear in mind that the movement-image and the time-image are already "material-forces" of the "Cosmic Age" in the distinction that Deleuze and Guattari make. My only claim is that the neuro-image makes this cosmic perspective much more explicit as a dimension of the third synthesis of time.

Julio Medem's *Earth* (1996) quite literally makes connections between the soil, the ground of the earth, and the ungroundedness of the cosmos, with lightning as its most important feature and sign, tracing various nonlinear zigzagging connections between these layers. At the beginning of the film Angel (Carmelo Gómes) arrives at an island where he is contracted to fumigate woodlice from the soil. The landscape he drives through is struck by lightning: the trees and a herd of sheep are electrocuted. During the title sequence, just before Angel's arrival, the camera has moved from a cosmic spatial position toward the island and into the soil:

Camera moves through a cosmic night. Angel's voice-over:
Death is nothing, but if you were completely dead, you wouldn't hear me. So you're here Angel, in the middle of the widest, most unknown ocean you can imagine. Existence is accompanied by an inevitable background noise called anguish, which we can only half bear. But don't despair, you live in the only known light in the universe.
Camera moves through clouds to descend towards the earth, seen from above:
A tiny island, which is at your eye-level, but riddled with holes of mystery.
Extreme close-up view of woodlice in the soil:
A mystery: the woodlice, less than an inch, with twelve legs, it is what gives the wines of this area their earthly flavor.
Back to the cosmos again:
Another mystery—me. I am the part of you that died and I speak from the cosmos. You have transcended in life like the woodlice in wine. But you're the one who's here for something.
Angel driving in his car, vocalizing the same stream of consciousness:
Come on! I'm half-man, half-angel, half-alive, half-dead. I'm the voice that speaks from your mind, uncontrollably.

Here, from the very beginning of the film, earthly qualities are mixed with celestial forces: the connection between the woodlice and the angel; Angel declaring himself half-man, half-angel, half-alive, half-dead. Within the film a logical explanation is given for this: Angel has been a psychiatric patient with a vast imagination and a split personality. He is on the verge of being cured and—perhaps as a sort of therapy—he has been given the assignment to fumigate the woodlice from the soil of the island. Here he will meet two women, Angela (Emma Suárez) and Mari (Silke). He feels attracted to both of them (his angel side loves Angela; his man side prefers Mari), and a beautiful strange love story unfolds in which reality and surreality blend perfectly.

At the level of the film's story we see through Angel's eyes, as his schizophrenic brain tells us what to see and how to understand the images. However, it is also possible to do a metaphysical reading of the film that goes beyond the idea of a disturbed mind, or at least of a disordered mind that has an "antenna for the invisible forces of the universe." At the end of the film Angel refers to the brain explicitly. At the breakfast table with Angela, Mari, and Alberto (Mari's brother, played by Nancho Novo) he asks:

Did you know that our brain contains a universe of 10,000 million neurons and 1,000 billion circuits? It only occupies 1,500 cubic centimeters. And it hides a black ocean that's unknown. There is no light. But it generates disorder. Its laws obey chance, so it makes a lot of mistakes. And it's a machine that makes noise, although you don't hear mental noise. Like cosmic dust, which I've never seen, have you?

This and other remarks by Angel point us further toward the film's philosophical ideas of the neuro-image's brain-screen and its relations to the cosmic forces of life.

Medem's images in *Earth* show that the material and immaterial aspects of subjectivity are two distinct yet indiscernible sides of the same fold. In this sense they are time-images, but their explicit references to the cosmic has them belonging even more to the third synthesis of time of the neuro-image. Especially in relation to Angela, Angel's virtual side literally enters the picture. Three scenes in *Earth* illustrate this particularly well. In the first scene Angel talks to Angela on the phone. Just as in the beginning of the film, this scene starts with the camera moving from the cosmos to Earth, while on the soundtrack we hear the voices of Angel and Angela in conversation. When the camera has entered Angela's house, we see her on the phone. When Angel (invisible on the other side of the phone line) tells her that he wants to imagine her, his virtual double suddenly moves from the left side of the screen into the image and kisses her face. Angela does not see him, although he does seem to touch her with his voice and words. The second scene in which the virtual and the actual are both present and expressed is again a scene in Angela's house, right after her father tries to kill himself because he cannot get over the loss of his wife. Angel saves him and then wants to console Angela. He stands behind her, while she is sitting at the kitchen table. He stares at her back and we hear his thoughts, expressing his profound love for her. The camera movements suggest he is touching her with his vision and thoughts, and just before he actually embraces her, his virtual self detaches from his body and puts his arms around her shoulders. The last scene takes place at the local bar, where Angel's virtual side seduces Angela, and Angela is again touched by Angel's angel side, this time through his looks. But his man side chooses to go and visit Mari. He leaves his angry virtual double behind at the bar.

All these scenes show quite literally a doubling of the virtual and the actual, but they could still be considered as imaginings in Angel's schizoid mind. The end of the film, however, clearly puts these moments in a temporal metaphysical perspective. In the penultimate scene Angel is in the hospital after a stone has hit him in the head. He has just left both Angela and Mari. Nevertheless, Mari comes to visit him and promises to leave the island with him. Then the camera moves into Angel's head. We see Angel walking behind Angela and her daughter while his virtual side says farewell:

Listen to me for the last time. I'm not going with you. If you ever need me, you'll find me here, beside Angela, under these skies we like so much. Never forget this island. Even if it's just a memory lost in the vastness, like the woodlouse under the earth, like the earth in the midst of the cosmos, like a tiny particle in the depth of your imagination. I'll live here if you don't forget me.

Then the scene changes; the colors shift from the dark brownish red of the earth to the deep blue of the sea. Angel and Mari are driving along the coast, leaving the island. In these last scenes it becomes evident that we can see the split personality of Angel not just as a literal projection of his schizophrenic mind but also as a temporal image, in which time is split up between a present that passes (Mari) and a past that preserves itself (Angela). Perhaps Angela died and Angel keeps her alive as a memory (like a tiny particle); perhaps Angel did die from the blow to his head, and

Angela keeps him alive in her memory while Angel now meets Mari in heaven (the color changes could indicate this and the cosmic references of the rest of the film allow this view). Or perhaps Angel and Mari do leave, and Angela will feel Angel's presence forever, just as she did before. The point is that all of these alternatives are possible, folded into one another as three levels of the syntheses of time; it is up to the spectator to choose an option.

What is crucial is that this kind of temporality that opens up to cosmic spirituality occurs more explicitly in the third synthesis of time. In his article "The Scattering of Time Crystals" Michael Goddard addresses this relationship between time and spirituality: "Like an iceberg, the majority of which remains submerged beneath the surface of the ocean, mystical experience gives rise to a form of temporality that crystallises powerful virtual forces, beyond the power of an individual body or discourse to actualise: the body plunges into the virtual or spiritual depths which exceed it, rather than containing the spiritual as a personal property."[72]

Therefore, while the virtual as a dimension of all image types (movement-image, time-image, neuro-image) opens up to spirituality, the neuro-image seems to make more explicit references to a cosmic perspective. (Here again, precursors to this explicit cosmic perspective can be acknowledged, including Stanley Kubrick's metaphysical cerebral time-images in *2001: A Space Odyssey*, which I will discuss in the next chapter.) Another scene in *Earth* seems to address this cosmic temporal spirituality explicitly. After Angela's father has tried to commit suicide, Angel asks him to look for his deceased wife:

You're separated by an enormous distance. Your wife is 20 million years from here. That's how old the universe is. And as she has ceased to exist she's had to go back all that time.

They watch the sky. The camera sees them from a low angle at the back.

It's an enormous loss.

They turn to each other and look each other in the eye, the framing still from below.

We live at our own eye-level midway between the stars and the atoms. We can only move with our thoughts.

Angel looks at Angela, who feels she's being watched.

Tomás, imagine a woodlouse. Do you see it? If your mind can reach the smallest thing, it can reach the biggest. Then you can see the edge of the universe. You must do that with your wife. Ask her to come close.

Angel asks Tomás to travel in his mind and embrace the enormous vastness of time and cosmic spirituality. Spirituality in this sense is related to a temporal movement of the mind. Medem's film makes this sensible to us.

In *What Is Philosophy?* Deleuze and Guattari relate spirituality to the sensation of the material-forces of the cosmic age. When they discuss how sensation in art responds to chaos by contracting "the vibrations of the stimulant on a nervous surface or in a cerebral volume," they explain: "Sensation itself vibrates because it contracts vibrations. It preserves itself because it preserves vibrations. Sensation is the contracted vibration that has become quality, variety. That is why the brain-subject is here called soul or force, since only the soul preserves by contracting that which matter dissipates, or radiates, furthers, reflects, refracts, or converts."[73] A sensation is therefore a contraction, a contemplation of elements of matter that preserves the before in the after. Deleuze and Guattari relate this aspect of sensation not just to humans but also to all kinds of organisms. Plants and rocks do not possess a nervous system, but they seem to share chemical affinities and physical causalities that constitute "microbrains" or an "inorganic life of things" as they put it.[74] In this vitalistic conception of spirituality, when speaking of the soul or force of life that art can make us feel, the cosmic universe is full of microbrains that are constantly moving, acting and reacting, but that find in sensations a moment of pause, where all options are still open and a decision has to be made to live our life. Angel's schizophrenic brain, speaking half as a dead man from a virtual place in the cosmos, half as a living man on Earth, shows us in a more "cosmic" way than Claude in *Je t'aime, Je t'aime* that "between the two sides of the absolute, between the two deaths—death from the Inside or past, death from the Outside or future—the internal sheets of memory and the external layers of reality will be mixed up, extended, short-circuited and will form a moving life . . ." We can now see why Deleuze continues this sentence with " . . . which is at once that of the cosmos and of the brain, which sends out flashes from one pole to another."[75] The third synthesis of time relates explicitly to the cosmic. With the neuro-image, cinema has perhaps died, indeed, but only to return in a new way in the digital age, anticipated by Resnais's cerebral screens in a digital cinema without digits, and renewed with differences and repetitions in the more explicitly cosmic dimensions of contemporary screens. The fundamental metaphysical openness of the third synthesis of time in the neuro-image also relates to a corresponding epistemology that acknowledges this openness, an aspect of the neuro-image to which we now turn.

5

Degrees of Belief

EPISTEMOLOGY OF PROBABILITIES

We have seen that the cinema of Alain Resnais expresses a Bergsonian metaphysics with an emphasis on the second synthesis of time but also that it opens onto the third synthesis of time, reprising the future, death, and new beginnings (eternal return). Furthermore, Resnais's films anticipate a digital logic: reassembling the past or even presenting various futures; setting up database-like alternatives of images and objects, biographies and ages; and delegating the creation of the story to the spectator's mind. Resnais's images show the temporal metaphysics behind contemporary digital screen culture in its incipient form. They also point to the fact that the fundamental openness of such metaphysics introduces uncertainty into the image. "Time has always put the notion of truth into crisis," Deleuze says in *The Time-Image* when he discusses the powers of the false.[1] In this chapter I investigate how such "powers of the false" elicit epistemological questions: How can illusions be (taken as) real? How can we decide what is true? My key reference will be David Hume's empiricism and especially Deleuze's recognition of Hume as the philosopher who introduced the idea that knowledge is based on principles of probability and degrees of belief. Hume's skeptical empiricism may seem at odds with Bergson's vitalistic metaphysics of intuition and duration; however, I will show that these thinkers can be brought together productively.

As Deleuze argues, the novelty of Hume was to conceive of humankind as an "inventive species."[2] This recognition of human inventiveness makes it possible to look at stories and myths as expressions of fundamental human needs. Our imagination of desert islands is such an expression. "What must be recovered is the mythological life of the deserted island," Deleuze argued in an early text.[3] Attending to desert islands in contemporary culture, I argue that the popular television series *Lost* (ABC, 2004–10) is an audiovisual recovery of the mythological life of the desert island, presenting ways of imagining rebirth and second beginnings. Humian concerns with knowledge and belief run through the *Lost* series as a whole, while a temporal metaphysics is expressed in its aesthetics. Furthermore, *Lost* is a typical example of transmedial storytelling in the digital age, in which ambiguities in the plot and metaphysical questions not only are distributed to the mind of the spectator but also correspond with other forms (and agents) in media culture more broadly. After considering another mythological island story transformed for our age, the metamorphosis of Odysseus into a cosmic astronaut that lands on a "deserted planet" in James Cameron's *Avatar* (2009), in the final part of this chapter I will show how Humian approaches to knowledge and belief might be brought to the problems of destiny, free will, and choice.

Hume's Modern Empiricism: Associations, Passions, Belief

Hume's empiricism seems highly relevant to our comprehension of contemporary media culture. Although not a main reference point for film studies, empiricism has been connected to cinema previously. Stanley Cavell, for instance, has taken up John Locke's empiricism in his book *Pursuits of Happiness*.[4] Locke is well known for the development of his ideas on both the Laws of Nature and the Social Contract. Cavell emphasizes in Locke the import of mutual consent for a social contract and the inherency of trust to this, and he reads classical Hollywood comedies of remarriage in terms of the constant need to reestablish consent (and trust). Cavell also briefly mentions Hume as the philosopher who picks up Locke's suggestions that the idea of Nature is a useful fiction. The self according to Hume is only a fiction or artifice: through habit we come to believe in it as a sort of incorrigible illusion of living; through this artifice the self becomes fully part of nature. According to Hume, social relations are not so much governed by a social contract (as expressed in classical Hollywood films described by Cavell) but by experiment and creativity, which corresponds even more closely with contemporary media realities. To comprehend the value of Hume's modern and revolutionary form of empiricism, Deleuze's work is particularly clarifying.

In 1953 Deleuze published his first book, *Empiricism and Subjectivity*, on the work of David Hume.[5] Also in a very concise but rich article in 1972, "Hume," Deleuze summarizes the achievements and ideas of Hume that centrally influence his own development of a transcendental empiricism.[6] Deleuze argues that empiricism is more than a critique on the a priori of innate ideas and a revaluation of the primacy of sense data (think of Locke's plea for the idea of the human mind as a "tabula rasa" that gives knowledge about the world after being inscribed by experience). Deleuze sees in Hume other concepts and relations manifold in empiricism but undertheorized in that tradition of thought itself: the nature of relations as external to their terms, knowledge as degrees of belief, and the role of creativity and invention as fundamental to the human mind, culture, law, politics, and economy. Hume's central concern, Deleuze argues, is to understand the relation between things or "sense data." Deleuze gives the example "Peter is smaller than Paul" to illustrate why, according to Hume, relations are exterior to their terms. Hume's proposition is an answer to the paradox of relations that, until Hume, had been considered as either belonging internally to the terms (aspects of Peter or Paul that make one smaller than the other) or to a larger composition of the Idea of Peter and Paul. Empiricism has always argued for the exteriority of relations but usually by opposing the terms (sense data, impressions) to the ideas (operations of the mind on these data). For Deleuze Hume radicalizes the empirical claims of exteriority in proposing that it is not between impressions and ideas that one has to make the distinction but "between the impression or ideas of terms *and* the impression or ideas of relations": "Now the empiricist world can for the first time truly unfold in all its extension: a world of exteriority, a world where thought itself is in a fundamental relation to the Outside, a world where terms exist like veritable atoms, and relations like veritable external bridges."[7]

Hume's thought is founded on this dual register, according to Deleuze: *atomism* addresses how ideas or sense impressions refer to discrete minima that produce time and space (physics of the mind), and *associationism* addresses how relations are established between these terms (logic of relations). This dual register of atomism and associationism produces "a Harlequin world of colored patterns and non-totalizable fragments, where one communicates via external relations."[8] In the foreword to the English translation of *Empiricism and Subjectivity* Deleuze describes Hume's universe in this way: "We start with particles, atoms, but these atoms have transitions, relations and tendencies that circulate from one to the other."[9] (We can begin to see the continuities between Bergson and Hume here, which I will return to in the next section.) Relations can be considered as those which allow passage from a given impression or idea to the idea of something not given. Hume asserts that these passages are the effect of principles of association that are universal in human nature. We infer on the basis of principles of contiguity, resemblance, causality. The famous example, that when watching the sun come up, I say that it will come up tomorrow, makes clear how we construct knowledge on the basis of what we experience: "*I infer and I believe*, I await, I expect."[10] To think in an empiricist way is therefore not to be certain (of given sense data) but, on the contrary, to *believe* where we cannot be sure. So here we see how belief becomes the basis of knowledge: different yet similar cases of certain instances are observed and in the imagination (by principles of association) are fused in the mind, coming to constitute a habit. Degrees of belief can then be calculated based on experience and probability.

Deleuze elaborates that the principles of association work in both nature and fiction alike, which gives a schizoanalytic flavor to Hume's empiricism: if it is true that the principles of association determine the mind by imposing on it a nature to discipline its delirium or fictions of the imagination, conversely the imagination uses these same principles to pass off its fictions and fantasies as real, lending them a surety they would otherwise not have—making us believe in tales of madness.[11] If delirium and fiction can exist just as easily on the side of human nature, then it is essential to Hume to see that we are not so much threatened by error but by delirium, and therefore by powers of the false. The illegitimate belief in the World, Self, and God appears as the horizon of every possible legitimate belief; Hume posits such belief as a useful or unavoidable fiction required by our nature. The principles of association (which derive from relations) make sense only in relation to principles of passion (which derive from inclinations): "Association gives the subject a possible structure, but only the passions can give it being and existence."[12] He emphasizes that the principles of passion are absolutely primary, even though principles of association (as habit) may come to feel as natural (and first). Deleuze's essay on Hume explains how our natural inclinations are partial and limited in sympathy (to family and friends) and need to be stretched into extended generosity. Here the principles of passion lead to the invention of social institutions that force the passions to go beyond their partiality, producing moral, juridical, and political feelings. This is because institutions as bodies of social power can amplify feelings of intensity and belief in government, customs, and taste through the impact of rules like permission, punishment, and reward. Here we see, Deleuze argues, how "Hume is one of the first to have posed the problem of power and government in terms of credibility, not representativity."[13] Differently, the mostly wild and indeterminate passions can also be "ruled" through the softer or more implicit pressures of associations of norms and tastes. Further, aside from the force of institutions and norms, the imagination (artifice) can also help to stretch the passions beyond their natural limits. Fiction and imagination act upon passions like a percussion instrument, "making them resonate, and causing them to go beyond the limits of their partiality and presentness. . . . By reflecting the passions, the imagination liberates them, stretches them very thin, and projects them beyond their natural limits."[14] This is why the world of artifice or culture is so important to Hume.[15] Before turning to contemporary culture and the ways in which Hume appears relevant for us today, I want to clarify the connection between Bergson and Hume and to consider how both philosophers relate to the findings in neuroscience that I have discussed in previous chapters.

Bergson, Hume, and Neuroscience

If Hume's epistemology of knowledge as degrees of belief is important for the neuro-image, it should be consistent with the temporal metaphysics of Deleuze's Bergsonianism. However, it has been noted that Bergson's rejection of Hume's conception of exteriority of relations, in favor of the indivisible continuity of duration, seems to make their positions irreconcilable. In his perceptive book, *Deleuze's Hume*, Jeffrey Bell addresses this issue extensively to argue that in many respects Hume and Bergson are actually not so discordant. We have already seen that according to Deleuze, Hume does not make a distinction between sense impressions and ideas but between the impression or ideas of terms and the impression or ideas of relations. In other words he claims that there is a "dualism between 'hidden powers of nature and the principles of human nature.'"[16] Bell demonstrates convincingly that this double tendency corresponds with Deleuze's work on the relational movements of the virtual and the actual:

> There is first the movement of imagination forging beliefs that extend beyond the given, with the attendant risk of delusion and superstition. In the context of Deleuze's project, this would be the movement of the virtual to the actual. . . . Second, there is the movement of reason that progressively checks these beliefs, reducing them to nothing if "left alone." This is the movement of the actual to the virtual, the movement whereby reason relates the identity of belief, the identity of that which is believed, to the identities that make this belief possible.[17]

Deleuze has shown that both Hume and Bergson pose the problem of the creation of the new as this plays out in the mind. As I mentioned in the previous chapter, in *Difference and Repetition* Deleuze refers explicitly to Hume's thesis that "repetition changes nothing in the object, but does change something in the mind which contemplates it" at the beginning of his discussion of the syntheses of time.[18] In addition, Bell argues that Hume's double tendencies of nature (impression of perceptions) and human nature (mind) can be related to the double movement of intuition and intellect in Bergson. Furthermore, both philosophers seem to agree that it is "the demands of the actual, most notably the demands of life, that play the key role in filtering and selecting. The "double movement of contraction and expansion," and the extent to which the creativity of the virtual is increased or diminished, "is the result of the fundamental needs of life."[19] Metaphysics, therefore, is transcendental empiricism; "rather than deduce the conditions for possible experience," both Bergson and Hume "seek to arrive at the conditions for real, actual experience, and these conditions are themselves experienced." Schizoanalysis, according to Bell, is just this very strategy, to "effect a Bergsonian intuition, through an experimentation that accesses the virtual multiplicity inseparable from the actual."[20]

This double tendency or dualism in transcendental empiricism/ schizoanalysis (between intuition and intellect, principles of passion and principles of association, virtual and actual) resonates with findings in contemporary neuroscience. In Chapter 3 I referred to affective neuroscience and the difference between (unconscious) emotions and (conscious) feelings, as well as the primacy of bodily emotions that behave in accordance with the principles of passion to which Hume refers. Additionally, the discussion of mirror neurons has made clear that a "subpersonal architecture of simulations" based on sensorimotor actions shows how *as if* body loops, "through the internal activation of sensory body maps, create a representation of emotion-driven body-related changes," which are also triggered by external impressions (the behavior of other people).[21] At the end of his article on mirror neurons Gallese suggests that to reconcile this embodied account of representation with reason and thought, we should turn to Hume: "As already pointed out by Hume, inductive reasoning is a large part of our explanatory approach to the world in which we live. By inductive reasoning, we can apply the results of our previous experiences to unprecedented events and novel states of affairs. Inductions, although not necessarily referentially sound, determine our pervasive tendency to detect cause-effect relations."[22]

Findings in recent neuroscience call for a revival of Humian transcendental empiricism. Apart from the sympathetic orientation of affective neuroscience, cognitive neuroscientists, studying conscious experience in split-brain patients, have also come to conclusions that match Hume's philosophical ideas. Earlier I discussed Michael Gazzaniga's research into the interpretive functions of the left hemisphere. It seems that "the interpreter" rules over the hemispheres according to Hume's principles of association, to constantly risk the making of delirious connections:

What is the system that takes the vast output of our thousands upon thousands of specialized systems and ties them into subjectivity through secret channels to render a personal story for each of us? It turns out that we humans have a specialized system to carry out this interpretive synthesis, and it is located in the brain's left hemisphere. The interpreter is a system that seeks explanations for internal and external events in order to produce appropriate behaviors in response. . . . It allows for the formation of beliefs, which in turn are mental constructs that free us from simply responding to stimulus-response aspects of every day.[23]

Like Hume, Gazzaniga poses the principle of belief as an important element in the assessments and interpretation of our actions. Furthermore, both in Humian transcendental empiricism and in contemporary neuroscience, fiction (however illusory and illegitimate or even dangerous it may be) is a necessary feature of conscious human experience, holding our life story and even culture at large together. As Deleuze foresaw, Hume seems to indicate a path for the future of philosophy, a philosophy both scientific and popular that gives "a decisive clarity, which is not the clarity of ideas, but that which comes from relations and operations."[24] This philosophy involves operations of the mind—establishing the relation between the various sense data that comes to us via (unconscious and conscious) selections—to provide the narrative of our lives.

The Need for Fiction: Myths of Desert Islands

The problem of fiction as narrative technique seems initially at odds with Deleuze's approach to images in his cinema books. Contrary to classical film studies, Deleuze has never shown much interest in narrative analysis. For Deleuze a narrative always follows from a particular combination of movement-images or pierces through the more illogical combination of time-images or, we could add, can be distilled (in multiple variations) from the overflow of neuro-images. I will investigate the particular aesthetics of storytelling in the neuro-image in more detail in Chapter 6. For now, it is important to note that for Deleuze, "cinema" emerges from the particular images on the screen. Considering the ways in which the mind works as described in transcendental empiricism and cognitive neuroscience, we can argue that for Deleuze film narratives are perhaps "secondary articulations," forms of actualizations that follow from articulations of the virtual. At the same time, these stories have direct effects in operating on the mind through habit formations or by opening up new perspectives. Therefore, although Deleuze did not explicitly address the problem of narrative, stories are nevertheless important in his film-philosophy. In

The Time-Image Deleuze has given storytelling, as acts of fabulation, an important micropolitical power to summon a "people to come."[25] Similarly, mythological stories might continue to play a role: not to repeat in nostalgic fashion what has been but as "seeds of thought" that grow every time anew, as a repetition of difference. As Brian Boyd argues in his book *On the Origin of Stories*, many stories present familiar elements, but as stories, they have an evolutionary function, showing a "necessary link between problems of historical knowledge and universal aspects of human nature."[26] It is interesting to look at Deleuze's short text "Desert Islands" in this respect, to see how the myth of the desert island undergoes transformation in contemporary media culture.

Deleuze begins this essay by distinguishing between two kinds of desert islands. Geographers distinguish continental islands (accidental islands, derived from broken-off pieces of land separated from the continent by sea winds) and oceanic islands (originary, essential islands, erupted above the sea from the deep ocean floor below). This distinction corresponds to the ways in which the imagination dreams of desert islands in different ways: on the one hand desert islands can be a form of the dream of pulling away, separating from the continent, being lost and alone. On the other hand they can be dreams of starting from scratch, recreating, beginning anew. These islands are not in complete opposition, though one of the two tendencies is usually dominant. Furthermore, Deleuze states that even if the desert island is inhabited, it does not stop being a desert island, since these creatures should be considered as part of the deserted island itself:

Human beings live there already, but uncommon humans, they are absolutely separate, absolute creators, in short, an Idea of humanity, a prototype, a man who would almost be a god, a woman who would be a goddess, a great Amnesiac, a pure Artist, a consciousness of Earth and Ocean, an enormous hurricane, a beautiful witch, a statue from the Easter Islands. . . . A consciousness of the earth and the ocean, such is the deserted island, ready to begin the world anew.[27]

Deleuze emphasizes that the essence of the desert island is imaginary, not actual, mythological and not geographical; it "require(s) the collective imagination, what is most profound in it, i.e., rites and mythology."[28] Mythologies of desert islands can fail, in the sense that they fail to create or begin anew. *Robinson Crusoe* and *Suzanne and the Pacific* are in that sense failed mythologies, according to Deleuze.[29] In *The Logic of Sense*

Deleuze analyzes Michel Tournier's *Friday* (1969) as a successful originary myth of a desert island: "an amazing novel of comic adventures and cosmic avatars," where Robinson becomes one with the island and the elements, where the Other becomes the expression of a possible world and where Robinson becomes perverse when he no longer needs the Other.[30] In his article on Deleuze's reading of *Friday*, Ronald Bogue gives a beautiful quote from Tournier's autobiographical book *The Wind Spirit* that emphasizes once more the fundamental importance of fiction and myths: "Man rises above animality only by [the] grace of mythology. Man is nothing but a mythological animal. He only becomes man—he acquires a human being's sexuality and heart and imagination—only by virtue of the murmur of stories and kaleidoscope of images that surround him in the cradle and accompany him all the way to the grave."[31]

What is especially important in the mythology of the desert island as prototype of the collective soul is that rather than referring to an origin, it is the imagination of a second origin, a rebeginning. This presupposes that the world happens in two stages, Deleuze argues: birth and rebirth, both implicated in one another, "born for renewal and already renounced in catastrophe. It is not that there is a second birth because there has been a catastrophe, but the reverse, there is a catastrophe after the origin because there must be, from the beginning, a second birth."[32] This second birth, says Deleuze, is more important than the first because it gives us the law of repetition. We can understand this myth perhaps as an intuition of the third synthesis of time, the eternal return and the creation of the new after death: "In the ideal of beginning anew there is something that precedes the beginning itself, that takes it up to deepen it in the passage of time. The desert island is the material of this something immemorial, this something most profound."[33] As John Rajchman indicates in his introduction to Deleuze's essays on immanence, this myth also relates to Hume and his insistence on the necessity of fictions to "experiment with that in life [which] is prior to both possessive individuals and traditional social wholes."[34] Fictions of desert islands are just such experiments, which can either succeed or fail.

Contemporary screen culture has not forgotten the myth of desert islands. The popularity of reality shows like *Expedition Robinson* and *Survivor* as global television formats can perhaps be explained by the universal mythological attraction of the imagination of desert islands in the human mind. However, one wonders if these shows, like *Robinson Crusoe* and *Suzanne and the Pacific*, do not equally fail to grasp the originary sense of the desert island by repeating nondeserted life. At best, such shows are interesting psychological experiments to study human behavior out of habitual contexts. At worst, they are exploitative formulas that repeat the competitive format of global television, dividing the world into winners and losers (also by audience numbers).[35] A more interesting attempt to restore the mythology of the deserted island is to be found in audiovisual fictions such as the film *Cast Away* (Robert Zemeckis, 2000) and the popular television series *Lost*. In *Cast Away* Tom Hanks plays Chuck Noland, a workaholic FedEx employee who becomes marooned on a deserted island after a plane crash. Like Tournier's *Robinson*, he learns to live with the island and the elements. Unlike the character from the novel, Chuck does not turn into a "pervert": a volley ball serves as a surrogate friend he can talk to, and an unopened FedEx package keeps the hope alive of a "possible world of the other"—the notion that one day he will be able to return to society and deliver the package. Chuck finds a way back home and literally comes back from the dead (his friends, family, and fiancée have already held a funeral for him). At the end of the film, after he delivers the package, he finds himself at a crossroads. He is reborn and has to begin anew, on a new path.[36] It is unlikely he will become the same workaholic businessman, but all options are left open. *Cast Away* is said to have inspired the makers of *Lost*, the television series that also presents a contemporary originary myth.

Lost as Originary Myth and Humian Experiment

Lost was a popular television series created for ABC by Danon Lindelof and Carlton Cruse (and a whole creative team) about a group of people who survive a plane crash (Oceanic Flight 815) and land on a mysterious deserted island. The series' archetypal characters include Jack (Matthew Fox), the doctor; Kate (Evangeline Lilly), the trickster girl on the run; Sawyer (Josh Holloway), the con man; Hurley (Jorge Garcia), the funny overweight guy; John (Terry O'Quinn), the man who regained his ability to walk after the crash; Sayid (Naveen Andrews), the former Iraqi

Republican Guard member; Jin and Sun (Daniel Dae Kim and Yunjin Kim), the Korean couple; Charlie (Dominic Monaghan), the addiction-troubled rock star; and Claire (Emilie de Ravin), the pregnant girl. In the course of the show's six seasons many more characters, such as the fertility scientist Juliette (Elisabeth Mitchell) and the leader of "The Others," Ben (Michael Emerson), join the cast.[37] The series stirred countless speculations and theories, some more compelling than others, about the significance of the island and the interpretations of the strange events that occur across seasons.[38] Of the many interpretations that could be brought to *Lost* here, the series' exploration of mythological powers alongside specific philosophical references allow its extended and transmedial storytelling to be considered as belonging to the neuro-image.

Lost has created its own mythology, as indicated on the wiki page:

The show's mythological elements include a "Monster" that roams the island, a mysterious group of inhabitants the survivors call "The Others," a scientific organization called the Dharma Initiative that placed several research stations on the island, a sequence of numbers that frequently appears in the lives of the characters in the past, present, and future, and personal connections (synchronicity) between the characters they are often unaware of.[39]

While these strange inhabitants can be seen as "the desert island itself," it is also possible to argue alongside Deleuze that all of the show's characters have survived the catastrophe of the plane crash because each had already some compulsion toward a second birth. The series' narrative structure and movements support this view. The first two seasons of the series mix in a creative way the life on the island with flashbacks of the characters to reveal what happened to them before the crash. Each episode is more or less seen through the mind-set of one of the main characters. What becomes evident from these histories of mind-sets is that it is always very difficult to begin anew. Even if there are no more external ties that connect their experience to their previous life, the past keeps on creeping up on them and in large parts determines their feelings, decisions, and actions on the island.[40] Much in the series indicates, indeed, that it is impossible to "escape the tyranny of our memories" and "to reinvent ourselves when the only thing that remains from our past is the remembrance of our actions and choices."[41] The first three seasons present nonchronological flashbacks, but in season 4, episodic flashbacks are replaced by flash-forwards, where characters are depicted in the lives that follow their return from the island. These flash-forwards similarly inform or question the present in which the characters are stranded but from the perspective of the future. In season 5 the characters literally jump through layers of time. (Each jump gives them a splitting headache, and they have no control over the moment of the jump or the moment in time that they return to.) This goes on until they land in 1974 at the beginning of the Dharma Initiative, where they will try (in vain) to prevent a hydrogen bomb from detonating. The sixth season has two (parallel) time lines, exploring two possible outcomes of the detonation of the hydrogen bomb: in one time line the past and future are changed, and Oceanic Flight 815 never crashes (the makers call this a "flash sideways"); in the other time line the characters have to deal with the results of the bomb in the present. The show thus deals on a narrative level with the problem of time and, through that narrative, addresses fundamental questions about second beginnings and the (im)possibilities of renewal and creation of the new. Nothing is certain, and many questions remain open.

Lost is known for its countless implicit and explicit references to science, philosophy, and literature and, as such, diagrams and gives tribute to "humanity as an inventive species." Characters are named Rousseau, Faraday, Hawkins, Burke; references to books such as *Catch 22*, *The Fountainhead*, *Heart of Darkness*, *The Odyssey*, and *Ulysses* have led to *Lost* book clubs.[42] All these references are significant; however, it is just as important to note that the characters do not completely embody the scientists or philosophers after whom they are named. This does not mean that they are (un)faithful representations of metacharacters (or of the books that are read or discussed) but that they can be seen instead as signs or signals of the fictional universes that they evoke. More thematically, the main problems that *Lost* addresses are precisely the empiricist problems of knowledge, skepticism, and belief: Can we trust our sense data and rational explanations, or do we have to find a basic belief in ourselves, in the world, in others, in the island? From the series' beginnings, *Lost* develops these problems as a choice between science and belief and, on a deeper level, between free will and determinism. At the same time, as we will see, it also problematizes these oppositions. Signaling the fundamental empiricist questions posed by the series, one of the main characters is named after the philosopher John Locke; as I have mentioned, his relation to Locke's empiricism is not straightforward.[43] Let me briefly analyze a fragment of the show to indicate how it deals with the question of knowledge and belief. In season 1, John (Locke) discovers an underground hatch that seems impossible to open. At the end of the first season he, Jack, Kate, and Hurley find some dynamite and set out to open the hatch by force. They believe the hatch will provide a shelter for everybody to be safe from The Others, apparently very dangerous people who also live on the island. On the way to the hatch the group is besieged by strange forces from nature. John is smothered by black smoke and almost literally swallowed by the island. He seems to want to surrender to the island, but Jack and Kate rescue him just in time. The dialogue that Jack (the doctor) and John (the miraculously recovered quadriplegic) then have opposes them as a "man of science" and a "man of faith" at counterpoints:

JACK. What the hell was that all about John? I need to know what's going on in your head.

JOHN. You're a man of science Jack.

JACK. And what does that make you John?

JOHN. That would make me a man of faith. Do you really think all this is an accident? We're brought here for a reason.

JACK. And who brought us here John?

JOHN. The Island . . . Destiny. All this happened so that we can open the hatch.

JACK. No, we open the hatch so that we can survive!

JOHN. Survival is a relative thing Jack.

JACK. I don't believe in destiny.

JOHN. Yes, you do, you just don't know it yet.

The two then head toward the hatch, and season 1 ends with the cliff-hanger of John and Jack having opened the hatch, staring into a deep shaft that seems to lead into dark nothingness.

Move now to the opening of season 2. The precredit sequence shows an unidentified man going through his morning rituals (making a protein shake, doing pull-ups, injecting himself with an unknown substance); he suddenly draws a machine gun after being alarmed by something inside his home (an intruder perhaps). Season 2's first episode, "Man of Science, Man of Faith," goes on to address the empiricist question of what counts as scientific proof, as opposed to faith. "Man of Science, Man of Faith" is told from Jack's perspective. While Jack refuses to go into the hatch, John continues to question the reasons for his refusal and the nature of the scientific proofs he needs to do so, while Jack continues to be skeptical about John's faith in destiny. In flashback scenes we see Jack at the hospital: a badly injured woman, Sarah, is brought in, and Jack is determined to save her. On the island Jack and Hurley walk back to the other survivors. Hurley tells Jack why he believes it was not a good idea to open the hatch: he was once in a mental hospital where one of his fellow patients kept on repeating the sequence of numbers "4 8 15 16 23 42." After his release Hurley filled out a lottery form with these numbers, won the lottery, and became a multimillionaire, but he was equally struck with bad luck. Hurley explains to Jack that when he saw the hatch, he discovered the same sequence of numbers and considered this a bad omen.[44] Jack listens to the story, looks at Hurley, and asks, "You said you were in a mental hospital?" To which Hurley replies, "How about you believe me man?" reproaching him for his grating rationalist bent. In a flashback we then see Jack's relentless bedside manner, when he tells Sarah that she has practically no chance of ever walking again. As a true traditional empiricist, Jack has calculated the probabilities of a successful operation and is very skeptical about a positive outcome.

Clearly, the traditional empiricism of Jack, as man of science, is opposed to the belief of John, as a man of faith (and of Hurley, who has a schizophrenic paranoid "faith"). However, in the course of this episode and in the season that follows, it becomes clear that this opposition is not at all clear-cut and that perhaps belief might indeed be the zero degree of knowledge. In any case both Jack and John must revise their positions constantly, based on what happens on the island, even taking into account the possibility of miracles. In another flashback in "Man of Science, Man of Faith" we see Jack after an unsuccessful operation on Sarah exercising on the steps of a football stadium to get rid of his frustration at not being able to help her, when he encounters a man named Desmond, who is also exercising. Desmond tells him that perhaps a miracle could happen, and upon leaving, gives an upbeat farewell: "See you in another life, brother!" In yet another flashback we see how Jack, after operating on Sarah, tells her that her surgery was unsuccessful. She takes the terrible message in and then asks quietly: "Why then can I move my toes?" Jack's skepticism gets a severe blow here. Perhaps he cannot be sure of what he knows after all, if what he knows is based only on scientific proofs and probabilities alone. He gives in to his emotions. The scene where this happens is quite beautiful; one feels that it is because Jack gives in that there is a moment of reciprocation, that "the universe gives something back."[45] The whole scene also is like (the cliché of) a delivery scene, drawing on all the emotions that are involved in the arrival of new life, except that here we are witnessing a *second* birth: Sarah can walk again. For Jack this moment marks (however skeptical he may remain) the beginning of a new empiricism (based on belief) that he will have to face much more fully on the island.

It is significant that at the end of this episode the identity of the man who lives in the hatch is revealed. When Kate, John (Locke), and finally Jack descend into the hatch, they receive an unfriendly welcome from the man we saw at the very beginning in the precredit sequence of "Man of Science, Man of Faith"; he is Desmond, the man Jack also met in the football stadium, the man whose full name is Desmond David Hume (played by Scottish actor Henry Ian Cusick). However humorous and playful this reference may be, I suggest that the introduction of Desmond David Hume is significant in introducing the idea of belief as being imbricated with the bases of knowledge. Knowledge has to be inferred from hard sense data, but even Jack has to admit that in order to know what will happen, one has to go beyond the given, which introduces uncertainty and the necessity of at least a small degree of belief. In the course of season 2 the fragilities of knowledge and belief are persistently brought into overlapping force fields of dynamic relation in the form of Jack (who starts doubting his reliance on scientific facts), John (who begins questioning his faith and at the end of the season has lost it completely—only to find it again in the next season), and Mr. Eko (Adewale Akinnuoye-Agbaje), a Nigerian war lord and fellow survivor who becomes a priest and defends a Christian point of view on faith. These characters can perhaps be seen as the aesthetic figures that actualize and transform the virtual dialogues on faith performed by David Hume's conceptual personas of Cleanthes, Philo, and Demea in his *Dialogues Concerning Natural Religion*, first published posthumously and anonymously in 1779.[46] It is not my intention to look at the exact correspondences between these aesthetic figures and their conceptual personas (this could be a whole separate study). But we can perhaps easily note that Cleanthes's experimental theism could be compared with John Locke's faith in the island after he miraculously is able to walk again, that Jack Shephard's skepticism corresponds to that of Hume's Philo, and that Mr. Eko's Christianity defends the a priori arguments of religious belief, which he shares with Demea. These positions, moreover, as in Hume's work, are not static points of view. More generally, Hume's concerns with religion and the probability of miracles seem to mainframe the problems *Lost* addresses through the different attitudes of its characters. In "Of Miracles" Hume argued:

A wise man, therefore, proportions his belief to the evidence. In such conclusions as are founded on an infallible experience, he expects the event with the last degree of assurance, and regards his past experiences as a full *proof* of the future existence of that event. In other cases, he proceeds with more caution: He weighs the opposite experiments: He considers which side is supported by the greater number of experiments: To that side he inclines, with doubt and hesitation, and when at last he fixes his judgment, the evidence exceeds not what we properly call *probability*.[47]

Hume goes on to describe all kinds of evidence, classifying testimonies, witness reports and experiences of (super)natural principles, holding on to the possibility of miracles (and prophecies) but cautioning against taking miracles as the foundation of any religious system.[48] Nevertheless, he concludes that mere reason can never be enough: "whoever is moved by Faith to assent to it, is conscious of a continued miracle in his own person, which subverts all the principles of his understanding, and gives him a determination to believe what is most contrary to custom and experience."[49] Hume's empirical skepticism shows that we can never be completely sure of what we know, and therefore all options, even those of miracles and religious beliefs, have to remain open.

Lost takes up these age-old philosophical problems in a new form, through the confrontations and transformations of the degrees of belief of its aesthetic figures. Questions of faith and belief structure season 2 not only through this conflict of characters and their flashbacks but also across the plots and episodic mise-en-scène. After Jack and Desmond recognize each other, Desmond explains to Jack and John that every 108 minutes, one of them must type the numbers "4 8 15 16 23 42" (a fictional mathematical equation, the "Valenzetti Equation") into the hatch's computer and press enter; otherwise something terrible will happen. This task and its import is also explained to visitors of the hatch on a videotape left there by a scientist of the Dharma Initiative, who had been doing scientific research and experiments on the island. Desmond, who drove his sailboat against the rocks of the island three years ago and has been performing this button-pushing ritual ever since, at this point abandons the hatch, leaving Jack and John with the task and the choice to perform it. "To push the button, or not to push the button" presents Jack and John again with this tortuous dilemma that puts their positions in sharp relief. There is no evidence at hand of what could happen, nor any great reason to develop a high degree of belief as to what is even at stake. Even though he is skeptical, Jack consents in performing the ritual, and he and John begin to take shifts typing in the numbers every 108 minutes. On a narrative level this device provides many suspenseful "deadline moments." All the characters can possibly know is that every time they enter the numbers and push the button the alarm starts sounding (always four minutes before the deadline), the counter sets back to 108 minutes, and everything remains the same. It could all be a joke, but with various degrees of belief, they each take it seriously. Of course, within the problem of choosing to enter the digits and push the button (or not), the problem of belief looms, suggesting that: "To think is not to be certain, but, on the contrary, to believe where we cannot know for sure."[50] *Lost* can be seen as a Humian experiment in positioning belief as the basic principle of knowledge.

Other factors that make *Lost* quite Humian are the frequent references to hallucinations and deliria. As Deleuze has shown, Hume's transcendental empiricism takes the strange battle between fiction and reality quite seriously. He warns us that we are "swimming in delirium" and that human nature can make us believe tales of madness. Many characters have supernatural visions (Kate sees a horse from her past and, in a different episode, believes that she hears her stepfather speak through Sawyer's feverous voice; Charlie has vivid dreams about Aaron, Claire's baby; Jack sees his dead father in the jungle). In an episode of the second season called "Dave," the delirious nature of the human mind is explicitly connected to schizophrenia. This episode is centered on Hurley, whom we see in flashbacks as a patient in a psychiatric hospital with a friend. This friend, Dave, all of a sudden also appears on the island. Dave has always already been an imaginary but real friend of Hurley's. In this episode Hurley expresses the idea that everything happening on the island is just a mind game: the island and everybody on it are just a fantasy in Hurley's own head. However, this idea is rejected by both the episode itself and the series as a whole. Rather than remaining uniquely in the mind of one single character, *Lost* presents us with a more general skeptical image of a (the) world that questions and tests the principles of knowledge and belief, while also attending to the truth of the delirious possibilities and connections connate with our perceptions, thoughts, actions, and choices. It therefore testifies explicitly to the schizoanalytic implications of the neuro-image.

In *Mind-Energy* Bergson recognized these relationships similarly:

The dream is not something fantastic hovering above and additional to the reality of being awake; on the contrary, that reality of the waking state is gained by limitation, by concentration and by tension of a diffused psychical life, which is the dream-life. In a sense, the perception and memory we exercise in the dream-state are more natural than those in the waking state: there does consciousness disport itself, perceiving just to perceive, remembering just to remember, with no care for life, that is, for the action to be accomplished. But the waking state consists in eliminating, in choosing, in concentrating increasingly the totality of diffuse dream-life at the point where a practical problem is presented.[51]

With its incredible emphasis on the possibly delirious nature of our perceptions and its questioning of knowledge—proposed as a degree of belief that can never give complete assurance—*Lost* can be considered a neuro-image. The particular mythological power of the island in this contemporary fiction may well point us to the "second birth" of Hume. This second birth is perhaps necessary precisely because of the proliferation of cinematographic images in the course of the twentieth century and its dispositive (see Chapter 1) on other screens. Although Hume had already developed such thinking in the eighteenth century, it could be argued that, like Bergson, he was startlingly ahead of his time, envisioning what the cinematographic dispositive has merely made more evident: the transformation of the world into an object of belief. Gregg Lambert emphasizes the role of cinema in this shift: "[Cinema] has participated in the transformation of the world into an object of belief—even if this belief should prove illusory. It is precisely because everything that I see and hear is capable of being false, the expressions of deceit or trickery, of false oaths and betrayal, that only my belief is capable of connecting with what I see and hear."[52]

The world of *Lost* is a strange world, full of metaphysical and epistemological questions that relate to the delirious nature of contemporary screen culture. By presenting its characters with difficult choices, this world asks us to reconsider what we think we know:

The modern subject is faced with a terrible choice: either to continue to live in such a way that he or she can no longer believe anything he or she sees or hears (resulting in the loss of any connection to the world), or actively to cultivate reasons to believe in this world of which fools, con men and tricksters are a part. Restoring our connection to the world, but also assuming a constant vigilance over clichés and ready-made linkages—these are the tasks of the cinema that emerge today from this new situation of thought.[53]

Hurley, the fool; Sawyer, the con man; and Kate, the trickster, belong to the "prototypes and the Idea of humanity" heralded by the originary myth of desert islands. They cannot struggle to be "reborn" without consideration for the questions asked by Locke and Hume. Moreover, as I hope to have shown, Deleuze and his vision on the myth of desert islands has come to assist with this.

Lost in Digital Culture

The objection may be raised that *Lost* is not artful cinema worthy of film-philosophical analysis, but instead highly commercial television drama. While the series has high production values and all episodes are shot on location in Hawaii with a 35 mm Panavision camera, it is indeed made for television.[54] However, as paradoxical as it may seem, besides introducing many medium-specific changes, the digital turn also allows transversal jumps between media formats and modes: film's dramatic potential, and cinematographic aesthetics, may now even be seen in an intensified and extended form on television. Complete seasons of high-quality television drama, available on DVD, and large digital home screens with Dolby surround sound turn the living room into a "hypercinema," where we can engage with the lives of characters onscreen not just for two hours but for hundreds of hours. Considered on this level, *Lost* is a prime example of our changed relationship with many more characters of high-quality television series that come to "grow on you" (quite literally, if we take our mirror neurons into account); these relationships can be seen as "cinematographic" in the sense that they produce images that put thought into movement, just as Deleuze argued about cinema. Although *Lost* and other television dramas are part and parcel of the vertiginous machinery of capitalism, as cinema also always has been, it is far too easy to reject the whole media industry (and its "product") on the basis of its merely feeding consumers with senseless or superficial entertainment (which it does as well). As Lipovetsky and Serroy have argued, in the excessive age of hypercinema and hypercapitalism, the most astonishing fact is that "the society of mass consumption, emotional and individualistic as it is, allows an adaptable spirit of responsibility to coexist with a spirit of irresponsibility incapable of resisting either external temptations or internal compulsions."[55] Responsible and irresponsible, creative and exploitative media production and consumption go hand in hand, and the boundaries are not clear-cut. Humanity is all the more fragile confronted with all these excessive choices. As I have indicated, television's popular forms can contain heightened questioning and acute observations about life in the twenty-first century.[56]

Lost encapsulates the digital age additionally in its position at the forefront of new television distribution methods: it delivers its images on all types of screens. In addition to traditional terrestrial and satellite broadcasting, it was one of the first series issued through Apple's iTunes Store service for playback on Apple products. Since October 2005 new episodes without commercials have been available for download by American audiences the day after they air on ABC, and these episodes have eventually been made available for international audiences as well.[57] Moreover, *Lost* is a particularly good example of a form of storytelling that Henry Jenkins in *Convergence Culture* has called transmedial storytelling, typical for the twenty-first century. Jenkins discusses the new media landscape in terms of its slippery and ubiquitous characteristics of media convergence, collective intelligence, and participatory culture. Referring to the "Bert and Bin Laden" controversy in which a photoshopped image of Sesame Street's Bert with Bin Laden posted on a homepage by a Philippine

American young man is picked up by anti-American demonstrators in Pakistan, whose demonstration in turn is picked up by CNN, leading to new controversial images on the Internet, Jenkins sketches the scope of his arguments: "Welcome to convergence culture, where old and new media collide, where grassroots and corporate media intersect, where the power of the media producers and the power of the media consumer interact in unpredictable ways."[58] Although Jenkins's analysis is often seen as uncritical of capitalism, it closely attends to how corporate capitalism and grassroots consumer actions are now entangled far beyond the total control of corporate media itself. Jenkins's book argues against straightforward notions of convergence such as that expressed by the "black box fallacy" (the idea that convergence would mean that all media come together in one big black box) and in doing so clarifies the complexity of changes occurring within the contemporary media landscape:

Media convergence is more than simply a technological shift. Convergence alters the relationship between existing technologies, industries, markets, genres and audiences. Convergence alters the logic by which media industries operate and by which media consumers process news and entertainment. Keep this in mind: convergence refers to a process, not an endpoint. There will be no single black box that controls the flow of media into our homes. Thanks to the proliferation of channels and the portability of new computing and telecommunications technologies, we are entering an era where media will be everywhere.[59]

In other words the idea of converging media and transmedial storytelling does not mean there is no medium specificity. On the contrary, social network media such as Facebook and Twitter do have different properties and cover different aspects of media culture than the hypercinematic images of the digital age that are the central focus of this book. What does crucially mark the difference of a "convergence culture" and its applicability to film media, however, is that films are less and less to be considered as closed texts. While Resnais's *Last Year in Marienbad* carried its openness into the mind of the spectator, it remained a "closed object" in itself. Films and other media texts in the digital age operate more like seeds that grow and spread rhizomatically with other parts of culture, including in their relation to images from the past that are recycled and transformed, a process I discuss more specifically and politically in Chapter 7.

Characteristic of convergence culture is this way in which media is increasingly based on "world building"—the creation of a fictional universe across different media, incorporating combinations of films, cartoons, television series, video games, online games, toys, and trading cards. The typical examples Jenkins mentions are Pokemon and *The Matrix*. Another characteristic is that convergence plays on the powers of the false through hoaxes. Here *The Blair Witch Project* is the prime example, but one can also think of *The Truth About Marika*, *The Linda Tapes*, the genre of mockumentaries or many viral advertisement campaigns. Typically, the narrative proceeds by clues that can be found in different media, providing new developments, additional information, different versions, or alternative points of view. Compared to the narrative of a classical Hollywood film that the audience can take in with their popcorn and still be able to follow the plot, transmedial storytelling never delivers the full story and always contains other clues. As discussed in Chapter 1, theorists such as Paul Virilio have marked this as the infernal density and speed of media culture that does not permit any break (or brake), unless by prolepsy or epilepsy. Sure enough, this convergence culture can be viewed in terms of the schizophrenic nature and overflow of contemporary screen culture in which we are all "swimming in delirium."

These media forms might be caged in capitalist relations. Nevertheless, convergence culture bursts with creativity, both on the "corporate" side of media professionals, writers, artists, and filmmakers and on the "grassroots" side of fans, "prosumers," and engaged spectators. So the story of *Lost* is presented, commented on, analyzed, parodied, augmented, and recreated across many different media forms and platforms, through top-down and bottom-up initiatives that influence each other ad infinitum. Combinations of *Lost* media objects online build a larger world where characters have extended life and significance: biographies and information about the show can be found and tracked across Lostpedia and wiki pages, and discussed on blogs such as The Fuselage, on Twitter, in *Lost* radio communities, and across countless fan sites. Games and other augmented experiences allow us to join the survivors of Oceanic Flight 815, mixing and collaborating with the digital avatars of Jack, Kate, Hurley, John, and others. On YouTube, unofficial and official parodies of the show (*Lost Untangled*) summarize and comment on the story in playfully mocking ways. Hoaxes, too, are part of the mind game of the show's own transmedial storytelling: billboards for Oceanic Airlines appear along Los Angeles highways; the website of the last season invites us to enroll in the *Lost* University; fake television programs appear on the DVD extras; and so much more. A *Lost Symphony* played live by the Honolulu Symphony (presented as audiovisual performances on the DVDs of season 5) shows the dedication of the composer and musicians to create and perform the series' characteristic score.

Transmedial storytelling is perhaps the schizophrenic "Gesamt-kunstwerk" of participatory media culture. Not every message on Twitter or Facebook is a neuro-image in the sense I have discussed. As I have noted, there are other matters regarding medium specificity that I am not addressing here. However, the larger set of relations in which these images are embedded is important to take into account as the surrounding collective network of the neuro-image. Capitalism may be ruling it, but capitalism cannot contain its forces. As Jeffrey Bell has argued, this is because

capitalism risks unleashing desire as multiplicity, a revolutionary desire that will undermine and transform the immanent system of capitalism itself. In *Anti-Oedipus* this unleashed desire, this multiplicity that cannot be normalized, homogenized, and reduced to a commodity to be bought and sold, is referred to as schizophrenia. Thus Deleuze and Guattari state, in terms that echo Marx's revolutionary thought: "The schizophrenic deliberately seeks out the very limit of capitalism: he is its inherent tendency brought to fulfillment, its surplus product, its proletariat, and its exterminating angel."[60]

Capitalism and schizophrenia are immanent systems of production and antiproduction that cannot be contained or controlled by any single panoptic eye. It takes a collective brain to keep the checks and balances and choose what we can believe legitimately, productively, sustainably.

Odysseus's Cosmic Transformations and Desert Islands in Space

While *Lost* refers to the originary myth of desert islands and creates its own mythological figures for that island, it also refers to another ancient mythical figure, Odysseus, the hero of Homer's *Odyssey*.[61] Contemporary culture contains many other versions of this ancient myth that has so profoundly captured the links between our specific historical age and the problems of this time, and universal aspects of human nature (as Brian Boyd suggests is the evolutionary purpose of stories). A classic film that has also updated the *Odyssey* journey, by the other great director of a "cinema of the brain" (discussed by Deleuze in *The Time-Image*), is Stanley Kubrick's *2001: A Space Odyssey* (1968). "Earth is the cradle of mankind, but one cannot live in a cradle forever," Arthur C. Clarke proclaimed in a television interview in the 1960s when he was working with Kubrick on the film.[62] James Cameron's *Avatar* (2009) can be considered the cosmic neurocinematic follow-up to Kubrick's masterpiece. Astronaut characters, Dave Bowman (played by Keir Dullea in Kubrick's film) and Jake Sully (Sam Worthington in *Avatar*), are modern mythological figures that produce the respective futures of their own age. Not only are both films technological and aesthetic milestones of cinematographic imagination, offering a breathtaking celebration for the senses, but they are also both mythological narratives about the human desire to leave "the cradle" and begin anew.

Cameron's admiration for Kubrick's film is well known. Aesthetically, *2001* took the (conventionally) B genre of science fiction to a new level, not only because of its beautiful composition and the meticulous craftsmanship in the special effects of spaceships and the solar system but also because of its realistic portrayal of state-of-the-art space technology and of orbital conditions in the 1960s. Before men actually landed on the moon in 1969, Kubrick's space travelers coped with zero gravity and floating objects. The beginning of *Avatar* is clearly a tribute to *2001*. After several years of traveling, former marine Jake Sully is awakened from a hibernation state; doctors around him keep themselves from floating randomly in zero gravity by grasping handles on the walls. The floating bodies and the exterior view we get from the spaceship that arrives at the distant planet Pandora consciously recalls Kubrick's film.

Whereas Kubrick shows us the mysteries of space exploration in the 1960s, Cameron sets his science fiction in the year 2154, a perspective from the future typical for the third synthesis of time, in which the colonization of distant planets is under way. Jake Sully is taken to the base station at Pandora to neurologically operate an Avatar, a hybrid creature made from a combination of his DNA and the DNA of a Na'vi, the tall blue-skinned inhabitants of Pandora. Unlike Dave Bowman in the 1960s science fiction, Jake Sully seems to know exactly what he has to do: infiltrate the Na'vi people and make sure the earthlings can maintain access to the valuable resources of Pandora. The story that unfolds, as many critics have noted, is indeed quite familiar: Jake meets Na'vi princess Neytiri (Zoe Saldana) and gains respect for the Na'vi way of living, which causes him to question the value of his mission.[63] However, this does not make the film superficial. On the contrary, in its combination of massive popular appeal and huge aesthetic endeavor, *Avatar* has Homeric mythological power. Odysseus's fabulous adventures address aspects of security and survival, and social problems specific to the ancient Greek world, which have strong universal currency and power today. Kubrick's and Cameron's mythological travelers are similarly influenced by the problems of their historical times. *2001: A Space Odyssey*, for example, has to be seen in connection to the politics and aesthetics of the 1960s: the space race between the United States and the USSR, the sense of alienation around modern design and technology, and unresolved narratives being typical for films of that period (Antonioni's *Blow Up* and Coppola's *The Conversation* are also cases in point).

Avatar's references to contemporary concerns about the ecology of the world are obvious but at the same time very powerful. Aesthetically, the film connects to our time, because it can be considered a neuro-image: contrary to *Lost*, the images are quite literally the product of Jake Sully's mind (the Avatars are called "dream walkers"). Moreover the images at every level reproduce our neural system: the Na'vi relate to their animals, plants, the past, and each other through "synaptic connections" and energetic fields when they literally connect their long braids to another entity; the film's images stretch out in all directions like an overflowing brain and tend to visually connect like neural tissue (consider the hammocks that look like axons that enable the Na'vi to sleep in a neural network). Transparent touch screens, LED lights, and the immersive quality of the 3D viewing experience additionally make Cameron's film, in spite of the age of 3D technology, and in spite of the 1990s VR concept of avatars, unmistakably a film of the twenty-first century.[64]

Compared to the abstract compositions and beautiful but sober aesthetics of *2001*, *Avatar's* aquatic digital jungle images are actually closer to the universe of *Lost*. In its reliance on the mysteries of nature *Avatar* thus also relates to another fundamental mythological figure, the figure of the desert island, just as the epic myth of *Lost* relates to the fundamental desire to begin anew, the desire for a rebirth. As I have indicated, Deleuze connects this rebirth always to a catastrophe that creates the necessary conditions from which the world can begin anew: "It is an island or a mountain, or both at once: the island is a mountain under water, and the mountain, an island that is still dry."[65] When Deleuze described the mythological power of the figure of desert islands, it is as if he looked into the future and saw how Kubrick's space odyssey could arrive at the floating mountains of Cameron's Pandora, finding a "cosmic egg," the "mythological maternity of parthenogenesis" of Eywa (the mother goddess of Pandora's biosphere).[66] Perhaps he could guess how the Star Child would grow from its cradle to transform into "Jake Sully, the Na'vi," imagining man's rebirth as another kind of being after the exhaustion of the earth—the problem and imminent catastrophe of our cosmic age to which the neuro-image is fundamentally connected.

Providence Lost? Destiny, Freedom, and Necessity in the Neuro-Image

There is a final element of *Avatar*, addressing age-old questions revived in the neuro-image, that I want to mention by way of conclusion. When Neytiri spots Jake for the first time in the jungle of Pandora, her first impulse is to kill him with one of her poisoned arrows. However, when she is about to shoot, a white, octopus-shaped feather lands gently on the tip of her spear. Taking this incident as a sign of providence (the "feather" is a seed of the Holy Eywa tree), she holds her shot and decides to take Jake with her back to her tribe. Jake's incidental fortune seems to indicate a destiny of which neither of them is yet aware; in the course of the story his status as a mediator between humans and Na'vi becomes crucial for the survival of Pandora. This reintroduction of the questions of providence and destiny in the space odyssey relates to the temporal metaphysics and transcendental empiricist epistemology of the neuro-image that I have been describing.

In a beautiful book on this question, *Providence Lost*, Genevieve Lloyd demonstrates how Western philosophy has slowly lost its belief in providence and necessity. By rereading ancient Greek myths, plays, and Stoic philosophy, Lloyd makes her plea to restore a Spinozan conception of necessity that does not completely oppose free will. At the heart of Lloyd's book is Spinoza's claim that we can find true freedom in understanding ourselves as part of a necessary whole, in finding a "free necessity." Comparing the dominant legacy of Descartes, of extending the free will into dominion and control over necessity, to the reemerging views of Spinoza, Lloyd argues that (even if we do not accept all of Spinoza's worldview) we can learn from Spinoza's view on necessity: "In trying to make such reconnections now through Spinoza to ancient ideals of necessity—of freedom without free will, acceptance without passivity—we might rediscover the capacity to be reassured rather than terrified by necessity. We might again find delight in the mind's recognition of its own movement in perceiving how things must be."[67]

Spinoza's Stoic acceptance of "free necessity" in terms of the "mind's recognition of its own movements" might also be understood in terms of Deleuze's discussions of destiny in *Difference and Repetition*, and of Humian epistemology based on principles of belief. Deleuze argues that the continuing present and the virtual pasts that ground it give us a temporal vision of destiny that enables freedom and necessity to be embraced without contradiction. Deleuze cautions that destiny is not the same as determinism:

Destiny never consists in step-by-step deterministic relations between presents which succeed one another according to the order of a represented time. Rather, it implies between successive presents non-localizable connections, actions at a distance, systems of replay, resonances and echoes, objective chances, signs, signals and roles which transcend spatial locations and temporal successions. We say of successive presents which express destiny that they always play out the same thing, the same story, but at different levels: here more or less relaxed, there more or less contracted. This is why destiny accords so badly with determinism but so well with freedom: freedom lies in choosing the levels. The succession of present presents is only the manifestation of something more profound—namely, the manner in which each continues the whole life, but at a different level or degree to the preceding, since all levels and degrees co-exist and present themselves for our choice on the basis of a past that was never present.[68]

In his profound and precise reading of *Difference and Repetition* as Deleuze's philosophy of time, James Williams explains this view of destiny further by making a comparison with film:

The meaning of freedom in relation to destiny in Deleuze is then not the freedom to add to a sequence, for instance, when a new director adds a new film to an established franchise (*My Life IV*). Instead, we are free to make a new cut of an existing film (*My Life, The Director's Cut*) . . . though a new cut retains all of the scenes from the earlier versions, it can change their sense, value and emotional significance through a novel ordering (*put death in the middle and birth at each end*).[69]

I will return to this interesting analogy in respect to the database logic of digital culture in Chapter 7. For now, however, I would like to draw this Deleuzian understanding of destiny back to *Lost*.

It is possible to see the epic story of the *Lost* series as a sign of renewed interest in the age-old questions of freedom and destiny, filtered through the philosophical problems of mind that resonate with Deleuze's readings of Bergson, Hume, and Spinoza. The last season of *Lost* centers on the acceptance of our ultimate destiny: death. The season opens with the death of Juliette in the arms of Sawyer, leaving him devastated. In several other episodes of this season, the acceptance of the destiny of death returns. Sayid sells his soul to the devil in order to be reunited with his lost loved one but will find out that the price is too high and is reminded of this by Desmond. In an episode called "Ab Aeterno" (From Eternity) we are given the backstory of Richard (Nestor Carbonell), a character who seemingly travels without aging through all time layers of the series and who, in the nineteenth century on the island of Tenerife, lost his wife, Isabella. In the course of this episode Richard meets Isabella again, who tells him to accept her death because it was her time to go. The questions of knowledge and belief also return on many levels. Several of the main characters are offered the choice to become the protector of the island (which is suggested to be a source of life and eternal return). It is Jack who fully accepts his destiny to take this task on himself. All of his character's doubts, skepticism, and experiences that give him reasons to *necessarily* accept belief as the basis of knowledge make his choice quite plausible and true to his destiny. At the same time, Jack does not escape his final destiny: while saving the island, he dies. Thereafter, he sees his deceased father again in a chapel, where he also meets all his friends from the island and finally unites with Kate. While the symbolism of this version of the future as "after life" is overtly Christian, this is also derided (Jake's father's name, Christian Shephard, is mocked by Kate). Moreover, a stained-glass window in the chapel shows symbols of all religions in one frame, undermining any privileged religious certainty. As such, the series remains very much engaged with the Humian framework with which it began. In *Providence Lost* Genevieve Lloyd discusses Hume's skeptical view on providence, miracles, and religion extensively, reminding us how Philo, the most skeptical of Hume's conceptual personae, keeps on shifting positions in *Dialogues Concerning Natural Religions*. Philo comes to side with Demea to acknowledge the "adorable mysteriousness of the divine nature," provided this mysteriousness is located in the realm of the imagination rather than in the realm of religious certainty.[70] Moreover, this ending of *Lost* puts the whole show in the overall dimension of the third synthesis of time, the time of the future, retaking all of the past (all of the characters revisit their pasts) and all of the present, moving on in an eternal return of rebeginnings.

The mythological narratives of "Desert Islands" in *Lost* and *Avatar* quite literally "put death in the middle and birth at each end." These are the rebeginnings and reorderings Deleuze imagined as necessary to find our way back to the freedom of choice we have *within* the necessity of our lives and deaths. On a different (material) level neuroscientific discussions about freedom and determinism also begin to be reformulated in the same ways. As the illusory and affective principles of the brain discussed in the previous sections indicate, we are not able to consciously control our life with a "free-floating" free will independent from its encounters with the world or from largely unconscious internal brain mechanisms. We are, however, free to choose (unconsciously, and consciously, even if we are not aware of it) from the overflow of data that reaches us (from the Inside and Outside), those levels of contractions and extensions, those imaginations and understandings and those degrees of belief that help us to accept (stoically) the necessities of our destiny with reassurance rather than with frustration, anger, or anxiety.[71]

So we see that Hume's empirical transcendentalism, posing knowledge as degrees of belief with varying scales of probability and acknowledging the role of imagination in humanity as an inventive species, can help us to consider what has been lost and to reinvent our conceptions of destiny and choice as "free necessity." In the next chapter I will further investigate the suggestion that destiny is related to creativity (of the mind, of society, of art) by looking at the aesthetic dimensions of the neuro-image.[72]

Expressions of Creation

AESTHETICS OF MATERIAL-FORCES

As we have seen, Hume's epistemology of degrees of belief assigns an important role to the imagination and the power of creation. This creative power is critical to any engagement with the aesthetic dimensions of the neuro-image. Here I want to follow up on my analysis of *Lost* (and its Humian empiricist themes) as a transmedial Gesamtkunstwerk by examining the typical neuroaesthetic style of contemporary cinema.[1] Compared to the linear clarity of the movement-image and the ambiguous soberness of the time-image, the contemporary neuro-image is characterized by overabundance. Its saturated aesthetics have been referred to as neobaroque or digital baroque. Philosophically, this aspect of contemporary culture can be connected to Leibniz and to Deleuze's reading of him in *The Fold*.[2] Like Bergson and Hume, Leibniz is a "philosopher of the brain" who had astonishing intuitions that correspond with contemporary neuroscientific insights. Leibniz's brain philosophy of folds and pleats has much to offer to our discussion of aesthetics and to our neobaroque interest in mathematics. The beauty and power of infinite numbers and geometric patterns of spiral and fractal figures are the basis of baroque aesthetics. These patterns and figures are related to the limitless powers of thought, through which madness and metaphysics fold and unfold into each other; they point toward an "ungrounded ontology" typical of the neuro-image.[3]

To investigate more closely the particular aesthetics of baroque material-forces on our contemporary screens, I want to attend to the current fascination with mathematics in popular culture and, in particular, our seeming obsession with the mind of the genius/mad scientist in cinema. The popularity of mathematics is evident from television series like *Numb3rs* (CBS, since 2005) and Hollywood films about mathematician figures, including *Good Will Hunting* (Gus Van Sant, 1997), *A Beautiful Mind* (Ron Howard, 2000), and *Proof* (John Madden, 2005). Of course, it is a classic trope to feature the scientist as a mad mind; however, contemporary cinema shows that something quite different is now at stake. The mathematician in contemporary popular culture may be socially maladapted and even schizophrenic, but in recent films this particular mind is no longer depicted as completely deranged or opposed to a typically functioning brain. Rather, in line with the schizoanalytic premises of this book, the "mad scientist" mind in popular culture seems to indicate deep metaphysical and epistemological truths. To consider how cinema has expressed these concerns with the brain aesthetically, I will investigate the changing relationships between cinema and the (neuroscientific) brain, tracing cinema's development from the movement-image and the time-image to a contemporary neuro-image. I will develop the brain aesthetics of the neuro-image more profoundly by looking at two illuminating films by Darren Aronofsky: *Pi* (1997) and *The Fountain* (2007). These films present quite cogently, yet in two opposing ways—from the Inside and from the Outside—direct access to a "scientific brain" that reaches out to the universal questions of the genesis of the universe: life, death, and belief. I will argue that these two neuro-images exemplify the two extreme poles of contemporary neuroaesthetics in cinema, revealing its profound relations to the material-force unity of the cosmic age, to powers of creation, and to the eternal return typical of the third synthesis of time.[4] I will conclude by showing how these aspects configure to create new forms of "monadic" storytelling, alongside the transmedial narrative forms discussed in the previous chapter. Although I focus on the aesthetic dimensions of the neuro-image in this chapter, we should keep in mind that this aesthetics is an expression of the affective dimensions of the deliriously saturated media culture we live in today.

Neobaroque Cinema and Leibniz's Monadic Folds

When we look at the aesthetics of contemporary cinema, it is worth recalling Deleuze's own predictions. The characteristics he gives at the end of his cinema books of a new type of cinema are recognizably neobaroque. First, Deleuze argues, the organization of space in a new cinema is different. Instead of having privileged directions, space will become omnidirectional; accordingly, there will no longer be an outside or out-of-field to any image: "[images] have a right side and a reverse, reversible and non-superimposable, like a power to turn back on themselves."[5] Second, the screen itself can no longer be considered a window or a painting, but it rather constitutes a table of information, a surface inscribed with "data," where information replaces nature. In Deleuze's terms: "the image is constantly being cut to another image, being printed through a visible mesh, sliding over other images in an 'incessant stream of messages,' and the shot itself is less like an eye than an overloaded brain endlessly absorbing information: it is the brain-information, brain-city couple that replaces that of eye-Nature."[6] Finally, the new image gives way to a new psychological automaton, already present in the time-image, where characters are no longer psychologically (or psychoanalytically) motivated but become the performers of a speech act. Deleuze talks about Bresson's "models," Rohmer's puppets, Robbe-Grillet's hypnotized ones, and Resnais's zombies of the time-image that no longer have memories (in flashback) but instead have feedback loops and failed feedback that is largely involuntary.[7]

The changed image characteristics Deleuze predicted all accord with what is now commonly understood as the neobaroque of digital aesthetics.[8] Apart from the fact that such films and figures are all now part of a network of transmedial storytelling and world building, the aesthetics of the films themselves can also be recognized as baroque. In her admirable book *Enfoldment and Infinity* Laura Marks also engages with contemporary neobaroque aesthetics when she explores a hidden genealogy of new media art in ancient Islamic art. Marks not only traces the countless points of contact between Islamic aesthetics and new media art in Western art history (such as Paul Klee's abstract lines) but also locates the origins of typical aspects of digital culture (algorithm, pixel, morph, virtual reality, artificial life) in Baghdad, Cairo, Herat, and Karabagh. Marks demonstrates how mathematics and the algorithm specifically ("a statement of instructions that, when carried out, will bring about a new state or new information")[9] create algorithmic aesthetic experience, in which a certain rational but awe-inspiring structure unfolds images in accordance with patterns and rules. Islamic aniconic art, Marks discovers, incorporating patterns and forms, can be considered as applied geometry or, indeed, socialized mathematical knowledge:

Mathematics, and the new technologies they enabled, became popular culture throughout the Muslim world in the ninth and tenth centuries. . . . A textile pattern occurring all along the Silk Road, a design of coin-like roundels arranged in a grid, embodies applied mathematics. . . . This pattern demonstrates algebraic problems of addition, subtraction, multiplication, and squares and square roots. Wearers of this luxurious cloth might have enjoyed using it to demonstrate their grasp of the new mathematical knowledge, just as in our times some knowledge of how computers work is valuable cultural capital."[10]

The algorithmic aesthetics of complex repeated patterns and harmonic shapes is awe-inspiring because it occupies a "middle position between the intelligible and the sense worlds and exhibits within itself many likenesses of divine things and also many paradigms of physical relations."[11] In other words mathematics can unfold a sense of infinity—a characteristic of baroque aesthetics. Marks engages with Steven Soderbergh's *Ocean's* film cycle—*Ocean's Eleven* (2001), *Ocean's Twelve* (2004), and *Ocean's Thirteen* (2007)—comparing the virtuous and algorithmic plotting of the (most) neobaroque *Ocean's Thirteen* to the complex layered patterns of Persian carpets form the Seljuk and Safavid periods. Indicating how the group of thieves and daredevils around the leader, Danny Ocean (George Clooney), in the *Ocean's* films set up a complex heist in a casino, using and outsmarting artificial intelligence surveillance systems, Marks concludes:

The new casino movies, the caper genre more broadly, and the newly pervasive multiplot narratives show that the contemporary cinema is becoming ever more like Persian carpets in that its pleasures are not narrative but algorithmic and sensuous. In their baroque fascination, they point our attention, if not to God or to the void, then at least to the information based economy that is their outer limit. Often . . . in digital media, the "universe" is flattened, via algorithmic repetition, to a field of articulated sameness. The exceptions, like *Ocean's Thirteen*, are those works that augment the algorithmic space with humanity, mystery, and . . . "tactile values."[12]

Marks shows that digital technology makes a renewed unfolding of mathematical and baroque patterns visible again. It is also worth noting that the *Ocean's* films signal another form of resistance to the control society of surveillance culture, not by creating a wider range of affects (as in *Red Road* and *Evidence Locker*) but by thwarting the system's logic with trickery, heists, and cons. This relates to the neuro-image's acknowledgment of illusions, fictions, tricks, and manipulations as natural and everyday aspects of human brain function (see Chapter 2).

In *The Fold* Deleuze engages philosopher and mathematician Gottfried Wilhelm Leibniz and considers the close connection of his work to the baroque. Leibniz developed in his *Monadology* (1716) a philosophical understanding of the striving for the infinite in the finite beings that we are. With his concept of the monad Leibniz conceptualized how each finite being enfolds the whole (the infinite, the cosmos). As James Luchte has argued, Leibniz's interpretation of "substance as a monadic body, which . . . contains all of its aspects (necessary and contingent), past, present and future," is "deeply wedded to a temporal problematic."[13] His "monadology" is founded on the proposition that it is only possible to conceive and contain all aspects of time from a divine (Infinite) perspective, a point of view finite beings can never completely obtain. Monads, therefore, enfold a particular point of view of the whole. The point of view is not determined by a pregiven subject; on the contrary, it "will be what comes to the point of view. Or rather what remains in the point of view."[14]

The baroque aesthetic, Deleuze argues in *The Fold*, endlessly produces folds: it "twists and turns its folds, pushing them to infinity, fold over fold, one upon the other" (3). As we saw in Chapter 4, the temporal containment of all times is also related to a cosmic perspective (perhaps similar to the divine and the infinite). In the cosmic age, which Deleuze calls our time, this baroque aesthetic is the expression and construction of direct "material-forces."[15] Deleuze presents a Leibnizian understanding of our negotiation of these times and forces, in terms of bifurcating parallels: "by moving along two infinities, as if infinity were composed of two stages or floors: the pleats of matter and the folds in the soul" (3). Deleuze describes how for Leibniz matter is infinitely porous, containing all kinds of vaporous fluids, flows, and waves that are folded twice: under elastic forces ("when a boat reaches a certain speed a wave becomes as hard as a wall of marble" [6]) and under plastic forces (that organize mass but also deconstruct form). The soul, however, is an expression of the world, and the world is what the soul expresses. Together the pleats of matter (the lower floor) and folds of the soul (the upper floor) compose the "baroque house." The lower floor (body) has windows, several small openings that stand for the five senses and are connected to the "pleats of matter." The upper floor (soul) is a dark room, has no windows, and is decorated with a "drapery diversified by folds": "Placed on the opaque canvas, these folds, cords or springs represent an innate form of knowledge, but when solicited by matter they move into action" (4). Deleuze also suggests that the folds of this matter might duplicate (more or less) the folds in the soul; thus, it is possible to argue that material-forces of the lower floor and immaterial resonating forces of the upper floor relate to one another in intimate and formative ways.[16]

What is important to take from this is that a baroque aesthetics of enfolding and unfolding entails matter and soul, physical and meta-physical forces that are all enfolded into one another.[17] These complex patterns are fractally related to a profound connection between microcosmic and macrocosmic perspectives, held together "mid-way" in our brains.[18] Fractal repetitions are not always completely the same (otherwise nothing new would be produced); and Mandelbrot shapes and Julia-sets are the geometric figures of the digital age. Of course, fractal forms have always existed (coastlines, ferns, walnuts, broccoli, and other natural forms are shaped fractally) and can be identified and calculated without compu-tational machinery (Laura Marks's book is full of sublime examples of ancient Islamic art). However, it is only since the super calculating powers of the computer that they have become such common geometric figures in mathematics and in culture. Scientists seem to agree that the brain, too, is fractally structured.[19] Before homing in on the particular ques-tions of aesthetics all this raises, I want to first address Leibniz's monadic "neurophilosophy" of the finite and the infinite, which, just like Bergson's metaphysics and Hume's transcendental empiricism, is deeply concerned with the problem of the brain.

For Leibniz the mediation between the lower and upper floor (body and soul) functions through a membrane—a screen in the upper floor that has both innate ideas and is formed by what it receives. This membrane is a screen between Inside and Outside and can be considered a brain diversified by folds. Sjoerd van Tuinen insightfully elaborates these relations and characteristics of Leibniz's brain-screen concept, developed in *New Essays on Human Understanding* (especially the section where Leibniz critiques Locke's idea of the mind as a "tabula rasa"), in his article "Leibniz und das psychophysische Gehirn":

To increase the resemblance we should have to postulate that there is a screen in this dark room to receive the species, and that it is not uniform but is diversified by folds representing items of innate knowledge; and, what is more, that this screen or membrane, being under tension, has a kind of elasticity or active force, and indeed that it acts (or reacts) in ways which are adapted both to past folds and to new ones coming from impressions of the species. This action would consist in certain vibrations or oscillations, like those we see when a cord under tension is plucked and gives off a musical sound. For not only do we receive images and traces in the brain, but we form new ones from them when we bring "complex ideas" to mind; and so the screen which represents our brain must be active and elastic. This analogy would explain reasonably well what goes on in the brain. As for the soul, which is a simple substance or "monad": without being extended it represents these various extended masses and has perceptions of them.[20]

This conception of the brain as a filter or screen, continuously and infinitely oscillating between the Inside and the Outside, corresponds in important ways with the 4EA conceptions of cognitivist schools and with contemporary cognitive neuroscientific insights into the embodied brain and neuroplasticity, as discussed in the first three chapters of this book. Just as Bergson's and Hume's "neurophilosophies" operate on a dual level (actual/virtual), Leibniz discusses how body and soul are different yet interconnected. Let us look now more directly at how these discussions inform (the image of) the brain and its aesthetic expressions in cinema.[21]

From Action-Thought to Problem-Theorem
in an Immersive Brain-World

As Deleuze reminds us in *The Time-Image*, cinema has always had a profound relation with thinking, the connection to the brain being cinema's essence: "It is only when movement becomes automatic that the artistic essence of the image is realized: *producing a shock to thought, communicating vibrations to the cortex, touching the nervous and cerebral system directly.*"[22] Cinema produces "nooshocks" to the brain; cinema and the brain enter into a circuit that produces new thoughts. The cinema of Eisenstein, which combines emotional images of attraction with intellectual montage, is for Deleuze the paradigmatic example of the organic way in which the movement-image connects to thought. In cinema of the movement-image, thinking proceeds by tropes, metonymies, metaphors, inversions, oppositions, attractions, and so forth. Deleuze calls this a form of action-thought where there is always a relation between man and the world; hence its organic qualities, always relating to a synthetic Whole in which everything is associated. Classic American cinema operates mainly through metonymical principles of continuity editing (we look through a character's eye, follow her or his point of view or actions in space, and infer what we do not see through sensorimotor recognition). Eisenstein's films produce shocks to thinking through metaphorical montage. The prime example here is the intellectual montage in *October* (Eisenstein, 1927) in which images of the commander-in-chief, Kerensky, entering a room in the Winter palace are intercut with a peacock, producing the synthetic thought of the commander's vanity (and eventual downfall).

Another way in which classical cinema or the movement-image is related to the brain and to mental processes is in its relation to memory and the imagination (dreams and fantasies). Here also the organic composition of the Whole determines the place of memory and imagination. Memories are presented out of the necessity of a clearly defined point in the present to which we always return. The flashbacks in *Daybreak* (Marcel Carné, 1939), for instance, are motivated by the character's fate in the present. Movements back and forth in time relate to the organic Whole of the tragic conditions of the present and explain how this present has come about. Hitchcock's *Spellbound* (1945) most famously shows how dreams figure in our unconscious. Here the main character suffers from amnesia and anxiety attacks whenever he sees black stripes on a white surface (a fork scratching on a white table cloth, stripes on pajamas, ski marks in the snow). The famous dream sequence designed by Dalí is shown as an oneiric flashback and decoded by the psychoanalysts in the film to discover its significance, forming (again) the composition of a Whole that makes sense.

If we look at more literal images of the movement-image in which the brain and the mind of the scientist feature, we find that classical cinema presents us quite frequently with the trope of the mad scientist or brain as metaphors for all kinds of fears. In the 1950s a whole range of horror movies produced the B genre of so called brain movies. A telling example is *Fiend Without a Face* (Arthur Crabtree, 1958), in which a mad scientist secretly experiments in "thought materializations" in order to detach consciousness from the body and give it an entity of its own. The experiments he performs on his own brain are literally boosted when his instruments are struck by lightning (another trope of mad science since James Whales's 1931 adaptation of *Frankenstein*), and he strategizes that the atomic plant near his laboratory would be an even more powerful source of energy for his project. Somewhat predictably (for brain cinema of this era), the experiments soon become uncontrollable, and the scientist discovers that he has created an invisible fiend of expanded intelligence, a mental vampire that feeds on atomic power and the brains and spinal cords of human beings. While the representation of materialized thought as literal disembodied brains is way over the top, the metaphoric relations between the unleashed brain and the dangers of nuclear power during the Cold War are still powerful. Again, we see in the movement-image how thought, tropes of experimental thinking, and the brain are connected in an organic way. The mad scientist soon regrets the effects of his thought experiments when they disturb the Whole.

With the arrival of the time-image, cinema's relationship to the brain takes on a different form. Deleuze turns at this point to Artaud, who argued that cinema can be brought together with the innermost reality of the brain. "But this innermost reality is not the Whole, but on the contrary a fissure, a crack," Deleuze adds.[23] This crack is quite literally related to a break with the organic sensorimotor link of humans with the world:

the time-image produces "seers" (the precursors of the Sensing Alices I proposed in Chapter 3) who find themselves struck by something intolerable in the world and confronted with something unthinkable. The "task" of cinema from this point is no longer to produce thought showing the connections to the Whole but, instead, "the psychic situation of the seer, who sees better and further than he can react, that is, think."[24] When the sensorimotor link of humans with the world is broken and we can no longer be sure of the exact relationships between ourselves and the world, of the great organic links between what is seen, heard, and known in and of that world, it is *belief* that becomes the ontological basis of the image. As we have also seen in the previous chapter, belief becomes a schizophrenic power of thought that redefines knowledge as degrees of probabilities and belief. I will return to the schizophrenic nature of this belief, but first it is important to recall Deleuze's observation that thought in the time-image no longer operates through figures and tropes but instead becomes "theorematic" and problematic. The cinematographic image ceases to merely present images in association; hereafter, "it also has the mental effect of a theorem, it makes the unrolling of the film a theorem. . . . It makes thought immanent to the images."[25] In this description of the image as theorematic thought Deleuze refers to mathematics:

A problem lives in the theorem, and gives it life, even when removing its power. The problematic is distinguished from the theorematic (or constructivism from the axiomatic) in that the theorem develops internal relationships from principle to consequences, while the problem introduces an event from the outside—removal, addition, cutting—which constitutes its own conditions and determines the "case" or cases: hence the ellipse, hyperbola, parabola, straight lines and the point are cases of projection of the circle on its secant planes, in relation to the apex of a cone. This outside of the problem is not reducible to the exteriority of the physical world any more than to the psychological interiority of a thinking ego.[26]

I will return to the theorem and the problem in the neuro-image in my discussion of *Pi* and *The Fountain* momentarily. At this point it is important just to see how thought in the time-image is related to the exteriority of a belief, a choice that has to be made outside any mode of certain knowledge (as in Hume's basic principle) or individual psychology.

Another important characteristic of the time-image is that it no longer refers to the Whole as an organic totality (as it did in the movement-image, defined by montages of associations, or by attractions between parts, the set, and the changing Whole). In the time-image the Whole is the Outside, which means that what is important now is what happens in between images, a spacing that according to Deleuze means that each image is plucked from the void and falls back into it:

Given one image, another image has to be chosen which will induce an interstice *between* the two. This is not an operation of association, but of differentiation, as mathematicians say, or of disappearance, as physicists say: given one potential, another one has to be chosen, not any whatever, but in such a way that a difference of potential is established between the two, which will be productive of a third or something new.[27]

Thought becomes irrational and not necessarily organic. In relation to the time-image, Deleuze has demonstrated how this inorganic power of thought and belief is related to the unsummonable in Welles, the inexplicable in Robbe-Grillet, the undecidable in Resnais, the impossible in Duras, and the incommensurable in Godard. In all these types of time-images the power of thought is related to a confusing and confused experience of time and to the reality of the virtual that crystallizes with the actual.

The time-image's relation to the brain and to thought are by and large also dominant in the neuro-image, albeit in a baroquely transformed and schizophrenically intensified form. As we have seen, contemporary screen culture at large is populated with schizos, delirious and delusional characters, and characters that suffer from amnesia and other brain disorders. I have shown how contemporary cinema has quite literally entered the mind of its characters to play all kinds of tricks with spectator's minds simultaneously. In *Fight Club* we enter the movie as a ride through the brain's neural network, only to find out at the end that the two protagonists are actually one: a "crystal character," so to speak, whose virtual and actual sides are both real. *The Butterfly Effect* deals with blackouts and the schizophrenic hallucinations of time travel; *The Illusionist* and *The Prestige* show how perception is illusionary and can be toyed with; *Red Road* can be considered a "neurothriller," creating suspense between emotions and feelings; in *Earth* the main character is schizophrenic or perhaps even (returning from the) dead; *Lost* is populated with tricksters, con artists, and schizos; *Avatar* presents its events as a mental world, directly fed by the minds of its characters. Other examples of how cinema has turned into a schizophrenic "machine of the invisible" can be added: in *Eternal Sunshine of the Spotless Mind* (Michel Gondry, 2004) the classic screwball theme of remarriage is literally played out in the minds of the two main characters, who have their memories of one another erased by a company called Lacuna; similarly, *The Machinist* (Brad Anderson, 2004) presents events from the traumatized mind of its protagonist. *Inception* (Christopher Nolan, 2010) and *Source Code* (Duncan Jones, 2011) are other popular examples of how cinema has become a brain-city, or brain-world. Playing inside the architecture of the brain, *Inception*'s layers and levels fractally enfold its stories, all from the point of view of the future (shown at the beginning and end of the film) when its protagonist is old and dying. *Source Code* is a digital brain story of the eternal return of difference and repetition.

Many more examples can be found of contemporary film characters that seem to have lost their minds or are, as Anna Powell indicates, in "altered states" and whose mindscapes we have literally entered, without warning, from a more stable point of view of reality.[28] The looking and acting characters of the movement-image and the wondering and wandering characters of the time-image seem to have evolved into the delusional or overwhelmed characters of the neuro-image. These "schizophrenic" characters become lost in the vertiginous monadic multiplicities and vortices of screens, data, and information of contemporary globalized media culture. They are Leibnizian in the sense that in a fractally dynamic folding and unfolding reality, they might think that they have "reached the port" only to realize they have been "cast back again into the open sea."[29] The image of the brain in the neuro-image can be considered from the deepest and most inner folds and pleats of the soul *and* from its most external field of expression, as I will try to demonstrate in the next sections by looking at two films by Darren Aronofsky. Characters in both films are obsessed with something deeper than any explanation can give. Therefore, I am not proposing the films in opposition (depth versus external field) but as two variations that can be placed at different ends of the spectrum of expressions resulting from the changed aesthetic of the neuro-image.

The Inner Pole of the Neuro-Image: *Pi* and the Visceral Qualities of the Schizobrain of a Mathematician

Pi is a subjective movie.[30] Its images are entirely composed from the perceptions of its main character, Max Cohen (Sean Gullette), who is a mathematician obsessed with finding a universal pattern in numbers. He is especially fascinated with the number π (pi), the ratio of a circle's circumference to its diameter, 3.1415926535 . . . (on to infinity), and with predicting the fluctuations in the stock market; consequently, he is wanted by both a Wall Street company and a group of Hasidic Jews. Max suffers from paranoid schizophrenia (the initial idea for the film was to explore paranoiac schizophrenia).[31] The mathematical theories and numerological references to the Kabbalah (the Gematria) to which Aronofsky refers are accurate and true, but the film is not about mathematics. Rather, as the filmmaker declares, it is an exploration of "cool math theories" and the belief that mathematics is related to the divine.[32] When asked if *Pi* is a science fiction film, Aronofsky emphasizes that it is sci-fi in the tradition of Philip K. Dick—of storytelling through inner exploration: "It's pushing science forward within the fiction realm, so I think ultimately it is a science fiction film."[33] The film then presents the dynamics of pop mathematics while linking these to larger questions about the origin of the world and cosmic or divine spirituality, as is typical for the neuro-image.

Pi refers to the brain on three different levels. First, as a subjectively schizophrenic film, the image itself is completely mental (the screen immediately relays brain images). At the same time, metaphorical references to the brain are everywhere. The brain no longer stands for the dangers of nuclear power and mad scientists. It is now seen as a complex computer network that can malfunction. In one scene Max discovers a literal bug in Euclid (Max's homemade computer), which can be read in relation to the "bugs" in his mind. Inside Max's delirious hallucinations, which always follow his seriously affecting headaches, he sees literal brains: on the floor in the underground, and in the washbasin ("that was Rudolph Guiliani's brain that we borrowed," Aronofsky jokes in the DVD commentary about this brain).

Most striking about *Pi*'s different relation to the brain are the film's visceral qualities. The choice of the film stock is remarkable: *Pi* is shot in black and white reversal film; this stock is difficult to develop and has no gray tones, only sharply contrasted black and white. Furthermore, the camera angles and movements bring the camera into Max's headspace by always staying in close proximity to him or showing his point of view (often hallucinating or affectively charged with panic and fear). Sometimes a little camera on his body (a Snorri-cam) gives the sense of agitated movement (for instance when he is chased in the underground). "We wanted the audience to experience how it was to be a renegade genius mathematician standing on the verge of insanity," Aronofsky says.[34] The soundtrack is another important element that affects the senses directly. Max's headaches are announced by an uncontrollable shaking of his thumb, followed by what Aronofsky calls a "hip hop montage" of Max taking pills, where the images and music are thrown about by a fast rhythm. When the pain kicks in, the spectator (with Max) physically experiences this through a sharp invasive sound that penetrates our brains. When Max opens his computer and gets the bug (an ant) out, his fingers are sticky with a sort of slimy substance that Max first looks at, listens to, smells, and then tastes. Max is also somehow able to touch (with a pen) the three pounds of brains in his hallucinations, causing the sharp sound again; he even attacks and smashes this cerebral matter toward the film's end. In *Pi*, contrary to many of the brain-films in the time-image where the mental landscape is more often expressed in a more distant conceptual way (even if violently or passionately), such as in Kubrick, the mental spaces and brains of the neuro-image are much more physical and sensuous indeed.[35]

If we take Deleuze's definition that a theorem develops internal relationships from principles to consequences, we can consider *Pi* a theorematic film. At several points in the movie Max's voice-over states his assumptions: "1. Mathematics is the language of nature. 2. Everything around us can be translated and understood through numbers. 3. If you graph the numbers of any system, patterns emerge. Therefore everywhere in nature there are patterns." Clearly this is the theorem the film proposes: the principle of mathematics, because underlying principles of everything, should make it possible to decode and predict the patterns of the stock market, which, according to Max is "a living organism, screaming with life." This is also the theorem Max's character explores.

How should we consider the numbers and geometric figures in the film? In "Notes on the Number π" in the DVD extras, it is indicated that the obsession with the number π is related to our attraction to the circle: a circle is probably the most perfect and simple form known to humans. Lying at the heart of it is a specific, unchanging number that also manages to appear everywhere in functions of geometry, statistics, and biology. It just keeps popping up, reminding us that it is there and defying us to understand why. Pi is a nonrepeating decimal that reaches out into infinity, and our continuing challenge is to compute this number farther than it has been computed, farther than the many billions of endless digits it has reached already. Aside from the circle and the number π, the Fibonacci sequence and the spiral are other mathematical figures that return in the film. The Fibonacci sequence is a string of numbers in which each succeeding number is the sum of the two preceding ones (1, 1, 2, 3, 5, 8, 13 . . .). It appears that many phenomena in the world reproduce Fibonacci sequences (flower-head arrangements, the human body, DNA, even voting patterns). In *Pi* Max also analyzes the Fibonacci patterns of the stock market. The spiral logarithms in *Pi* are also frequent patterns of nature (seashells, whirlpools, hurricanes, an embryo, the galaxy). Many have argued that these patterns must have a meaning, perhaps a divine meaning.[36]

In *Pi* these mathematical formulas and symbols are not just the theme of the film; they are also repeated in the style of the film: circles, spirals, and Fibonacci sequences are frequently expressed in the mise-en-scène and in the camera movements. The title sequence is a graphic design of circles, spirals, and other figures, including neurons that shift over moving digits belonging to the number π. Elements of these graphic figures reappear later in the film. Spirals appear in the mise-en-scène, for instance, in a dash of milk in coffee, in cigarette smoke, and in the arrangement of a game of Go that Max's friend Saul leaves behind after he has committed suicide. Fibonacci sequences are drawn on the financial paper and by the Jewish numerologists, and circles feature for instance in zeros on the computer screen while the camera encircles Max in a 360-degree pan. In this very consistent style, form and content repeat each other or are enfolded in one another.

Pi has several endings, or more accurately, it remains ambiguous about what has actually taken place, which is again a characteristic that the neuro-image shares with the time-image. We don't know whether Max actually sees the divine light, if he literally drills his own brain, or if from his hyperactive state of positive symptoms of schizophrenia he falls into a catatonic state, nor whether he actually has freed himself from his "brain power" and can accept life on a phenomenological scale, enjoying nature as it appears and the company of the neighbor girl. Conspicuously, the brain Max attacks at the end of the film is crawling with the presence of ants, the same kind found in his computer and throughout his apartment. In the DVD audio commentary Aronofsky explains his motivation for including this theme: on a holiday in Mexico he visited a small, unknown Mayan temple and discovered that it was literally covered with ants. He suddenly envisioned that humans (this important civilization of the Mayans) and ants were all the same; he saw the groundlessness of the "I," which is also a groundlessness Max discovers the closer he comes to the mysteries of the universe. Aronofsky's revelation and the way the ants are present in *Pi* also resonates with Deleuze's conclusions in *Difference and Repetition*, which develop a nonrepresentative, preindividual way of thinking difference: "The ultimate, external illusion of representation is this illusion that results from its internal illusions—namely, that groundlessness should lack differences, when in fact it swarms with them. What, after all, are Ideas, with their constitutive multiplicity, if not these ants which enter and leave through the fractured I."[37] Before turning to *The Fountain*, I just want to reiterate the connection between *Pi*'s means of dissolving Max's identity by introducing ants into the image: the ant moves beyond being a metaphor for a "bug" in the system and becomes instead a rhizomatic connection between different forms of life without a determined "I." All this is experienced from a most subjective mental point of view, situating *Pi* at the inner pole (or circle) of madness of the neuro-image.

The Outer Pole of the Neuro-Image: *The Fountain*, the Third Synthesis of Time, and the Calculus

Madness transforms into metaphysics more explicitly in *The Fountain*, strongly pronouncing the concerns of the neuro-image, such as the problem of time and cosmic spirituality. Like *Pi*, *The Fountain* is a particular kind of science fiction film. Even though it takes place (partly) in outer space, it is actually taking place in inner space. Here again, the film presents the mental landscape of its main male character, but this time we are not accessing a mad brain but a metaphysical brain that reaches out to the past and the future. Moving between three layers of time (sixteenth-century Spain, twenty-first-century North America, and a twenty-fifth-century somewhere in outer space), *The Fountain* is essentially the story of the same couple, played by Hugh Jackman and Rachel Weisz. In the twenty-first century Tommy is a brain surgeon who tries to find a cure for his wife, Izzy, who has a brain tumor. This story unfolds into the past, where conquistador Thomas wants to save Spain and Queen Isabelle by finding a holy tree in the New Spain; and into the future, where the astronaut Tom travels through space in a biospheric "bubble-ship" and tries to deal with the previous stories.

As a new type of image, the film shows how the organization of space itself has differentiated to become omnidirectional. This is most obvious in the futuristic sequences, where bulbs, spheres, and lights float in and out of the frame from all directions, an effect that is repeated in the mise-en-scène of the lights in other parts of the film. As we will see shortly, many elements in the composition of the image tend to return. The elements that create spatial omnidirectionality are thus also part of the other layers of time. *The Fountain* no longer gives us a window to the world but has become a "brain-information" table. Similar to *Pi*, this brain has to be seen as a very sensuous one: touch, smell, and taste are frequently emphasized in close-up. These combined elements do not present a filmic setting for a story to unfold within; rather, they present a new tapestry of thoughts and affects. I will show how these aspects of the film push it beyond the digital possibilities of contemporary cinema (though such possibilities remain extremely relevant) to engage with the question of a will to art. Finally, I will argue that *The Fountain*'s characters can be understood as sensuous adaptations of Resnais's zombies. This is especially the case with the character of Izzy, who, in fact, is dead most of the time we see her and who returns in feedback loops.

Perhaps the most important general characteristic of the film that makes it a new type of cinematographic image is that, despite its dealing with death and seemingly outer space issues, it makes us believe in the world, in love and life. This is the true quest of the brain surgeon, who wants to find a cure for the "disease of death" but will discover beauty in *believing* love and life will continue in an eternal return. Whereas *Pi* is a theorematic film, *The Fountain* is "problematic." Its central problems are the Big Questions that come from the Outside: life and death. What does it mean to live? What would it mean to live forever? What does it mean to die? Obviously, the film cannot give any answers, but these universal questions are enfolded in the singular love story of the two main characters and are offered up in three variations. The way in which the film proceeds to unpack the thoughts and affects connected to the problem of life, love, and death is by repeating the same story in different layers of time. Here we must return to the three syntheses of time that Deleuze developed in *Difference and Repetition*. Deleuze explicitly relates repetition and the synthesis of time to art:

Beyond the grounded and grounding repetitions, a repetition of *ungrounding* on which depend both that which enchains and that which liberates, that which dies and that which lives within repetition. Beyond physical repetition and psychic or metaphysical repetition, an *ontological* repetition? . . . Perhaps the highest object of art is to bring into play simultaneously all these repetitions, with their differences in kind and rhythm, their respective displacements and disguises, their divergences and decenterings; to embed them in one another and to envelop one or the other in illusions the "effect" of which varies in each case. Art does not imitate, above all it repeats; it repeats all the repetitions, by virtue of an internal power.[38]

We have seen that Deleuze develops these points by arguing that all repetitions are ordered in the pure form of time (creating different forms of differences in the repetition). However, we can consider here also his proposition that the "Before" (second synthesis of the past) and "During" (first synthesis of the present) depend on the third time, the Future. The Future is the proper place of decision ("a decision on which everything depends, deeper than all the explanations that can be given for it," quoted earlier in connection to the Outside of the problem). If the neuro-image belongs to the third synthesis of time, this means that all other times are implicated in its artistic forms as well: "There is only eternal return in the third time: it is here that the freeze-frame begins to move once more, or that the straight line of time, as though drawn by its own length, re-forms a strange loop which in no way resembles the earlier cycle, but leads into the formless, and operates only for the third time and for that which belongs to it."[39]

Typical of the neuro-image is this tendency for the three syntheses of time to play out in "strange loops," repeating and differentiating in a sort of culminating or vortical movement of all times. Deleuze's ontological ideas on repetition, art, and time shed light on the ontological questions and problems that *The Fountain* poses. The film clearly brings into play the different kinds of repetition Deleuze delineates: physical, metaphysical, and ontological. In the film, too, it is only in the third time, the literally ungrounded future (where everything is floating), that "all times" come together, as Deleuze suggests. Only in the future do we see the "Historical Isabelle" from the Before and "Present Izzy" from the During appear in Tom's hallucinations and feedback loops that are several times repeated, leading up to his final decision to end the other two times by choosing the eternal return. As paradoxical as it may seem, but in line with the demands of the third synthesis of time, the eternal return happens by accepting death and returning to the Unicity of being.

Many scenes are repeated throughout the film. Most striking perhaps is the scene, repeated three times, where Izzy suddenly appears, dressed in a white winter coat and a white knitted cap, to ask "Take a walk with me?" The first time Tom replies from the future (Tom looks different in every layer of time), saying, "Please Izzy," as if he wants her to leave him alone. The second time the scene plays out, it is Tommy (in the present) who replies, "Please Izzy," and explains that his colleagues are waiting for him for an operation. We move more deeply into that layer of time, discovering "the problem" and how Tommy is obsessed with curing her fatal illness. With the third repetition of the scene Tommy changes his mind and does follow Izzy into the snow. This will lead to Tom(my)'s final decision to finish the story of the conquistador in the past (a story Izzy was writing and repeatedly asks him to finish), to finally die in the future (the climax of the film where Tom dies in the nebula of a dying star and becomes a celestial particle) and accept her death by planting a seed on her grave in the present time. The final image of the film is another repeated scene from the present: in extreme close-up Tommy whispers into Izzy's neck, "Everything is fine." The eternal return has selected the affirmative powers of love, life, and belief.

Aronofsky invokes a certain mathematical order in this film also, an order that seems to underlie all these repetitions of scenes. The formal mathematical principle that gives *The Fountain* its particular style is the recurrent baroque geometrical figure of the neuro-image: the fractal. As I have indicated, fractal formulas produce complex geometric shapes that are very different from the Euclidean geometric lines and points of Renaissance perspective (but do resonate with Arab aesthetics). Fractals can be subdivided into parts, each of which is a differentiated reduced-size copy of the whole, following a mathematical logic of difference and repetition. We can also understand how the screen, as window projecting onto a plane (following Renaissance perspective) in the movement-image and the time-image, has in the neuro-image turned into a table of data, in accordance with Deleuze's explanation of baroque mathematics: "Transformation of inflection can no longer allow for either symmetry or the favored plane of projection. It becomes vortical and is produced later; deferred, rather than prolonged or proliferating: the line effectively folds into a spiral in order to defer inflection in a movement suspended between sky and earth."[40] Not coincidentally, this is one of the many occasions where Deleuze's own philosophy appears itself fractal—similar patterns and principles are repeated in endlessly complex variations throughout his entire work.

The Fountain's style is fractal on several levels. I have already mentioned the striking repetitions and differences of entire scenes in different syntheses of time. Also, cinematographically and in the composition of the image, patterns recur throughout the film. The different layers of time are connected through formal shapes and mathematical figures by stylistic enfolding, and each layer of time has its own particular predominant motif. Throughout the film, low and high camera angles (characters looking up into the celestial star field, the camera looking down on the scene below) are repeated frequently, emphasizing the infinity of the cosmos, the abstract beauty of the composition of the scenes on Earth, and the connection between the two. Microcosmos and macrocosmos are also repeatedly connected at a purely visual level, for instance in the image of a brain cell under a microscope that is very similar to the movements and lights in the film's sky. I have mentioned the particular arrangements of lighting in the first and second layers of time that match the omnidirectional cosmic lightbulbs in the third time. Other elements in the mise-en-scène are also very subtly repeated, such as the patterns on Isabelle's royal dress that are like the roots of a tree, which connect her to the tree in the space bubble and to the tree of life. Furthermore, the whole design of the film is the shape of a crucifix, or mathematical "cruciform," including vertical and horizontal planar shifts that return in all layers. Of course, as indicated by Aronofsky, each layer in itself also has a different predominant mathematical motif.[41] In sixteenth-century Spain and in Mayan civilization the triangle (the three-point star in Mayan cosmology, arches in the queen's palace) is recurrent and sometimes returns in a picture on the wall in Tommy and Izzy's apartment in the twenty-first century. Here the most repeated form is the rectangle or square (computer screens, windows, pictures, doorways, etc.), emphasizing our screen culture, while in the third layer of time of the future, it is the circle, bulb, or sphere that is presented in many variations.

Finally, the film stock itself is used in a fractal way. Although the idea of fractal logics goes back to Leibniz, fractals can only actually be mass-produced aesthetically by means of computer technology with immense calculating powers. It seems appropriate, then, that the neuro-image, having access to the endless possibilities of CGI, would be fractal. Yet the power of *The Fountain* is certainly also due to the fact that Aronofsky has made only very limited use of digital effects. This is another indication that technology is not the cause of aesthetic change, nor the agent of this specific film's aesthetic difference, even though it can be profoundly related to it. It is striking that the cosmic images of the third layer of time are not computer generated, even though that is the most current way of showing outer space. Instead, Aronofsky and his team hired Peter Parks, a specialist in macrophotography, to brew chemicals and bacteria to create a fluid dynamic on the film stock, which affected the substances photographed. Parks explains: "When these images are projected on a big screen, you feel like you are looking at infinity. That's because the same forces at work in the water—gravitational effects, settlement, and refractive indices—are happening in outer space."[42] Without utilizing computer imagery, even the ontological status of the film material itself is in this way deeply fractal.

Recalling Deleuze's metaphor of the Leibnizian monad, *The Fountain* can be seen as a "baroque house" in which the different layers of time are its lower and upper floors. Deleuze holds that Leibniz constructs a great baroque montage that "moves between the lower floor, pierced with windows, and the upper floor, blind and closed, but on the other hand resonating as if it were a musical salon translating the visible movements below into sounds up above."[43] In this sense *The Fountain* presents monadic images, where only the third layer, the third synthesis of time of the future, contains all other syntheses. This image layer includes all series and states of the world, the organizing principles of which lie outside the monad itself and outside the world. The neuro-image does not imply the extinction of the other two images. They remain possible variations of the image, but they will also increasingly be implicated in a third image, the image of the third time.

The aesthetics of the neuro-image implies that the virtual resides in the soul but requires matter in order to be actualized and incarnated in the subject, repeating the folds of the soul. As Claire Colebrook argues, Deleuze envisions a double commitment: everything begins from the sensible, but the task of thinking is to go beyond the sensible into the potentials that make the sensible possible, into the extension of any possible series outside actual experience.[44] We could argue with Deleuze that the subject is formed in the folds of matter and soul, physically and metaphysically, but that its formative principle lies outside both these points, in the mathematical principle. If the movement-image gives us (nonpersonal) material aspects of subjectivity (the physical) and the time-image (nonpersonal) immaterial aspects of subjectivity (the metaphysical), the neuro-image goes beyond subjectivity, opening up to the *infinite possibilities* of universal series (the mathematical).[45] In the last chapter of *Difference and Repetition* Deleuze explicitly connects mathematics to a cosmic awareness when he explains that difference is not the same as diversity:

Diversity is given, but difference is that by which the given is given, that by which the given is given as diverse. . . . It is therefore true that God makes the world by calculating, but this calculation never works exactly, and this inexactitude or injustice in the result, this irreducible inequality, forms the condition of the world. The world "happens" while God calculates; if the calculations were exact, there would be no world.[46]

Deleuze indicates that the world could be regarded as a "remainder," and the real as fractional numbers, (micro)differences of levels, temperature, pressure, tension, potential, intensities,[47] which makes *Difference and Repetition* the philosophical counterpart of chaos theory. Difference of intensity is the condition of all that appears, as "every phenomenon flashes in a signal-sign system" that contains its conditions of appearance.[48] Mathematics, God, the infinite all point toward these fundamental questions.

In final analysis the search for principles of infinite possibility is the fundamental theorem and problem posed by *Pi* and *The Fountain*. This search for the "beginning of the universe" is also the reason why both *Pi* and *The Fountain* refer to the book of Genesis. In *Pi*, when Max is close to breaking through the code, the first page of Genesis in Hebrew and numerical translations appear on his computer screen. *The Fountain* refers to the tree of life (as opposed to the tree of knowledge) that is described in the book of Genesis.[49] In both cases the implication of a universal mathematic pattern of infinite possibilities is the force of the virtual that is immanent in the power of the images. *Pi*'s theorematic nature brings the neuro-image to its most dangerous pole, where a breakthrough turns into a breakdown: madness. *The Fountain*'s presentation of the problem of death resurrects life and love in a repetition of eternal return and a truly becoming-imperceptible, becoming-world that reaches into a cosmic ontology. As such, these films can be considered as exemplifying the two most extreme poles (Inside and Outside) of the contemporary neuro-image, with infinite possible variations in between. Most strikingly, the neuro-image seems to acknowledge an increasing consciousness, bridging across the three domains of thinking (art, science, and philosophy), that we are only temporary subjects formed by the encounters and experiences we have in the world. Beyond the groundedness of our being that we can experience in the first and second synthesis of time, we are connected to a universal and ungrounded eternal return of a fractured "I" that is "swarming with difference" and the infinite virtual potentialities of mathematical calculations that are at the basis of our madness and our metaphysics.

Creation and Monadic Narration
in the Neuro-Image

If the connection to the third synthesis of time makes it possible to see how Leibnizian baroque aesthetics are related to a temporal metaphysics (and a mathematical ontology), another aspect of the neuro-image that *The Fountain* reveals makes possible a return to Hume's insistence on the creative and inventive nature of humanity. *The Fountain* reflects on storytelling and artistic creation. If the universe is conditioned by differences and repetitions, differences of intensities, repetitions of three passive syntheses of time, there is also an active form of (artistic) creation and of choice (which in the previous chapter was explored as destiny, the form of a free necessity). Aronofsky has indicated that *The Fountain* is diversely inspired by the myth of the fountain of youth and the tree of life, Spanish conquistador stories, and ancient Mayan culture, as well as "Space Oddity's Major Tom" (David Bowie) and cowriter Ari Handel's PhD in neurosciences. "I'll take different threads from different ideas and weave a carpet of cool ideas together," Aronofsky says.[50] This rhizomatic way of thinking and creating leads to the story of Tommy and Izzy, but the film exceeds its narrative on all sides and levels, as I hope to have shown in the analysis of its fractal style above. Within the narrative of the film the process of storytelling is an important metanarrative thread, or signal, which itself weaves the stories of the film together. In the time of the present, Izzy is writing the fictive story of Isabella and the Spanish conquistadors in the past. Not being able to accept Izzy's death, Tommy first refuses to finish the story; in this sense Tommy is like a tragic Greek hero who refuses to accept as destiny the "untimely" death of his loved one (resembling the character of Richard in *Lost*, who also refused to accept the death of his Isabella). The moment he chooses to finish the fictive story, Tommy "chooses to choose" and act creatively within the bounds of fate, creating as such the eternal return of the differential intensity of their love and life. While Tommy continues to write the story in the present, the conquistador Thomas of the past is swallowed by the earth and the tree of life that he too greedily wanted to obtain, and "Major Tom" of the future returns (fully accepting his fate) to celestial stardust. This emphasis on the act of creation in the present suggests that in this way we can actively relate to the passive synthesis of time and choose the eternal return. We see that in spite of all its literal cosmic and outer space references, the neuro-image is deeply concerned with (learning from) the past and (creating and choosing in) the present. *The Fountain* addresses the metaphysical questions of time, creation, destiny, and eternal return in a wonderfully baroque way that does not give away folded secrets easily. It is only after a second or third viewing that these depths start to reveal themselves (and resonate with powerful intensity).

It is worthwhile pursuing further the (meta)reflections in the neuro-image on the creation of stories, because it is a significant feature of this cinema that I will argue differs from metareflections in the movement-image and the time-image. Let us briefly look at two other neuro-images that explicitly address their creative process. *The Fall* (Tarsem Singh, 2006) and *Southland Tales* (Richard Kelly, 2006) are two films that have met a mixed reception because of their (at some points) overly exaggerated baroque aesthetics. These films are indeed less metaphysical than Aronofsky's films, but they are nevertheless interesting in their (meta)reflections on neurocinematic narration. Both explicitly address the creative process of storytelling when referring (like *The Fountain*) to the *mental* genesis of stories via rhizomatic combinations of heterogeneous elements formed into something new. I want to closely describe and analyze this kind of repetition, so that its difference from other forms of self-referentiality becomes tangible. Both films are set in a fictitious Los Angeles. *The Fall* brings us back to 1918 and is the story of a depressed stuntman, Roy Walker (Lee Pace), and a young migrant girl, Alexandria (Catinca Untaru), who are both in the hospital because of a fall. Containing countless references to the early slapstick movies of Buster Keaton and Harold Lloyd, *The Fall* pays explicit tribute to the power of early cinema to set the body in motion, to fly, jump, and fall as had never been seen before. At the same time, paralyzed in his hospital bed, Roy tells a story to Alexandria in which fiction and reality blend in fantastic ways. *Southland Tales* is set in Los Angeles in 2008. Here the story centers on an amnesiac action hero, Boxer Santeros (Dwayne Johnson), who encounters a reality television presenter/ porn star Krysta Now (Sarah Michelle Gellar). As a political cartoonesque satire, *Southland Tales* suggests that the magic of early cinema has been replaced by the paranoia of surveillance culture. (In the film, following a nuclear attack on Texas, the government institute USIDent has total control over the population, and only a clumsy group of neo-Marxists still holds on to the idea of resistance.) As in *The Fall,* fiction and reality begin to mix when the film script (as story element) written by Santeros appears increasingly to predict events to come.

Like all neuro-images, the films in themselves can be considered monadic forms of storytelling. If in the movement-image stories are likened to bricks that are connected in a particular order and invested with the function of building a house (telling a story), and if in the time-image these bricks begin to shift and break, leaving empty spaces and cracks that are more telling than the bricks themselves, then in the neuro-image the house itself has fallen into ruins, the debris flying around in disorder, while any stray piece becomes a (fractal) version of the (Whole) story.[51] Several aspects can be distinguished in this monadic form of narration, noticeable in *The Fall* and *Southland Tales.* First, both films are part of a transmedial logic, whereby different versions of the story are scattered like debris in media culture at large; as such, they are part of an open and growing network that contains both powerful and banal versions.[52] *Southland Tales* is part of a serial story, the fictional forms of which include prequels in three graphic novels, an animation film, a making-of featurette, and many YouTube clips, among which are compelling video clips. ("I've Got Soul but I'm Not a Soldier" by Justin Timberlake, who plays a traumatized Iraq veteran in the film, is especially popular.) These fictional forms fold in and over references to political reality: 9/11 has transitioned into a nuclear attack on Texas, the Patriot Act has morphed into the ultimate homeland security of USIDent, and left-wing America has turned into a parody of itself. *The Fall* equally engages such baroque serial logic. The film is a variation of the Bulgarian movie *Yo Ho Ho* (Zako Heskija, 1981), and its sequences have an "independent life" as video clips playable on YouTube alongside behind-the-scenes conversations with the director and time-lapse videos of the sets, which showcase the powerful mise-en-scène.

Stylistically, also, these films show how the storytelling process operates monadically. In *The Fall* many patterns and details in the mise-en-scène are repeated with variation: a coffee stain on a napkin transforms into the blood of a dying hero in the fictional story that Roy tells the little girl; a radiologist in a black leather harness morphs into a whole hostile army of soldiers in black uniforms; the fantastic costumes made by Eiko Ishioka, such as the butterfly coat of Darwin (Leo Bill) and the flower veil of Princess Evelyn (Justine Wadell), are like nature. Indians and cowboys from early westerns, the people and objects in the hospital and in Los Angeles in the late 1910s, as well as the elements and heroes in the fictional stories, perform as rhizomatically connected variations of each other. For example, the Indian man who works with Alexandria on the orange plantation turns into a hero of the fictive story; India and Hollywood mix when the Indian man falls in love with a beautiful squaw and his Taj Mahal–like palace is revealed as a wigwam. Similarly, in *Southland Tales* the countless screens of surveillance cameras, television sets, and computers repeat story elements. Additionally, the film's mise-en-scène and narrative elements recall other films. Director Richard Kelly mentions *Brazil* (Terry Gilliam, 1985) and *Dr. Strangelove* (Stanley Kubrick, 1964) as important references. The exorbitant setting, the apocalyptic ending, and the double role of the blonde and brunette lovers of Santeros are also reminiscent of early neuro-images such as *Strange Days* (Kathryn Bigelow, 1995), *The Fifth Element* (Luc Besson, 1997), and *Mulholland Drive* (David Lynch, 2001). These films are not quoted directly, but they do seem to function like the (unconscious) background "noise" from which new images arise here.

As baroque aesthetics prescribe, these films are self-referential, not only in their reference to other (Hollywood) films but also in their reflection on the process of their own creation. Of course, this is in itself not new. From its beginnings cinema has reflected on itself. Buster Keaton's *Sherlock Junior* (1924) and Dziga Vertov's *Man with a Movie Camera* (1929) are but two of the most well-known examples of movement-images that explicitly address the cinematographic apparatus, displaying the camera, the cutting room, the projector, the screen, and the audience in the theater. Classical Hollywood was already self-reflexive. The introduction of sound is central in the plot of *Singin' in the Rain* (Stanley Donen, 1952). In *Paris When It Sizzles* (Richard Quine, 1964) Audrey Hepburn helps a scriptwriter to write a film script, and the building blocks of the classical narrative are literally laid out on the floor (each empty page of the script representing a segment, narrative development, or turning point). *Sunset Boulevard* (Billy Wilder, 1950) is another classic in the self-reflexive genre. Here the main character and narrator of the film has drowned in a swimming pool at the beginning of the film. In a long flashback scene we come to know exactly how this came about. Within the plot of the film the main character works on a film script as well. However, the film does not reflect on the process of storytelling but on the social cruelty of the Hollywood factory. The time-image has equally produced self-reflexive images. *Le mépris* (Jean-Luc Godard, 1963) and *Day for Night* (Francois Truffaut, 1974) are noteworthy examples. In both films the process of film production and cinephilia is important and entirely interwoven with complicated love stories of the characters involved. Many more examples could be given, but my point is that in the movement-image and the time-image self-reflexivity addresses for the most part the rules of filmmaking itself (giving the building blocks of a story, showing the filmic apparatus, reflecting on the film process or the film business).

Although all these elements continue to be part of neurocinematic self-reflexivity, the difference now is that the *mental* processes of storytelling are being displayed onscreen. Many neuro-images show how creative processes work when elements of reality and cultural objects are blended in the imagination and rendered as new images (which in turn then impact our perception of reality, memory, and imagination to infinity—or *ad nauseam* perhaps). "The future is what you imagine," reads the tagline of *Southland Tales*. References to Robert Frost's "The Road Not Taken" indicate that the film presents an alternative scenario of contemporary reality: this could have happened, perhaps is happening, or still could happen. In *The Fall* we literally witness how a story unfolds from elements in reality. More important, however, this film seems to argue that stories are of vital importance to restore a belief in life. In the end Roy does not commit suicide. Saved by creative powers of the false, he watches a movie together with Alexandria and other patients, in which he performs as an actor. Even the apocalyptic conclusion of *Southland Tales* is an open (albeit tongue-in-cheek) ending. By reflecting on the mental processes of creativity and the strange interweaving of fiction and reality in this way, neuro-images signal the important role of fiction and artistic creation in expressing a belief in the reality of life. Here, the essential, experiential, co-responding Outside of mathematics and the brain is, in fact, the very process of storytelling *and vice versa*, a fact that these latest neurocinematic stories are now beginning to take into account. The cosmic age that Deleuze signaled is therefore this age in which mathematics, the brain, and the storytelling process itself come most profoundly together in intimate and knowing coarrangements.

Now that we have seen how principles of the brain can help to assess contemporary digital screens and explored the metaphysical, epistemological, and aesthetic dimensions of the neuro-image, the next three chapters will examine the ways in which neuro-images operate in reality and, as such, have (micro)political power.

PART 3

NEUROPOLITICS
Transnational Screen Connections

7

The Open Archive

CINEMA AS WORLD-MEMORY

Although I have already touched on the political dimensions of the neuro-image, especially in my discussion of affective resistance against the controlling forces of surveillance screens (in Chapter 3), in these final three chapters I address larger questions about the politics of the neuro-image. As a general preliminary remark I would like to emphasize that neuropolitics is not to be confused with politics in an ideological sense. Ideologies are an overarching aspect of the political, of course, but they are formed on the basis of all kinds of schizoid, "real illusionary," and affective-aesthetic principles at work on our brain-screens, which involve micropolitical movements and are largely connected to (collective or individual) unconscious operations. Concurrently, these micropolitical movements are very much entangled with macropolitical and ideological forces. Therefore, to consider the political dimensions of the neuro-image, we must pursue a multilayered analysis of various political lines of forces that are at work simultaneously, taking into account the manifold levels on which images can operate in reality.[1] I want also to emphasize that in discussing the political dimensions of the neuro-image, I certainly do not wish to imply that all things neuropolitical are simply "good," let alone propose something like a neuronal ideology.[2] The fundamental openness and dynamic character of the neuro-image allows a diversity of appropriations, adaptations, and operational strategies, good and bad, productive and counterproductive (these are precisely its schizoid characteristics). Nevertheless, coming to grips with some of these complex and mostly invisible dimensions of how images work on our brains, and how (consciously or unconsciously guiding our memories, perceptions, and actions) they operate in the world, is important if we are to disentangle their political dimensions.

I concur here with William Connolly, who, in his book *Neuropolitics: Thinking, Speed, Culture*, has addressed the complexity and speed of contemporary life in terms of what he calls a democracy of "deep pluralism" that is "nourished by a generous ethos of engagement" that recognizes first and foremost the micropolitical operations of our brains.[3] Connolly identifies that in spite of the potentially negative aspects of "the accelerated pace of life, inscribed in public media, military weaponry, Internet communications, technological development, cinematic practice, air travel, population mobility, and cultural exchange," these are the very same changes that are "indispensable to pluralization and democracy."[4] The up-tempo world will make people more fluid and creative, even if that creativity can also be used to reinforce state power or can create all kinds of fundamentalisms to pose blocks of fixed identities (as "safe havens") in the sea of data, images, and possible ways of life. Neuropolitics is thus related to a micropolitics of the mind (both the individual and collective mind), macropolitical norms, institutions, ideologies, and strategies. It acknowledges many directions and dimensions at the same time (not just the ideologically "right" one). When elaborated within these political dimensions, our schizoanalysis of the neuro-image will point out both its creatively empowering and dangerous aspects.

Connolly, too, links neuroscience, cinema, and Deleuzian philosophy. In developing his theory of deep pluralistic democracy, however, his main reference is Nietzsche, who, though by no means regarded as a democrat himself, nevertheless experimented productively with refashioning democratic thought.[5] One particular contribution of Nietzsche's that is fundamental to Connolly's work is a conception of the present moment as a "rift of time." Connolly's description enables a political perspective to be applied to the temporal metaphysics of the neuro-image as a manifestation of the third synthesis of time and the eternal return (described in Part 2 of this book). It is worth quoting Connolly here at length. Referring to Nietzsche on "the Moment" from *Thus Spoke Zarathustra*, Connolly states:

It appears at first that Zarathustra supports a linear conception of determinism against the dwarf's cyclical picture of eternal return. That would be ironic for the thinker himself reputed to be a proponent of eternal return. But such a reading soon dissolves into another that folds eternal return into an acyclical philosophy of time. What returns is the dissonant conjunction of the moment. In every moment, the pressure of the past enters into a dissonant conjunction with uncertain possibilities of the future. The fugitive present is both constituted by this dissonant conjunction between past and present and rendered uncertain in its direction by it. Often enough that uncertainty is resolved through continuity, but below the threshold of human attention indiscernible shifts and changes have accumulated, sometimes finding expression in small mutations and sometimes in large events. So occasionally time forks in new and surprising directions. A rift in time, engendered by the dissonant conjunction between complex systems with some capacity for self-organization and unexpected events not smoothly assimilable by them. A rift through which at any moment a surprising fork *may* emerge, ushering microscopic, small, large, or world historical shifts into an open future unsusceptible to full coverage by a smooth narrative, sufficient set of rules, or tight causal explanation. . . . Politics is rendered possible and dangerous by the constitutive rift in the moment.[6]

Translated into the terms I have put forward in connection to the neuro-image, it is possible to argue that Connolly demonstrates how neuroscreens (the indiscernible shifts and changes in our brains) and neurophilosophy (the rifts in time within the syntheses of time) relate to neuropolitics (small, large, or world-historical shifts). The difference that emerges in the rift of time (however infinitesimal it may be) leads to the "deep pluralistic" possibilities and dangers of the contemporary moment to which the neuro-image both testifies and contributes.

The three chapters in this last part of *The Neuro-Image* address different aspects of this deep pluralism of political engagement that results in all kinds of creative and possibly dangerous cultural forms. In Chapter 8 I look again at "the powers of the false" by addressing the fabulating powers of political cinema (in particular the Humian "divine interventions" of Palestinian filmmaker Elia Suleiman), putting these powers in the contexts of postcolonial theory and the critiques on Deleuzian philosophy from this branch of political cultural philosophy. In Chapter 9 I read the multiple screen aesthetics and "powers of affect" of the Iraq War to argue that multiplied screens present monadic perspectives of the war that engage in an infernal nomadic battle of screen realities but also call for affective engagement in a more democratic image regime. In the present chapter I return to the temporal dimensions of the neuro-image through a consideration of history as collective memory, or "world-memory," and in relation to the "archive fever" of contemporary culture. I will focus in particular on the strange "archival life" of *The Battle of Algiers* to show how time can change the "political life" of a film. I will conclude this chapter with a discussion of the political use of Deleuzian theory in real combat situations, addressing questions this has raised about the (im)possibility of artistic counterstrategies. The basic neurological and philosophical implications discussed in the previous two parts of the book are still at work as basic and implied principles informing these last chapters. In focusing on the political aspects of the neuro-image, however, those prior-developed principles and dimensions are assumed but not (often) discussed explicitly. The underlying position throughout, of course, is that images *as images* (documentary, fiction, analog, digital) operate on the mind, can change our perception, and are therefore a "political player," with consequences that range from imperceptible to global, from the most liberating to the most destructive.

The Open Archive and Hyperhistoricity

In his seminal book *Archive Fever* Derrida indicates in an important footnote that all engagements with archives are political: "There is no political power without control of the archive, if not memory."[7] He argues that the performances of democracies can indeed be measured by their level of participation, the access permitted to their constitution, and the level of interpretation permitted in relation to their archive(s). Furthermore, having always been critically attentive to the ways in which new technologies shape and manipulate our understanding of the world, Derrida refers in this book to new electronic media (such as email), and points out how these technologies give rise to new kinds of archives that involve new kinds of memory practices. While the traditional definition of the archive as "a place in which public records or other important historic documents are kept" (*Oxford English Dictionary*) is still valid, Derrida has argued that the archive is not just a (closed) place to shelter the past but that it is at the same time fundamentally open to the present and, especially, anticipates the future:

The archivist produces more archive, and that is why the archive is never closed. It opens out of the future.

How can we think about this fatal repetition, about repetition in general in its relationship to memory and the archive? It is easy to perceive, if not to interpret, the necessity of such a relationship, at least if one associates the archive, as naturally as one is always tempted to do, with repetition, and repetition with the past. But it is the future that is at issue here, and the archive as an irreducible experience of the future.[8]

Contemporary archival studies have taken Derrida's formulations of the dynamic openness of the archive further, analyzing very specific transformations of the archive and various memory practices these involve. Geoffrey Bowker, for instance, has studied memory practice in the sciences in terms of the relation between archival practices in different "memory epochs," as these correspond with scientific knowledge about the world (ranging from geology to biodiversity).[9] Bowker emphasizes the importance of the openness of archival systems and of access to any elements hidden in the "mnemonic deep" of the archive, that allow us, and it, to "unlock the present and to free the future."[10] Discussing biodiversity databases, he demonstrates that all elements in a database "contain complex histories folded into them, histories that must be understood if the data is to persist."[11] These hidden histories, including the forces behind the construction and disclosure of archival categories, selections, and (intended and unintended) uses, are important aspects of the open archive in a culture that is marked by a frenzy of the archive—a frenzy that is always already private and personal but is also a collective impulse.

In a comparable way Eric Ketelaar has discussed the openness of the archive in terms of the tacit narratives it contains. Each future use of the archive will change all of its previous meanings, and new meanings will continue to be added: "once we no longer assume that there is only one reality or meaning or truth, but many, no one better than the other, we can try to find these multiple meanings by interrogating not only the administrative context, but also the social, cultural, political, [and] religious contexts of record creation, maintenance, and use."[12] Working in a juridical context, Ketelaar demonstrates the openness of the archive by referring to the archives of the International Criminal Tribunal for Former Yugoslavia and the International Criminal Tribunal for Rwanda as "living archives." The archives are alive because judges, prosecutors, defense counsels, and other stakeholders engage them actively and ongoingly; their contents therefore will be "challenged, contested and expanded."[13] In this sense archives and other memory practices (such as memorial museums and films that in one way or another address historical reality) are political battlefields that contain and construct history and collective memories and allow the questioning of "monolithic Truth, History, and Memory," with the attendant risk that memories and identities are not arbitrated through one common version.[14] Such archives should be expanded, Ketelaar argues, by linking content to other (non)governmental agencies that continue to collect material about the conflicts involved; by gradually releasing classified documents as far as protection of witnesses, privacy, and state security permit this; and by allowing people to enrich the official records with their comments and stories.[15] Clearly, new media technologies are important tools for opening up the past of archival memory into the needs of the present and the future. In another text, "Exploitation of New Archival Materials," Ketelaar refers to other media technologies that extend the records of the archive: "The use of new archival materials often implies the construction of a new document. Still pictures, moving images and recorded sound from one or from different archives are used to create a documentary film. The user of a data film creates a new file, in which the data from the archives are merged with data from other documents."[16] This re-use is part of the dynamics of the living archive. Open archives, therefore, are characterized by ongoing contestation and extension that is increasingly facilitated by different new media technologies.

One last aspect that I want to bring into this outlining of the openness of the archive is specific to the audiovisual archive and, in particular, cinema's relation to time. In *The Emergence of Cinematic Time* Mary Ann Doane gives a rich account of early cinema and its double movement of capturing the instant (by chance) and archiving the past. Among many other early films, Doane refers to one of the earliest screened for an audience, the famous *Workers Leaving the Factory* (Lumière Brothers, 1895), and asks what exactly is being archived in the preservation of this early film: the details of costumes in 1895, the gestures of the workers, the patterns of light and shade across the entrance, or the film as a meaningful artifact? Arguing that "the two salvaging or preservative processes—that of film as historical artifact and that of the moment as historical event, as lost presence—are inextricably intertwined," Doane demonstrates that film not only preserves time (the past), but also preserves an experience of temporality, a "now" that has become "then." Additionally, referring to Derrida, she argues that the archive is "always a wager about the future: a future screening, a future interpretation."[17] So cinema, because of its inherent temporal dimensions, seems to be an object par excellence of archival openness. Here it has to be noted again that this temporal dimension is a characteristic of cinema in general; since its beginnings, this complex temporality has been part of cinema's fascination. The movement-image, time-image, and neuro-image only offer different dimensions of this aspect (dimensions based in the motor-sensory present, the coexistence of the past, or the open future; all discussed in connection to Deleuze's three syntheses of time in Chapter 4).

Doane's insistence on the interpenetration of film's archival function and its instantaneity and contingency is even more evident in contemporary image culture, where anything can be filmed at any time and uploaded to the Internet—now a giant open archive (or "viral archive," as opposed to institutional archives, which in their openness tend to offer more mediation).[18] Doane mentions the demolition of the bombed-out Alfred P. Murrah Building in Oklahoma City that was filmed by live television but is also available in many digital forms. The countless images of the falling towers of the World Trade center on 9/11 are, of course, another case in point, showing that in spite of the differences of filmic, electronic, and digital technologies, all these images "hold in common a core and formative indexicality and a strong investment in the lure of instantaneity."[19] As Doane explains, indexicality and the power of chance lie in "the absolute discontinuity of the instant, which enables the emergence of the new."[20] It is remarkable how Doane's reference to the Peircian index as an "absolute discontinuity of the instant" corresponds to the Nietzschean "rift of time" that Connolly describes as a "dissonant conjunction of the moment." Deleuze's "pure difference" seems to be hidden somewhere in the indexical moment that makes its renewed repetition possible and that makes the archival filmic image open for the future.[21]

It is important to note that, once understood as a temporal sign, the indexical aspect of the moving image does not change in analog, electronic, or digital images, even if the *belief* in a link between the image and the world becomes more apparent or important in the digital age. Digital images can be more easily manipulated than analog ones, and because of their accessibility, their indexical relations are open to more interpretations; however, as powerfully demonstrated by Doane, analog images also already carry this contingency inside of them. This does not mean that there are no differences between analog movement-images and time-images, and digital neuro-images, but the differences are of temporal dimensions and transformations, not of essence. In her book *From Grain to Pixel* Giovanna Fossati discusses the problem of indexicality from the perspective of film archivists. She, too, does not see the transition to the digital as a fundamental change in film as an archival object; even though the digital offers important new (or more effective) tools and new questions for archival practice, including new means of providing access, film has always in a sense been dynamically "in transition." Being conscious of the fundamental openness of the archive and its object, rather than merely recalibrating that openness backward from the present (i.e., through a digital lens), Fossati calls for a theory of archival practice that can offer an understanding of "the archival life of film, namely for understanding films once they have been archived, restored, digitized, in other words, historicized by archivists."[22] We will, perhaps, grasp such an understanding of the "archival life of film" in the next section by delving into the many projections, vectors of rediscovery, and transformed reception of *The Battle of Algiers*, a film that has become part of world-memory through so many complex archival processes and movements.

Before looking in depth at this film, I wish to emphasize that in our discussion of the open archive, the concept of "archive fever" as an intense desire for historical images is not only relevant to documentary images but also relates to fictional forms that equally contest and expand the open archive. Contrary to Fredric Jameson's argument in *Postmodernism, or, The Cultural Logic of Late Capitalism* that history is disappearing in Hollywood's nostalgia for the past and that we live in posthistorical times, contemporary cinema (as fictional form) can be frequently seen to offer new perspectives in a living archive.[23] Here I agree with Gilles Lipovetsky and Jean Serroy, who in *L'écran global*, hold that in the frantic logic of our hypermodern times and excessive image culture, memorial practices and "hyperhistoricity" are deeply engrained into our screen culture. Instead of seeing this as a loss of history, Lipovetsky and Serroy show that there is a fundamental democratic potential in these (fictional) additions to the archive of world history. The "monolithic truth of history and memory" is increasingly contested and transgressed: "In cinema one has passed from the standard genre of the historical film, to a much more dispersed historical thematic that is impregnated in all genres, from comedy to drama. A new cinema is developing, moved by a political or transpolitical will to reappropriate historical 'blocks' that were previously hidden and to celebrate different collective identities."[24] In other words, although the question of the indexical is even more open in fiction films than in, for instance, documentaries, many contemporary films refer more or less indirectly to historical events—questioning official versions of history or offering powerful and affective insights and perspectives that are important in understanding the complexities of history, memory, and their political implications.

Lipovetsky and Serroy give further explanations for this change. First of all they recall the classical historical films that are well established generically: the peplum film, the sword film, the pirate film, the biopic, and the western are all classic genres that evoke the past as past, mostly as a glorious past. Slowly, however, this past as clichéd past has given way to the larger traumas of history. Even if Resnais in 1956 in *Night and Fog* had to remove images that implicated the French police in the deportations of the Jews, this remains one of the first films to indicate the shifted interest of cinema toward history. Lipovetsky and Serroy also mention films such as *Apocalypse Now* (Francis Ford Coppola, 1979) and *Shoah* (Claude Lanzmann, 1985): "The film that speaks of yesterday, does so for today: the past is contested and judged. The ways in which cinema now approaches history testifies to the great change in respect to history in hypermodern society: history, told as a past past, becomes memory, in other words a past that is problematized in the present."[25] In other words, "contested and judged" history becomes a living memory in an open archive.[26] Lipovetsky and Serroy further specify this new memorial cinema in two categories: films that put the present in the past (the neohistorical film) and films that give a past to the present (the memorial film).

Films that put the present in the past no longer try to recreate the past to "look old" (faire ancient), as did classical historical movies such as *The Ten Commandments* (Cecil B. DeMille, 1956) or *Cleopatra* (Joseph Mankiewicz, 1963). In the neohistorical film, characters speak the language of today; the present is perceptible everywhere in the past. Lipovetsky and Serroy mention Sofia Coppola's *Marie Antoinette* (2006), with its modern soundtrack, and *Braveheart* (Mel Gibson, 1995), in which Mel Gibson's William Wallace appears more like a punk rocker than a thirteenth-century Scottish warrior. As Lipovetsky and Serroy argue, this cinema gives a punch in the face to the myths of history. Contemporary memorial cinema focuses not on great legendary events or heroes but on the history of peoples. Presenting a humanized past, this type of historical cinema also revisits the past but adjusts it according to the insights and changed needs of the present, giving the present a different past. The examples Lipovetsky and Serroy give are mainly French and most contest France's colonial past.[27] They mention in particular *Indigènes* (Rachid Bouchareb, 2006), a film that brings back into memory the forgotten or even occluded involvement of North African soldiers in the liberation of the French from Nazi Germany. Besides the fact that this film led to the actual belated funding of veteran North African pensioners, the point that Lipovetsky and Serroy make is that through filmic fiction, the particular memories of North African combatants become part of the national French collective memory. Unanimous history has now given way to polemical forms of memory (which can prove dangerous when taking the form of a battle of closed identities, yet can just as easily have potential emancipatory power).

In terms of Deleuze's syntheses of time and image types, it is possible to say that the classical historical film described by Lipovetsky and Serroy gives a habitual image of the past in a first synthesis of time. The time-image's relation to the past is actually not so explicitly discussed by Lipovetsky and Serroy; however, if we consider films like *Hiroshima mon amour* or *Muriel*, we can determine that the past returns in these films differently, as a dimension of the second synthesis of time—involving the pure past, the nonchronological coexistence of layers of time—which confuses the characters and renders relations to the past unstable, opening it up. I argue that the neohistorical and memorial images Lipovetsky and Serroy define and describe are also the dimensions of the past of the neuro-image, or the third synthesis of time. They bring the past not only to the present, but also to the future (perhaps a people to come, to be created or recreated from the "mnemonic deep" of the open archive). These are the broad developments in film's relations to historical time. It is also possible to see these transformations within and around one single film: *The Battle of Algiers*. This film is particularly interesting to follow through history because it not only shows aspects of hyperhistoricity but also engages the database logic of contemporary culture. As such, it is a powerful example of the openness of the archival object and of how images can operate as political world-memory.

The Battle of Algiers as Hyperhistorical and "Prehistorical" World-Memory

For a long time *The Battle of Algiers* (Gillo Pontecorvo, 1966) has been one of the few Algerian films widely available (on film, video, and DVD) and with English subtitles. Besides its cinematographic qualities (which I will discuss shortly), this exceptional quality of archival disclosure and accessibility has made it possible for the film to occupy a central place in the imagination not only of the Algerian War of Independence but also of other wars of decolonization and of liberation in general. What I want to show in this section is how Pontecorvo's film has developed into what Deleuze calls in the time-image a "world-memory." Discussing the cinema of Resnais, he observes: "The different levels of the past no longer relate to a single character, a single family, or a single group, but to quite different characters as to unconnected places which make up a world-memory."[28] I will discuss the unpredictable journey and relations that *The Battle of Algiers* traces and articulates as a film, as it engages this definition of *world-memory*. I will also address the film's further development within the database logic of the neuro-image, a logic marked by hyperhistoricity on the one hand and a new form of posthistoricity, perhaps better conceived as "prehistoricity," on the other hand.

"A Memory of a Single Group"

The Battle of Algiers is a fiction film based on real events that took place in 1957 during the Algerian War of Independence (1954–62). The film shows the mounting tensions between the Algerians and the French, leading to torture and other unorthodox measures from the French side, terrorism and the killing of French civilians from the Algerian side. Many of the characters are based on real historical figures. Ali La Pointe (Brahim Hadjadj) was a leading figure in the Casbah during the actual Battle of Algiers in 1957. Ben M'Hidi (who was killed by the French in 1957) and Yacef Saadi (who was imprisoned but survived and plays himself in the film) were actual leaders of the FLN (*Front de la Libération Nationale*). Colonel Mathieu, the French colonel who is brought to Algiers to fight the FLN resistance, is based on Colonel Jacques Massu (played by the film's only professional actor, Jean Martin). The tortures and bombings staged in the film also took place in actuality. However, the film is not a documentary, and aspects of the history it references have been altered and staged for the sake of cinematographic rhetoric and poetry. For instance, the ending of the film suggests that after a period of relative calm following France's victory at the Battle of Algiers, sudden spontaneous popular resistance in 1960 finally drove the French away. In reality the French withdrawal was caused by a sustained and bloody insurrection by the Algerian people over the entire country, in terse conditions that took over a million lives. The augmentation of beautiful and haunting music by Ennio Morricone adds a powerful affective dimension to the events. Nevertheless, scenes were indeed staged in the actual Casbah of Algiers and were so realistically performed that many Algerians believed themselves confronted with the actual return of the French. Shot in black and white, and with an authoritarian voice-over commentary, the film looks in some sections like a newsreel, so much so that for the American release a disclaimer had to be added before the beginning of the movie, explaining that the film does not contain a single frame of newsreel footage and is not a documentary.

At its original reception *The Battle of Algiers* was considered one of the prime examples of so-called Third Cinema, a political film movement that came into existence in parallel to various movements and wars of decolonization in the Third World in the 1950s and 1960s. In their manifesto from 1969, Argentinian filmmakers Fernando Solanas and Ottavio Gettino gave this type of militant cinema its name and argued for its methods and impact as a cinema that would decolonize culture from the former colonizers. "We have to film with a camera in one hand and a rock in the other," they wrote.[29] *Third Cinema* refers to the minority political position of the Third World as it is explicitly addressed in these films, but the term is also coined as an aesthetic opposition to what Solanas and Gettino call First Cinema (Hollywood) and Second Cinema (European art cinema). First Cinema is Hollywood genre cinema, what Deleuze calls the action-cinema of the movement-image, in which events are plotted through the experience of one or two central characters who overcome a challenge in the course of their actions.[30] Second Cinema is auteur cinema, often an idiosyncratic reworking of classical genres, sometimes with nonprofessional actors. Second Cinema pays more attention to specific class realities, but the stories are also poetically universal, taking on the human condition in general. In Deleuzian terms the seamless montage (continuity editing) of the action-image has become a "montrage" of long takes and deep staging, and irrational cuts make it difficult to distinguish between the actual and the virtual. This type of cinema is broadly categorized by Deleuze as the modern cinema of the time-image.

In his book *Political Film* Mike Wayne gives several characteristics of Third Cinema.[31] It considers history as a Marxist dialectic process of change and contradiction. The raising of political consciousness is also very important in Third Cinema. There is always a critical engagement with the minority position. Finally, the film always speaks from a position within the culture that it speaks for. We find the hopes of Che Guevara for a united South America in films of Solanas and Gettino; in Egypt Yussef Chahine in 1963 directs the film *Saladin* to commemorate Nasser's nationalization of the Suez Canal; and in Algeria the struggle of the FLN is captured in liberation films, of which *The Battle of Algiers* is the most famous, with Ali La Pointe as an Algerian Che Guevara. In all these early Third Cinema expressions the idea of "the people" as a united force that can be represented and addressed is very strong. As Deleuze has famously argued, this sense of a united people no longer exists in the modern political film (which is instead based on a fragmented or even missing people, and marked by the disuniting forces of new dictatorships, poverty, civil wars, diaspora, and migration). I will return to this contention in the next chapter. Here I want to remain with *The Battle of Algiers*, which, as Third Cinema in its original conception, is considered as the proud "memory of a single group": the Algerian people. It is for this reason, too, that the film was initially forbidden in France. Only in 1971, after protests by Louis Malle and other filmmakers, was *The Battle of Algiers* released. Throughout the 1970s such screenings remained heavily contested.

"A Memory of Multiple Groups"

In the 1960s and 1970s several revolutionary groups all over the world used *The Battle of Algiers* as training material, lifting from it specific guerilla tactics against oppression and lessons in revolutionary cell organization. The Black Panthers, the Maoist Weather Underground Movement, the PLO, and the IRA are reported to have organized regular screenings of the film for their members. Apparently, the film was also Andreas Baader's favorite movie.[32] In this way *The Battle of Algiers* became paradigmatic for many other revolutions. In the film FLN leader Ben M'Hidi is accused by French journalists of cowardly using women's baskets and handbags to carry explosive devices that kill innocent people. M'Hidi's response, "Give us your bombers, and you can have our baskets," resonates with a guerilla approach in many different contexts. Here we see how a single film can turn into a transnational memory, part of a collective open archive, shared by multiple groups with similar political aims. The way in which the film gives political recognition to struggles for freedom and the emancipatory rights of independence partly explains its power and reception. The fact that *The Battle of Algiers* places much of its allegiance with the (Algerian) revolutionaries makes appropriation by other similar fights possible. Yet this is not the only reason for the overall impact of the film.[33] Much of its language is poetic and therefore touches universal affective powers. As Pauline Kael argued in her review in the *New Yorker* in 1973, the film shows the strength of the oppressed in a most dangerous kind of Marxism, a poetic Marxism.[34]

Mike Wayne and Murray Smith similarly argue that the film is not just told in the militant cinematographic language of Third Cinema.[35] Influences of Italian neorealism and European auteur cinema of the 1960s are clearly present in the film. It won the prize for Best Film at the 1966 Venice Film Festival and has strong elements of Second Cinema as well, in the mise-en-scène and montage style of certain scenes and with its black-and-white film stock. A prison scene at the beginning of the film, for instance, shows in a very restrained and sober Bressonian close-up sequence of eyes, how Ali La Pointe becomes a revolutionary at the sight of the execution of a compatriot. A famous image of Ali La Pointe sitting with a small child on stairs in the Casbah resembles the mise-en-scène and sequence of the father and son in *Bicycle Thieves* (Vittorio De Sica, 1948); the use of nonprofessional actors also helps to create a feeling of neorealist authenticity. All these elements contribute to the poetic force of *The Battle of Algiers*, opening up this very particular struggle to a level of universality that allows connections to and appropriations by other contexts.

The film also contains First Cinema elements. The plot is loosely constructed around Ali La Pointe as the film's hero, a criminal-turned-revolutionary of the Casbah of Algiers, who after serving some time in a French prison becomes a member of the FLN. Several scenes invite suspenseful identification, such as the famous sequence where Algerian women, dressed up like French girls, pass French checkpoints with bombs in their baskets and place them in crowded spaces in the French part of the city. The film itself is presented as a duel between two parties. In spite of the predominant allegiance with the Algerians, French points of view are not excluded. Indeed, while it can be argued that the film owes its existence to FLN leader Yacef Saadi approaching Italian director Gillo Pontecorvo and script writer Franco Solinas to film his memoirs of the battle (also passing on the book that he wrote in prison as a guide), it is noteworthy that Pontecorvo and Solinas pieced the film together using the memories of a disenchanted French paratrooper. Accordingly, the film also addresses the motifs and strategies of the French militaries against the guerilla attacks of the Algerian FLN. The original trailer of 1966 is clearly also edited in a Hollywood style. Over four minutes, the trailer classically sets up two opposing camp positions in a typical Hollywood narrative of reckoning between arch opponents. These "Hollywood" elements make the film even more open and accessible to a larger audience. In sum, it is possible to argue that, besides its explosively political contents and its grounding in political Third Cinema traditions, much of the film's acclaimed success and influence is due to the formal openness of its cinematographic language and its inclusion and specific mix of Second and First Cinema elements within the dimensions of Third Cinema.[36]

"A Memory of Quite Different Characters"

French-Algerian power relations in *The Battle of Algiers* have often been compared to similar relations underlying the Israel-Palestine conflict. In 1988, during the First Intifada, the film was shown for several months at the Tel Aviv cinémathèque and used in political arguments both for and against the occupation and escalation of violence against Palestinians.[37] After 9/11 and the chaotic dynamics of the global war on terrorism, *The Battle of Algiers* found yet a new audience: in 2003 the film was screened at the Pentagon. In 2004 it was rereleased theatrically in the United States and Great Britain, and a new Criterion DVD edition was brought into distribution. The film was found useful among members of the US government as a tactical lesson for military operations in Bagdad. As reported in the *Washington Post* and *New York Times*, one of the Pentagon invitation flyers read, "How to win a battle against terrorism and lose the war of ideas. . . . Children shoot soldiers at point blank range. Women plant bombs in cafes. Soon the entire Arab population builds to a mad fervor. Sound familiar? The French have a plan. It succeeds tactically, but fails strategically. To understand why, come to a rare showing of this film."[38]

Here, instead of lessons in revolutionary guerilla tactics, the film is used as a prime example of antiterrorist tactics and strategies. The fact that both Ali La Pointe and Colonel Mathieu can be viewed as (action) heroes (and matched rivals) certainly makes reverse or dual political identifications possible. Stephen Hunter suggests this in his comments on the presumable attraction of the "elegant, swift paratrooper" and the equally presumed secret admirations for the "well-motivated urban guerilla fighter" among the "boys and girls with metal on their shoulder boards in that five-sided horizontal skyscraper where the Defense Department nests."[39] Apart from this, what more does *The Battle of Algiers* have to do with Baghdad? Charles Freund explains:

Terror. The Mideast learned the efficacy of insurgent terror from Algeria. The PLO, Hamas, and other groups are indebted to the Algerian strategy of so-called "people's war." Its lessons are now apparent in Iraq, too. Yet the film treats the Algiers terror campaign as a failure: its later bombings and shootings are made to appear increasingly desperate and strategically pointless. "Wars aren't won with terrorism," says one key revolutionary. "Neither wars nor revolutions." But that depends at least in part on how the other side reacts to terror, whether the other side is France in Algeria or the United States in Iraq. Wars may not be won with terror, but they can be lost by reacting ineffectively to it. This is where *The Battle of Algiers* is potentially most valuable and most dangerous as a point of comparison for the U.S. military. While *The Battle of Algiers* has next to nothing to say about the overall strategy of the French in Algeria, its most obvious military lesson—that torture is an efficient countermeasure to terror—is a dangerous one. Aside from its moral horror, torture may not even elicit accurate information, though the film seems to suggest it is foolproof.[40]

The prologue of the film immediately connotes unorthodox interrogation methods as "foolproof" when we see how an old Algerian man, after having been tortured, reveals the actual hideout of Ali La Pointe. Colonel Mathieu's "cool" tactic is to make the enemy speak and then put him in a French uniform. In a later scene Colonel Mathieu replies to a critical question from a French journalist with a counterquestion: "Should France remain in Algeria? If your answer is still 'yes', you must accept all necessary consequences," implying torture as a necessary means of interrogation. Although the situation of the French in Algeria and the Americans in Iraq is not the same, from Algiers to Abu Ghraib and Guantanamo Bay is not such a long way to travel, historically or imaginatively. At its very end, however, the film also implies that these violent military strategies will not stop the (Algerian) people, even if the continuing violence and bloodshed that came with the remainder of the war is not shown. We might surmise that in spite of all the differences between the French-Algerian war and the American-Iraq war, *The Battle of Algiers* could be said to function like a "strange attractor" in collective memory, operating in the present in micro- and even macropolitical ways.[41]

In the last chapter of this book I will return to the war in Iraq and its multiple mediating screens. At this point, however, I want to make two additional remarks about *The Battle of Algiers*. The first concerns its interpretive limits, and the second takes account of its continuation and transformation in digital culture. The cinematographic qualities and political influence of *The Battle of Algiers* are undisputed, but the "script" of the film can be said to be limited in terms of the identifications and referentiality it promises. Although the film's allegiance with the Algerians is obvious, Mike Wayne notes that the film has an even larger field of view that continues also from the outside, "from the perspective of the bewildered Europeans."[42] Because much of its language is poetically abstract (those Second Cinema qualities), we never attain much insight into the motivations, ideas of, or conflicts between the FLN guerilla fighters. Another aspect that makes *The Battle of Algiers* less a Third Cinema film is its inattention to key historical circumstances and events. For example, the unbearable conditions of colonialism that led to massive unemployment, illiteracy, and poverty in Algeria, and the massacres in Setif on 8 May 1945 (the day France was liberated from the Nazis), when an Algerian demonstration for freedom in Setif was met by extreme violence from the French (with casualties estimated between five hundred and forty-five thousand, depending on the source), are not at all part of the affectively powerful and universally poetic rhetoric of *The Battle of Algiers*. This does not make the film less relevant for our analysis; instead, it indicates that there are many indexical moments left open in the film that both enable and demand extension and contestation. As Lipovetsky and Serroy have argued, much of the film's historical or contextual limitations are overcome by other media that give additional information, alternative points of view, and revisions of the causes, events, and consequences of this specific war of decolonization. Our audiovisual archive and collective memory continue to grow in hyperhistorical media culture.

The role of the Internet as information source (such as historical websites on Setif) and distribution channel cannot be underestimated in this respect (nor can DVD distribution or online distribution networks). The Criterion edition of *The Battle of Algiers* comes with two additional DVDs that provide background information about the war, its players, the making of the film, the director, and the actual events that followed 1962. Some of the older Algerian films made about the War of Independence are now available. *Chronicle of the Years of Embers* (Mohammed Lakhdar-Hamin, 1975), for instance, shows the background and material circumstances of the revolution mixed with different thoughts about the armed revolt among the Algerian people. *Un peuple en marche* (René Vautier, 1963) shows unique historical material about the war from the perspective of the guerilla fighters in the Algerian mountains and the incredible hope and dignity of the Algerians in the year that followed their victory. In addition to these and other early films that were hidden in film archives and finally distributed thanks to digital technologies, later films have taken up many "forgotten" aspects of the Algerian War and thus added new images to the collective memory and popular consciousness of the past. In the Algerian civil war in the 1990s, fundamentalists strictly prohibited cameras, and almost no images were produced during this period (this war is known as "The War Without Images").[43] In France the historical archives of the Algerian War are still not completely open, although the continuing protest of historians contributes to the impossibility of their closure, for example in the persistent attention given to the terrible events on 17 October 1961, when many peaceful FLN demonstrators in Paris were beaten to death and thrown into the Seine.[44] Filmmakers of second-generation migrants, who came to be known in the 1980s as Beur filmmakers, filmed the deplorable situations of young men in the French suburbs and started to go back to the past and return to events of the War of Independence according to their families' experiences. *Vivre au paradis* (Bourlem Guerdjou, 1998), for instance, tells the story of the filmmaker's father's generation, who lived in the slums of Paris during the events of 17 October 1961. More recently, in films such as *Nuit noire, 17 octobre 1961* (Alain Tasma, 2005), made for French television, the involvement of the French police is explicitly addressed. Through Michael Haneke's *Hidden* (2005)—not by accident a typical ("universal") Second Cinema film with political dimensions—the traumatic event of the Algerian War has definitively become part of world-memory. It goes without saying that traditional historical and archival research remains of basic importance, but it seems that the disclosure of history in both fiction and documentary images puts *The Battle of Algiers* in a hyperhistoric context that allows many more perspectives to open up the archive and images to exert their own influence on our collective memories. In this way *The Battle of Algiers* and its additional images has increasingly become "a memory of quite different characters."

"As to Unconnected Places"

There is one other aspect that is striking and necessary to mention regarding the transformations of *The Battle of Algiers* as an open archival object. Comparing the trailer of the rerelease of the film in 2004 to the original trailer, it is interesting that the film's new context is explicitly addressed in textual inserts, which proclaim: "The most explosive film of the 1960s is now the most important film of 2004" and "Banned in France in 1965. Screened in the Pentagon in 2003." Further, it is striking that the length of the trailer is considerably shorter (almost half the length of the original at 2.23 minutes), and most of the narrative exposition is now cut to a rhythmic montage of image flashes. Although there are still clearly two camps, the French and the Algerians, it is much more difficult to distinguish in this trailer—which uses the same images of the film but to a different intensity and in a different order—which bombs and explosions are the work of which camp. In line with the schizoanalytic logic of contemporary culture, the affective dimensions of the images have become more important. We see here how quite literally the rerelease of *The Battle of Algiers* is constructed in the form of a retake of the past, without changing actual events that have happened, but that selects and reorders the past according to different intensities. With its rhythmic affective impact, the new trailer draws out this changed intensity. The reedit also reveals that the original film is actually composed via a database logic that allows these recombinations. Of course, it is possible to see any film as a collection of images that are combined in a certain way, mostly according to a narrative logic.[45] Nevertheless, *The Battle of Algiers* seems to carry this logic very explicitly in its open aesthetics. As such, it behaves "as a machine that winds time and folds place into complex configurations that stream multiplicity, ambivalence, play."[46]

Marc Laffia and Fang-Yu Lin have taken this database logic of *The Battle of Algiers* as the core conceptual inquiry of their online artwork that they conceived for the Tate Intermedia Art program, entitled *The Battle of Algiers* (2006).[47] Their project description states:

This *The Battle of Algiers* deemphasizes the film's dramaturgic components, focusing on the film's modes of movement, its meanderings and collisions, its speeds and drifts, its points of intensity, its lines of force, its fluxes and flows. This *The Battle of Algiers* brings the database to the fore, articulating and amplifying the film's multiple trajectories. The film's images become the cells of this piece—echoing the cellular structure of the FLN—and we are able to see the film's dynamics more clearly.[48]

This version of *The Battle of Algiers* mixes its images not only according to the stylistic logics of Third, Second, and First Cinema but also on a molecular ("cell"ular) level, folding and unfolding in many directions. Ali La Pointe, for instance, appears as much as he disappears in the film's ambiguous layers. As Laffia's and Lin's work shows, the images are like a database flow. Visitors to the website can experiment with this database, clicking on different cells that form algorithmic patterns. Narrative chronology and identifiable locations disappear in a dynamic flow that instead delivers the "pathos of war,"[49] as world-memory comes about through lines and actions that traverse "unconnected places."[50] Here, on the other side of hyperhistoricity, occurs a sort of "prehistoric" floating of history, the elements of which can be recombined in unpredictable ways, bringing out many additional perspectives on history itself, making us more conscious of the complex layers of historical events and their relation to the present. It also shows that at the basis of this hyperhistoric consciousness is a nonhistoric or prehistoric molecular (cellular) dimension of a database logic— one that becomes more explicit within the database logic of contemporary digital culture. On the one hand this database logic allows the opening of the archive to more and revised historical knowledge,[51] and on the other hand it makes history more vulnerable to an overflow of seemingly unconnected data, pure pathos, and "inappropriate appropriations" that make contextual information (about the various perspectives) all the more important. These seem to be the benefits and risks of the increased openness of the archives of history, which sees images operating more and more in our collective consciousness. In respect to *The Battle of Algiers* we can conclude that it has become a "strange attractor" of history. As an open cinematographic archival object, Pontecorvo's film is another neuro-image avant la lettre, which, in its digital afterlives, reveals its "neuro-image-aspects" even more powerfully. It forms our imagination of the Algerian War of Independence, other wars of decolonization, terrorism, and counterterrorism in the past and the present. But, as shown in this section, this imagination (as creative micropolitical movements of the mind, including powers of the false), insofar as it is strongly connected to political realities, also informs macropolitical actions and reactions.

Walking Through Walls: Two Forms of "Smoothing Out Space"

In its report on the Pentagon's screening of *The Battle of Algiers*, the *Washington Post* announced that "one hopeful sign is that the military is thinking creatively and unconventionally about Iraq."[52] Creative and unconventional thinking in military warfare is also the subject of Eyal Weizman's remarkable article "The Art of War," which discusses the ways in which the Israeli Defense Forces are influenced by contemporary philosophy.[53] Weizman mentions especially the military's familiarity with Deleuze and Guattari's concepts of smooth and striated space in *A Thousand Plateaus*, Guy Debord's concepts of *dérive* and *détournement*, and contemporary theories of architecture. I have traced some of the creative and political implications of *The Battle of Algiers* as "world-memory" by looking at the different groups that have taken the film as a strategic model for quite different battles, but there are other "creative lessons" hidden in Pontecorvo's film that relate urban guerilla tactics to the philosophies mentioned by Weizman. *The Battle of Algiers* shows a form of unconventional warfare that is not fought on a battlefield but in the urban environment of narrow and labyrinthine streets, where the enemy can be anywhere, unexpectedly turning up around a corner, on a rooftop, or from points on all sides. The organization of the enemy is cellular and nonhierarchical, and women, too (or men dressed up as veiled women), can turn out to be enemy forces. Furthermore, having more knowledge about the urban environment, space is for the Algerians in the Casbah "smoother" than for the French. One of the military "microtactical actions" that *The Battle of Algiers* demonstrates as an effective strategy is to simply blow up entire walls; through this means of drawing out Ali La Pointe and other resistance fighters from their urban hideouts, the French essentially recreate the urban space. Such methods are quite similar to the "operational architecture" of the Israeli Defense Force, which understands urban fighting as a spatial problem and refers to the concepts of smooth and striated space.[54]

Although Deleuze and Guattari proposed smooth space as that which escapes from striation in measurements and other forms of capture, control, or blockage (and thus can have resisting power), the smooth and the striated are never meant as fixed oppositional concepts but designate two coexisting forces in any environment.⁵⁵ Additionally, as Colonel Mathieu in *The Battle of Algiers* and the Israeli Defense Force make perfectly clear, the state can very well appropriate "smooth spatial tactics." Weizman has interviewed Brigadier General Kokhavi of the Israeli Defense Force, who described the attack conducted by his units on the city of Nablus in April 2002 as "inverse geometry" and "infestation" whereby they "moved horizontally through walls and vertically through holes blasted in ceilings and floors."⁵⁶ Weizman argues that militaries and military theorists are reconceptualizing the city more than architects are. Weizman quotes Kokhavi when he explains military spatial methodologies:

This space that you look at, this room that you look at, is nothing but your interpretation of it. Now you can stretch the boundaries of your interpretation. How do you interpret the alley? . . . We interpreted the alley as a place forbidden to walk through and the door as a place forbidden to pass through, and the window as a place forbidden to look through, because a weapon awaits us in the alley, and a booby trap awaits us behind the doors. This is because the enemy interprets space in a traditional, classic manner, and I do not want to obey this interpretation and fall into his traps. I need to emerge from an unexpected place. I want to surprise him. This is the essence of war. I need to win. . . . This is why we opted for the methodology of moving through walls. . . . Like a worm that eats its way forward, emerging at points and then disappearing. . . . If until now we used to move along roads and sidewalks, forget it! From now on we all walk through walls!⁵⁷

"Smoothing out space" is the tactical term frequently referred to. Nonlinear and fractal swarming operations, nomadic terrorism, and the war machine are but a few other Deleuze-Guattarian concepts utilized by the Israeli army that show an understanding that "belief in a logically structured and single-track battle-plan is lost in the face of the complexity and ambiguity of the urban reality."⁵⁸ Deleuze and Guattari have described that contemporary reality extremely well with their concepts, which, like *The Battle of Algiers*, are robust and open enough to accommodate extension into quite different contexts. When Weizman explains the attraction of Deleuze and Guattari's concept of complexity and ambiguity for contemporary warfare, it seems as if he describes scenes from *The Battle of Algiers* directly:

Identity can be changed as quickly as gender can be feigned: the transformation of women into fighting men can occur at the speed that it takes an undercover

"Arabized" Israeli soldier or a camouflaged Palestinian fighter to pull a machine-gun out from under a dress. For a Palestinian fighter caught up in this battle, Israelis seem "to be everywhere: behind, on the sides, on the right and on the left. How can you fight that way?"[59]

The only difference is that the guerilla fighting tactics of the Algerians in the Casbah have now been taken over by the Israeli army, and micropolitics have turned into state operational tactics, fluidly and creatively appropriated in a macropolitical matrix.

Now does this mean that Deleuze and Guattari's concepts are useless for political resistance? While many political and postcolonial theorists argue this is the case, a position that I will address in the next chapter, here I would like to suggest two preliminary answers. First of all, schizoanalysis has always accepted that production and antiproduction, resistance and counterresistance, are implied in one another, that the complex dynamics of the contemporary world both necessitate and make possible the creative uses of micro- and macropolitical strategies, and that each and all of these aspects can occur in strange combinations. Deleuze and Guattari continue to offer invaluable concepts to understand these dynamics—even if their concepts can be used in many different ways. (That is precisely the schizophrenic and potentially dangerous logic of the contemporary world.) Second, because the "archive" remains fundamentally open and dynamic, concepts, spaces, and images can also be reappropriated. It is here also that art remains of fundamental importance. As William Connolly has extended Spinoza's famous dictum about the unknown capabilities of the body: "Nobody has yet determined the limits of cultural capability." In his video *Walking Through Walls* (2010) Tom Tlalim investigates the Deleuzian conceptualization of space as taken up by the Israeli Defense Forces. The video shows images of new urban spaces in Amsterdam (Amsterdam South train station captured through a hole between two walls through which urban traffic is also visible), alternated with images of unidentified ruins and destroyed houses filmed by a mobile camera that "shoots" through walls and falls through holes. The soundtrack layers the images with ominous and anonymous electronic zooming, buzzing, and scratching sounds. At one point, footsteps, the sound of typing on a keyboard, and a copying machine become audible. These sounds indicate yet other spaces.

Halfway through the twenty-minute video, Tlalim cites in voice-over Weizman's quote of Commander Kokhavi, given above. The spaces that until then have been ambiguous and anonymous become appropriated in some way. Without context the viewer is unlikely to know at this point in the film that these are the words of an Israeli commander (they could just as well be the words of a guerilla leader). Soon, however, Tlalim refers explicitly to the influence of contemporary philosophy on the Israeli Defense Forces and their military reconceptualizations of the urban domain. The images from this point juxtapose as commentary on the devastating spatial strategies of the Israeli army but go further to reference the counterinfluence of the military on contemporary models of urban architecture and business strategies. At the same time, however, the way these sources are used serves to contrast the artist's way of roaming spaces, as being without (military) purpose, drifting. The end of the video explicitly states an artistic desire: "Beyond borders and roadblocks to be able to walk following her ears and nose, without the repetitive urge to turn back and settle in one place. To be able to see into the future, the horizon, straight through her walls, to interpret the space as she wants." Although it is not completely clear, this is most likely a quote from Raja Shehadeh's "Palestinian Walks, Notes on a Vanishing Landscape" (mentioned in the credits of the film) and another counter to the military interpretation of "walking through walls." Tlalim presents a metareflection on the military appropriation and artistic reappropriation of the concept(s) of smooth space, as it (mis)translates across very different domains. What is most important is that Tlalim's *Walking Through Walls* indicates how art can continue to resist and, as art, can continue to operate on the micropolitical level of our neuroscreens, changing our perceptions and memories, thus relating to history and macropolitics, however small or imperceptible that resistance may seem, however tiny the opening toward the future may be. William Connolly has to be acknowledged here again in a summary of what is at stake in neuropolitics:

We simply know that it is important today to strive to actualize an ethos of deep, multidimensional pluralism. This is a domain where political speculation, experimentalism, and enactment draw upon resources of history, knowledge, and experience while stretching beyond them. As the great experiment proceeds, it is wise to pay attention to the registers upon which the cultural dispositions to closure or pluralism are established. Any vision of pluralism that fails to come to terms with the layered texture of being remains imprisoned in a narrow intellectualism insufficient to the world.[60]

In the next chapter I turn my attention to the films of Palestinian filmmaker Elia Suleiman to offer a much closer look at the ways in which art can offer nomadic experiments of resistance.

8

Divine In(ter)vention

MICROPOLITICS AND RESISTANCE

The radical complexity of Deleuzian philosophy and its concepts, including especially the schizoanalytic acknowledgment that any production carries with it its own immanent counterproduction (exemplified by the schizoid trajectory of *The Battle of Algiers*, becoming world-memory in the previous chapter), has caused many misunderstandings about its political implications.[1] In the summer of 2009 journalist Stephan Sanders wrote a devastating critique of Deleuze as a political philosopher of difference, a critique that exemplifies oft-heard objections against Deleuze's philosophy in general and its political implications in particular.[2] According to Sanders, the twenty-first century has indeed become Deleuzian, as Foucault once famously predicted, but only in the worst possible sense. Sanders argues that in our globalized age people have locked themselves up in radical differences (ethnic, sexual, and religious), and the world has consequently turned into a fragmented nightmare of minishelters, catering to microidentities or Crusoes conscious only of their own individual islands, living in ignorance of each other and connecting only in opposition through threats and terror.[3] Deleuze, he argues, is to blame for this: "[not to condemn Deleuze for his political views is] a crime, because precisely Deleuze, the revolutionary, who described himself as a pragmatist and a vitalist, needs to have his nose put in the misery that he, in a political-philosophical sense, has produced."[4]

Contemporary reality does indeed know multiple identitarian wars (the War on Terror being the most prominent), and the individualization of contemporary digital media and Web 2.0 does carry risks of creating millions of Crusoes, each on their own island. Cass R. Sunstein, for instance, in *Republic.com 2.0*, claims that Internet culture makes it possible to listen and speak only to the like-minded, with each person mixing and matching his or her own "Daily Me."[5] But is Deleuze's philosophy really to blame for all this? Isn't his philosophy of difference and repetition very much written against the conceptualization of difference as the difference of multiple identities, and an attempt to overcome established concepts of identities, by looking at a deeper level of reality situated below the threshold of the visible? In this chapter I will take up the "tribunal challenge" posed by Sanders and other political philosophers and postcolonial theorists who have rejected Deleuze's concepts because they are not politically accountable or, worse, supposedly only lead to the disasters of microidentities, ignoring one another or warring with each other. I will argue that the tragedy of Deleuzian philosophy is not that Deleuze's radical thinking has undesirable practical political effects in contemporary (media) reality but that his work is not yet fully enough understood in its metaphysical, epistemological, and aesthetic depths. In particular, the necessity of artistic vision and its relation to micropolitics causes much confusion. While Deleuze fully acknowledges that philosophy and art have very limited direct political power, he does not simply see them as forces that are separate from the realities of life.[6] On the contrary, as Joshua Delpeche-Ramey also has indicated, philosophical and artistic creativity in Deleuze is not something optional or of personal choice or taste: "it is a matter of survival; the visions filmmakers invent allow us to once again believe in this world."[7]

This oft-recited statement of Deleuze's about the necessity of cinema to recreate a belief in the world is rather enigmatic. To fully comprehend what it means, and how it can be seen as political, it is necessary and useful to call again for a cinematic partner in dialogue to offer up the important contributions and insights. Predominately, the work of Palestinian filmmaker Elia Suleiman guides my readings in this chapter. The films of Suleiman's trilogy—*Chronicle of a Disappearance* (1996), *Divine Intervention* (2002), and *The Time That Remains* (2009)—are considered here as creative redescriptions of a political situation (Israel/Palestine) that through their very construction show how art and philosophy engage seriously with the contemporary globalized world.[8] Further, I will show how the political implications of such constructions are situated on quite a different level than Deleuze's prosecutors prefer to conceptualize.[9] This chapter will come to show Suleiman's trilogy, and especially *The Time That Remains*, as a neuro-image of the third synthesis of time that is political in its creative relation to the future. To show how Deleuze can be understood politically, I begin by addressing some of the common objections to Deleuzian concepts raised from the perspective of political philosophy and postcolonial theory, especially Deleuze's take on representation and his concepts of (political) reality, the nomad, becoming-minoritarian, and the impersonal. These concepts are critical to our understanding of Suleiman's films. As in the previous chapter, my references to the brain and the neurosciences are indirect, although I remain within the overarching premise that artistic interventions work first and foremost on the (invisible) creation of new percepts, affects, and thoughts that are at the basis of any (political) change.

Deleuze and the Political: A Problematic Relation

As I have already indicated, Stephan Sanders is not alone in his critique of Deleuze. Since Gayatri Spivak's rigorous dismissal of Deleuze in her seminal article "Can the Subaltern Speak?" the significance of Deleuzian philosophy for postcolonial studies has been heavily contested.[10] Several postcolonial critics have argued that Deleuzian philosophy cannot take account of the political. Two basic charges are made against Deleuze (and Guattari). First, Deleuze's critique of representation as developed in *Difference and Repetition* and his emphasis on desire, lines of flight, and the virtual are seen to prohibit real material contact with, and any commitment to or navigable route through, concrete postcolonial and political reality. Second, Deleuze's philosophy is said to leave no room for the specific voices of (Third World) others; the political concepts he (often with Guattari) developed, such as the nomad, becoming-minoritarian, and the impersonal (or asubjective), are deemed problematic from a postcolonial point of view.

The first critique is formulated by Spivak, who writes against Deleuze's rejection of representation as the dominant "image of thought." Deleuze argues that thinking difference based on the principle of representation always reduces difference in relation to "a conceived identity, a judged analogy, an imagined opposition or a perceptual similitude," which makes the real, deep, and immanent difference, below the level of representation that conditions any representation, impossible to grasp.[11] Spivak, however, emphasizes the importance of both political representation (speaking for, *Vertretung*) and representation as in art and philosophy (*Darstellung*), which together make representation the most important concept for understanding the ideological nature of reality and hence for speaking about reality itself. Theory cannot afford to overlook representation in these two senses, Spivak argues. It "must note how the staging of the world in representation—its scene of writing, its *Darstellung*—dissimulates the choice and need for 'heroes,' paternal proxies, agents of power—*Vertretung*."[12] Deleuze's critique of representation is seen by Spivak as a refusal to deal with the real world (and accordingly, to act on it politically through the actual use of representation). Additionally, Deleuze's emphasis on desire (or "desiring machines") as the unconscious basis of culture and his claim that "we never desire against our interests, because interest always follows and finds itself where desire has placed it" is unacceptable to Spivak.[13] The suggestion that people could perhaps desire certain political regimes (such as fascism) downplays the role of ideology in forming the political subject. In a similar criticism of refusing to deal with reality, Christopher Miller reproaches Deleuzian thought for provoking a mystification of the virtual that leaves reality in a "now-you-see-it-now-you-don't limbo." According to Miller this imprecise "limbo" means that only "certified Deleuzians" can ever say whether reality and representation are left behind or if there is still contact with reality.[14]

The second general objection to Deleuzian (political) philosophy is that Deleuze also ignores the real (local) voice of experience and knowledge of the colonial or postcolonial subject, which remains absent in favor of a so-called universal, but in the final analysis Eurocentric, theory. Spivak argues, "The clearest available example of such epistemic violence is the remotely orchestrated, far-flung, and heterogeneous project to constitute the colonial subject as Other."[15] Miller also points to the problematic abstraction of "the other" in Deleuze's thinking: "Colonial and postcolonial studies have taught us, perhaps above all else, that 'the other' cannot be so quickly and permanently dissolved in abstraction."[16] In this respect Deleuzian concepts such as the nomad and becoming-minoritarian are considered particularly problematic. These concepts, which I will address more extensively in the following sections, are often considered part of a "politics of disappearance of local or indigenous knowledge systems."[17] The general fear is that becoming-minoritarian (understood here as becoming part of a minority) might lead to a literal becoming-imperceptible, a condition too familiar for so many minority individuals and groups and something that should instead be overcome rather than pursued. Similarly, the nomad concept is often argued incorrectly to romanticize mobility and fragmentation at the margins. This romanticizing is said to coincidentally perpetuate the terms of colonial discourse by holding on to a universalized and unmarked Western norm.[18]

In *Out of This World* Peter Hallward has developed such critiques even further to argue that Deleuze's ultimate aim is to reach escape velocity and disappear into an impersonal cosmic vitalism. According to Hallward, Deleuze's philosophy "inhibits any consequential engagement with the constraints of our actual world." He, too, argues that Deleuze has no concept of the other: "Deleuze writes a philosophy of (virtual) difference without (actual) others."[19] Concrete historical time or actuality cannot, according to Hallward, be taken into account, and Deleuze's emphasis on the loss of the subject in favor of asubjective vitalistic creation is considered "politicide."[20] In the conclusion of his book Hallward explicitly advises those who "still seek to change the world and to empower its inhabitants" to look elsewhere.[21] A more devastating "philocide" is hard to imagine. Many have already commented elaborately on the interesting one-sidedness of Hallward's reading of Deleuze, so I will not repeat those arguments here.[22] Nevertheless Hallward's negative reading of Deleuze's work as a philosophy of creation is useful to review, given that it brings together the key postcolonial critiques of political accountability and its lack in Deleuzian philosophy, including the claim that abstract notions such as "the virtual" and "the impersonal" are problematically situated "out of this world."

One problem that should immediately be cleared in response to the postcolonial critiques is the conception of the virtual as something "out of this world" and as "not related to actual reality." This is simply a classic misunderstanding of the virtual (perhaps a remnant of 1990s cyberculture conceptions of "virtual reality" perception as disembodied, otherworldly experience), in which the virtual is assumed to be opposed to the actual. For Deleuze the virtual is always connected to the actual but in a far more intimate way than by opposition. As I indicated in Chapter 4, the Bergsonian movements of the present that passes (actual) and the past that preserves itself (virtual) are tightly interwoven in "actualizations" and "crystallizations" in the first and second syntheses of time. This is particularly relevant in contemporary image culture, where all images (actual and virtual) refer to other images (actual and virtual). In a Deleuzian system of thought, then, it is wrong to see the virtual as "out of this world"—the virtual is an immanent force that has to be taken into account in *this* world. The consequence of this circulation between the virtual and the actual is that the virtual is also real (albeit on a more invisible level: in our minds, in memories, in fantasy or imagination, in the invisible layers of images and culture). The Deleuzian conception of the virtual is an important contribution to political theory precisely because of this different conception of the relationship between "reality" (actual) and "imagination" (virtual) that it offers up, when more typically, the political is conceptualized in terms of a relationship between representation and ideology. How to conceive this relation between the virtual, actual, and reality in a politically accountable way (the critical aspect that postcolonial critics have queried) will here be concretely developed through reference to the films of Elia Suleiman.

Burlesque Political Style:
The Violence-Laughter Circuit

In *Chronicle of a Disappearance, Divine Intervention,* and *The Time That Remains* Elia Suleiman returns to his native village in Palestine, Nazareth, which he presents in fragmented, sometimes tableaux vivant–like, scenes. He himself is the voiceless protagonist who acts as a silent mediator looking at the world, receiving images from the world and giving them back to us filtered through his consciousness. By way of this general aesthetic setup, Suleiman's films are often noted for the passivity

of their protagonist/director, who is argued to seem incapable of extending comprehension of the films' images into (political) action(-images).
Chronicle of a Disappearance "measures the gradual disappearance, following the Oslo Agreement, of Palestinian identity and agency in Israel. . . .
The main sense of the film is of passivity, in-fighting (reflecting the cor-
ruption of the newly established Palestinian Authority), and paralysis."[23]
In *Divine Intervention* there is similarly "no progression, development or
resolution. . . . Progression has no currency here, there is only action and
reversal, an endless dialectic of aggression and response. . . . There is no
narrative structure to perform a revelation of 'truth' that suggest[s] an appeal to justice. There is simply repetition, accumulation of acts and no
'greater' meaning."[24] The films relate to a concrete political situation but
not in a classic representational way. Suleiman neither stands for all Palestinians (as *Vertretung*), nor does he follow the rules of classical representation (as *Darstellung*); these films do not give us heroes and agents of power.

It is possible, however, to read these dimensions of inertia and passivity in the performance of the director/protagonist more actively, as a
performative style that creates a distance from the director's own subjectivity. "I did not cast myself," Suleiman points out in an interview on the
Divine Intervention DVD. Rather, he explains being coaxed into the film
by the film: specific selections of images, actions, and situations, through
the impact of their data in conjuring meaning and still other data, create
a moving political document that in the end is quite radically *under*determined by the director's personal subjectivity. The result is a sort of
invented self-portrait, composed through the force and layers of meaning
delivered to the filmmaker by such specific selections. This downplaying
of his own (autobiographical) subjectivity turns his "absent'" and silent
acting into a "politics of the impersonal" that is also at the heart of Deleuzian philosophy. In his very last text, "Immanence: A Life," Deleuze pays
homage to the impersonal aspects of any individual life: "The life of the
individual gives way to an impersonal and yet singular life that releases a
pure event freed from the accidents of internal and external life, that is,
from the subjectivity and objectivity of what happens: a 'Homo Tantum'
with whom everyone empathizes and who attains a sort of beatitude."[25]

Let us have a closer look at *Divine Intervention* to see how Suleiman
addresses concrete political reality while going beyond representation, any

notions of the subject, and signification (a style that is consistent, in fact, across all of Suleiman's films).

Suleiman's style could be considered a "small form" (ASA) of the action-image, as described by Deleuze in *The Movement-Image* in a section addressing the contributions of Buster Keaton and Charlie Chaplin to action-image aesthetics.[26] Suleiman's unspeaking face could indeed be said to resemble Keaton's approach. However, in the way he performs and films, Suleiman is more of an heir of Chaplin, if we consider Deleuze's description of Chaplin's genius:

Because he knows how to invent the minimum difference between two well-chosen actions, he is also able to create the maximum distance between the corresponding situations, the one achieving emotion, the other reaching pure comedy. It is a laughter-emotion circuit, in which the one refers to the slight difference, the other to great distance, without the one obliterating or diminishing the other, but both interchanging with one another, triggering each other off again.[27]

Every scene in *Divine Intervention* actually appears in this way to set up a play between several associations or double meanings of a visual scene, creating with a minimum of difference a maximum of effect. The first time we meet the protagonist in *Divine Intervention* (at the beginning of the second part of the film), he is driving in his car, eating an apricot. We see him in profile, filmed close from the interior. When he has finished the apricot, he tosses the stone out of the window. It's a very simple and ordinary gesture. The image then cuts to a position outside the car: from a distance we see the car driving away, and we hear the stone of the apricot hitting something hard; a giant tank on the side of the road is briefly visible. At the sound of the apricot stone hitting it, it suddenly explodes. The image becomes a giant sea of fire. The protagonist does not notice the effect of his small gesture. He was only discarding the inedible remains of his fruit. He continues to drive. The contradiction between the small gesture and the enormous effect it has creates a Chaplinesque effect. We enter a laughter-emotion circuit, or more precisely a laughter-violence circuit, that is as comic as it is shocking.

Here we have an "impersonal performance": the director embodying his character as a man eating an apricot has little to do with his own subjective self, while at the same time he traces lines of life and lines of resistance that have everything to do with a life in Palestine. In this burlesque political style the question of the film's reference to reality is not irrelevant. At the same time, the spectator is delegated the decision of how many layers of reality one wants to see. Of course, the sudden appearance of a tank on a deserted road is significant, and its explosion is as well. Paradoxically, the blowing up of a tank can be seen as a pacifist gesture (getting rid of machines of war). The scene can be read as a figure of thought as well (the stone of the apricot symbolizing stones of the intifada; the tank a symbol for Israeli occupying forces). It might also produce a "bitter-sweet" reversal of the actuality of tanks destroying apricot (and olive) trees, with the virtuality of an apricot destroying a tank. In itself the whole scene is hilariously absurd, crystallizing allegorically the absurdity of the entire political situation . . . and the possible readings continue to grow.[28] The reader need not be aware of all readings to appreciate the scene in its rhythmic timing of the gag, but the possible layers of significance add to the pleasures and pains of watching the film. It would be just as erroneous to argue that reality here is in limbo, that the virtual leads us "out of this world," or that the impersonal or asubjective is apolitical or purely Eurocentric (as Miller, Hallward, and Spivak have argued). Instead, it is the level of virtuality—consisting of so many larger links *to* reality—surrounding the actual images that makes them so powerful, infusing them with sociopolitical and historical layers and weight. This is precisely the immanence of the virtual at work; it is ultimately political and of this world.

There are many other examples in which Suleiman plays with the ambiguities and multiple meanings of images in order to powerfully activate and construct the significance of the film in the mind of the spectator. Just before the apricot scene, three men in a garden are shown violently hitting something on the ground with sticks. The camera is at a distance and the garden fenced, so we can't know exactly what they are beating. "Knock out the vermin," we hear one of them say. Watching this scene, infamous video images of Israeli soldiers hitting Palestinians begin to resonate in our brains. A fourth man arrives with a gun and shoots at the "vermin" on the ground. More images of beatings and killings that circulate on the world news and YouTube pop up from our virtual/mental storage rooms. Then we see one of the men take two sticks and pick up the poisonous snake they have just killed. . . . The difference of the actual image from all the virtual images that had crossed our minds previously is not so great; the difference in the actual situations is enormous. Again Suleiman has played effectively with the "mist of virtual images" surrounding the actual images that he shows.[29]

A final example from *Divine Intervention* I want to mention in this respect occurs at the end of the film, where the protagonist pulls up at a traffic light. On the other side of the road, there is a giant billboard with a picture of a woman covered in a Palestinian Arafat shawl and text that invites Israelis to "come and shoot when you are ready." Then, next to the filmmaker's vehicle, a man wearing a kippah stops his car, the Israeli flag waving on the rooftop. Our artist-protagonist opens the window, puts on a music cassette, and looks (with dark sunglasses shading his eyes) at this man. Natacha Atlas sings her Arabic trance version of "I Put a Spell on You" as they keep on staring at each other; the traffic lights turn green and then red again, until the cars behind them start to hoot. This is a battle without words, without violence, a battle of pure image and sound, an exchange of ambiguous but loaded looks and music. The scene immediately following this one shows two forcefully gripped hands in an extreme close-up, which might easily be interpreted as a metaphoric commentary on the standoff between the two men we just saw, or even the two countries. However, just when we take on that reading of the image sequence, the frame shifts and the hands appear to be those of the protagonist helping his sick father (played by Nayef Fahoum Daher) get out of bed in the hospital, where he is staying after suffering a heart attack. This image of the "wrestling/helping hands" now also begins to resonate with a scene from *Chronicle of a Disappearance* in which Suleiman's (actual and at that time healthy) father's hands are captured wrestling with his friend's, and always winning. Whereas in many other scenes of Suleiman's work the images that seem to be private or ordinary turn out to be (virtually) political, here an image that seems to be political turns out to be a very private affair. The actual image of the father's hand as he is being helped out of bed is reminiscent of the strong hands he used to have. At the end of the film the father dies. The virtual brings in a notion of generational time.

In terms of the syntheses of time, we see here how *Divine Intervention* relates concretely to the virtuality of the pure past. In terms of Suleiman's own past (films), images from those pasts (such as the wrestling hand, images of his father at the kitchen table) return with a different intensity. But also in terms of the images of the past we have in our collective consciousness, the whole of the past is virtually present. Furthermore, all these scenes indicate the ways in which Suleiman reaches the impersonal dimension of immanent life by taking distance from himself and the political situation simultaneously (to which there remain obvious and continuous connections), as he constantly shifts between events in his personal life and observations that have collective and political resonances. He creates images that enter into circuits of the virtual and the actual and therefore are "swept towards the asubjective."[30] He does this (in part) by employing a burlesque composition of the image, typical for the small form of the action-image. Suleiman's inert performance and the images that open up to so many virtual dimensions could perhaps be considered the "burlesque of the time-image." The burlesque does not so much depend on small sensorimotor differences (as in Chaplin) but on small differences between the virtual and the actual. Violence and laughter therefore enter into a circuit of what could be called an impersonal burlesque political style.

Political Cinema: Fabulation and Double-Becoming

Suleiman's films can also be considered political in other respects, without following the laws of representation. As we saw in the previous chapter, Deleuze refers in *The Time-Image* to modern political cinema, especially films that address contemporary political issues such as decolonization, migration, and globalization.[31] Consistent with Deleuze's conception of cinema as movement-images and time-images that have immanent power independent of representation, this modern political cinema does not *represent* reality but instead operates as a performative speech act that plays a part in *constructing* reality.[32] In a postcolonial world characterized by fragmentation, migration, transnational movements, and intercultural encounters, some postcolonial scholars, including Stuart Hall, have suggested that representation in the classic sense is no longer possible or even desirable and that there has developed instead a "burden of representation."[33] For the filmmaker this implies that he or she can no longer *represent* a people but that, instead, his or her "fabulating" films can contribute to the *creation* of a people. A fabulation is an act or element of storytelling that is "not an impersonal myth but neither is it a personal fiction."[34] The relation between the filmmaker and his or her characters is one of becoming: "the author takes one step towards his characters, but the characters take one step towards the author: double-becoming."[35]

In his films Elia Suleiman is both director and character; a kind of double becoming takes place in his own performance, through which he becomes his own character. *Chronicle of a Disappearance, Divine Intervention,* and *The Time That Remains* are modern political films that create fabulations between the personal and the collective, between the objective and subjective, and between fiction and reality, expressing and addressing *both* the actual *and* the virtual as part of reality. In several interviews Suleiman discusses his way of working and the way in which he wants to renew the story of Palestine with his films. He explicitly addresses the question of fiction and reality, arguing that a film is real (it exists), but, at the same time, dreaming and the imagination are very much a part of reality:

What I'm trying to do is bring the imagination down and put the supposed reality up so that they are moving on the same, let's say strata. There is no rupture between one and the other, but they are blurred territory. The spectator imagines and decides for him- or herself what's real and what is not real. This is always an open question; we can never know for sure.[36]

Suleiman's reference to the "strata" and (at another moment in the interview) the layers (that is, the virtual, memories, associations) in his images corresponds to Deleuze's claim that time-images can link-up in an infinite number of ways and are therefore "stratigraphic":

In this sense, the archaeological, or stratigraphic, image is *read* at the same time as it is seen. . . . Not in the sense that it used to be said; to perceive *is* to know, is to imagine, is to recall, but in the sense that reading is a function of the eye, a perception of perception, a perception which does not grasp perception without also grasping its reverse, imagination, memory, or knowledge.[37]

Deleuze here calls for a new analytics of the image, one that is able to read this stratigraphic condition of the image in all its richness and virtuality. This implies, indeed necessitates, a different relation to the political than has traditionally been sought through the classic models of representation. As Deleuze has famously argued, the modern political film is based on the condition that "the people are what is missing."[38] Nowhere is this political fact of a "missing people" more explicitly acknowledged in Deleuze's work than in the case of the Palestine people. In a short article titled "Stones" Deleuze wrote:

Europe owes its Jews an infinite debt that Europe has not even begun to pay. Instead, an innocent people is being made to pay—the Palestinians. . . . We are to believe that the State of Israel has been established in an empty land which has been awaiting the return of ancient Hebrews for centuries. The ghosts of a few Arabs that are around, keeping watch over the sleepy stones, came from somewhere else. The Palestinians—tossed aside, forgotten—have been called on to recognize the right of Israel to exist, while the Israelis have continued to deny the fact of the existence of a Palestine people.[39]

Suleiman's films are modern political films in that they contribute to the "invention" of a missing people by "renewing its story" in a nonrepresentational and impersonal, stratigraphic way that allows a free play between reality and imagination, memory, and knowledge, with often humorous and empowering effects.[40]

An impressive symbol of that empowerment through imagination is the pink balloon the protagonist in *Divine Intervention* inflates at the checkpoint in Ramallah at which he normally meets his female lover, who comes from the checkpoint's other side. As the balloon grows bigger inside of his car, the face of Arafat printed on it becomes visible. The rooftop of the car is opened and the balloon escapes, crossing the checkpoint. The Israeli soldiers, baffled, wait for orders to act on a balloon crossing the border unauthorized as it travels over Jerusalem to land softly on top of the golden mosque. Here we see how a very simple balloon (its journey digitally enhanced by CGI to travel in perfect accordance with the filmmaker's wishes) can transform into a powerful image of resistance; and in the same moment, we truly perceive the fragility of the kind of resistance art can provide (it is a balloon; moreover, its journey is fictionalized in order to be successful). Suleiman's images here again open up to a whole range of virtual dimensions and references, including the globe balloon that Chaplin (as Hitler) plays with in his visionary *The Great Dictator* (1940), but also to the Second World War that was the start of the deep problems *Divine Intervention* addresses—the terrible extermination policies of the Nazis and the unimaginable confinements, invisibility, and genocide of the Jewish people. Most important, the film shows how explosively all of this past has recombined into a new present in which the stakes are very different.

Besides the burlesque strategy of *Divine Intervention* that puts us in a politically engaged circuit of violence-laughter, the stratigraphic conflation of imagination and reality is another way in which the political is taken into account in a virtual/actual circuit. One does not need to be a Deleuzian to disentangle these layers. It is precisely that the actual and virtual layers *cannot* be disentangled and are always so mixed that makes the film so powerful, aesthetically and politically. And we have seen how other Deleuzian concepts, such as the paradoxical combination of the violence-laughter circuit, the impersonal fabulating powers of political cinema, and the stratigraphic layering of (political) images, are useful for understanding this complex interweaving of the virtual and the actual in contemporary media culture.

Nomadic Thinking: Mixing Codes, Outside, Intensity, Humor

The Deleuzian concepts of nomadic thought and nomadic subjectivity "have led to a plethora of work within poststructuralist theorizing that strongly privileges notions of mobility, movement and becoming over conceptions of being, essence or stable subjectivity."[41] This Deleuzian notion of the nomad is also the one that has perhaps most stirred postcolonial debates about the politics of his philosophy. As I have mentioned, a general concern regarding the poststructuralist conception of the "nomad" is that it becomes yet another unmarked universalized Western subject that does not acknowledge the voice and experience of the (indigenous or minoritarian) other: it marginalizes local knowledge and experiences.[42] Taking these objections seriously, let us look again at Deleuze's essay "Nomadic Thought," so that we might first discern Deleuze's original thinking and then consider whether or how those principles of the nomad find concrete and specific expression in *Divine Intervention*.

"Nomadic Thought" was published in 1973 and developed as a consideration of the importance of Nietzsche for the contemporary world.[43] Deleuze points out that Nietzsche's key concern is to address cultural codes (family codes, state codes) in a new way, for the purpose of "getting something through in every past, present, and future code, something which does not and will not let itself be recoded. Getting it through on a new body, inventing a body on which it can pass and flow" (253). Clearly, Deleuze is drawing connections here between the fundamental import of creativity in Nietzsche, the repetition of difference developed in *Difference and Repetition*, and the temporal implications of the syntheses of time (discussed elaborately in Chapter 4 and at the end of this chapter). "Nomadic Thought" suggests that such valuable production of the new can be achieved by "mixing up all the codes," an activity that is especially noticeable in the artistic style of a work (a style of writing, a style of filming). This mixing up of codes into something new that is not coded is, according to Deleuze, "what style as politics means" and what he calls "the beginning of the nomadic adventure" (254, 260).

Importantly, Deleuze actually defines nomadic thought in terms of an artistic experimentation in style that nevertheless has political relevance—precisely because of its rendition of the escape from established codes. In this sense *Divine Intervention* is a nomadic adventure, not because it represents a "nomadic" (in the sense of a fragmented, multiplied, drifting) people but because it stylistically mixes several codes in the way that Deleuze outlined. If the dominant code in cinema is Hollywood, this film plays with the cinematographic codes and escapes them by seeking to, in Suleiman's words, "Bresson-ianise *The Matrix*. I wanted to break away from the ghettoisation between the *auteur* film and commercial cinema. . . . You can entertain aesthetically, politically, authorially. Entertainment is not necessarily superficial or ephemeral."[44] The scenes discussed so far demonstrate the ways in which the filmmaker mixes expected codes to create something new by bringing the actual and the virtual, private and public, violence and laughter together in challenging mixed circuits of a burlesque political style.

The scene that most clearly mixes the stylistic codes of the auteur film, the political film, and Hollywood cinema, but also the codes of religion, politics, and pop culture, is the much-discussed scene at the end of

Divine Intervention. Israeli soldiers are captured as they are target training, firing at targets that depict the image of a Palestinian woman (previously seen on the billboard earlier), dressed in a long black Matrix-style
coat and covered in a Palestinian shawl, who magically comes to life. Janet
Harbord comments on the sequence:

The action sequence of a human figure rising magically into aerial combat recalls the martial arts set pieces of recent transnational films, the potency of the
body matched with special effects, a particular configuration of technology and
the body from popular film. This is mixed with the symbols of a Palestinian national state, and the Christian reference as a reminder of the history of this space
as a "Holy land."[45]

This image, first observed by Suleiman when driving in Israel, is described
by the director as a "sparkle from reality." In this final scene he takes it
"up" into the realm of the imagination, adjusting the movements of the
soldiers to appear more like choreographed dances and the image of the
woman to come alive and participate in a martial arts combat scene. This
nomadic mixing of codes enacts a virtual, fantastic, entertaining escape
from what may have otherwise existed in this scene of target practice as
always-already "death by representation."

A second principle of nomadism that Deleuze distinguishes in "Nomadic Thought" is its relation to "the outside." This principle does not
refer to a state of being or of thinking that is "out of this world." On the
contrary, it refers to the ways in which a work of art shares something with
worlds and experiences "outside" of its apparent or internal frame of reference and, further, the ways in which the work of art or film itself actually
heeds those forces of life outside itself. At the same time, the outside is
not a feature of completed (artistic or philosophical) "works" specifically.
Deleuze explains the concept using the example of psychoanalyst Donald
Winnicott's realization, in relation to a patient, that at a certain point he
is no longer translating, interpreting fantasies into signifiers and signi-
fied, but instead has put himself in the patient's shoes. In the same way,
philosopher and artist do not simply represent reality but share in the
experiences they present:

We are in the same boat: a sort of lifeboat, bombs falling on every side, the lifeboat drifts toward subterranean rivers of ice, or toward rivers of fire, the Orinoco,
the Amazon, everyone is pulling an oar, and we're not even supposed to like one

another, we fight, we eat each other. Everyone pulling an oar is sharing, sharing something, beyond any law, any contract, any institution. Drifting, a drifting movement or "deterritorialization."[46]

Deleuze goes on to point out that we find something beautiful when it relates to something beyond its frame:

What is this: a beautiful painting or a beautiful drawing? There is a frame. An aphorism has a frame, too. But whatever is in the frame, at what point does it become beautiful? At the moment one knows and feels that the movement, that the line which is framed comes from elsewhere, that it does not begin within the limits of the frame. It began above, or next to the frame. . . . Far from being the limitation of the pictorial surface, the frame is almost the opposite, putting it into immediate relation with the outside.[47]

The outside opens up the interiority of the text or the image (or Winnicott's own person), relating it to the invisible because virtual, but very real, forces in the world.

   At other instances in Deleuze's thought these virtual forces are specifically related to a universal consciousness of becoming-minoritarian (to which I will return in the next section) and also to the external forces of intensity. Intensity is thus a third principle of nomadism and closely related to the outside:

The lived experience is not subjective, or not necessarily. It is not of the individual. It is flow and the interruption of flow, since each intensity is necessarily in relation to another intensity. In such a way that something gets through. This is what is underneath the codes, what escapes them, and what the codes want to translate, convert, cash in. But what Nietzsche is trying to tell us by this writing of intensities is: don't exchange the intensity for representation.[48]

The coappearance of love and pain, as this opens to the intensity that refuses to supplant such intensity with representation, is in Suleiman's film our signal of this political nomadic aspect: love for the land, love for the father, love for a woman; pain for the land, pain for the violence and frustrations in the Israeli-Palestinian conflict, pain for a lost love. In the interview provided on the *Divine Intervention* DVD, Suleiman is asked about the meaning of the title of his film. Suleiman's answer is itself nomadic, in that it indicates a poetic license to mix codes. "Divine intervention" does not so much refer to something holy "but to something close to that," the director argues, namely imagination, which allows one to cross borders and checkpoints. When the protagonist loses both his father and his lover, the lover returns as an imaginary heroine. Whereas earlier in the film she has crossed the checkpoint just by walking past the soldiers in a sexy pink dress and high heels (which makes the watchtower collapse), in the martial arts sequence at the end of the film she returns as comic and aestheticized violent form, able to carve out a new story, a fabulated story, for the Palestinian people. In fact, such divine intervention (or divine invention) engages closely with Hume's concepts of fabulating powers and the divine that I developed in Chapter 5, which concluded by making a case for the contemporary relevance of Hume's Philo: recognition of the return of the mysteriousness of the concept of the divine, locatable in the realm of the imagination.[49]

The subtitle of *Divine Intervention: Chronicle of Love and Pain* relates to Suleiman's previous film, *Chronicle of a Disappearance*, which clearly addresses the disappearance of Palestine. (Its closing image, of Suleiman's elderly parents asleep in front of the television set as an Israeli flag marks the end of a broadcasting day onscreen, has been the subject of much political comment.) In Suleiman's words *Divine Intervention*'s subtitle "grounds the film's imagination," precisely by addressing lived experiences outside the frames of the image. Once more we see that the Divine and the Outside do not refer to an abstract virtual realm out of this world but to an interpenetration of the world, the outside and intensity of the text, the work of art and cinema. It is therefore through the artwork that we can share this "divinity." Joshua Delpech-Ramey points out something similar when he notices that if Deleuze talks about "God as light" in the cinema books, he means the light of film: "The 'divine part in us' Deleuze is thinking of here is not that which removes us from one another, but that which joins us most intensely together in the creation of a work of art: it is the efforts which culminate in the projection of a film—as Deleuze himself once put it, there is no intersubjectivity except an artistic one."[50]

In addition to the mixing of stylistic codes, the relation to the Outside, and the notion of intensity contrasted with representation, Deleuze indicates in "Nomadic Thought" that humor is the fourth characteristic of nomadism:

Call it the "comedy of the superhuman" or the "clowning of God." There is always an indescribable joy that springs from great books, even when they speak
of ugly, desperate, or terrifying things. . . . You cannot help but laugh when you
mix up the codes. If you put thought in relation to the outside, Dionysian moments of laughter will erupt, and this is thinking in the clear air. . . . Laughter in
Nietzsche always harks back to the external movement of humours and ironies,
and this is the movement of intensities.[51]

This other kind of *playing* with codes and with spectator's coded expectations is clearly part of the joy of *Divine Intervention*, making it such a
wonderful nomadic experience. Clearly, this "nomadic" film experience
does not literally take us on a journey, nor is it about a diasporic movement of people. Even if the journey goes nowhere and takes place in a
single space (the "Holy Land"), *Divine Intervention* infuses our perceptions and thoughts with its visionary nomadic and impersonal wander-
ings/wonderings. Its laughter is laughter in the midst of the intolerable, in
the midst of violence, and hence is laughter that is necessarily and vitally
related to the world.

The Splendor of the Impersonal: Becoming-
Minoritarian as an Affair of Everyone

Let us acknowledge that Deleuze's concepts are particularly difficult to accommodate within institutionalized postcolonial frameworks of
political representation and the critique of ideology, since they ask for a
philosophical framework capable of perceiving and affirming the reality
of both the virtual and the actual rather than a framework that critiques
the opposition between reality and ideological representation. The difference does not mean that Deleuze's work is apolitical; it is obvious that
his complex articulations of fundamentally mixed states, where the world
and our perception and consciousness are always layered with multiplicities, visions, memories, knowledge—in short, with virtualities—contribute something quite new to political theorizing. To more profoundly clarify and comprehend this difference between a representational framework
and a Deleuzian nomadic framework of thinking and artistic practice,
I would like to return once more to the "politics of the impersonal" by
comparing the violence in *Divine Intervention* to the violence in a recent

French television film, *Pour l'amour de Dieu* (*For the Love of God* [Ahmed Bouchaala and Zakia Tahri, 2006]), which in a very different way calls for "divine intervention."

In an essay on Deleuze's impersonal politics René Schérer explains that the impersonal power of Deleuze's philosophy of immanence implies a paradoxical logic. First, the impersonal of "a life" reveals itself most explicitly in a confrontation with death.[52] Think of the example in Dickens, given by Deleuze in "Immanence: A Life," of doctors trying to save the life of a rogue: "Between his life and his death, there is a moment that is only that of *a* life playing with death."[53] A second paradox lies in the implication that the most original and authentic expression of "self" can only be expressed by the impersonal, where "I" no longer has a subjective significance. To illustrate such "splendour of the impersonal," Schérer refers to the use of the impersonal pronoun *on* ("one") in a poem by Arthur Rimbaud: "On n'est pas serieux quand on a dix-sept ans" (One is not serious at seventeen). This "one" is not an "I" nor a "we" but the impersonal of "anyone" of which Rimbaud speaks; it addresses anyone young and in love, an "anyone" that is nobody in particular and yet exists as any body.[54] This paradox of the impersonal sets the stage for many other paradoxes implied in nomadic thought and is not easy to grasp from within a representational image of thought.

The television film *Pour l'amour de Dieu* takes this poem by Rimbaud as its framing device. At the beginning of the film the poem is read in a classroom, and the teacher explains that when one is young, one doesn't yet understand all the dimensions of love, life, and the future. *Pour l'amour de Dieu* is a film that follows a representational logic and directly addresses important ideological, religious, and identity problems of our times. It is the story of seventeen-year-olds Kevin and Meriem, both born in France of Algerian parents, thus representing second-generation migrant young people. Kevin is attracted to Meriem because she practices the religion from which he is completely alienated. He feels lost in postcolonial French society and finds certitude, purity, and pride in his Islamist brothers, who give him strict rules to adhere to and a recognizable, stable religious identity (so also the politics in the film is an identity politics). He seemingly is not conscious of the complexity of messages in the Koran, which include instruction in values such as tolerance, simplicity, and freedom of religious choice. When Meriem returns from a visit to Algeria, where she has seen her grandmother for the first time, Kevin, who now calls himself Mohammed, asks her to marry him. Referring to Rimbaud's poem again, Meriem reminds him that they are too young, not only to marry but also to be able to make decisions about more political issues, such as whether or not to wear the headscarf. (Meriem, in fact, decides to stop wearing a headscarf until she has developed a fuller understanding of all the dimensions encompassed by such an act.) Pushed by his friends, Kevin/Mohammed then kills Meriem, who they consider unfaithful. In the desperate aftermath of his deed and Meriem's death, Kevin/Mohammed turns on the gas in the kitchen of the Islamist meeting place. When he reconsiders this second act of violence and wants to call his friends to warn them, his eye catches a passage from the Koran that he could never fully comprehend when Meriem had quoted it: "If God had wanted it, everybody would believe." Kevin/Mohammed breaks down, imprisoned in a phone booth that frames him in his failed attempt to create a stable self. Not understanding the impersonal One of Rimbaud's poem, and replacing it with a destructive identity quest, Kevin/Mohammed can only find a "way out" when he breaks down, leaving a trail of violence without any laughter. The film shows in a classic realistic way, following a classic image of representational thought, that shelters and Crusoes/crusaders on their islands are no solution for the multiple identity crises and political challenges the contemporary world faces. To avoid this logic, one (as One) has to recognize a movement beyond it, to become nomadic in a Deleuzian sense. Indeed, it is the consequences and contexts of the lack of that impersonal movement beyond that this film explores and captures so poignantly and tragically.

In his essay on violence Fanon suggested that it was "the naked truth of decolonization that evoked the searing bullets and bloodstained knives which emanate from it";[55] in other words, violence was a necessary component of national decolonization processes in the Third World. As *Pour l'amour de Dieu* also indicates, in an ideological representational framework, this violence has turned into a postcolonial religious violence, where God is called on as a higher authority to justify a human judgmental and avenging violence based on identity politics. Such a call for divine intervention from "out of this world" does not seem to bring about any kind of greater good, nor any change of perception, nor a restoration of a positive belief in this world. In his own work Fanon himself powerfully acknowledges that in the long run violence makes life, any life, impossible, despite being necessary to reintroduce humankind into the world at specific historical moments. He explicitly addresses European peoples' roles in this process of working toward a global sense of humankind's presence to humankind: "To achieve this, the European people must first decide to wake up and shake themselves, use their brains, and stop playing the stupid game of Sleeping Beauty."[56] Nomadic thought and nomadic political art have a significant impact on such kinds of political awakening. By affecting us on an impersonal, universal level of One, anyone can be reached by the paradoxical pleasures and pains of violence and laughter, enabling the transformation of established visions of the actual world, and restoring our belief in a "divine intervention" that belongs to this world, is not the property of any one in particular, and, paradoxically, helps to create a people that are missing.

The "splendor of the impersonal" thus needs to be seen in connection to a becoming-minoritarian, which is always a process of disidentification and defiguration, indeed a flight from a (representational) image of thought of the face, which in its final stages will reach a becoming-imperceptible. This does not so much imply the becoming-imperceptible of a minority group (as postcolonial critics have interpreted and feared) as it does a change for anybody who enters into contact with this asubjective, impersonal level on which becomings take place. As Paola Marrati explains, the "man of becoming" must go unnoticed; there must be nothing special to be perceived from the outside. Becoming involves a becoming-everybody,

but "becoming-everybody" (*devenir tout le monde*) is not just a matter of being unrecognisable, of being like "everybody else." Deleuze and Guattari are playing here with the different possible meanings allowed by the French expression "tout le monde." Thus *devenir tout le monde* also entails a *becoming of everybody*, a *becoming-everything* and a *becoming of the world itself*. . . . Deleuze and Guattari oppose the figure of a *universal minoritarian consciousness* that in principle concerns everybody to the majoritarian "fact" that itself is the product of a state of domination, but is the analytical fact of *nobody*.[57]

Becoming-minoritarian is what Deleuze and Guattari call nomadic micropolitics, which is not related to any form of representation, either of majorities or of minorities. Its aim is to resist: resist power, resist the intolerable, resist fear and shame, resist the injustices of the present. Contemporary nomadic films function precisely as such micropolitical acts of resistance, first and foremost by proposing for the spectator an intensive, affective encounter that can provide a slightly new perception of the world. Becoming-minoritarian is shown in such films to be an affair of or for anyone. It does not lead us out of this world but directs us (through works of art) precisely to that which we share in this world, outside the framework of the work of art.

Kay Dickinson, in "The Palestinian Road (Block) Movie," gives an extended overview of this particular nomadic way that Palestinian films explore what contemporary cinema can do on a micropolitical scale:

> There is little sense that Palestinian movies will change anything—what films ever do in these earth-shattering terms—but the situation is constantly creatively picked over. For certain directors, making these rather anarchic films is a product of freedom of expression. . . . The movies are also conceived of as an archive of resistance for present as well as future use, concretizing its benefits in a location where change is rapid and destructive."[58]

With this emphasis on the creative reconstruction of reality comes the opening toward the future and hence the notion of time and the syntheses of time.

The Time That Remains: Nomadic Resistance in the Third Synthesis of Time

In an interview at Cannes on the occasion of the premiere of his film *The Time That Remains*, Suleiman relates humor (one of the characteristics of nomadic thought and nomadic art identified in this chapter) explicitly to the notion of time. Certain forms of humor, he suggests, including humor under oppression, help to gain time—time to sustain yourself a little longer in a situation of despair.[59] He adds that humor is related also to rhythm, tempo, musicality, and poetry, each being possible elements of resistance that aesthetically escape ideological representation, while nevertheless addressing political reality. Humor is thus part of a nomadic strategy of creating a "new time," a time for the future. Considering such comments, the "time that remains" can be seen in a double way: on the one hand it is the time that is preserved and thus time(s) from the past that remains, but on the other hand it can be considered the time that is still left open, the time still remaining to come, the future. I will come back to these senses of the title of Suleiman's film a little further on. First, let us consider Suleiman's trilogy as a whole in the framework of the different temporal dimensions of the syntheses of time that I have argued are so important in the conception of the neuro-image. Indeed, the three films in Suleiman's trilogy can be seen to belong to three different syntheses of time. As such, they invoke different temporal relations to resistance.

Chronicle of a Disappearance, the first film of the trilogy, is the film that belongs most to the first synthesis of time of the present (that has passed). The film is also partially rooted in the second synthesis of time, as Laura Marks has shown in her discussion of *Chronicle of a Disappearance*'s "thin-looking images" that call for attentive recollection of their hidden stories as "memories of images" in the time-image.[60] But every image type, even if it has its own dominant synthesis of time on which it is based (that synthesis's particular forms of relating to the past, present, and future), *also* relates (or can open up) to the other syntheses of time (with their respective forms of past, present, and future). In our comparative analysis of the films of the trilogy, then, we can quite accurately address *Chronicle of a Disappearance* as a time-image, which, next to its strong relations to the virtuality of the past, has significant openings to the first synthesis of time as well. The film is set in 1996, a present in which, after a long stay abroad, the filmmaker returns to his hometown, Nazareth. Suleiman films his (real) parents, Fuad and Nazira Suleiman, in their home as they meet with neighbors, clean fish in the kitchen, or sleep in front of the television set. The director himself (as his character) meets with two friends and sits with one of them for hours in front of the friend's souvenir shop, Holyland, silently observing passersby. The political present is the present of the 1990s: radio or television broadcasts address the Oslo Accords, the Balkan War, and the Algerian civil war. On these very concrete levels *Chronicle of a Disappearance* (as a time-image) addresses the first synthesis of time that roots the whole film also in the present of 1996. Openings toward the third synthesis of time are also noticeable, especially in the last part of the film. A Hebrew-speaking Arab woman gets hold of a walkie-talkie from the Israeli police and starts sending messages and directions to the police units in the streets that make the police cars seem to dance. Also throughout the sequence that captures the long drive to Jerusalem (the Golden Dome being sometimes visible) while Natacha Atlas sings "Leysh Nat'arak?" ("Why Are We Fighting?"),[61] the viewer is delivered a creative "picking over" of real situations that allows us to see things in a different way in the imagination, opening us to hope for the future.

Divine Intervention, the second film of the trilogy, is clearly anchored in the second synthesis of time. It is made in memory of Suleiman's father and, at a very personal level, restages the events of his illness and death (the father is played by an actor, who represents a present of the past). The filmmaker's love affair (real or imaginative) also comes to an end (or this is what is suggested when, toward the end of the film, the lover no longer arrives at the parking place next to the checkpoint, which makes the scene a restaging of a past present). *Divine Intervention*'s nomadic mixing of codes, its relations to intensities outside the frame, and its humorous use of fragile political symbols discussed earlier in this chapter are effective because they are based on the virtual (the past) adding layers to actual images. These images refer simultaneously to the virtual of history and politics outside the frame (the Israel-Palestine conflict), to the history of cinema (Chaplin, the burlesque), and to Suleiman's first film (the hand wrestling, but also the frequent images of men in their pajamas, the sound of a walkie-talkie, perhaps even the Golden Dome that appears again, this time as the landing point of the pink balloon). But from this second synthesis, the first synthesis also sometimes intercedes in moments where repetitions of habitual behavior are repeated: a man throwing garbage into his neighbor's garbage, boys playing soccer in a narrow street, repeated encounters between the lovers at checkpoints—these are all moments of habitual presents of the first synthesis of time. (And they become important elements in the timing of the visual gags when such habitual gestures are slightly differentiated from their previous repetitions.) The third synthesis creatively opens up the future when the lover returns transformed by the imagination as a ninja warrior to make the Israeli soldiers dance; less optimistically the future is announced in the final image of a pressure cooker that is not removed from the stove.

The Time That Remains can be considered a neuro-image by way of its temporal dimensions based in the third synthesis of time. At this point of creation both parents of the director have died; the subtitle is translated as *Chronicle of a Present Absentee*, which could refer not only to their continuing presence following their death but also to the presence of the past in the future. The film is partly based on Suleiman's father's memories, which Suleiman asked his father to write down before he died. In line with the hyperhistoricity of the neuro-image (discussed extensively in the previous chapter), *The Time That Remains* dramatizes and restages the past in ways that were previously only implicit as the virtual pasts of the time-image. Only now do we see the father as a young man, rebelling against the handing over of Nazareth to the Israeli forces in 1948, at the cost of torture. We see his mother as a young woman, writing letters to a relative in Amman, commenting on personal and political events in the course of that time (how young Elie is doing at school, how difficult it is to survive). Other political historical periods that are recalled include Radio Cairo announcements of Arab nationalism in the 1950s; the televised mourning of Nasser in 1970, depressing the whole neighborhood (one of the neighbors keeps on trying to set himself on fire); and the First and Second Intifadas. We access here "all of the past" leading to the construction of the Wall and to the increasing tensions of the contemporary situation in the Middle East.

Throughout these historical periods Elia—as a child, as a young adult, and as the adult filmmaker—is played by three different characters (Zuhair Abu Hanna, Ayman Espanioli, and Elia Suleiman himself). The scenes of the dramatized past are clearly written "from the future" because they announce what is going to happen later: Elie as a little boy is punished several times for calling American policy colonialist, or imperialist in another variation; this will lead to his expulsion from Israel when he is a young adult and his turn to filmmaking. The father is seen smoking like a chimney, despite frequent warnings from the doctor, and we know he will die of a heart attack. The mother complains as a young woman in one of her letters about her diabetes, and in the (globalized) present of the film she has an Asian caretaker who gives her insulin and is cross with her when she secretly eats ice cream at night (mother will die of diabetes). Further, this film's relation to "all of the past" is emphasized in the repetitions of scenes from the previous two films. As in *Divine Intervention*, we see the protagonist (with his back turned to the camera) staring out of the window of the hospital room where his father is taken, but here a different actor plays the younger Elia. Several other scenes are repeated from the previous two films but always with a difference that implicates (knowledge of) the future. The first part of the film can also be considered a long episodic flashback. Characteristics of the movement-image (and its past) return, too. Additionally, many time-images persist in frequent instances of the protagonist simply observing what is taking place. The fractal layering of times and image types becomes complicated and enfolded, which is typical for the neuro-image.

As I indicated at the beginning of this section, the "time that remains" can also be seen as the time of the future. We have just seen how in the neuro-image, in the third synthesis of time, the future is the basis of the past and present. Meanwhile, in the other two films we have seen how moments of imaginative recreation open the possibility of the future as a dimension of the third synthesis of time. Natacha Atlas singing for a reconsideration of the past and the cessation of fighting on the way to Jerusalem, the daring and simultaneously absurd image of the pink Arafat balloon over Jerusalem—both are moments in the first two films where hope for the future is called on. *The Time That Remains* also ends on a hopeful note. The protagonist, Elia Suleiman himself, characteristically observes scenes in a hospital yard where doctors, patients, visitors, and police officers walk, talk, and exchange cigarettes and greetings. The soundtrack then plays an Arabized Mirwais remix of the famous Bee Gees song "Stayin' Alive." Another moment of regained time is here nomadically playing out into the future.

There is one additional powerful image from *The Time That Remains* that should be mentioned here, which utilizes imagination to create dimensions of the future.[62] Between the historical time of the present of the 1990s captured by the hopeful drive toward Jerusalem in *Chronicle of a Disappearance* and the moment when the fragile balloon floats over the city in *Divine Intervention*, Palestine has increasingly turned into a prison through the construction of the Wall. In a dialogue with documentary filmmaker Simone Bitton, whose film *The Wall* (2004) has captured most powerfully to date the disastrous effects of the Wall, Suleiman praises Bitton for her famous opening images, which capture "the weight of time in the weight of the cement of the wall."[63] "This wall has to be filmed,"

Bitton insists. Bitton searches within the documentary tradition itself to show how cinematographic language can help fight the despair of another ghettoization.[64] Suleiman indicates that if he would (or could) film the Wall, he would have to find some small and personal way to relate to its reality from within his own fictional language. In *The Time That Remains* he discovers this technique. In one scene near the end of the film the protagonist stands in front of the wall. Then he simply runs toward it and takes a high jump—right over the wall. Like the computerized balloon over Jerusalem, the jump over the wall is digitally imagined but crucial for the imagination of a future. The wide-ranging conversation between Bitton (who is of Moroccan descent but grew up and lived in Israel) and Suleiman is interesting in many respects.[65] Yet what seems most profound about it, for the purposes of our discussion here, is that in their conversation around such a difficult topic, an Israeli and a Palestinian point of view are able to meet around cinematographic images. Furthermore, those cinematic images themselves are capable of addressing—via the micropolitical levels of our percepts, affects, and feelings—the experiences of living under the unbearable weight of history that has brought us to where we are now, as well as the qualities and dimensions of imagination and creation that find openings for the future.[66] In the next chapter I address the problem of perspective even more explicitly as we confront the multiple screens mediating the war in Iraq and the ways in which contemporary cinema addresses their conflicting and opposing perspectives.

Logistics of Perception 2.0

MULTIPLE SCREENS AS AFFECTIVE WEAPONS

Throughout this book the Algerian postcolonial situation, the Palestine-Israel conflict, and the war in Iraq have been discussed as important schizoanalytic world-historical political backgrounds for the neuroimage.[1] Indeed, as we have moved from the schizoid visions of *Alienations* (Bensmail's filmed mental patients discussed in the first chapter), to consider the spatial imaginative practices of the Israeli army, as well as the nomadic forms of resistant thought or divine intervention proposed by Elia Suleiman in his political trilogy, the Algerian model of terror and counterterror in particular has seemed to arise constantly to form different specific alliances with media. In *Watching Babylon*, Nicholas Mirzoeff's book on the war in Iraq and visual culture, Mirzoeff also refers to *The Battle of Algiers* and the Palestine-Israel political situation as explicit models and reference points for the contemporary global War on Terror. He rightly states that if Algeria is still the model, "the country's subsequent history of Islamic resistance to the Front Liberation National (FLN), culminating in the suppression of elections of 1991 and the violent civil war that followed, is a grim warning."[2] Mirzoeff further argues that the contemporary world can be considered as "the empire of camps." His analysis shows how Iraq has transformed into a refugee camp based "on the model of Israel's permanent war with the Palestinians in the Gaza Strip and on the West Bank." He critically explores the visual culture connected to the war in

Iraq, which, according to him, is characterized by a "banality of images" that renders us immune to the spectacle of war. "In the second Gulf War, more images were created to less effect than at any other period in human history," he argues.[3] Mirzoeff shows, in fact, how the "cinemania" of the contemporary world (to use Lipovetsky's words) has transformed war into the logic of a Hollywood script, whereby "Saving Private Lynch" is the lesser rerun of *Saving Private Ryan* (Steven Spielberg, 1998), and Bush's landing on the USS *Abraham Lincoln* appears as an afterimage of *Top Gun* (Tony Scott, 1986). This emphasis on the devaluation of the image in contemporary visual culture is a position Mirzoeff shares with Jean Baudrillard and Paul Virilio, who have both argued that reality disappears in the ever more accelerated simulacra of the real. Through these arguments (Hollywood) cinema might be deemed limited to roles of projecting (manipulating) images without value, or overshadowing concrete reality, perceiving the world as a bleaker version of spectacular Hollywood. Undeniably, much of contemporary media culture works according to this logic.

This, however, is not the whole story of the processes of visual culture. While Mirzoeff analyzes a small number of graphic cartoons, such as the series *In the Shadow of No Towers* (Art Spiegelman, 2003), as examples of exceptional and less banal images able to offer resistance, in this chapter I would like to look at the ways in which cinema itself has responded to the Iraq War. Recent (Hollywood) feature films about this war include *Redacted* (Brian De Palma, 2007), *In the Valley of Elah* (Paul Haggis, 2007), *Battle for Haditha* (Nick Broomfield, 2007), *Stop-Loss* (Kimberly Peirce, 2008), and *The Hurt Locker* (Kathryn Bigelow, 2008). I will also discuss *Valley of the Wolves: Iraq* (Serdar Akar and Sadullah Sentürk, 2006), which presents the war in Iraq from a Turkish point of view.[4] Among the many documentaries, *Fahrenheit 9/11* (Michael Moore, 2004), *The War Tapes* (Deborah Scranton, 2006), *Iraq in Fragments* (James Longley, 2007), and *Standard Operating Procedure* (Errol Morris, 2008) are of note.[5] All these films present strong investigations not only of the effects of the war but also of war's (digitally) filmed images, which operate through an overwhelming variety of contemporary mediated screens. Accordingly, they can be considered paradigmatic for the omnipresence of screens in the neuro-image.

The presence of multiple cameras and multiple screens in the Iraq War films is of course not a coincidence of surface-level stylistic decisions (at the level of production). As Paul Virilio demonstrates in his book *War and Cinema*, "the history of battle is primarily the history of radically changing fields of perception."[6] While Virilio addresses the "logistics of perception" of the First and Second World Wars, recent films of the Iraq War support his theorem of the relationship between war, technology, and changing fields of perception, which might now be called a logistics of perception 2.0. These films testify—in a less harmonious way than the transmedial storytelling and neobaroque aesthetics discussed in Chapter 6—to the ways in which contemporary culture is also a terrifying "schizo-Gesamtkunstwerk" in which Leibnizian monadic perspectives come together in the form of nomadic interventions to contest a battle played out across multiple screens. The screen has become a weapon in the sense that it works on our minds, in a psychological warfare. This oversaturation of spectacularized images and perspectives creates on the one hand an effect of disconnection or distance from reality as "pure spectacle." On the other hand, as this chapter will show, actual reality keeps on returning, as mediated by affective screens, to mobilize us politically and ethically in many different ways.

Cinemania at War: Waning of Reality in an Aesthetics of Disappearance

Virilio's work demonstrates how war and technologies of perception are closely connected and develop in mutual feedback. He further presents arguments for how perceptual technologies directly enter our brain-screens: "There is no war, then, without representation, no sophisticated weaponry without psychological mystification. Weapons are tools not just of destruction but also of perception—that is to say, stimulants that make themselves felt through chemical, neurological processes in the sense organs and the central nervous system, affecting human reactions and even the perceptual identification and differentiation of objects."[7]

Discussing the First and Second World Wars, Virilio gives many different aspects and examples of this relationship between war and cinema that works in both directions. Spectacle and propaganda are closely related: the first film studios in Germany were established during the First World War, and color films multiplied during the Second World War, when "they were the direct result of acts of logistical piracy" in a competition between Agfa and Technicolor.[8] Inversely, military observation techniques have historically led to creative cinematographic applications. The first battlefield observation balloon in 1794 used during the French Revolution indicates the close connection between the development of perceptual instruments and aviation. The military study of movement inspired the chronophotographic rifle camera of Jules Marey, one of the founding fathers of the cinematograph. These are but a few examples that demonstrate a larger history of entanglement of cinema technology and war logistics, wherein "aerial reconnaissance both tactical and strategic became chronophotographic and cinematographic";[9] film directors (e.g., D. W. Griffith) became war filmmakers; war pilots (e.g., Howard Hawks) became filmmakers. Virilio's argument in *War and Cinema* is much more elaborate than I can detail here, but his main observations give a first-level explanation of the remarkable presence of all kinds of perceptual technology in the most recent war films of Iraq. The military is an important source for the development of all kinds of perceptual technologies.

Meanwhile, of course, the situation has changed dramatically since the First and Second World Wars and the beginnings of cinema. In the context of the war in Iraq in 2003 (and after), it is crucial to go back to the perceptual logistics of the First Gulf War of the early 1990s, a war whose visual regime was most famously discussed by Jean Baudrillard, in addition to Virilio. Virilio's thesis about the ultimate implications of the war/spectacle logistics of perception is that it leads to an "aesthetics of disappearance." A similar argument is made by Baudrillard. In *Simulacra and Simulations* he describes the development of (mediated) images into pure simulacra in four successive phases: the reflection of basic reality, the masking and perverting of basic reality, the masking of the absence of basic reality, and finally the complete lack of relation to any reality whatever.[10] In his 1991 essay "The Gulf War Did Not Take Place" Baudrillard argues that the Gulf War was distanced and cleansed by image technology to the point that it became a purely virtual war (where he considers the virtual as not real, pure spectacle): "So war, when it has been turned into information, ceases to be a realistic war and becomes a virtual war, in some way symptomatic. . . . Everything which is turned into information becomes the object of endless speculation, the site of total uncertainty."[11]

The logical outcome of our increased spectacular warfare (and technologized society at large) is the dissolution of reality.

It is important to recall that the First Gulf War (1990–91) had a completely different strategy toward perceptual logistics than the Vietnam War (1959–75). In both wars television played a crucial role. As is well known, during the Vietnam War, photo journalism and television images changed the perception of the war internationally: images of the atrocities of napalm attacks and other horrific events effected a turning point in public opinion, which shifted from acceptance of the conflict as a "just war" to rejection of it as a "dirty war." Having learned from this, military perceptual logistics were quite different in the First Gulf War. In the intervening years television became a twenty-four-hour business, and the Gulf War made CNN the internationally (in)famous model of constant reporting. Television spectators worldwide were glued to their screens, which actually showed very little. Operations Desert Storm and Desert Shield were of a so-called clean war, and the camera remained at a distance to emphasize such a view of the war. Baudrillard therefore characterized this war as a nonwar,[12] where reported hostages took the place of combatants and "hostage value" became synonymous with the media simulation of the war: "We are all hostages of media intoxication, induced to believe in the war . . . and confined to the simulacrum of war as though confined to quarters. We are already all strategic hostages *in situ*; our site is the screen on which we are virtually bombarded day by day, even while serving as exchange value."[13] Comparing CNN to a stethoscope attached to the hypothetical heart of the war, Baudrillard denounces the specular and spectacular (cinemaniacal) logistics of a war that has no other object than deterrence and deception: "The war, along with fake and presumptive warriors, generals, experts and television presenters we see speculating about it all through the day, watches itself through a mirror: am I pretty enough, am I operational enough, am I specular enough, am I sophisticated enough to make an entry onto the historical stage?" Baudrillard concludes that our screens are invaded by an uncertainty,

in the image of that blind sea bird stranded on a beach in the Gulf, which remains the symbol-image of what we are in front of our screens, in front of that sticky unintelligible event. . . . We are left with the symptomatic reading on our screens of the effects of the war, or the effects of discourse of the war, or completely speculative strategic evaluations which are analogous to those evaluations of opinion provided by the polls.[14]

In other words television screens have become spectacular shields that hide the reality of war to the extent that that reality disappears, leaving us with nothing but speculations on reality.

Virilio makes similar remarks alongside Baudrillard in the 1990s: that the Gulf War has turned war into a spectacle that can only take place in a stadium, as a show.[15] Both Baudrillard and Virilio agree that the image has been dehumanized by a farewell to both the subjective eye behind the camera and the human subjects in front of the camera. As Virilio explains in *The Vision Machine*, the culmination of the progress of representational technologies in their military instrumentalization is "the complete evaporation of visual subjectivity into an ambient technical effect, a sort of permanent pancinema. Which, unbeknown to us, turns our most ordinary acts into movie action, into new visual material, undaunted, undifferentiated vision-fodder . . . [the total effect of which is] a waning of reality: an aesthetics of disappearance."[16] He calls this pancinematic aesthetics of disappearance the "dromoscopy" of contemporary visual culture, "the optical illusions experienced by the motorist whereby what stays still appears to recede while the interior of the moving vehicle appears stationary."[17] Our vision machines transform the world into accelerated spaces of perception that threaten to implode, in a logic of the "great lockdown, where inside and outside merge where the world is nothing but a gigantic phantom limb of hypertrophied humanity," which amounts to there being nothing to see.[18] In other words, according to Baudrillard and Virilio, the First Gulf War culminated in what could be retrospectively considered the logistics of perception 1.0.

This recognition that spectacularization leads to virtual wars of deterrence, and that the impersonal effects of surveying candid cameras leads to an aesthetics of disappearance, remains critically valid today. Nicholas Mirzoeff compares the spectacle of the Iraq War to the spectacle of the horror movie: "the constant return of the horror within each horror film, and its subsequent seeming eternal return in sequels, is the feuilleton of our times, chronicler of our boredom and fear alike."[19] Mirzoeff's notion of "constant return" is different from the concept of the eternal return that I have outlined in the previous chapters as the eternal return of difference in Deleuze's conception of the third synthesis of time. For Mirzoeff the constant return is conceived as the horror of the return of the same: nonprogression, exemplified by Babylon (Iraq) in opposition to the American narrative of progressive history. The image of Saddam Hussein, in particular, is analyzed in this way:

What is intriguing in all this is to ask why Hussein's body became uncanny for American viewers. Its uncanniness was a consequence of the doubled Holly-wood-style plotting of the war as a story. In the Hollywood action film formula, the complexities of the plot are reduced to a conflict between two leading men, often causing the villain to make mistakes in his pursuit of the hero. From the American point of view, this plot makes sense in interpreting the otherwise apparently "irrational" behavior of Hussein. This plot then intersects with that of the horror film in which, as every movie-goer knows, the monster proves remarkably hard to kill and keeps coming back from the dead.[20]

Here Saddam is seen as the ultimate uncanny oriental body that perpetually returns as a monster in the horror film. Mirzoeff considers the image as a weapon-image that, like the deadly videotape in *The Ring* (Gore Verbinski, 2002), jumps out of the screen and annihilates its viewer.[21] At the same time, he argues that the sheer quantity of such images during the Iraq War made no image of special importance, which leads to what he calls the "banality of images," a devaluation of images in their effect. Nevertheless, Mirzoeff also fully acknowledges the importance of the image, not just as a classic propagandistic tool but also as a performative operation: "The war image performs the American victory as an image and it is done. One might say that the war image asks its viewers to pledge, . . . 'in truth and in falsity,' the visual equivalent of the loaded dictum 'my country right or wrong.'"[22] According to Mirzoeff, then, the cinemaniacal logic of contemporary warfare makes all images flat and banal on the one hand, causing underlying reality to bleach and dim. On the other hand that same specular logic leads to wars being fought increasingly via images that become performative: the staged pulling down of the statue of Saddam Hussein is his (real) defeat, even if we know it is manipulated. The image may be banal, but it is on everybody's mind-screen. This power of the image is fully understood by the military propaganda machines. As Deepa Kumar argues in an analysis of war, media, and propaganda, "faulty and unverified information was repeated enough until, in true Orwellian fashion, falsehoods came to be accepted as truth. In order to keep these lies alive in the public imagination, the administration relied on the support of several well-funded think-tanks with easy access to the media."[23] In all these respects the "aesthetics of disappearance" announced by Virilio in his important analysis of the logistics of perception in war and media is clearly still at work in our contemporary wars, wherein an excess of information and images has caused both a devaluation of meaning and a reinforcement of the powers of the false in a manipulating sense. How to resist this deadly schizoaspect of contemporary culture?

Mirzoeff draws on Benjamin, who in his time turned to the epic as a "form of interactive story-telling that involved 'hand, eye, and soul' to find an alternative form of expression" that could resist too much spectacularization.[24] Mirzoeff argues that perhaps the graphic novel could provide a means of (what Benjamin called) preparing to survive civilization. Marjane Satrapi's *Persepolis*, Art Spiegelman's *In the Shadow of No Towers*, and a 2003 collection of comics from Israeli Dimona Comix are the epic graphic novels discussed by Mirzoeff that offer resisting points of view precisely in their aesthetics.[25] Of course, there will be other strategies as well. In the previous chapter I argued that a nomadic type of cinema can create little war machines that resist the madness of impossible political situations. Deepa Kumar hints at the emergence of participatory culture. In spite of the persisting logics of perception 1.0, something has also changed in our twenty-first-century logics of perception. Looking at recent war images, their multiple cameras, multiple screens, and multiple human subjects, it becomes difficult to maintain this concept of an ever-retreating reality, a desubjectification of the pancinematic spectacle of banal images as described by Virilio, Baudrillard, and Mirzoeff. Let me turn to one of the most striking Iraq War films, Brian De Palma's *Redacted* (2007), to begin my investigation into the contemporary logistics of the perception of war and assess what is at stake in the new visual regime of participatory multiple screen culture.

War and Contemporary Media: Battle of Screens, Explosion of Points of View

Redacted is based on a real event that took place in Samara in 2006 when a group of young American soldiers raped and killed a young girl and her family and set their house on fire. To tell this story De Palma changed the characters and some of the details; nevertheless, the plot does follow the real events, while also eerily resembling his earlier Vietnam film *Casualties of War* (1989). Indeed, history seems to repeat itself in the consideration of war-crime horror scenarios. Meanwhile, just as important as the story of the film is the way in which the story is told. In this, *Redacted* differs significantly from *Casualties of War*. In an interview the director explains that the material he wanted to use was that which is so widely available on the Internet: news stories, documentaries, pictures, blogs, video diaries of soldiers posted on YouTube—everything of relevance is already out there online, he says.[26] Yet, in bringing all these media together for his film, he had to fictionalize this existing material. He needed to restage not only events but also the different media screens themselves, with which such events are truly imbricated.

From its first moments *Redacted* foregrounds its perceptual technologies as the story unfolds through many different types of screens. A video diary by Private Angel Salazar (clearly staged but referring to the countless actual video diaries of Iraq soldiers) plays a central, focalizing role in absorbing and narrating the events. A French documentary with voice-over narration is another format through which the story unfolds. There are also Arab news channel reports, vérité camera recordings played on Al Qaeda sites, embedded journalist reports, Western news channel items, clips from Soldiers' Wives websites and from Get Out of Iraq campaign websites, military surveillance cameras, recordings from military hearings, Skype conversations, and actual pictures of collateral damage (that were redacted from De Palma's film for legal reasons). All these different formats and screens are entangled in complex ways and present different points of view of the same events told more or less chronologically, albeit with a few feedback loops that retell the same event from a different point of view.

Compared to the spectacular television screens of the First Gulf War, this aesthetics of *Redacted* is striking. As indicated above, in Virilio's writing the screen serves as a locus of the technological transformation of space and time, as a metaphorical site of acceleration and disappearance. However, as Anne Friedberg has argued, in the course of his work Virilio never makes any distinctions between cinema, television, and computer screens: "As Virilio's screens have multiplied in global extension, distinctions between them disappear, are lost," Friedberg points out.[27] We can recall here Henry Jenkins's urgings to consider media convergence not as the merging of all screens into a black box but in terms of a transmedial coexistence of multiple screens that are connected yet distinct in a vast global network. Accordingly, it seems the Iraq War films suggest that different types of screens, while interrelated, have different aesthetic, epistemological, and ethical implications. At the heart of their new logistics of perception there is a battle of different screens that translates into a literal conflict composed of points of view. Looking back to Virilio (and Baudrillard), it is possible to still consider parallels here with the logic of dromoscopic disaster and the implosion of reality. I want to zoom in further, however, to see if the different screens, while indeed all operating in a technomediated schizologistics of perception, can offer up any variations on these arguments.

Redacted shows us first of all that if we can speak of media convergence, it takes place on a metalevel in the sense that all different screens repeat, quote, or "remediate" other screens.[28] The computer screen, for example, "re-versions" television programs as streaming data or downloads. It offers a huge databank of cinema images ranging from the avant-garde to blockbusters, from experimental films to advertisements, from early cinema to the latest hypes. It offers information (wiki pages, articles), social spaces, blogs, and networks. Television, besides its own shows and news programs, also broadcasts old and new films and increasingly relates to websites, YouTube, and other digital media. Film aesthetics, in turn, are heavily influenced by digital media, not only in production, postproduction, and distribution but also in terms of the aesthetic remediation and citation of other media. This does not mean, however, that all these remediated screens lose their specific properties when they appear in another medium. *Redacted* includes a large number of other screens in its aesthetics, but it still is and performs as a film screen. Indeed, this film's reflexive "metascreen" aspect is now typical for the contemporary cinema screen of the neuro-image in general and of war cinema in particular. Therefore, before focusing on some particular types of screens, let me briefly investigate more specifically the most salient characteristics of multiple-screen conflicts as they are presented in a self-reflexive way in *Redacted*.

The war diary footage with which *Redacted* opens and which forms its narrative thread presents shaky images with lots of movement and handheld camera work. Through combining statements by the soldiers, such as "you are making a video of me making a video of you," with promises to take care of each other's videos should they die in combat, these war diaries confirm the soldiers' existence. Furthermore, the video diaries serve as testimonies of incredible day-to-day experiences. "No Hollywood narrative but the real shit," promises Private Salazar (Izzy Diaz), paraphrasing videographic desire for authenticity and truth (*Tell Me No Lies* is the title of the diaries). "Truth is the first casualty of war," Private McCoy (Rob Devaney) says to the camera of his friend. This may seem a cliché, but in view of the new logistics of perception, this aphorism seems not only to relate to the truth of what actually happens but also refers to the truth of the psychological experience of the reality of war. These images ultimately convey not a perceptual (spectacular) truth but an affective truth. I will return to this point later.

A quite different screen is presented by the French documentary in *Redacted*. Entitled *Barrage* (Checkpoint), its reflexive documentary mode comments on the realities of routines at a checkpoint in Iraq and has more distance from the events than do the war diaries.[29] The filmmaker is clearly an observer and not a participant in the action. The images are filmed in a classical cinematographic style, using stable camera work; the nondiegetic music is pacifying, and a female voice-over reflects on the soldiers' daily life-or-death decisions and on the difficulty of determining who is an enemy. There is also critical commentary about the number of innocent Iraqis killed at checkpoints. From a much more distant perspective than the war diaries, then, *Barrage's* images reflect on the moral decisions and ethical dilemmas the soldiers face, as well as the mistakes, impossible situations, and injustices of war.

Television news channels (Arabic channel ATV and European channel CEN) clearly present an additional media layer of conflicting points of view on the events of Samara. Compared to CNN's televisual monopoly on reports of the first Gulf War, it becomes a crucial factor that Arabic voices and discourses now reach the world through satellite television and online channels and sites. Biased truths presented as objective seem to be the main business of all such news channels during wartime. Military surveillance images introduce yet another type of screen that in De Palma's film shows the private thoughts of individual soldiers when they themselves speak among each other about their actions. The aesthetic of these images is typically grainy and mostly given as night shots. Other types of grainy images in *Redacted* include secret recordings produced near a checkpoint where a bomb is hidden. This camera also films the moment an explosion kills one of the American soldiers (an event we have first seen through the camera of Private Salazar's digital video). The recording is then shown on an Al Qaeda website as part of their guerilla tactics. Here, then, we see how the same event is for one camera a shocking accident and for another a weapon in the resistance against the Americans. Internet websites are also seen to serve multiple purposes: obviously as a means of communication—soldiers' wives leave video messages for their loved ones, and Skype video conversations allow direct contact with home—but also their political use is particularly striking. Both Arabic and American activists against the war publicize and network their images online to present videos of war crimes committed on both sides as evidence and as a call for action.

A particularly important aspect of contemporary media is that they are no longer monopolized by Western broadcasters, as I have already indicated. Not only official news channels but also insurgents and all kinds of activists have access to cameras and distribution channels. In their article "Filming Resistance" Walid el Houri and Dima Saber analyze the use of video images as a Hezbollah strategy in the fight against Israeli occupation in Lebanon.[30] They demonstrate how since 1986, when the first video of the securing of an Israeli outpost in Soujoud in occupied southern Lebanon was broadcast, Hezbollah has consistently filmed military operations that work like weapons, insofar as they have an empowering effect on the occupied population (the Lebanese, Arab, and Palestinian people) and a threatening effect on the Israeli population. (This latter effect is then picked up by Israeli and international media in its turn, and used again in different media contexts to show the dangers of Arab fighters and justify counter or preemptive actions; the spiraling logic is clear.) The same video, in other words, can be seen either as resistance or as terrorism. As El Houri and Saber indicate, "the videos have a double discursive power and are addressing two publics whose understanding of the visual message is opposed to the very opposition of terrorism and resistance and the 'cultural recognition' of each targeted group."[31] The battle of screens becomes a true battle of psychological warfare played out on many more brain-screens. Insurgent video propaganda is consciously used in this way: "Hezbollah soon discovered that its broadcasts had an effect not just on the Lebanese people but on the Israelis as well. 'On the field, we hit one Israeli soldier,' a Hezbollah official explained, 'but a tape of him crying for help affects thousands of Israelis. We realized the impact of our amateur work on the morale of the Israelis.'"[32]

By projecting for a viewer a single war story through its manifold refractions, *Redacted* grants its viewers metareflective access to the nature of psychological warfare as it takes form through strategic mediation and multiple perspectives. It is typical of the Iraq War films, which show us the micropolitical stakes of the neuro-image by putting ever-multiplying and ever-accelerating images on pause or replay to reflect on media aesthetics and their political implications. Each narrative event in *Redacted* is presented on one or another type of screen, telling the story quite literally as a battle of screens and points of view. Individual screens present fragments and perspectives of the whole narrative, which makes it important to both distinguish between screen typologies and image sources, as well as to understand the communications among them. Contrary to the visions of Virilio and Baudrillard in the 1990s, the relationship between war and media is here more dynamic than their analyses of a disappearing reality allowed. No longer can we speak purely with Baudrillard of masquerading images that give us a virtual war without human targets and real combat (the discourse of a clean war)—even if the spectacularization of the war is captured in a cinemaniacal logic. No longer is it possible to say with Virilio that the screen gives us only automatic images without human agency in an aesthetics of disappearance, even if this is indeed still a very concrete aspect of the new logistics of perception. With the multiplication of screens the logistics of perception have been reincarnated: version 2.0. Most characteristic of this new logic of perception exemplified by Iraq

War images are relations of dynamic multiplicity, a battle of screens of massively proliferating points of view, each with its own particular, different (resisting, violently traumatizing and "banalizing") effects.

In the Soldier's Shoes: Affects of Video War Diaries

At the level of perception we can see that images of points of view have multiplied exponentially; at the same time, the affective impact of such images has increased exponentially, too. A second characteristic of the Iraq War films is therefore the affective intensity that hits our brain-screens directly (see Chapter 4 for a more screen-neurological discussion of these effects of "neurothrills"). Contrary to the distant "objective" and "empty" images of the First Gulf War, images have become highly subjective and chaotically intense (countless combat images filmed by helmet cameras are a particularly salient example). Deleuze and Guattari's argument that "weapons are affects and affects are weapons" becomes all the more important in our oversaturated screen culture that mediates warfare.[33] This is another aspect of cinemania: gruesome effects (at least on one side of its image spectrum). In her article "Affective Imagery: Screen Militarism" Felicity Colman discusses the images of screen-based militarism by examining in particular the military trophy video.[34] One of the videos she discusses is the Aegis Video of snipings in Iraq from the back of a car, overlaid with Elvis Presley's song "Mystery Train."[35] As Colman argues:

That someone has—impulsively or otherwise—chosen to accompany the images of a shooting-spree with this particular song, displays a certain formless aesthetic that we have come to associate with our news media's realm of infotainment, where montage images of [insert your disaster of choice] are overlaid with popular music according to the most basic of stylistic criteria. . . . We smile blindly at death because the infectious rhythm of the song masks the horror of the image, and moves us into the emotive environment of the hillbilly hunter.[36]

What Colman describes is the technodelirious aesthetic of militarism that has left the battlefield and entered our daily screens: "The grasp of such militarism's affective zones reaches its sticky fingers into our brains, creating . . . media-zombies."[37] It is the absolute exploitative pole of schizoid

cinemania that is connected to war technology and the psychomecha-
nisms of contemporary war screens.

Many Iraq War films are based on actual diaries that can be found
on YouTube and other social media online. Internet culture appropriates
cinema technology for aesthetic effect, just as much as the inverse is true of
cinema appropriating Internet-based image relations. In one of the online
Iraq War diaries made by the US Marine battalion the Alpha Company
("From the creators of *My War Diary*," the video announces), we can see
how fast editing and upbeat soundtracks construct the war diaries in Hollywood style. Contrary to Hollywood productions, however, these films
are no longer dependent on hierarchical structures for their distribution.
Their images can be viewed (and remixed or mashed up) online by anyone
with access to the Internet (and bandwidth above dial-up speeds). This is a
completely different logistics of perception to the much more hierarchical
logistics of perception 1.0. The content of the images varies: men showing off their tattooed bodies in front of their barracks walls covered by
pictures of naked women; tours of duty at checkpoints; the rounding up
of suspected insurgents; house searches, violent raids, and shootings—
much of this filmed with helmet cameras. As Colman indicates, these
"digital-media war-events" posted online by soldiers in combat and under military operations "have formed new social networks, complete with
their own laws and affective directions. . . . It is a militarized delirium
that has produced a community of unseeing voyeurs; the war-impacted
schizophrenics."[38]

All these types of war diary images return in the war films. The
Iraq War films reframe these diaries in larger narratives that achieve the
expression of the affective and traumatic intensities of war experiences
within less detached, less fragmentary, and more reflexively adrenalized
ways. Many of these films give their multiple images a critical context
they often lack when consumed as fragmentary snippets found online.
Redacted, *Battle for Haditha* (2007), and *The Hurt Locker* (2008), for instance, present the intensity of an urban guerilla fight in a way that accounts for all its atrocities. Cinematographic technologies not only show
the emotions of the people involved—so that we can engage with them
and their situations—but these war films also make clear how the combat situation is governed by rage, panic, and reflex that can have serious

traumatic impacts. *The Hurt Locker* shows further how such experiences of war can become addictive (making the home front, after all the adrenaline of the battlefield, seem bleak and pointless). In his article "Affect, Agency and Responsibility" John Protevi explores the particular desubjectified states that soldiers need to enter into in order to kill: "most soldiers must leave the state of 'cold blood' in order to kill one-on-one at close range—they have to dump their subjectivity. They burst through the threshold of inhibition by super-charging their bodily intensity" (7).[39] A common method of combat preparation is to actually trigger soldiers' berserker rage (in itself already a traumatic experience, Protevi rightly insists), which easily leads to a frenzy of killing. The berserker rage is more "naturally" triggered by the death of a comrade, but it is here a trained mode of action also. Protevi also mentions "reflex training" as a common strategy used to desensitize and "enrage" the soldiers in preparation for a fight. Reflex training, which includes the rhythmic chanting of combat cries while running, creates group subjectivity and desensitizes the soldier to a dehumanized enemy. A further method is through computer simulation, where soldiers-cum-cyborgs learn to make instant shoot-or-refrain decisions based on the gestalt of the situation and a networked chain of commands. Protevi explains:

Such instant decisions are more than reflexes, but operate at the very edge of the conscious awareness of the soldiers and involve complex subpersonal processes of threat perception. In addition to this attenuation of individual agency, cutting edge communication technology now allows soldiers to network together in real time. With this networking we see an extended/distributed cognition culminating in "topsight" for a commander who often doesn't "command" in the sense of micro-manage but who observes and intervenes at critical points. In other words, contemporary team-building applications through real-time networking are cybernetic applications of video games that go above the level of the subject. (12)

Many of the most violent scenes in *Battle for Haditha* and *The Hurt Locker* bear a striking resemblance to first-person shooter games. Military training through video games is well known. The US Army has posted a free game, *America's Army*, online, which serves to entertain, educate, propagandize, and even recruit for the army.[40] The game aesthetic is another important dimension of the logistics of perception 2.0. Video games look like war, and war looks like a video game. Protevi indicates that the number of ex-soldiers who suffer from severe posttraumatic stress disorder (PTSD) multiplies once combatants are released from the military mode of reflex and group subjectivity and are unable to cope with other existent affects, such as guilt.

In *Battle for Haditha* this struggle is evident in one of the soldiers involved in revenge raids. Private Ramirez (Elliot Ruiz), who enters a berserker rage when he sees his friend dying from a landmine explosion, enters into a desubjectified, almost hallucinatory, mode in which he kills several civilians. After the fight he takes personal responsibility for the killings and experiences a subjective feeling of guilt that he cannot get over in the aftermath. In a commentary on *The Hurt Locker* Kathryn Bigelow indicates that by "putting the audience in the soldiers' shoes," she wants the audience to experience the psychology of warfare.[41] It is now possible to conclude that in the logistics of perception 2.0, the affective intensities and the pathos of war relate in two different ways to the spectacle of cinema. On the one hand contemporary media culture is saturated with images that follow the logic of cinemania, spectacularizing and desensitizing us to the atrocities of war through fast editing, pop soundtracks, and video-game aesthetics. On the other hand the contemporary war film reenacts the intensity of combat in a contextualizing narrative, giving important insights into the psychology of warfare, such as the effects of desubjectified precognitive reflexes and feelings of subjective traumatic guilt after combat, and in this way resensitizes us to the images of war.[42]

Other Iraq War films bring the war video diaries back home (as undeletable recollection-images) to focus on what happens after the combat. In *Stop-Loss* (2008) war diaries are also the basis of the film's aesthetic and narrative style. Director Kimberly Pierce says in an interview that she wanted to create the feeling of the video diaries captured by a film camera: everything handheld, fast-cut, and overlaid with music. In terms of mise-en-scène, similarities between Pierce's recreations and the war diaries on YouTube are striking (especially the familiar repetitive images of the soldiers' barracks and the "Death Before Dishonor" tattoos). Pierce's film could be considered a follow-up film to *Redacted*, *Battle for Haditha*, and *The Hurt Locker* in that it deals with the traumatic aftereffects of the war. The film takes up with a group of Texan soldiers when they arrive back home and cannot forget what they have experienced. Each returnee breaks down in one way or another, digging trenches to sleep in the garden, having traumatic flashbacks, committing suicide. When they get "stop-lossed" (the military term for being recalled back into combat beyond the initial call of duty, which happens often during the Iraq War), the sergeant of this particular platoon, Brandon King (Ryan Philippe), refuses to return and goes AWOL. The event in the central war diary of this particular film (depicted with all the affective intensities described above) is a horrific instance of urban warfare: a group of soldiers at a checkpoint chase insurgents and become trapped in the narrow streets of Baghdad. Three soldiers lose their lives, and one is badly wounded.[43] Many Iraqis (men, women, and children) are killed inside their houses while the rest of the soldiers escape, heavily traumatized. Back in the United States, images of this war diary return in constant flashback loops on Brandon's mindscreen. When he is in New York trying to obtain false-identity papers to escape the country, the huge city screens present other war diaries inviting young men to sign up for the fight in Iraq. There seems to be no escape from these images. If the soldiers' bodies are not destroyed in the combat, their minds nevertheless break down once they are back at home. The war diaries become traumatic memories. Here we could say that the film puts us in the soldier's mind and, in so doing, presents a critical reflection on the effects of the video game logistics of war perception.

In the Valley of Elah also deals with the effects of the war on the home front. The video diaries in this film are in first instance not so much undeletable memory flashbacks as traces to cling to for Hank Deerfield (Tommy Lee Jones), whose son Mike (Jonathan Tucker) is reported missing after returning from Iraq. The father goes on a search to find out what happened to Mike and gets hold of his son's cell phone, left in his bedroom at the military base. At first, all that is visible from the media data of this phone are some scrambled images and a picture Mike had sent home. In Deerfield's repeating nightmares his son's desperate voice calls the phone, asking, "Dad, are you there?" In the course of the film Deerfield (himself a Vietnam veteran) receives the news that Mike was murdered, and he slowly finds out what the war did to his son and his fellow army comrades. In the background the television news constantly reports on Iraq, and surveillance images and a picture of the war later turn out to be crucial in finding out the truth of what happened. Deerfield, helped by a deputy police officer, Emily Sanders (Charlize Theron), has to put all the pieces of information together independently, combining declarations of witnesses, surveillance footage, statements of other soldiers, and bits and pieces of media data from the cell phone that Deerfield receives courtesy of a local hacker. He eventually makes sense of his material: the war had turned his son into a drug-using sadist who uses film to distantly explore and accentuate the pain he delivers to his victims; Mike was killed by his fellow soldiers in a pointless fight. As in *Stop-Loss*, we can see how the state of desubjectification necessary in combat is not a simple on-off switch but has lasting consequences on the mind. At the end of the film the video image of the son on his cell phone turns into the father's own recollection. When he finally understands what happened to Mike, he remembers how his son had actually called him for help to get him out of the army. In this recollection-image we see the initial event that caused Mike's breakdown. In a convoy he had run over a girl and, against standing orders, stopped his tank to take a picture with his cell phone, which he sent home. This was the undeletable image that destroyed all (ethical) sense in the soldiers' minds.[44]

Taken together, the war video diaries in these films are both testimonies of intensely affective experiences and traumatic memory flashes that show the enormous impact of war. Although they are part of the hypermodern logic of cinema's expanded dispositive and have a spectacular side, these war films as contemporary neuro-images are not distant or empty images. They put us in the soldiers' shoes and minds on an immediate affective level. They are part of but also reflect on the logistics of perception, version 2.0, to indicate how intensely and traumatically these images operate in the chaos of our overloaded brain-screens. Asked for a war story back home, one of the soldiers at the end of *Redacted* exclaims, "I have these images that are burned in my brain and I don't know what the fuck I'm gonna do with them." Filmed, distributed, and remediated on all kinds of different platforms and screens, these war diary images become the traumatic kernel of our collective screen culture. Because of its complex entanglement in the vortex of multiple screens and multiple perspectives, an ethics of the image seems to be related to a consciousness arising from the paradoxical affects of this new logistics of perception. Now, after being held hostage by the spectacle of the "nonwar," we can say that in the logistics of perception 2.0 we are all participants in a battle of screens that is quite literally mind-blowing.

Restaging the Traumatic Kernel: Images of Abu Ghraib in War Films

Perhaps the most symbolic images of the collective traumatic kernel of contemporary screen culture are the videos and the photographs taken with cell phones and digital cameras by soldiers in the Abu Ghraib prison in 2003. The photographs were first introduced to the mass television media on *60 Minutes* (28 April 2004) and have since circulated on the Internet. The hooded man standing on a box with electrocuting wires held in each hand has become a symbol for the unjustness of the war in Iraq. Other pictures of naked men with women's underwear on their heads, detainees in sexually humiliating stress positions, and seemingly endless other atrocities became widely publicized in all variety of media, while also being interpolated through further re/de-contextualized variations (including cynical parodies such as Abu Ghraib coffee tables or Lego versions of the hooded man). In his article "Invisible Empire" Nicholas Mirzoeff discusses the paradoxical fact that although a number of the images traveled the world, the most compromising photographs of torture, sodomy, and other forms of humiliating and perverse conduct of the US militaries in Iraq did not have much effect in the United States (or in "Empire," as Mirzoeff refers here to Hardt and Negri's concept of the transnational global power of capitalism).[45] At least, they did not have any effect on the subsequent presidential elections. None of the senior army figures involved have been held accountable for the crimes, and the majority of the eighteen hundred pictures and video documents remain invisible today by court order. For all the mass proliferation of images, the visuality of war remains profoundly undemocratic, Mirzoeff rightly argues.[46] Meanwhile the images of the "embodied spectacle" of war that have been traveling in the transnational networks are *continuously* barbaric and degrading. They can be considered a lasting confirmation of the worst forms of orientalism humiliating the "Oriental" as deviant body. As Mirzoeff argues, the images reenact the age-old stereotypical division between "mind" and "body" rendered spatially in Empire, "so that America becomes 'mind' and the rest of the world, especially the Muslim world, becomes 'body'."[47] Mirzoeff's arguments about the banality of images discussed earlier in this chapter are only confirmed at this point, as the "nothing to see" of contemporary Babylonian visual culture. But Mirzoeff also argues that if we want to respond to this kind of spectacle, we require a new form of politics. The question, of course, is what that new form of politics would look like and whether contemporary culture (including the Iraq War films I suggest) does not already contain within it such new forms of politics. I will return to this question.

First, I would like to address the question of the digital and the possible or impossible survival of cinema in the digital age that is also enfolded in these images (albeit on another level). David Rodowick argues that the Abu Ghraib images exemplify the way in which cinema "survives" in the digital age but only as information. While digital images continue to have documentary power (in spite of their digital manufacturing, nobody questions the authenticity of the Abu Ghraib images), their dissemination across the globe is remarkable and "express(es) an immediate, cumulative past that remains part of our historical present."[48] In Chapter 7 I examined how this accumulated past in the present (which is a form of the second synthesis of time) is recut and reordered in the third synthesis of time typical for the neuro-image. As free-floating images on the Internet, they become available for anyone. According to Rodowick, this aspect of a contemporary image's networked reality turns digital images in general (and the Abu Ghraib pictures exemplarily) into pure information: "digital capture devices convert images into information, and in doing so they accelerate and amplify their powers as communications, a process limited only by the availability of computing cycles, storage capacity, and bandwidth."[49] I agree that a great many of the images circulating on the Internet are information and communication (and as such they implicitly or explicitly always serve as tools for political or capitalist hegemonic powers); however, I would not draw the conclusion that cinema therefore only survives as information (the other direction for the "virtual life of film" that Rodowick distinguishes is that it survives as art—cinema as museum practice). As I have argued throughout this book, film as film survives in the form of the neuro-image. But if this is so, then digital images, specifically here the atrocious images of Abu Ghraib, must be reconsidered in the context of actual aesthetic film productions.

Valley of the Wolves: Iraq was the first feature film to depict the Abu Ghraib tortures in a popular feature film. Largely based on true events, the film depicts the war "hyperhistorically" in Iraq through Turkish eyes. It begins with the arrest of allied Turkish Special Forces soldiers and civilians in northern Iraq, a fictionalized version of the infamous "Hood event" that took place on 4 July 2003, when allied Turkish soldiers were hooded and detained for sixty hours. Other real-life incidents brought into the story include the raid of an Arab wedding, where the groom and many guests are shot dead by US Marines. The survivors (among whom is the bride) are brought to Abu Ghraib, where we see some of the infamous pictures restaged (such as the image of a pile of naked bodies). The bride later decides to become a suicide bomber and partakes in insurgent actions. Various other real-life events that have taken place during the war are condensed and combined for the fictional film, which shows the destructive power of war and violence as a downward spiral. Being one of Turkey's most expensive big-budget films, *Valley of the Wolves: Iraq* was immensely popular in Turkey and other parts of the Arab world, and it is one of the few widely viewed films of the Iraq War made by a non-Western director. In the United States the film was less well received and accused of racism, which (considering the blatant racism and abuses of power testified by the Abu Ghraib pictures) seems yet another perverse turn of the original images' impact. From Jewish sides the film was accused of anti-Semitism, especially because of the suggestions made of the trafficking of prisoners' organs to rich Jewish families. The Jews as organ thieves is indeed a classic anti-Semitic stereotype that is potentially very dangerous.[50] These are rightly debated issues. Nevertheless, *Valley of the Wolves: Iraq* is an important film, precisely because it presents the atrocities of the Iraq War and the traumatic Abu Ghraib events from a non-Western perspective. Similarly, among the feature films about Iraq by Western directors, *Battle for Haditha* is an exceptional example of a feature that presents events from prolific military (different perspectives of the coalition, Iraqi forces, and insurgents) and more diverse civilian perspectives.[51] It is precisely by gaining insights into the many facets of the psychology of war that any comprehensions of futures are best developed.

Errol Morris's documentary *Standard Operating Procedure* is another film that has explored the taking up of "informational" images into a filmic context specifically through the investigation of the Abu Ghraib pictures. In contrast to the feature films that reenact, more or less realistically, fragmented events and images of the Iraq War into a narrative structure, Morris employs a very constructed and analytical style in his documentary, moving between interviews with the interrogators and digital camera operators at Abu Ghraib, clearly staged setups of the prison scenes, and the actual photographs themselves. Here we get the restaged images contextualized by interviews and analyses that investigate the psychology of war and the role of images in this in a different way. *Standard Operating Procedure* can also be considered a type of neuro-image. In *Deleuze and Memorial Culture* Adrian Parr argues the Abu Ghraib pictures as cultural phenomena show that a Foucauldian perspective on the events is useful but not sufficient to capture the complexity of what the photographs carry in them beyond their frames.[52] Foucault "insists power is a system of subjectification that emerges out of social relations and that power can be revolutionary as much as coercive."[53] Many of the testimonies in *Standard Operating Procedure* can be read in this way: the military's acceptance of humiliating and cruel practices "legitimized" or in any case normalized the entirety of the atrocities (as "standard operating procedure"). The multiplicity of minor processes imitating and supporting each other "converge and gradually produce the blueprint of a general method."[54] For Foucault historical processes and circumstances produce behavior and identity in terms of the power relations (*pouvoir*) of disciplined bodies. The use of female interrogators to humiliate the detainees was even a conscious policy that reflects this Foucauldian logic of the body and biopower. Mirzoeff, in his analysis of the Abu Ghraib horrors, also emphasized the biopolitical aspects of enforced sodomy and other perverse performances on the bodies of the Iraqi prisoners.[55]

However, as mentioned earlier, Mirzoeff also calls for new frames of reference, revisions of cultural theory that might enable us not only to understand what is going on in global image culture but also to imagine ways of breaking out of its perpetual repetitions:

Such reworkings of cultural theory may seem futile in the face of the current global violence. But the imagination is a key terrain for violence, and indeed violence appeals most effectively to the imagination. The contest for the hegemony of empire has been dramatically engaged by making instrumental use of the embodied spectacle as appropriation, most notably as the suicide bomber. Whatever else it is, suicide bombing is a striking new way to imagine the use of the body as an instrument of politics. Attacks like those of 9/11, or the 3/11 attack in Madrid, require a willingness to imagine devastation on a grand scale that makes the violence shown in a film like *The Battle of Algiers*, once so shocking, seem almost without impact. . . . At present, both empire and its neo-Islamic opponents have an imaginary of radical alterity to each other that they have deployed effectively, whether as the Webcast killings of hostages taken in Iraq or as the Republican National Convention. The task that confronts the politics of visual culture in theory and practice is to create a new imaginary that refuses empire in all its manifestations, whether based on Christian, Islamic or Jewish extremism.[56]

Mirzoeff indicates that such reworkings of imagination start with very concrete refusals, such as the refusal of the 343rd Quartermaster Company to take contaminated oil into a center of insurgency in Iraq or the refusal of certain Israeli soldiers to serve in the occupied territories. In the visual field we might refuse the complete transformation of society into a surveillance system against presumed terrorism. In Chapter 4 I argued that such refusal may also consist of breaking through the presumed omnipotent power of the surveillance gaze by changing the perception of the surveillance apparatus itself.

Mirzoeff also mentions, albeit briefly, the value of Spinoza and Deleuze in reimagining relationships between power, bodies, and thinking.[57] As is well known, contrary to Foucault's emphasis on institutional power (*pouvoir*), Deleuze insists on the affective dimensions of power as force (*puissance*): "The key here is whether the organization of affects establishes a microfascism, for what makes fascism dangerous according to Deleuze and Guattari is its 'molecular or micropolitical power, for it is a mass movement: a cancerous body rather than a totalitarian organism.'"[58] According to Deleuze and Guattari, desire is a fundamental organizational power: the exchange of libidinal intensities, energies, and affects runs through every system. It is not so much, or not only, that individuals are formed by institutional power in a top-down movement from system to individual but that all sorts of affective dimensions feed the system at the bottom or on microlevels.

This conception of "affective powers" (at work in different ways in the soldiers' video diaries discussed above) enables us to comprehend the critical approach *Standard Operating Procedure* brings to the embodied spectacle of Abu Ghraib. At the level of the individuals, those involved in staging and taking the pictures, Morris's film hints at the multiple affective layers to which the pictures (already) relate. Of the many dimensions that can be detected here, I want to mention three of the most salient. First of all, it is revealing to hear Lynndie England, the woman infamously photographed holding a detainee on a leash, speak in Morris's film of being simply in love with Charles Graner, the ring leader of the interrogators, and thus easily convinced to pose in the photographs. Personal affects of sexual desire and (problematically) gendered power relations are elements in the forces beyond the picture frames. England adds to this that Graner would never have given her the leash if there had not been a camera. Here a second libidinal element comes into the picture. The affective role of the camera itself makes the pictures partial evidence for "good" (allegiant) behavior (Graner wanted to show that he prepared prisoners for interrogation), as well as a kind of trophy machine for a "winning team." Contrary to what Graner may have expected, the pictures became evidence used to incriminate him and the other soldiers. Instead of symbols of triumph, they became a symbol of the shame of America. However, in another twist of this view on Abu Ghraib, there is yet another affective dimension, which is the third point I want to raise. As I have already shown, schizo-analytical desire is always already social and has a collective dimension. Adrian Parr argues that the images of Abu Ghraib have to be read as a (collective, unconscious, and "bottom-up") counterstrategy to the humiliating images of the falling towers on 9/11:

The images of Abu Ghraib relentlessly counter the images of 9/11 fresh in American minds, testifying to an infrastructure of desire operating at the pre-dialogical and pre-personal level of social memory. . . . On that note, it is interesting that the American media and the US administration didn't even bother trying to get the public to forget what happened at Abu Ghraib. Instead it was amplified . . . [as] a way of countering the memory of 9/11 not on ideological grounds but as a way in which a battered nation saw a way out of the malaise.[59]

The photographs can be seen as a perverse antidote for the humiliating images of the collapsing towers of the World Trade Center. The Abu Ghraib pictures and the war diary videos, as the affective traumatic kernels of the logistics of perception 2.0, demonstrate how war and imaging technologies are fundamentally connected and, therefore, risk getting caught in an infernal and vicious circle of action and reaction of a repetition of the same.

Amid such turmoil we may indeed hope for Virilio's "aesthetic of disappearance" as some alternative point from which to develop room for a different type of imagination and the eternal return of difference as hope for the future. In Chapter 8 I showed how a nomadic aesthetic (in the films of Suleiman) can produce such different visual regimes that enable alternative forms of resistance. In this chapter I have focused on films that show the psychology of warfare, now played out across and through all kinds of screens. The Iraq War films do not so much deploy a nomadic aesthetic. Rather, they offer a (valuable, indeed otherwise-impossible for any monad) metareflexive position on the ways in which different types of screens operate both in the world *and* as brain-screens (and without excusing our own brain-screens as viewers from that experience). The crucial difference seems to be the different play between the virtual and the actual. While in Suleiman's films the virtual and the actual are equally lifted to a plane of composition (where the actual is lifted up or peered through, and the virtual is chronicled and grounded), in the Iraq War films the actual is quite dominant. In general, it can be said that the neuro-image has many ways of playing with the virtual and the actual and that perhaps sometimes the virtual, as condition for the actual, swaps places with the actual containing all virtualities, always already actualized as a point of view.

Multiple Screens, Affect, and Refractional Perspectivism

To conclude, I want to elaborate further on these varying relations between the actual and the virtual by engaging John Mullarkey's analysis of Bergson's Leibnizianism, which considers Bergson as a perspectivist philosopher. Mullarkey's article "Forget the Virtual" is relevant for understanding the neuro-image as part and parcel of contemporary digital screen culture at large in all its complex dimensions.[60] Mullarkey takes a provocative position toward the general dominance of the concept of the virtual in much of the critical work on Deleuze. As I have already emphasized, for Deleuze the actual and the virtual always belong together, but sometimes the (mistaken) impression seems to be that the virtual should be considered good (open, difference) and the actual bad (closed, identity). (Perhaps this positivity of the virtual is also assumed because it holds the promise of being a new and unfamiliar theoretical element introduced by Deleuze, in relation to his more common—but indeed quite differently theorized—notion of the actual.) Mullarkey returns to Bergson to convincingly argue that Bergson increasingly grounds the virtual in a play of actualities: "the virtual for Bergson becomes a well-founded perspectival and psychological phenomenon—an emergent product formed through the interplay between a multiplicity of actual entities (including spatial and temporal continuities and discontinuities, identities and differences, quantities and qualities)."[61]

Mullarkey emphasizes how, for Bergson, movement in consciousness "derives from that actual, or rather, from a multiplicity of *refractive actualities*" (472). Mullarkey's goal is to redeem the actual, including molar identities and forms of belongings, and open up the possibility for movement and becoming within the actual, within the molar, since Bergson sees such processes operating at every level. In other words, instead of actualizing the virtual, Mullarkey reads Bergson inversely as a philosopher who virtualizes the actual. Actualism is related to the concept of perspectivism and refraction in that we always occupy one point of view (which makes other things invisible): "everything has its own perspective (on it) and so what is hidden must be due to the perspective and what is revealed must be due to a movement beyond that point of view" (475). Because of refractions, perspectivism is therefore always also about multiple points of view. In the context of the neuro-images of the Iraq War films, we can see how this refractional perspectivism can be related to the multiple screens that are presenting their actual points of view. Mullarkey proposes to take refractionism as fundamental for Bergson, for "ours is a 'refractory planet'" (488). A present actuality as a particular point of view is a force, an affect that can be felt; it therefore can lead to an ethics, or an "open morality" as Bergson himself calls it. This is an affective openness that calls for an understanding not only of what virtually binds us (on a preindividual, unconscious level) but also of concrete actualities of multiple realities that are all refracted, slightly distorted, mediated by attempts to understand the actual confinements of our situated bodies. Mullarkey calls for a philosophy that can take these actualities that give rise to the emergence of virtualities into account:

It is as philosophers, however, that we can conceptualize in some small way what distortions we create through reflection, by occupying the shifting interval between extremes, and by acknowledging the need to open ourselves affectively to the actuality of others. Hence despite the ubiquity of refraction, Bergson offers us hope in the form of a refraction that is aware of its own distorting effects . . . and as such partly undoes them: in *The Two Sources of Morality and Religion* he calls this "open morality." (488)

In spite of all the capturing forces that operate on our multiple screens, it is possible to see the media as a gigantic network of baroque perspectives where particular points of view and the psychological effects they entail become affectively entangled. We can say that in the new logistics we are not passive spectators captured by institutional or ideological power, even though these are still powers that need to be taken into account. What the Iraq War films of the logistics of perception 2.0 show us is that contemporary culture is traversed by multiple affects that are for a large part social, collective, and unconscious. Our real and virtual bodies are involved in complex ways that cannot be translated into simple ethical rules; we need instead an affective openness to be brought to the idea of cinema and (into) the world itself. By creating images, or simply by being affected by these images, we can participate in bringing reality and feeling back to the vortex of our multiple screens. Paradoxically, it is possible to conclude that in the face of the multiplication of ever-increasing screens, as monadic nomads, reality does not disappear but returns with an affective vengeance.

Conclusion: The Neuro-Image

BRAIN-SCREENS FROM THE FUTURE

Between 11/9 and 9/11

Several historical circumstances inform the transformation of the soul of cinema as conceptualized by Deleuze in terms of the shift from the movement-image to the time-image. The Second World War, by and large, marks the crucial turning point of changed conditions toward a new type of image. Deleuze recognizes that cinema as movement-image was specifically hollowed out by propagandistic utility when fascism and Nazism turned politics into art.[1] But he does not suggest a simple cause-and-effect relationship between Hitler's election as chancellor of Germany in 1933, the subsequent Second World War, and the emergence of the time-image from the debris of the war (Rossellini's *Rome, Open City* in 1945). The crisis of the action-image depended on many other factors as well, "which only had their full effect after the war, some of which were social, economic, political, moral and others more internal to art, to literature and to the cinema in particular."[2] The circumstances and conditions Deleuze mentions include "in no particular order, the war and its consequences, the unsteadiness of the American Dream in all its aspects, the new consciousness of minorities, the rise and inflation of images both in the external world and in people's minds, the influence on the cinema of the new modes of narrative with which literature had experiments, the crisis of Hollywood and its old genres."[3] There is an always-fundamental but not always-straightforward relationship between the world, our brain-screens, cinema, and larger image culture, all of which interrelate in complex ways.

If, then, as I have argued throughout this book, yet another transformation of the image has taken place so that we can perhaps speak of a third cinema type, the neuro-image, what could be the (assemblages of) circumstances that we might recognize as conditioning these changes? In *A Thousand Plateaus* Deleuze and Guattari give a precise date for every plateau of assemblages and concepts they discuss. These dates always refer to a particular moment in history that marks a before and after, a moment that indicates a certain event, emerged in its fullness from a complex assemblage of conditions (which implies that these conditions and circumstances have been around much longer than the singular moment of the event). In thinking about the conditions for the emergence of the neuro-image, there are perhaps two dates that are connected to the transition of the cinematographic image into this third type: 9 November 1989 (11/9: the fall of the Berlin Wall) and 11 September 2001 (9/11: the collapse of the Twin Towers). Of course, the fall of the Berlin Wall and the collapse of the Twin Towers are not the direct cause of the neuro-image. However, these two dates mark specific events related to assemblages of conditions that are connected to the transition toward a new regime of images.

The fall of the Berlin Wall in 1989, 11/9—witnessed on millions of television screens and news broadcasts all over the world (even if most journalists arrived a day later than the actual fall of the wall)—marked the end of the Cold War and the beginning of a new era. Politically, the division of the world between the East and the West officially ended. In the same year the fatwa against Salman Rushdie by Ayatollah Khomeini, another complex historical event in itself, marked the start of a period in which Islamic fundamentalism, much less contained in East and West blocs between capitalism and communism, could be considered as the beginning of a new type of dispersed political divisions in the world. Obviously, Islamic fundamentalism is connected to a long history of colonialism and is a reaction to many aspects of the new world order after 1989, as Michael Hardt and Antonio Negri explain so powerfully in the first chapters of *Empire*.[4] Empire is the age of global hypercapitalism, in full speed following the end of the Cold War and facilitated also by the introduction of email around the same time and the large-scale commercial use of the Internet.[5] The year 1989 can in this way be seen to coincide with the beginning of the digital age (even if its history goes back much further). The PC becomes a common feature on every desk in offices and at home. In cinema the end of the 1980s marked the arrival of what Lipovetsky and Serroy call "hypercinema," discussed earlier in this book.[6] Digital methods entered cinema production and postproduction as special effects changed the possibilities of image manipulation and special effects (James Cameron's *The Abyss* from 1989 being an important case in point). Such methods more deeply penetrate our scientific (and "scientific humanities") knowledges, too: the 1980s see the rise of cognitive neurosciences and advanced methods of noninvasive brain imaging technology such as fMRI scans. It is also the era that leads to the ultimate spectacle of the First Gulf War in an aesthetics of disappearance. All these developments continued to transform our world at high speed in many different directions in the 1990s, a period during which we see the emergence of many early neuro-images.

But it was not until the second historical moment, 9/11—the attack on the Twin Towers and their dramatic collapse in 2001, caught on countless professional and amateur cameras and distributed in a dense global network across different media—that the conditions of the large-scale emergence of the neuro-image were amplified, its qualities having already been signaled in the preceding decade. This crisis marked the end of (relative) post–Cold War euphoria, during which time even war had seemed to become "nonwar" in a disappeared or faded political present. The violent attack by Islamic fundamentalists definitively transitioned US power toward the era of the War on Terror, with the war(s) in Iraq and Afghanistan as its most visible and dire consequences. With every attack, or seemingly apparent threat, increased measures of control and surveillance became more severe and invasive—ranging from the proliferation of millions of CCTV cameras to full-body scans at airports and hyperinvasive and expanded data-mining by governments and companies. The Internet bubble had already burst at the end of the 1990s, and on 9/11 the logistics of perception 1.0 came to a full-blown standstill. Baudrillard takes this spectacular series of cultural-logistical transformations to their ultimate conclusion when he argues that on 9/11 reality may have returned but that it is now further marked by that previous perceptual era's spectacular aesthetic power:

So did reality actually overtake fiction? If it appears to have done so, it is only because reality absorbed the energy of fiction and itself became fiction. One could almost say that reality is jealous of fiction and real events are jealous of images . . . a sort of duel between them, to see who will be the most inconceivable. . . . The real is added to the images as a bonus of terror, and extra shiver.[7]

Not only are these images of the collapsing towers terrifyingly spectacular, but they are also even real, Baudrillard argues. He relates Hollywood and terrorism here as tightly interwoven, as each other's ultimate consequences: "In the singularity of this event, in this Manhattan catastrophe film, the two elements of mass fascination of the twentieth century are fused to the highest degree: the white magic of cinema and the black magic of terrorism."[8] The End is marked, by the spectacular logistics of perception . . .

And a rebeginning is emerging as well: just as Rossellini's camera on the ruins of Rome after the Second World War captured a new type of cinema, Ground Zero marks the beginning of a new type of cinema related to participatory digital culture. The emergence of Web 2.0 coincided with 9/11's eventfulness precisely when people began the massive upload of many versioned images, points of view, and concerns directly online, to blogs and other transmedial sites.[9] We can see the contours here of several assemblages that provide the conditions for a new image type, which I have proposed to call the neuro-image. The exponential growth of the media matches the increase of the neurosciences that have provided important new findings and insights into the operations of the brain. As Michael Gazzaniga has noted, cognitive neurosciences have replaced departments of psychology and have entered many other fields as well.[10] At the same time, our conception of the brain has changed: from rational and disembodied agent, the brain is now sensuously and affectively embodied and extended, guiding our feelings and thoughts in probabilistic but often unpredictable ways. The digital turn and the neurological turn seem to have evolved separately but also perhaps in a close and not often explicitly addressed exchange with one another. As Warren Neidich argues in his article "Neuropower," the brain is sculpted by cultural experience:

Through the use of distributed, mediated circuits such as television and the Internet, formerly unrecognized concepts of time diffuse into mainstream culture, where personal and cultural effects are possible. Thus the brain's potential is sculpted as a result of changes not only in its static elements, the neurons and neural networks with their axonal flows, myelination, synaptic neurochemicals and tight junctions, but in the dynamic apparatus of coordinated oscillation potentials and temporal signatures as well.[11]

Neidich discusses these changes in respect to the possibilities of art to "redistribute sensibilities to compete with the institutional conditions of the mind's eye" (123). At the same time, it has to be acknowledged that neuroscientific findings and brain imaging technology can be utilized (politicized, rationalized, simplified) in quite problematic ways in many different systems of capture of contemporary culture, such as in already available "brain fingerprinting" software used at airports in Israel, and currently being researched for use in Europe, for supposedly detecting terrorist brain activity (and giving people with "cleared brains"—and presumably a lot of money—priority access).[12] Surveillance has quite literally entered our brain-screens and is future-oriented, scanning for behavioral intent. On an even larger political scale, the War on Terror is directed from the vantage of a "new complex future, an Extreme Future of disruptions, risks, threats" that allows for all kinds of preemptive measurements.[13]

The Future Is Now

I have developed the changed temporality of the brain's "temporal signature" in the neuro-image through a reading of Deleuze's philosophy of time, which he developed in *Difference and Repetition*. If the movement-image is founded in the first synthesis of time of the present, and the time-image is grounded in the second synthesis of the past, the neuro-image belongs to the third synthesis of time, the time of the future. This certainly does not exclude the other times. The past and the present are based on a vision of the future. To complicate matters, it also has to be noted that each image type—the movement-image, the time-image, and the neuro-image—can also open up to the other two syntheses of time. Moreover the neuro-image can include and repeat elements of the movement-image and/or of the time-image because it is only in the third synthesis of time that all other times can be revisited, reordered, and cut to new intensities, corresponding to a database logic of the digital age.

If we return now to *The Butterfly Effect*, it is possible to see this film, too, as based in the third synthesis of time. As a film dealing explicitly with clinical schizophrenia, the film is obsessed with time. The various pasts that the main character, Evan Treborn, returns to could be seen as flashbacks dependent on a present where Evan is at high school (which would make a case for the first synthesis of time). However, this present is actually too unstable (is he really at high school or already in a mental institution?) and does not form the foundational basis of the traditional flashback, which investigates the past from a fixed center in the present. (Think of the famous flashbacks in Marcel Carné's *Daybreak* from 1939, where all events lead to the situation in the present.) Could the variations of the past, then, be explained as dimensions of the pure past and thus be based in the second synthesis of time? There are arguments that can be made for this reading, too; after all, the present situation depends on what happened in the past (the children at age seven and at age fourteen). But that does not explain the series of time and the many variations of the pasts and presents the film produces. Therefore, I suggest, the past and the present have to be seen as dimensions of the (always speculative) future imagined on Evan's schizoid brain-screen. Each moment Evan changes something in the past, the present changes (in unpredictable ways) accordingly. At the beginning of the film Evan is put under hypnosis in order to allow him to regain his memory. "Think of this as a film," the doctor hypnotizing him suggests. "Go back, rewind, slow down, zoom in on every detail you like." This is what happens when we are in the third synthesis of time: the past and present are "recut" with different speeds, intensities, and orders—and always from the perspective of the future (every time Evan sees how the past changes its respective future, he returns to undo this future effect; but obviously, the tragedy is that there is no linear cause-effect, so the future remains unpredictable).

The third synthesis of time is related to the creation of the new, to hope for the future, an eternal recurrence of "difference," but also to death (death as the future for all of us, but a future that also calls for rebeginnings). After Evan has revisited "all of the past" and "all of the present," these dimensions play out like a database of options seen from the perspective of "all options for the future." We return to the beginning of the film, where Evan is in the psychiatric hospital and is told that the diaries (that enable his entrances into his pasts) are nothing but fantasies to cope with his guilt (of having killed Kayleigh, in what is most likely the "real" version of the past and the present). Here the director's cut differs significantly from the theatrical version. Evan returns to the moment before his birth and strangles himself in his mother's womb. It is a cruel ending and a pathologically creative one indeed. But reading for the metaphysics, it is also the absolute degree zero of the third synthesis of time: to have died before birth, in order to create a new present—all from the point of view of the future. Zero intensity of the schizoid brain-screen. *The Butterfly Effect* shows the pathological (deadly) dimensions of this Time of the Future, or indeed, the "Time that is now," to quote another schizoid character from the beginning of this book, Arthur Edens in *Michael Clayton*. Together these schizoid characters also show that both the family (Evan Treborn suffers from the mental heritage of his father and an experience of incest trauma) and culture at large (Arthur Edens's breakdown in respect to the immorality of hypercapitalism) can constitute the planes on which these characters break down as a form of resistance, anticipating a future with which they cannot cope.[14]

I have proposed to read the neuro-image in a Deleuze-Guattarian framework of a schizoanalysis of contemporary screen culture. Three "schizoelements" have structured my arguments and guided the selection of concepts, films, and neuro-scientific findings: schizophrenia as a neurological disease, its powers of illusion (in hallucinations and other delirious realities of illusions), and its affective powers (ranging between hyperconnectivity or oversaturation and catatonia) form the basis of the different chapters. Taking the relationship between the clinical and critical seriously, I have looked at schizophrenia as the "degree zero" of our brain that has become our "illness and our passion." It really is the borderline upon which we (individually and collectively) walk. "Madness is like gravity," Heath Ledger as The Joker says in *The Dark Knight*; "All it needs is a little push." Many of the characters and brain-screens discussed in this book are characterized by a certain consciousness of the fragility of human psyche, which easily crosses over into a delirious stage (experienced as very real and full of affect) in which spatial and temporal coordinates are lost. Here

I have looked at these schizoid elements beyond their clinical conditions and as they appear in culture at large.

Films of the twenty-first century show us brain-worlds, brain-cities, architectures of the mind. We no longer look through characters' eyes; we experience their minds. Contemporary culture is full of neuro-images based in the third synthesis of time. Bergson's dual-genesis theory of matter and intellect, the virtual and the actual, body and brain continually shaping each other was an important notion for Deleuze and has been one of the guiding principles in this book in situating the brain and the screen, the brain as screen, in a reciprocal, dialethical way.[15] I have suggested how a new type of cinema could be conceived by continuing Bergson's dual-genesis theory of matter and mind in the context of contemporary digital image culture and in the form of the neuro-image. Taking the absolute internalism of the schizophrenic hallucinations as one pole of the brain-screen and the absolute externalism of cosmic space as the other pole, the brain-screen is always situated at some point between these poles, shifting and sliding between them, inducing epistemological probability and belief as a zero degree of knowledge. We should call for and continue with this schizoanalysis of visual culture so that we might better our understanding of its many possible dangers and empowerments through complex, open-ended, and collective processes.

Notes

INTRODUCTION

1. See www.imdb.com/title/tt0465538/ for a transcription of this monologue.

2. See Gilles Deleuze and Félix Guattari, *Anti-Oedipus: Capitalism and Schizophrenia*, trans. Robert Hurley, Mark Seem, and Helen R. Lane (London: Athlone Press, 1984); Gilles Deleuze and Félix Guattari, *A Thousand Plateaus: Capitalism and Schizophrenia*, trans. Brian Massumi (London: Athlone Press, 1988). See also Ian Buchanan and Patricia MacCormack, eds., *Deleuze and the Schizoanalysis of Cinema* (London: Continuum, 2008).

3. See Scott McQuire, Meredith Martin, and Sabine Niederer, eds., *Urban Screens Reader* (Amsterdam: Institute of Network Cultures, 2009).

4. Gilles Deleuze, *Cinema 2: The Time-Image*, trans. Hugh Tomlinson and Robert Galeta (London: Athlone Press, 1989), 270.

5. Ibid., 266.

6. Gilles Deleuze, *Difference and Repetition*, trans. Paul Patton (London: Athlone Press, 1994).

7. Gilles Deleuze, "The Brain Is the Screen," trans. Marie Therese Guirgis, in *The Brain Is the Screen: Deleuze and the Philosophy of Cinema*, ed. Gregory Flaxman (Minneapolis: University of Minnesota Press, 2000), 365–73.

8. Daniel W. Smith, "'A Life of Pure Immanence': Deleuze's 'Critique and Clinique' Project," introduction to *Essays Critical and Clinical*, by Gilles Deleuze, trans. Daniel W. Smith and Michael A. Greco (London: Verso, 1998), xvii.

9. Ibid., xxv.

10. Here I still refer to Smith's introduction, although not in the exact order of his presentation.

11. Smith, "A Life of Pure Immanence,'" xxxviii.

12. Deleuze, *The Time-Image*, 201.

13. Ibid., 126–55.

14. Smith, "A Life of Pure Immanence,'" xxx.

15. Ibid.

16. Deleuze and Guattari, *Anti-Oedipus*, 337. Deleuze and Guattari write here that capitalism is an "immanent system where each act of production is inextricably linked to the process of antiproduction as capital."

17. Lev Manovich, *Software Takes Command*, www.softwarestudies.com/softbook, 3.

18. Ibid. Other books in software studies are Alexander R. Galloway, *Protocol: How Control Exists After Decentralization* (Cambridge, MA: MIT Press, 2004); *Gaming: Essays on Algorithmic Culture* (Minneapolis: University of Minnesota Press, 2006); and Matthew Fuller, ed., *Software Studies: A Lexicon* (Cambridge, MA: MIT Press, 2008).

19. Manovich, *Software Takes Command*, 11.

20. Galloway, *Protocol*, xviii–xix.

21. Ibid.

22. Henry Jenkins, *Convergence Culture: Where Old and New Media Collide* (New York: New York University Press, 2006). See also Geert Lovink and Sabine Niederer, eds., *Video Vortex Reader: Responses to YouTube* (Amsterdam: Institute for Network Cultures, 2008).

23. This deep remixability will only increase with the evolution of the Internet into Web 3.0.

24. See http://en.wikipedia.org/wiki/Dogme_95. See also Jan Simons, *Playing the Waves: Lars von Trier's Game Cinema* (Amsterdam: Amsterdam University Press, 2007).

25. Lev Manovich, *The Language of New Media* (Cambridge, MA: MIT Press, 2002), 219.

26. Jacques Derrida, *Archive Fever: A Freudian Impression*, trans. Eric Prenowitz (Chicago: University of Chicago Press, 1996).

27. Manovich, *The Language of New Media*, 15. The prime example of a software performance is the way in which Google maps changes according to navigation patterns every time you navigate its maps.

28. Anne Friedberg, *The Virtual Window: From Alberti to Microsoft* (Cambridge, MA: MIT Press, 2006).

29. Nicolas Rombes, *Cinema in the Digital Age* (London: Wallflower, 2009).

30. Lev Manovich and Andreas Kratky, *Soft Cinema: Navigating the Database* (Cambridge, MA: MIT Press, 2005).

31. Matthew Fuller, *Media Ecologies: Materialist Energies in Art and Technoculture* (Cambridge, MA: MIT Press, 2005), 4. Fuller is following Guattari in connecting ecology to "ecosophy," in which there is a cross-fertilization among mental, natural, and social phenomena related to software, information, and computer networks.

32. David N. Rodowick, *The Virtual Life of Film* (Cambridge, MA: Harvard University Press, 2007), 125. See also his article "An Elegy for Theory," *October*, no. 122 (fall 2007): 91–109.

33. Gilles Deleuze, *Negotiations, 1972–1990*, trans. Martin Joughin (New York: Columbia University Press, 1995), 149.

34. Gilles Deleuze and Félix Guattari, *What Is Philosophy?* trans. Graham Burchell and Hugh Tomlinson (London: Verso, 1994), 197.

35. Deleuze, "The Brain Is the Screen," 367.

36. Deleuze, *Negotiations*, 149.

37. Deleuze and Guattari argue that concepts need conceptual personae that help to define them, such as the Friend. Aesthetic figures are sensational figures that express an aesthetic universe. Partial observers function within systems of scientific reference, indicating that there is never a total observer. See Deleuze and Guattari, *What Is Philosophy?* 2, 177, 129.

38. Ibid., 218.

39. Eric Alliez, *The Signature of the World*, trans. Alberto Toscano (London: Continuum, 2004). In this book Alliez is concerned primarily with the connections between science and philosophy. He has explored in depth the relations between art and philosophy elsewhere. See, e.g. (with Jean-Claude Bonne), *La pensée-Matisse* (Paris: Le Passage, 2005).

40. Kevin Haug and Kevin Mack, "Behind the Scenes" (Visual Effects of the Main Title Sequence), commentaries, *Fight Club*, dir. David Fincher (1998; Twentieth Century Fox Home Entertainment, 2000), DVD.

41. Deleuze and Guattari, *A Thousand Plateaus*, 15. Deleuze and Guattari's key reference is Steven Rose, *The Conscious Brain* (New York: Knopf, 1975).

42. Deleuze and Guattari, *A Thousand Plateaus*, 20.

43. Antonio Damasio has demonstrated how the actual brain in respect to emotions is built according to nesting principles where aspects of prior levels are incorporated in higher-function levels: "The ensemble does not look exactly like a neat Russian doll because the bigger part is not merely an enlargement of the smaller nested in it. Nature is never that tidy. But the 'nesting' principle holds. Each of the different regulatory reactions we have been considering is not a radically different process, built from scratch for a specific purpose. Rather, each reaction consists of tinkered rearrangements of bits and parts of the simpler process below" (Antonio Damasio, *Looking for Spinoza: Joy, Sorrow, and the Feeling Brain* [Orlando: Harcourt, 2003], 37–38).

44. Joe Hughes, "Schizoanalysis and the Phenomenology of Cinema," in Buchanan and MacCormack, *Deleuze and the Schizoanalysis of Cinema*, 23.

45. Daniel Frampton, *Filmosophy* (London: Wallflower, 2006).

46. Ibid., 8.

47. John Protevi, "One More 'Next Step': Deleuze and Brain, Body and Affect in Contemporary Cognitive Science" in *Revisiting Normativity with Deleuze*, ed. Rosi Braidotti and Patricia Pisters (London: Continuum, 2012 forthcoming)

48. Damasio, *Looking for Spinoza*, 14.

49. Jonah Lehrer, *Proust Was a Neuroscientist* (Boston: Houghton Mifflin, 2008), 193.

50. Ibid., 194–95.

51. Deleuze and Guattari, *A Thousand Plateaus*, 342.

52. Josef Früchtl has observed that contemporary cinema is a "driving force toward a vivid discursivization of the invisible" (Josef Früchtl, *The Impertinent Self: A Heroic History of Modernity*, trans. Sarah L. Kirkby [Stanford: Stanford University Press, 2009], 209).

53. In "The Leap in Thought" Gregg Lambert argues that "the virtual is the Brain"; see *theory@buffalo* 13 (2009): 43.

54. See Rick Altman, *Film/Genre* (London: BFI, 1999).

55. See also Warren Buckland, ed., *Puzzle Films: Complex Storytelling in Contemporary Cinema* (Malden, MA: Blackwell, 2009).

56. Deleuze and Guattari, *What Is Philosophy?* 197. The complete passage is quoted earlier in this introduction.

57. Marta Kutas, interview by Liesbeth Koenen, "de Huh-Belevenis," *NRC Handelsblad*, 8 January 2006, 43. Kutas has discovered the so-called N400-response in the experience and anticipation of language, which measures the anticipation of probability in sentences. Paranoid schizophrenia (and lighter forms of distrust, but also emotions in general) influences our language capacity and understanding of, for instance, jokes. The N400-response is a subtle and gradual mechanism:

> We humans anticipate what is coming on all levels at the same time, not just the semantic level. The quality of sound, formal elements, the construction of sentences, we use it all. I'd rather not use the word "predict." The N400-reaction is not just an "oops"-response because you'd expected something else. It's much more subtle. It's not: I expected this, but I got that. It's rather: I expected this with a certain degree of probability, and at the same time something else in an equal degree of probability. Now I'm here approaching all options in such a way that I get closer to the pattern that I expect it is going to be. But I keep all options open. It's a gradual phenomenon" (my trans.).

What this shows is that the brain is a probabilistic and highly influential or plastic system.

58. Robert Pepperell, "Where Is the Screen?" in *Screen Consciousness: Cinema, Mind, and the World*, ed. Robert Pepperell and Michael Punt (Amsterdam: Rodopi, 2006), 181–97. As an example of a powerful internalist account Pepperell refers among others to Samir Zeki, *Inner Vision: An Exploration of Art and the Brain* (Oxford: Oxford University Press, 1999). The externalist position is strongly defended in, for instance, Kevin O'Regan and Alva Noë, "A

Sensorimotor Account of Vision and Visual Consciousness," *Behavioral and Brain Sciences*, no. 24 (2001): 939–1031. The dialethic position is proposed by Graham Priest in his book *Beyond the Limits of Thought* (Oxford: Oxford University Press, 2002).

59. Pepperell, "Where Is the Screen?" 192.

60. Deleuze, *Negotiations*, 176.

61. *L'Abécédaire de Gilles Deleuze*, with Claire Parnet, dir. Pierre-André Boutang (Video Editions Montparnasse, 1996). For an English summary of this video see www.langlab.wayne.edu/CStivale/D-G/ABC1.html.

62. Damasio, *Looking for Spinoza*, 115–16. See also Vittorio Gallese, "The Manifold Nature of Interpersonal Relations: The Quest for a Common Mechanism," in *Philosophical Transactions of the Royal Society B: Biological Sciences* 358 (2003): 517–28.

63. Deleuze, *Difference and Repetition*, 22–23.

64. Deleuze and Guattari, *What Is Philosophy?* 211.

65. Ibid., 213.

66. Deleuze, "The Brain Is the Screen," 366.

67. Deleuze, *The Movement-Image*, 114. See also Ronald Bogue, "To Choose to Choose—To Believe in This World," in *Afterimages of Gilles Deleuze's Film Philosophy*, ed. David Rodowick (Minneapolis: University of Minnesota Press, 2010), 115–32.

68. Deleuze, *The Movement-Image*, 116.

69. Deleuze, *The Time-Image*, 172.

CHAPTER 1

1. Portions of this chapter have been published in earlier versions as "Delirium Cinema or Machines of the Invisible?" in Buchanan and MacCormack, *Deleuze and the Schizoanalysis of Cinema*, 102–16; and "Synaptic Signals: Time Traveling Through the Brain in the Neuro-Image," in "Schizoanalysis and Visual Culture," ed. Philip Roberts and Richard Rushton, special issue, *Deleuze Studies* 5, no. 2 (2011): 261–75.

2. Deleuze, *The Time-Image*, 318n32. Deleuze refers here to Jean-Pierre Changeux's *L'homme neuronal* (Paris: Fayard, 1983) and Steven Rose's *The Conscious Brain* (New York: Vintage Books, 1976).

3. Deleuze, *The Time-Image*, 211–12.

4. Michael Gazzaniga and his colleagues begin their seminal overview of modern cognitive neuroscience with an example of a schizophrenic patient. See Michael Gazzaniga, Richard Ivry, and George Mangun, *Cognitive Neuroscience: The Biology of the Mind*, 2nd ed. (New York: Norton, 2002), 23–24.

5. See also Catherine Malabou, *The New Wounded: From Neurosis to Brain Damage*, trans. Steven Miller (New York: Fordham University Press, 2012).

6. Deleuze, *Two Regimes of Madness: Texts and Interviews, 1975–1995*, trans. Ames Hodges and Mike Taormina (New York: Semiotext(e), 2007), 24. Remo Bodei describes this as follows: "Psychoses take the place of reality, reshaping and remodeling the world via hallucinations and delirium, which hereby appear as modalities of a forced adequation: it is external reality that has at all costs to conform to internal reality. Hence the endless attempts to reformulate the perceptual, ideational and affective present in such a way as to nurture and strengthen the mind's new born reality" (Remo Bodei, "Logics of Delirium," *Pli* 13 [2002]: 65–78, 71.)

7. Deleuze, *The Time-Image*, 317n20.

8. Eugene Holland, *Deleuze and Guattari's "Anti-Oedipus": Introduction to Schizoanalysis* (London: Routledge, 1999), x. I will deal with "capitalist economy" as screen culture, following Jonathan Beller's suggestion that capital has realized itself as screen culture. See Jonathan Beller, "Capital/Cinema," in *Deleuze and Guattari: New Mappings in Politics, Philosophy, and Culture*, ed. Eleanor Kaufman and Kevin Jon Heller (Minneapolis: University of Minnesota Press, 1998), 77–95.

9. Deleuze and Guattari, *Anti-Oedipus*, 34.

10. Ibid., 362.

11. Félix Guattari, quoted in Gary Genosko, *Félix Guattari: A Critical Introduction* (London: Pluto, 2009), 13.

12. Ibid., 12.

13. Ibid., 13.

14. See Godfrey D. Rearlson, "Neurological Progress: Neurobiology of Schizophrenia," *Annals of Neurology* 48, no. 4 (2000): 556–66.

15. Ibid., 556.

16. Ibid., 557.

17. Ibid., 556. There are numerous studies on gender differences in schizophrenia. See, e.g., H. Häfner, "Gender Differences in Schizophrenia," *Psychoneuroendocrinology* 28 (2003): 17–54; Figen Atalay and Hakan Atalay, "Gender Differences in Patients with Schizophrenia in Terms of Sociodemographic and Clinical Characteristics," *German Journal of Psychiatry* 9 (2006): 41–47; and M. Hambrecht, K. Maurer, and H. Häfner, "Gender Differences in Schizophrenia in Three Cultures," *Social Psychiatry and Psychiatric Epidemiology* 27 (1992): 117–21.

18. See, e.g., Judy M. Versola-Russo, "Cultural and Demographic Factors of Schizophrenia," *International Journal of Psychosocial Rehabilitation* 10, no. 2 (2006): 89–103; "The Secret Life of the Brain: The Teenage Brain: Culture and Schizophrenia," www.pbs.org/wnet/brain/episode3/cultures/index.html; Perdiep Ramesar, "Dubbelleven Marokkanen fnuikt Psyche," *Trouw*, 27 October 2007, www.trouw.nl.

19. The issue was heavily debated in the Dutch media in 2007 when a schizophrenic young man of Moroccan descent, Bilan B., entered a police station in Amsterdam and stabbed a number of officers who then shot him dead. See Binnert de Beaufort, "Jullie het Debat, Wij het Drama," *NRC Handelsblad*, 28–29 April 2007, 41.

20. Karl J. Friston, "The Disconnection Hypothesis," *Schizophrenic Research* 30 (1998): 115–25. See also Gazzaniga, Ivry, and Mangun, *Cognitive Neuroscience*, 23–61.

21. Friston, "The Disconnection Hypothesis," 117–18.

22. Ibid., 118.

23. Ibid., 122. Another type of neurological evidence that Friston mentions (among others) is histopathological observations that include "(i) decreased hippocampal expression of the embryonic form of the neural cell adhesion molecule (NCAM) in schizophrenia. This form of NCAM has been proposed to be related to synaptic rearrangement and plasticity. (ii) Selective displacement of interstitial white matter neurons in the frontal lobes of schizophrenics that may reflect an alteration in the migration of subplate neurons or into the pattern of programmed cell death. Both could be associated with abnormal neural circuitry and connectivity" (123).

24. See Jill Bolte Taylor, *My Stroke of Insight: A Brain Scientist's Personal Journey* (New York: Penguin, 2008).

25. Niki Korteweg, "Communicatie tussen hersenhelften is nodig voor begrip," *NRC Handelsblad*, 26 February 2006, 45.

26. See, e.g., Alessandro Angrilli et al., "Schizophrenia as Failure of Left Hemispheric Dominance for the Phonological Component of Language," *PLoS ONE* 4, no. 2 (February 2009): 1–9, www.plosone.org; and Brigitte Rockstoh et al., "Failure of Dominant Left-Hemispheric Activation to Right-Ear Stimulation in Schizophrenia," *Neuroreport* 9 (1998): 3819–22.

27. Deleuze and Guattari, *Anti-Oedipus*, 37.

28. Ibid.

29. Deleuze, *Two Regimes of Madness*, 26.

30. Deleuze and Guattari, *A Thousand Plateaus*, 151.

31. Deleuze and Guattari, *Anti-Oedipus*, 329.

32. Deleuze, *Two Regimes of Madness*, 22.

33. Genosko, *Félix Guattari*, 92.

34. Hambrecht, Maurer, and H. Häfner, "Gender Differences in Schizophrenia in Three Cultures," 119. See also Versola-Russo, "Cultural and Demographic Factors of Schizophrenia; Häfner, "Gender Differences in Schizophrenia"; Atalay and Atalay, "Gender Differences in Patients with Schizophrenia in Terms of Sociodemographic and Clinical Characteristics."

35. Deleuze, *The Time-Image*, 222. In his next film, *China Is Still Far* (2008), Bensmail follows schoolchildren in a village in the Aures, but he gives them a camera so that they can make a film with the director, instead of being simply filmed by him.

36. Here an interesting comparison could be made to the function of the tape recorder in the consulting room of the psychoanalyst, a topic discussed by Deleuze and Guattari in *Anti-Oedipus*: "Leave your desiring-machines at the door, give up your orphan and celibate machines, your tape-recorder and your little bike, enter and allow yourself to be Oedipalized" (58). The introduction of the tape recorder ("after a schizophrenic flash") is a breaking of the Oedipal contract. In *Alienations* we see that the camera is not necessarily an intrusion into the Oedipal secret that releases schizoid flows of desire but a desiring-machine that also releases Oedipal traumas.

37. Deleuze and Guattari, *Anti-Oedipus*, 363.

38. For an elaboration on the changes of the family in migration and in media practices see Patricia Pisters and Wim Staat, eds., *Shooting the Family: Transnational Media and Intercultural Values* (Amsterdam: Amsterdam University Press, 2005).

39. Lodge Kerrigan's *Clean, Shaven* (1993) and Harmony Korine's *Julien Donkey Boy* (1999) both render the schizoid perception of the world of their main characters in painfully penetrating images and sounds. Both films also show their male principal characters in relation to their family situation and their unfulfilled desire to be a father. In *Clean, Shaven* the main character, Peter Winter (Peter Green), is a schizophrenic who has lost the ability to order and make recognizable patterns in his brain and who is searching for his daughter. *Julien Donkey Boy* presents in another uncompromising way the world of its schizophrenic main character, Julien (Ewen Bremner). Julien lives with his sister Pearl (Chloe Sevigny), brother Chris (Evan Neumann), and dominant father (Werner Herzog); the film ends with Julien holding his stillborn son in his arms, hiding in bed under the blankets. The film was approved as an official Dogme 95 movie by Lars von Trier and Thomas Winterberg and was shot on digital video. Like Bensmail, Kerrigan and Korine witnessed the delusional and disordered realities of schizophrenic minds from nearby (a friend, a family member) and translated the horror of clinical schizophrenia into the aesthetics of their unusual and powerful fiction films. Kerrigan and Korine discuss this on the DVD extras of both films. See the audio commentary of *Clean, Shaven*, dir. Lodge Kerrigan (1993; Criterion Collection, 1996), Kerrigan in conversation with Steven Soderbergh, DVD. See also the interview with Korine in *The Confessions of Julien Donkey Boy* (New Line Home Entertainment, 2001), DVD.

40. I will refer to the director's cut of the film as distributed in 2004 by New Line Cinema and Icon Home Entertainment on DVD, which includes a

commentary by the filmmakers and contextualizes the film with both scientific theories and insights, as well as film historical backgrounds. Besides the director's commentary, the DVD contains notable extra material such as "The Science and Psychology of Chaos Theory" and "The History and Allure of Time Travel Films."

41. In the DVD extras *The Butterfly Effect* is framed within the genre of time-travel movies.

42. See also Christian Kerslake, *Deleuze and the Unconscious* (London: Continuum, 2007). Freud defines the unconscious in terms of displacement, condensation, and repression, all related to sexuality. The Deleuzian unconscious is based on Bergson and related to the synthesis of memories and duration. Kerslake discusses the Deleuzian unconscious in relation to Jungian collective psychology.

43. Garrett Stewart discusses time and memory in *The Butterfly Effect*, as well as in *Donnie Darko* (Richard Kelly, 2001), as a Hollywood Gothic science fiction, as opposed to the European uncanny humanism of films such as *The Double Life of Veronique* (Krzysztof Kieslowski, 1991) and *Swimming Pool* (Francois Ozon, 2003). See Garrett Stewart, "Cimnemonics versus Digitime," in *Afterimages of Gilles Deleuze's Film Philosophy*, ed. David Rodowick (Minneapolis: University of Minnesota Press, 2002), 327–50.

44. Genosko, *Félix Guattari*, 167–73.

45. Deleuze, *The Time-Image*, 265.

46. Paul Virilio, *The Aesthetics of Disappearance*, trans. Philip Beitchman (New York: Semiotext(e), 1991).

47. In the theatrical version Evan scares Kayleigh away the first moment they meet so that they never cross paths again. The film ends eight years in the future, where Evan recognizes Kayleigh in a crowded city street but after a moment of hesitation lets her pass by.

48. Martin P. Paulus and David L. Braff, "Chaos and Schizophrenia: Does the Method Fit the Madness?" *Biological Psychiatry* 53 (2003): 3–11, 3.

49. Hambrecht, Maurer, and Häfner, "Gender Differences in Schizophrenia in Three Cultures," 119.

50. Jim Clark, review of *Fear of Fear*, http://jclarkmedia.com/fassbinder/fassbinder25.html, 8.

51. In one scene Margot's mother-in-law openly criticizes Margot's cuddling and affectionate behavior with her children. "That is not normal," she says. Michael Haneke's *Das Weisse Band* (2009) gives this remark about the norm of unaffectionate behavior intertextual weight and further political implications.

52. Vincent Canby, "The Screen: Fassbinder's 'Fear of Fear.'" *New York Times*, 15 October 1976.

53. Frank Starik, "Hoe verdriet eruit ziet," *NRC Handelsblad*, 23 October 2009, 8–9.

54. See Kerslake, *Deleuze and the Unconscious.*

55. Bodei, "Logics of Delirium," 74.

56. Here it is useful to refer to *The Five Obstructions* (Lars Von Trier and Jørgen Leth, 2003), which is more or less paradigmatic for Von Trier's approach to film-making. The premise of *The Five Obstructions* is that "Lars von Trier has created a challenge for his friend and mentor, Jørgen Leth, another filmmaker. Von Trier's favorite film is Leth's *The Perfect Human* (1967). Von Trier gives Leth the task of re-making *The Perfect Human* five times, each time with a different 'obstruction' (or obstacle) given by von Trier" (quoted at http://en.wikipedia.org/wiki/The_Five_Obstructions). With each film of his own, Von Trier has set himself similar sorts of rules or constraints (be it Dogme rules, or the use of hundreds of digital cameras in *Dancer in the Dark*, or the empty stage floor and chalk marks of *Dogville*). In *Antichrist* the "rules" seem to have been set by his own dark mental condition. Like *Melancholia* (2011) it is the pure expression of depressed affect.

57. *The Dick Cavett Show, Cassavetes, Falk, and Gazzara* on YouTube, www.youtube.com/watch?v=4NiThZ8tJLI.

58. John Cassavetes, *Hollywood 1965*, YouTube, www.youtube.com/watch?v=pcgWO-hxZls.

59. *I'm Almost Not Crazy—John Cassavetes—The Man and His Work* (1984), YouTube, www.youtube.com/watch?v=gSZVYOgKIwE.

60. *Cassavetes in 60 Seconds*, YouTube, www.youtube.com/watch?v=hwbgEO9d47w.

61. Consider the upscale production values of (among many other shows) *The Sopranos* (HBO, 1999–2007), *Six Feet Under* (HBO, 2001–5), *Lost* (ABC, 2004–10), *Desperate Housewives* (ABC, 2004–), and *Mad Men* (AMC, 2007–).

62. See http://en.wikipedia.org/wiki/Twin_Peaks.

63. See "The City of Absurdity: *Inland Empire*," www.thecityofabsurdity.com/inlandempire/index.html.

64. Dennis Lim, "David Lynch Goes Digital," *Slate*, www.slate.com/id/2172678/.

65. Mark Amerika, *Meta/Data: A Digital Poetics* (Cambridge, MA, MIT Press, 2000)

66. Deleuze, *The Time-Image*, 204.

67. Ibid., 205.

68. Ibid., 193. See also the documentary *To Risk Everything to Express It All* (Rudolf Mestdagh, 1999) on www.youtube.com/watch?v=nlSh8SXR2tI.

69. See Dern's comments at http://en.wikipedia.org/wiki/Inland_Empire_(film).

70. See www.saatchi-gallery.co.uk/blogon/art_news/david_lynch_at_the_fondation_cartier_paris/1496. Michel Chion visited the exhibition with Lynch. See *Inland Empire*, dir. David Lynch (2006; Cineart and Twin Pics, 2007), DVD.

71. Lynch's way of filming is marked by this uncertainty: "I never saw any whole, W-H-O-L-E. I saw plenty of holes, H-O-L-E-S. But I didn't really worry. I would get an idea for a scene and shoot it, get another idea and shoot that. I didn't know how they would relate" (www.thecityofabsurdity.com/inland empire/index.html).

72. Guy Debord, *The Society of the Spectacle*, trans. Donald Nicholson-Smith (New York: Zone Books, 1995).

73. See also Elena del Rio, *Deleuze and the Cinemas of Performance: Powers of Affection* (Edinburgh: Edinburgh University Press, 2008), 178–203.

74. "Television Sucks," www.youtube.com/watch?v=ePptcNqXRJA.

75. Dennis Lim, "David Lynch Goes Digital," *Slate*, www.slate.com /id/2172678/.

76. Deleuze, *The Time-Image*, 193.

77. Gazzaniga, Ivry, and Mangun, *Cognitive Neuroscience*, 25. On Lynch's *Axxonn* see www.lynchnet.com/axxonn/. Lynch has a new collecting project online, The Interview Project; see DavidLynch.com.

78. David Lynch, quoted at http://en.wikipedia.org/wiki/Inland_Empire _(film).

79. Bodei, "Logics of Delirium," 77.

80. Jill Bolte Taylor, quoted by Robert Koehler, "Hemorrhaging Nirvana," http://drjilltaylor.com/articles.html.

81. Deleuze and Guattari, *A Thousand Plateaus*, 15.

82. Gilles Lipovetsky and Jean Serroy, *L'écran global: Culture-médias et cinéma à l'âge hypermoderne* (Paris: Edition du Seuil, 2007). The other ages they distinguish are the Age of Primitive Modernity (silent cinema, where cinema struggled for artistic recognition), the Age of Classical Modernity (the Golden Age of Hollywood, the studio system, omniscient narration), and the Modernist Age (emancipatory modernity and New Waves). They situate the beginning of this age in the 1980s.

83. Gilles Lipovetsky, *Hypermodern Times* (Cambridge, UK: Polity, 2003).

84. Rodowick, *The Virtual Life of Film*, 141–63.

85. Deleuze, *The Time-Image*, 211–12.

86. Jean-Louis Comolli, "Machines of the Visible," in *The Cinematic Apparatus*, ed. Teresa de Lauretis and Stephen Heath (Basingstoke: Macmillan, 1980), 121–142, 133.

87. See also Linda Williams, *Hardcore: Power, Pleasure, and the "Frenzy of the Visible"* (Berkeley: University of California Press, 1989) for a historical analysis of cinema as belonging to this paradigm, connecting it to the nineteenth-century "frenzy of the visible."

CHAPTER 2

1. Part of this chapter has been published as "Illusionary Perception and Cinema: Experimental Thoughts on Film Theory and Neuroscience," in *Deleuze and New Technology*, ed. David Savat (Edinburgh: Edinburgh University Press, 2009), 224–40.

2. Hugo Münsterberg, *The Photoplay: A Psychological Study and Other Writings*, ed. Allan Langdale (1916; New York: Routledge, 2002), 61.

3. Edgar Morin, *The Cinema, or, The Imaginary Man*, trans. Lorraine Mortimer (Minneapolis: University of Minnesota Press, 2005), xi.

4. Ibid., 206.

5. I refer to "illusionary perception" and "visual illusion." Sometimes the phrase "optical illusion" is used. Strictly speaking, optical illusions refer to illusions or distortions of vision in the outside world and are related to the retinal system. Visual illusions refer to illusions caused by processes in the brain when the input is ambiguous or seemingly at odds with itself. These terms, however, are commonly used interchangeably.

6. Ira Konigsberg, "Film Studies and the New Science," *Projections* 1, no. 1 (2007): 6. See also Uri Hasson, Orit Furman, Dav Clark, Yadin Dudai, and Lila Davachi, "Enhanced Intersubjective Correlations During Movie Viewing Correlate with Successful Episodic Encoding," in *Neuron* 57 (2008): 452–62; and Uri Hasson, Ohad Landesman, Barbara Knappmeyer, Ignacio Vallines, Nava Rubin, and David J. Heeger, "Neurocinematics: The Neuroscience of Film," *Projections* 2, no. 1 (2008): 1–26.

7. In *L'Abécédaire de Gilles Deleuze*, with Claire Parnet, Deleuze refuses to say anything about the letter *W* (for Wittgenstein).

8. John Protevi, "One More 'Next Step': Deleuze and Brain, Body and Affect in Contemporary Cognitive Science" in *Revisiting Normativity with Deleuze*, ed. Rosi Braidotti and Patricia Pisters (London: Continuum, 2012 forthcoming); see also "Deleuze and Wexler: Thinking Brain, Body and Affect in Social Contexts," in *Cognitive Architecture: From Bio-politics to Noo-politics*, ed. Deborah Hauptmann, Warren Neidich, and Abdul-Karim Mustapha (Rotterdam: 2010), 168-183.

9. Protevi, "Deleuze and Cognitive Science," forthcoming.

10. Alva Noë, *Action in Perception* (Cambridge, MA: MIT Press, 2004), 227.

11. Robert Pepperell, "Where Is the Screen?" 192. See also the discussion of this question in the introduction of this book.

12. See Gazzaniga, Ivry and Mangun, *Cognitive Neuroscience*.

13. Langdale, "S(t)imulation of Mind: The Film Theory of Hugo Münsterberg," in Münsterberg, *The Photoplay*, 9.

14. Ibid., 26.

15. See, e.g., David Bordwell, *Making Meaning: Interference and Rhetoric in the Interpretation of Cinema* (Cambridge, MA: Harvard University Press, 1989).

16. Deleuze and Guattari, *What Is Philosophy?* 206–8.

17. Robert-Houdin was the first to perform magic tricks onstage in his theater on the Boulevards des Italiens in Paris, which he opened in the 1860s. The theater's last owner before its destruction in 1927 was Georges Méliès, the famous film pioneer who combined cinema and stage illusions.

18. Nikola Tesla (1856–1943) was a Serbian-U.S. inventor and electrical engineer whose work was critical for much of the electronic technology we make use of today, including radio, telephone, and television. For more information on him and the impact of his work see www.electricalternative.com/tesla.htm.

19. For a presentation of visual illusions see www.michaelbach.de/ot/. See also www.visual-media.be/ for an archaeological overview of media technology and visual illusions.

20. For a historical overview of this effect and its significance for modern neurosciences see G. Mather, F. Verstraten, and S. Anstis, eds., *The Motion Aftereffect: A Modern Perspective* (Cambridge, MA: MIT Press, 1998).

21. See David M. Eagleman, "Visual Illusions and Neurobiology," *Nature Reviews Neuroscience* 2, no. 12 (2001): 920–26; and Richard L. Gregory, "Knowledge in Perception and Illusion," *Philosophical Translations Royal Society of London* 325 (1997): 1121–27.

22. M. Bach and C. Poloschek, "Optical Illusions," *Advances in Clinical Neuroscience* 6, no. 2 (2006): 20–21, 20.

23. Ibid.

24. See Eagleman, "Visual Illusions and Neurobiology" *Nature* vol. 2 (2001): 920–25; and Alva Noë, ed., "Is the Visual World a Grand Illusion?" *Journal of Consciousness Studies* 9, no. 5–6 (2002): 1–12.

25. See Gregory, "Knowledge in Perception and Illusion."

26. Eric Alliez takes hallucination as a starting point for reconsidering the aesthetics of modern painting. See Eric Alliez, *L'oeil-cerveaux: Nouvelles histoires de la peinture moderne* (Paris: Vrin, 2007).

27. Gregory, "Knowledge in Perception and Illusion," 1121.

28. Joseph Anderson, *The Reality of Illusions: An Ecological Approach to Cognitive Film Theory* (Carbondale: Southern Illinois university Press, 1996), 48.

29. Konigsberg, "Film Studies and the New Science," 7.

30. Allan Langdale, introduction to Münsterberg's *The Photoplay*, 15–16.

31. Deleuze, *The Movement-Image*, 74.

32. Deleuze refers to this semisubjective quality of cinema as "free indirect discourse" (see *The Movement-Image*, 72–75; see also Patricia Pisters, "Arresting the Flux of Images and Sounds: Free Indirect Discourse and the Dialectics of Po-

litical Cinema," in *Deleuze and the Contemporary World*, ed. Ian Buchanan and Adrian Parr [Edinburgh: Edinburgh University Press], 175–93).

33. The plot summary of *The Illusionist*, according to the DVD cover: "The acclaimed illusionist Eisenheim (Edward Norton) has not only captured the imaginations of all Vienna, but also the interest of the ambitious Crown Prince Leopold (Rufus Sewell). But when Leopold's new fiancée Sophie (Jessica Biel) rekindles a childhood fascination with Eisenheim, the Prince's interest evolves into obsession . . . and suddenly the city's chief inspector Uhl (Paul Giamatti) finds himself investigating a shocking crime [the murder of Sophie]. But even as the inspector engages him in a dramatic challenge of wills, Eisenheim prepares for his most impressive illusion yet."

34. Deleuze, *The Movement-Image*, 72. Deleuze relates this characteristic to what he calls the perception-image, which is both a specific image type but also the "zeroness" of all images, a sort of "degree zero" at the basis of all cinematographic perception.

35. *The Illusionist*, dir. Neil Burger (2006; 20th Century Fox, 2006), DVD audio commentary.

36. The plot summary of *The Prestige* from the DVD cover: "Two young, passionate magicians, Robert Angier (Hugh Jackman), a charismatic showman, and Alfred Borden (Christian Bale), a gifted illusionist, are friends and partners until one fateful night when their biggest trick goes terribly wrong [and Angier's girlfriend drowns]. Now the bitterest of enemies, they will stop at nothing to learn each other's secrets. As their rivalry escalates into a total obsession full of deceit and sabotage, they risk everything to become the greatest magicians of all time. But nothing is as it seems, so watch closely." Additional cast: Michael Caine, Scarlett Johansson, Rebecca Hall, and David Bowie.

37. Münsterberg, *The Photoplay*, 78–80.

38. Ibid., 85–86. Münsterberg differentiates between voluntary attention, in which we actively seek something, and involuntary attention, which is sparked from something external. It is this type of attention that Münsterberg relates to cinema, but in both cases he relates attention to consciousness.

39. Ibid., 87.

40. Victor Lamme, "Why Visual Attention and Awareness Are Different," *Trends in Cognitive Sciences* 7, no. 1 (2003): 12–18, 12.

41. See also Raja Parasuraman, ed., *The Attentive Brain* (Cambridge, MA: MIT Press, 2000).

42. Victor Lamme and Pieter Roelfsema, "The Distinct Modes of Vision Offered by Feedforward and Recurrent Processing," *Trends in Neuroscience* 23, no. 11 (2000): 571–79, 571. See also Victor Lamme, H. Supèr, and H. Spekreijse, "Feedforward, Horizontal, and Feedback Processing in the Visual Cortex," *Current Opinion in Neurobiology* 8, no. 4 (1998): 529–35.

43. Victor Lamme, *De geest uit de fles* (Amsterdam: Vossius Pers, 2006), 35.

44. Ibid., 29.

45. Victor Lamme, "Neural Mechanisms of Visual Awareness: A Linking Proposition," *Brain and Mind* 1, no. 3 (2000): 385–406, 399.

46. Münsterberg, *The Photoplay*, 191.

47. Michael Gazzaniga, *The Mind's Past* (Berkeley: University of California Press, 1998), 128–29.

48. Ibid., 131.

49. Ibid., 133.

50. Ibid., 26.

51. Ibid., 172.

52. Also in *Memento* (2000) and in *Inception* (2010), Nolan has shown explicit interest in the brain-screen. *Memento* is a search through an amnesiac mind. *Inception* investigates the deepest layers of unconscious dream states.

53. When Ledger was found dead in his New York apartment, he was in the middle of recording another "insane" film, Terry Gilliam's *The Imaginarium of Dr. Parnassus* (2010). The film was completed with the help of Jude Law, Johnny Depp, and Colin Farrell stepping in to play Ledger's role as "The Hanging Man." One cannot help sensing that some of the eerie and forceful powers of fiction with which he was engaging as an actor affected Ledger significantly.

54. Deleuze, *The Time-Image*, 132. It is possible to object here that since Deleuze introduced the forger into the time-image, this character is not so typical for the neuro-image. On the one hand it is true that in this respect the neuro-image is rather an intensification of the time-image's powers of the false. On the other hand it is significant that the powers of the false are introduced via Nietzsche, who toward the end of the cinema books seems to replace Bergson. In Chapter 4 I will argue that the appearance of Nietzsche is a significant part of a changed perception of time that becomes more prominent in the neuro-image but that has its incipiency in the time-image. In that sense Welles's forging characters have to be seen as lucid precursors to later characters in contemporary cinema.

55. Ibid., 141.

56. Ibid., 145.

57. Raymond Van Ee, A. J. Noest, J. W. Brascamp, and A. V. Van den Berg, "Attentional Control over Either of the Two Competing Percepts of Ambiguous Stimuli Revealed by a Two-Parameter Analysis: Means Do Not Make the Difference," *Vision Research* 46, no. 19 (2006): 3129–41, 3129.

58. For a beautiful assessment of the ethical values of fiction see also Gregory Currie, "Realism of Character and the Value of Fiction," in *Aesthetics and Ethics: Essays at the Intersection*, ed. Jerrold Levinson (Cambridge, UK: Cambridge University Press, 1998), 161–79.

CHAPTER 3

1. See Michel Foucault, *Discipline and Punish: The Birth of the Prison*, trans. Alan Sheridan (New York: Vintage, 1979); and Gilles Deleuze, "Postscript on Control Societies," in *Negotiations*, repr. in *CTRL [space]: Rhetorics of Surveillance from Bentham to Big Brother*, ed. Thomas Levin, Ursula Frohne, and Peter Weibel (Cambridge, MA: MIT Press, 2002), 317–21. See also Greg Elme, "A Diagram of Panoptic Surveillance," *New Media & Society* 5, no. 2 (2003): 231–47; David Lyon, ed., *Theorizing Surveillance: The Panopticon and Beyond* (Devon, UK: Willan, 2006). See also the online journal *Surveillance and Society*, www .surveillance-and-society.org.

2. See Wendy Hui Kyong Chun, *Control and Freedom: Power and Paranoia in the Age of Fiber Optics* (Cambridge, MA: MIT Press, 2006).

3. Gilles Deleuze, "Control and Becoming," in *Negotiations*, 175.

4. Ibid., 176.

5. See Jill Magid, *Evidence Locker*, http://jillmagid.net/EvidenceLocker.php. The larger framework of surveillance art as "circuit breakers" is important here but falls outside the scope of this chapter. See http://en.wikipedia.org/wiki/ Surveillance_art.

6. Magid, *Evidence Locker*, Letter 4, received in personal mail, 28 July 2008.

7. The "affective turn" in science, culture, and theory will be an important background for the reflections and analyses in this chapter. In media studies and philosophy the affective turn is mainly related to a revaluation of the embodied phenomenology of Merleau-Ponty and to the influence of Deleuze and Guattari. See Laura Marks, *The Skin of the Film: Intercultural Cinema, Embodiment, and the Senses* (Durham, NC: Duke University Press, 2000); Anne Rutherford, "Cinema and Embodied Affect," *Senses of Cinema* 25 (2002): www.sensesof cinema.com/2003/25/embodied_affect/; Brian Massumi, *Parables of the Virtual: Movement, Affect, Sensation* (Durham, NC: Duke University Press, 2002); Vivian Sobchack, *Carnal Thoughts: Embodiment and Moving Image Culture* (Berkeley: University of California Press, 2004); and Del Rio, *Deleuze and the Cinemas of Performance*; see also Patricia Clough and Jean Halley, eds., *The Affective Turn: Theorizing the Social* (Durham, NC: Duke University Press, 2007).

8. Deleuze, *The Movement-Image*, 210.

9. *The Bourne Identity* (Doug Liuman, 2002), *The Bourne Supremacy* (Paul Greengrass, 2004), and *The Bourne Ultimatum* (Paul Greengrass, 2007) are all (loosely) based on Robert Ludlum's Jason Bourne novels. Bourne suffers from retrograde amnesia and has to rediscover who he is and why several groups are trying to kill him.

10. Dietmar Kammerer, "Video Surveillance in Hollywood Movies," *Surveillance and Society* 2, no. 2/3 (2004): 473. See also John S. Turner, "Collapsing the

Interior/Exterior Distinction: Surveillance, Spectacle, and Suspense in Popular Cinema," *Wide Angle* 20, no. 4 (1998): 93–123.

11. *The Last Enemy* website, www.bbc.co.uk/drama/lastenemy.

12. "Keeping Up with the Future," http://news.bbc.co.uk/2/hi/uk_news/magazine/7246763.stm. Richard Rogers and Sabine Niederer discuss this laziness in respect to consumer culture and consumer technology: "To participate in consumer society, you have to be watched. It's not so much that resistance is futile. It has more to do with the fact that there is just too much interactivity. (...) Eventually, one yields back to the default setting, and carries on with 'whatever'" (Richard Rogers, "Consumer Technology After Surveillance Theory," in *Mind the Screen: Media Concepts According to Thomas Elsaesser*, ed. Jaap Kooijman, Patricia Pisters, and Wanda Strauven [Amsterdam: Amsterdam University Press, 2008], 288–96, 289).

13. "Keeping Up with the Future."

14. Chun, *Control and Freedom*, 297.

15. Fuller, *Media Ecologies*, 131. Fuller adds that this type of dynamic relationality is always political and can never be accused of a flattening "relativism." Dimensions of relationality can be the classic "causations" like class, race, and gender. But they can also be something as simple as "being able to read, visualize, sense, record or otherwise apprehend an object, process, or event." Or they can be forces like norms, laws, or markets (131).

16. Del Rio, *Deleuze and the Cinemas of Performance*, 9.

17. The other directors are Mikkel Nørgaars and Morag McKinnon. Another way of describing the project would be to say that the directors are each asked to present a potential scale of a "dimension of relationalities" for the characters based on the same "data" that can be recombined in different ways. As such, Dogme films subscribe to a "database logic" typical of digital culture. In "Affinitive and Milieu-Building Transnationalism: The Advance Party Initiative," Mette Hjort discusses the transnational dimensions of the Dogme project in general and of *The Advance Party* in particular (*Cinema at the Periphery*, ed. Dina Iordonova, David Martin-Jones, and Belén Vidal [Detroit: Wayne State University Press, 2010], 46–66). David Martin-Jones describes the transnational feeling of the mise-en-scène, even though it is set in Scotland. See David Martin-Jones, *Scotland: Global Cinema—Genres, Modes and Identities* (Edinburgh: Edinburgh University Press, 2010), 229–30.

18. Andrea Arnold, interview by Michael Joshua Rowin, *Reverse Shot* 26, http://www.reverseshot.com/article/interview_andrea_arnold.

19. Kammerer, "Video Surveillance in Hollywood Movies," 466. See also Anne Friedberg's *The Virtual Window*, which gives an insightful taxonomy of multiple screen variations (202–39). The prime example of one of the first feature films using surveillance aesthetics is *Time Code* (Mike Figgis, 1994), a film told in four split screens, involving four digital video cameras following four separate

lines of action filmed in "real time" in one ninety-three-minute unedited take. Friedberg quotes from the *Time Code* website: "Digital Video has arrived. For the first time, a film shot in real-time. Who do you want to watch? A story that could be told in four dimensions" (218). Of course experiments in real time have been undertaken previously (think of Hitchcock's *Rope*), but the aesthetics of real time and simultaneity is typical for digital culture.

20. See Laura Marks's elaborate description of haptic visuality in *The Skin of Film*, 170–93.

21. "For all the Orwellian overtones, her film stresses that the people monitoring us aren't fascist snitches—they're underpaid drudges calling ambulances for stabbing victims," says Danny Leigh in the *Guardian*. See Danny Leigh, "I Like Darkness: Andrea Arnold Talks *Red Road* and Oscars," *Guardian*, 17 October 2006, www.guardian.co.uk/film/2006/oct/18/londonfilmfestival2006 .londonfilmfestival1.

22. Brian Massumi, "The Autonomy of Affect," in *Parables for the Virtual: Movement, Affect, Sensation* (Durham, NC: Duke University Press, 2002), 23–45.

23. Ibid., 25. Neuroscientists have begun to collaborate with artists to research precisely these effects, finding that images usually evoke more intensive affects than words alone. See Roel Willems, Krien Clevis, and Peter Hagoort, "Add a Picture for Suspense: Neural Correlates of the Interaction Between Language and Visual Information in the Perception of Fear," *Social Cognitive and Affective Neuroscience* 5, nos. 2–3 (2010): 404–16.

24. Massumi also refers to "stories of the brain" in his essay on affect. His philosophical references are to Spinoza and Bergson. I will refer to the philosophical dimensions of the neuro-image in the second part of this book.

25. See Gazzaniga, Ivry, and Mangun, *Cognitive Neuroscience*, 537–76.

26. Damasio, *Looking for Spinoza*, 80. Another leading expert in the field of affective neuroscience is Joseph LeDoux, who has conducted a range of experiments investigating the emotion of fear. See Gazzaniga, Ivry, and Mangun, *Cognitive Neuroscience*, 543; and Joseph LeDoux, *The Emotional Brain: The Mysterious Underpinnings of Emotional Life* (New York: Simon and Shuster, 1996). In 2004 LeDoux was named head of New York University's Center for Neuroscience of Fear and Anxiety.

27. Massumi, "The Autonomy of Affect," 30.

28. Niels Bohr, *Atomic Theory and Description of Nature*, quoted in Gazzaniga, *The Mind's Past*, 63.

29. These experiments are described in Gazzaniga, Ivry, and Mangun, *Cognitive Neuroscience*, 551–53. Also frequently mentioned in this respect is the famous experiment by Benjamin Libet, which indicated that "brain potentials are firing three hundred and fifty milliseconds before you have the conscious intention to act. So before you are aware that you're thinking about moving your arm,

your brain is at work preparing to make that movement" (Gazzaniga, *The Mind's Past*, 73). Libet's experiment is often raised to discuss the (im)possibility of free will; however, the only sure thing the experiment indicates is that consciousness takes time.

30. Damasio, *Looking for Spinoza*, 68. William James is another important reference for having proposed this view on the physical basis of emotions: "We feel sad because we cry, angry because we strike, afraid because we tremble," he says in "What Is an Emotion?" *Mind* 9 (1884): 188–205.

31. Spinoza, quoted in Damasio, *Looking for Spinoza*, 211.

32. Basic emotions in facial expression are anger, fear, disgust, happiness, sadness, and surprise. See Ralph Adolphs, Hanna Damasio, Daniel Tranel, and Antonio Damasio, "Cortical Systems for the Recognition of Emotion in Facial Expressions," *Journal of Neuroscience* 16, no. 23 (1996): 7678–87. Joseph LeDoux indicates how basic emotions help us to respond to environmental challenges, taking care of "defense against danger, sexual behavior, maternal behavior, eating and other things like this" (Gazzaniga, Ivry, and Mangun, *Cognitive Neuroscience*, 543). See also Jaak Panksepp, "A Critical Role for 'Affective Neuroscience' in Resolving What Is Basic About Basic Emotions," *Psychological Review* 99, no. 3 (1992): 554–60.

33. Most famously, Hitchcock explains the difference between surprise and suspense by giving the example of a scene where two people are having a conversation, sitting at a table. We watch them just talking, and suddenly a bomb explodes; the effect is "surprise." If we have the same scene, but filmed in such a way that the audience is given a shot of the bomb hidden under the table, the effect will be "suspense": the audience is now included in the knowledge of an impending danger and will want to warn the characters. Although Hitchcock provides the most clear narratological explanation of suspense, it also has to be acknowledged that Hitchcock was very conscious of the effects of film on the spectator's mind and of the affective dimensions of film aesthetics. If one compares the classical suspense thriller to the "neurothriller," one could say that in the former the narrative gives rise to feelings of suspense, while in the latter the emotional dimension comes first.

34. Andreas Bartels and Semir Zeki, "The Neural Correlates of Maternal and Romantic Love," *NeuroImage* 21 (2004): 1155–66, 1155. Bartels and Zeki made fMRI scans of mothers watching pictures of their own child versus an acquainted child, and pictures of their loved partner versus a friend, and then compared these findings, discovering significant overlapping activity regions in the maternal and lover areas: "The similarity of the results compared to those obtained in our previous study on romantic love is striking; several regions overlap precisely, while others are specific to each form of attachment" (1161).

35. Affective neuroscience in general has emphasized that emotions have to be seen in a distributed network of cortical and subcortical circuits that allow change, overlap, and plasticity. See Richard J. Davidson, "Seven Sins in the Study of Emotion: Correctives from Affective Neuroscience," *Brain and Cognition* 52 (2003): 129–32; and Richard J. Davidson, Daren J. Jackson, and Ned H. Kalin, "Emotion, Plasticity, Context, and Regulation: Perspectives from Affective Neuroscience," *Psychological Bulletin* 126, no. 6 (2000): 890–909.

36. Damasio rightfully warns that this does not mean that ethics (and laws and politics and other sociopolitical phenomena) depend solely on neurobiological factors. See Damasio, *Looking for Spinoza*, 159–60.

37. Gazzaniga, Ivry, and Mangun, *Cognitive Neuroscience*, 545. See also Jorge Moll et al., "The Neural Correlates of Moral Sensitivity: A Functional Magnetic Resonance Imaging Investigation of Basic Moral Emotions," *Journal of Neuroscience* 22, no. 7 (2002): 2730–36; and Joshua Greene and Jonathan Haidt, "How (and Where) Does Moral Judgment Work?" *Trends in Cognitive Science* 6, no. 12 (2002): 517–23.

38. Vittorio Gallese, "The Shared Manifold Hypothesis: From Mirror Neurons to Empathy," *Journal of Consciousness Studies* 8, no. 5–7 (2001): 33–50, 35.

39. Ibid., 36–37 (Gallese's emphasis). Gallese explains his hypothesis further: "My proposal is to interpret the motor activity of mirror neurons in terms of an efference copy of the motor program signal. Once the features of the object to be grasped are specified, and 'translated' by canonical neurons into the most suitable motor program enabling successful action to be produced, a copy of this signal is fed to mirror neurons. This signal would act as a sort of 'simulator' of the programmed action. This simulation of the action is used to predict its consequences, thus enabling the achievement of a better control strategy" (40).

40. Ibid., 41. Gallese argues here against the classic cognitivist idea of a "Theory of Mind" (TOM) in which other minds are conceived on the basis of inferential theories and hypotheses. See also Vittorio Gallese and Alvin Goldman, "Mirror Neurons and the Simulation Theory of Mind Reading," *Trends in Cognitive Science* 2, no. 12 (1998): 493–501.

41. Damasio, *Looking for Spinoza*, 117. Mirror neurons are also important in the study of autism, where they do not seem to function very well (thus no direct empathy can be established).

42. See, e.g., Marco Iacoboni, *Mirroring People: The New Science of How We Connect with Others* (New York: Farrar, Straus and Giroux, 2008); and V. S. Ramachandran, *The Tell-Tale Brain: Unlocking the Mystery of Human Nature* (London: William Heinemann, 2011).

43. See Christian Metz, *The Imaginary Signifier: Psychoanalysis and Cinema*, trans. Celia Britton, Annwyl Williams, Ben Brewster, and Alfred Guzzetti (Bloomington: Indiana University Press, 1984).

44. See, e.g., Laura Mulvey, "Visual Pleasure and Narrative Cinema," as well as other seminal articles of this important paradigm in film studies, in *Narrative, Apparatus, Ideology: A Film Theory Reader*, ed. Philip Rosen (New York: Columbia University Press, 1986).

45. See, e.g., Slavoj Žižek, *Looking Awry: An Introduction to Jacques Lacan Through Popular Culture* (Cambridge: MIT Press, 1991).

46. See Murray Smith, *Engaging Characters: Fiction, Emotion, and the Cinema* (Oxford: Oxford University Press, 1995).

47. As I indicated at the beginning of this chapter, theorists of the affective turn (including phenomenological perspectives) do acknowledge this embodied aspect of the viewer-screen relationship. See also Dieter Lohmar, "Mirror Neurons and the Phenomenology of Intersubjectivity," *Phenomenology and the Cognitive Sciences* 5 (2006): 5–16.

48. Gallese, "The Shared Manifold Hypothesis," 37.

49. Münsterberg, *The Photoplay*, 191–200. See also Chapter 2 above. Marco Iacoboni discussed the controversial issue of media violence and the power of advertisements in this respect (Iacoboni, *Mirroring People*, 204–42).

50. Gallese, "The Shared Manifold Hypothesis," 46.

51. Gallese distinguishes three levels: a phenomenological level, a functional level, and a subpersonal level, which he calls the "shared manifold" on which intersubjective communications through mirror neurons can operate. See ibid., 45.

52. Ibid., 38.

53. Norman Holland, "The Neuroscience of Metafilm," *Projections* 1, no. 1 (2007): 59–74. Paul Virno asks another important question. Referring to Gallese's work, he asks how it is possible that, given the intersubjective and empathic power of mirror neurons, this power can be negated. His political example is that of the Nazi officer who is unable to recognize the old Jewish man as a fellow member of the human species. Virno suggests that this incapacity is due to a linguistic power, the power of words that can counter the power of empathic mirror neurons. So language is a negation of empathy; it introduces the possibility of nonrecognition: "Negation certainly does not obstruct the activation of mirror neurons. But it renders the signification of these neurons as something ambiguous and reversible" (183–84). At the same time language can also be used as an antidote against this negation, a negation of a negation, and thus exert a "force that restrains" and that "ceaselessly postpones total destruction" (189). Paul Virno, "Mirror Neurons, Linguistic Negation, Reciprocal Recognition," in *Multitude: Between Innovation and Negation*, trans. Isabella Bertoletti, James Cascaito, and Andrea Casson (Los Angeles: Semiotext(e), 2008), 175–90.

54. Holland, "The Neuroscience of Metafilm," 70. Holland explains: "Dorsolateral prefrontal cortex is essential for planning, choosing among, and executing or inhibiting actions."

55. Fuller, *Media Ecologies*, 153.

56. This is not to say that voyeurism is no longer an issue or that the voyeur is always in control. Michael Powell's *Peeping Tom* (1959), often offered as an allegory of the psychoanalytic conception of the cinematographic apparatus, is a case in point. At the end of the film Mark Lewis's (Karlheinz Böhm) murderous voyeurism turns into masochistic identification with his victims, when he throws himself into the blade of the tripod of his own camera.

CHAPTER 4

1. A small portion of this chapter has been published as "Flashforward: The Future Is Now," in "Deleuzian Futures," ed. Nir Kedem, special issue, *Deleuze Studies* 5, no. 3 (2011): 98–115.

2. Alain Resnais, interview by François Chalais, 1961, www.youtube.com /watch?v=gTg_knL4cks.

3. Deleuze, *The Time-Image*, 270.

4. Ibid., 266. Gregg Lambert and Gregory Flaxman propose in a similar way that "the future of the cinematic brain lies in the development of the crystalline image" (Gregg Lambert and Gregory Flaxman, "Ten Propositions on the Brain," *Pli*, no. 16 (2005): 114–128, 124.

5. Deleuze, *The Time-Image*, 371. William Connolly argues that cinema can reveal things about the constitution of time that otherwise remain hidden. See William E. Connolly, *Neuropolitics: Thinking, Culture, Speed* (Minneapolis: University of Minnesota Press, 2002). I will return to Connolly's work in Part 3.

6. Henri Bergson, *Mind-Energy: Lectures and Essays*, trans. H. Wildon Carr (New York: H. Holt, 1920). I will refer to this original version. A new annotated edition with an introduction by Keith Ansell Pearson has been published by Palgrave (2007).

7. Christian Kerslake, *Deleuze and the Unconscious*, 32.

8. Deleuze, *The Time-Image*, 22.

9. Gilles Deleuze, *Difference and Repetition*, trans. Paul Patton (London: Athlone Press, 1994).

10. John Mullarkey, "'The Very Life of Things': Thinking Objects and Reversing Thought in Bergsonian Metaphysics," in Henri Bergson, *An Introduction to Metaphysics* (New York: Palgrave Macmillan, 2007), ix–xxxiii, xi. Bergson defines intuition as a kind of "intellectual sympathy by which one places oneself

within an object in order to coincide with what is unique in it and consequently inexpressible" (5).

11. Bergson, *Introduction to Metaphysics*, 44.

12. Ibid., 54.

13. Ibid., 7. "We may sympathize intellectually with nothing else, but we certainly sympathize with our own selves," Bergson adds.

14. Ibid., 6–15. Strictly speaking, Bergson does refer to perceptions, memories, and motor-habits but not directly to affects or emotions. However, he does refer to a continuous flux that is moving underneath perceptions and memories, which, arguably, can be connected to the intensive levels of affect discussed in the previous chapter. Deleuze discusses Bergson's critique of intensity as unconvincing in *Difference and Repetition* (239), showing that intensity and extensity in fact cannot be separated.

15. Bergson, *Introduction to Metaphysics*, 11.

16. In *Matter and Memory* Bergson develops a concept of the image beyond the dualism of Idealist versus Realist: "Matter, in our view, is an aggregate of 'images.' And by 'image' we mean certain existence which is more than that which the idealists call a representation, but less than that which the realist calls a thing—an existence placed halfway between the 'thing' and the 'representation'" (Henri Bergson, *Matter and Memory*, trans. Nancy Margaret Paul and W. Scott Palmer [New York: Zone Books, 1991], 9).

17. For an extended discussion see Deleuze's "Lecture Course on Chapter Three of Bergson's *Creative Evolution*," in "Henri Bergson's *Creative Evolution* 100 Years Later," ed. Michael Kolkman and Michael Vaughan, special issue, *Substance* 36, no. 3 (2007): 72–90.

18. Bergson, "The Soul and the Body," in *Mind-Energy*, 42.

19. This problem was dubbed as "Easy" and "Hard" by David Chalmers:

> Calling the first one easy is an in-joke: it is easy in the sense that curing cancer or sending someone to Mars is easy. That is, scientists more or less know what to look for, and with enough brainpower and funding, they would probably crack it in this century. . . . The Easy problem, then, is to distinguish conscious from unconscious mental computation, identify its correlates in the brain and explain why it evolved. The Hard Problem, on the other hand, is why it feels like something to have a conscious process going on in one's head—why there is first-person, subjective experience. . . . The Hard Problem is explaining how subjective experience arises from neural computation. The problem is hard because no one knows what a solution might look like or even whether it is a genuine scientific problem in the first place. (Steven Pinker, "The Mystery of Consciousness," *Time*, 12 February 2007, 39)

20. Bergson, "The Soul and the Body," in *Mind-Energy,* 58–59. Before Bergson, Leibniz also already addressed this problem in his monadology. I return to Leibniz in Chapter 6.

21. Bergson, "Life and Consciousness," in *Mind-Energy,* 12–13.

22. Ibid., 17.

23. See, e.g., Amy Herzog, "Images of Thought and Acts of Creation: Deleuze, Bergson, and the Question of Cinema," *Invisible Culture: An Electronic Journal for Visual Studies,* no. 3 (2000): 1–17.

24. See Herzog, "Images of Thought and Acts of Creation"; and Amy Herzog, "Affectivity, Becoming, and the Cinematic Event: Gilles Deleuze and the Futures of Feminist Film Theory," in *Conference Proceedings Affective Encounters: Rethinking Embodiment in Feminist Media Studies,* ed. Anu Koivunen and Susanna Paasonen, 83–88 (Turku: University of Turku, 2001), e-book at www.hum.utu.fi/oppiaineet/mediatutkimus/tutkimus/proceedings_pienennetty.pdf.

25. Deleuze, *The Movement-Image,* 3.

26. Ibid., 6.

27. Ibid., 8.

28. Ibid., 59.

29. Ibid., 66.

30. Deleuze, *The Time-Image,* 46.

31. Ibid., 98. Bergson discusses this splitting of time in relation to the phenomenon of "déjà-vu" as a "memory of the present" in *Mind-Energy* (167).

32. Deleuze, *The Time-Image,* 99.

33. Gilles Deleuze, "The Virtual and the Actual," trans. Eliot Ross Albert, in *Dialogues,* ed. Gilles Deleuze and Claire Parnet, 2nd ed., trans. Hugh Tomlinson and Barbara Habberjam (London: Continuum, 2002), 149–50.

34. James Williams, *Gilles Deleuze's "Difference and Repetition": A Critical Introduction and Guide* (Edinburgh: Edinburgh University Press, 2003), 85.

35. Deleuze, *Difference and Repetition,* 70. Alia Al-Saji also refers to the influence of Bergson in *Difference and Repetition,* referring mainly to the second synthesis of time. See Alia Al-Saji, "The Memory of Another Past: Bergson, Deleuze, and a New Theory of Time," *Continental Philosophy Review,* no. 37 (2004): 203–39.

36. Deleuze, *Difference and Repetition,* 71.

37. Deleuze's argument is complex and extended. For insightful discussions of *Difference and Repetition* see the indispensable references Williams, *Gilles Deleuze's "Difference and Repetition": A Critical Introduction and Guide* and Joe Hughes, *Deleuze's "Difference and Repetition"* (London: Continuum, 2009). See also James Williams, *Gilles Deleuze's Philosophy of Time: A Critical Introduction and Guide* (Edinburgh: Edinburgh University Press, 2011).

38. Deleuze, *Difference and Repetition*, 73. In contrast to Bergson Deleuze conceives the syntheses of time not only in respect to the human mind but to all processes of life (human and nonhuman).

39. Ibid., 80.

40. Williams, *Gilles Deleuze's "Difference and Repetition,"* 101.

41. Ibid.

42. It is known that Proust assisted frequently with Bergson's lectures. See, e.g., Lehrer, *Proust Was a Neuroscientist*, 75–95.

43. Deleuze gives the ground of the past the characteristics of the sky: "the foundation concerns the soil, it shows how something is established upon this soil . . . whereas the ground comes rather from the sky, it goes from the summit to the foundations" (*Difference and Repetition*, 79).

44. Ibid., 76.

45. We can see now how the present is different in the first and second syntheses of time: "In one case, the present is the most contracted state of successive elements or instants which are in themselves independent of one another. In the other case, the present designates the most contracted degree of the entire past, which is itself like a coexisting totality" (Deleuze, *Difference and Repetition*, 82).

46. Ibid., 90.

47. Ibid., 91.

48. Williams, *Gilles Deleuze's "Difference and Repetition,"* 101.

49. Ibid., 103. Williams further explains: "identities fall into the past but that part of them that is pure difference returns (a cut between the same and difference that forms a whole)." Also in his article "Science and Dialectics in the Philosophies of Deleuze, Bachelard and Delanda" (in *Deleuze and Science*, ed. John Marks, Special Issue, *Paragraph: A Journal of Critical Modern Theory* 29, no. 2 [2006], 98–114), he clarifies this differently: "When thinking of the future (F) as different from the past (P), we may be tempted to think that the difference lies between P and F. However, Deleuze's point is that in a selection we move from an assembly P/F to a new assembly P'/F'. We select a new past and a new future. So any difference is between P/F and P'/F'" (112).

50. Deleuze, *The Time-Image*, 275.

51. Moreover, each synthesis also opens up to the other syntheses (each with their own respective dimensions of times). In his article "Passions and Actions: Deleuze's Cinematographic Cogito" (*Deleuze Studies* 2, no. 2 [2008]: 121–39), Richard Rushton also refers to the syntheses in time, indicating how the virtual and the actual can be read as the first and second syntheses of time in the movement-image in *Letter from an Unknown Woman* (Max Ophuls, 1948). Rushton's focus is (in a discussion with Mark Hansen) on spectatorship, and he relates the time-image to the third synthesis of time and the dissolution of the subject. I propose in this chapter

and the remainder of this book a more metatheoretical perspective by arguing that the movement-image, the time-image, and the neuro-image are each based in a different synthesis of time; that each has its own relation to past, present, and future; and each can open up to the other syntheses. However, it is only in the third synthesis that all other syntheses can be repeated. Therefore, the neuro-image can include (elements of) the movement-image and of the time-image.

52. Deleuze, *Difference and Repetition*, 119. In the video interview with Claire Parnet, *L'Abécédaire de Gilles Deleuze*, Deleuze discusses this phenomenon for the letter *z* of *zigzag*. "L'éclair qui fait voir," the flash of insight (of the connection between two things, of change), is preceded by a dark precursor. The *z* of this lightning is perhaps the most elementary movement, says Deleuze. He even proposes (only half-jokingly) to replace the Big Bang by Le ZigZag. For an English summary of this interview see Charles Stivale's website: www.langlab.wayne .edu/CStivale/D-G/ABC1.html.

53. Deleuze, *The Time-Image*, 82. The other two films are Hitchcock's *Vertigo* (1958) and Dovzhenko's *Zvenigora* (1928).

54. The DVD is distributed by Editions Montparnasse, 2008. It has no subtitles but interesting extras, such as an interview with Claude Rich (main actor), Jacques Sternberg (writer), and Alain Resnais, as well as written commentary and interviews.

55. See Barbara Creed, *The Monstrous Feminine: Film, Feminism, Psychoanalysis* (New York: Routledge, 1993). Deleuze's argument in *Difference and Repetition* that the second synthesis of time of the Mnemosyne is erotic ("It is always Eros, the noumenon, who allows us to penetrate this pure past in itself, this virginal repetition which is Mnemosyne," 85) might be relevant here also.

56. Neuroscientific research has recently discovered the material aspects of the transformation of memories. Memory-making processes need proteins to construct new cells that can be incorporated into the neural network. Karim Nader, Glenn Shafe, and Joseph LeDoux have conducted experiments that indicate that the act of remembering changes us and that the process of making a memory can be interrupted by injecting a protein synthesis inhibitor. This is even the case for long-term memories that seem to disappear completely once the recollection process is interrupted. Memories are not stored in a safe location in the brain but are altered with each recollection. See Karim Nader et al., "Characterisation of Fear Memory Reconsolidation," *Journal of Neuroscience*, no. 24 (2004): 9269–75; and Karim Nader et al., "Fear Memories Require Protein Synthesis in the Amygdala for Reconsolidation After Retrieval," *Nature*, no. 406 (2000): 686–87.

57. Deleuze, *The Time-Image*, 119.

58. Ibid., 125.

59. Note that Deleuze distinguishes several types of repetition: an intracyclic repetition for the first synthesis; a cyclic repetition for the second synthesis

(the main form of repetition presented in *Hiroshima mon amour*); and the repetition of the third synthesis, which is the repetition of the eternal return. See Deleuze, *Difference and Repetition*, 93. These repetitions are connected but do not coincide.

60. Deleuze, *The Time-Image*, 209.

61. Deleuze, *Difference and Repetition*, 94.

62. Here it would be possible to connect the neuro-image and its relation to a speculative future that is not necessarily related to (individual) consciousness (the inside, the past as memory) but also to the future as speculative reality (the outside as cosmic temporality) to the "speculative turn" in continental philosophy. See Levi Bryant, Nick Srnicek, and Graham Harman, eds., *The Speculative Turn: Continental Materialism and Realism* (Melbourne: re.press, 2001).

63. Manovich, *Software Takes Command* (see above, Introduction, note 17).

64. Manovich, *The Language of New Media*, 218–43.

65. As Manovich notes, databases are not new (seventeenth-century Dutch still lifes can be seen as databases of food or flowers, arranged as a catalogue; libraries have worked with databases for ages; encyclopedias are organized in a database logic). The point, of course, is that with the arrival of computers, databases become the dominant organizational form of culture (not limited to screen culture) and knowledge.

66. This is not to say that all database culture is art. Many entrance points on a website lead to (useful or commercially abusive) information.

67. Resnais interview, www.youtube.com/watch?v=gTg_knL4cks.

68. Deleuze, *The Time-Image*, 102.

69. Deleuze, *Difference and Repetition*, 91.

70. Deleuze and Guattari, *A Thousand Plateaus*, 337–50.

71. Ibid., 342. Perhaps scientifically this started when Einstein discovered the fundamental relationship between energy and matter in the formula $E = mc^2$.

72. Michael Goddard, "The Scattering of Time Crystals: Deleuze, Mysticism and Cinema," in *Deleuze and Religion*, ed. M. Bryden (New York: Routledge, 2001), 53–64, 57.

73. Deleuze and Guattari, *What Is Philosophy?* 211.

74. Ibid., 213.

75. Deleuze, *The Time-Image*, 209.

CHAPTER 5

1. Deleuze, *The Time-Image*, 130.

2. Gilles Deleuze, "Hume," in *Desert Islands and Other Texts, 1953–1974*, ed. David Lapoujade, trans. Michael Taormina (Los Angeles: Semiotext(e), 2004), 162–69, 167.

3. Gilles Deleuze, "Desert Islands," in *Desert Islands and Other Texts*, 9–14.

4. Stanley Cavell, *Pursuits of Happiness: Hollywood Comedies of Remarriage* (Cambridge, MA: Harvard University Press, 1981). David Rodowick has elaborated on the productive encounter between Cavell and Deleuze, arguing that it is precisely in the empirical problem of skepticism that Cavell and Deleuze agree on the double role of cinema in posing skepticism as the modern problem and its overcoming. See David Rodowick, "An Elegy for Theory," *October*, no. 122 (2007): 91–109.

5. Gilles Deleuze, *Empiricism and Subjectivity*, trans. Constantin V. Boundas (New York: Columbia University Press, 1991).

6. Deleuze, "Hume." For the summary of Hume's main ideas I will refer to this text.

7. Ibid., 163.

8. Ibid. Resnais's kaleidoscopic mosaic film style comes immediately to mind.

9. Deleuze, *Empiricism and Subjectivity*, x.

10. Deleuze, "Hume," 164 (Deleuze's emphasis). "Awaiting" and "expecting" are just as important because they introduce the notion of time in Hume's thought and, again, make the link to Bergson more justifiable.

11. Ibid., 165.

12. Deleuze, *Empiricism and Subjectivity*, 120.

13. Deleuze, "Hume," 168. One only needs to think of *The Queen* (Stephen Frears, 2007), in which Helen Mirren as Queen Elizabeth at the death of Lady Di discovers that the Queen as the Country ("I am England") is not as influential as the Queen of Hearts, to understand how principles of passion are related to credibility and contemporary forms of power. Consider also the ways in which contemporary politicians can only win elections or remain in power when they can sustain media credibility.

14. Ibid., 168.

15. In *Deleuze's Hume* Jeffrey Bell makes extended references to Bruno Latour, whose vision is close to Hume's in Latour's conception of the reality of the artifact (albeit more in the world of science): "As Latour will argue at length in *Pandora's Hope*, what needs to be challenged is the assumption that being constructed implies artificiality or lack of reality, when for Latour 'it is because [reality] is constructed that it is so very real, so autonomous, so independent of our own hands'" (Jeffrey Bell, *Deleuze's Hume: Philosophy, Culture and the Scottish Enlightenment* [Edinburgh: Edinburgh University Press, 2009], 69).

16. Ibid., 29. Bell quotes Deleuze here.

17. Ibid., 50.

18. Deleuze, *Difference and Repetition*, 70.

19. Bell, *Deleuze's Hume*, 52.

20. Ibid., 55.

21. Gallese, "The Shared Manifold Hypothesis," 46. The references to Damasio, who refers to the parallels between neuroscience and Spinoza, allow us to consider Hume and Bergson also in relation to the three types of knowledge in Spinoza, who distinguishes knowledge through the senses and emotions, knowledge through rational scientific explanations, and the highest form of knowledge through intuition. Such parallels are more elaborate than this, of course, but the primacy of embodied perception is common in all three philosophers.

22. Ibid. Brian Massumi also points out the possibilities of induction and transduction in "The Autonomy of Affect," where he discusses the conditions and emergence of ideology: "One way of conceptualizing the non-ideological means by which ideology is produced might deploy the notions of induction and transduction—induction being the triggering of a qualification, of a containment, an actualization, and transduction being the transmission of an impulse of virtuality from one actualization to another and across them all (what Guattari calls transversality). Transduction is the transmission of a force of potential that cannot but be felt, simultaneously doubling, enabling and ultimately counteracting the limitative selections of apparatuses of actualization and implantation. This amounts to proposing an analog theory of image-based power: images as the conveyors of forces of emergence, as vehicles of existential potentialization and transfer" (42–43).

23. Gazzaniga, Ivry, and Mangun, *Cognitive Neuroscience*, 672, 674.

24. Deleuze, "Hume," 169.

25. Deleuze, *The Time-Image*, 215–23. See also Ronald Bogue, *Deleuzian Fabulation and the Scars of History* (Edinburgh: Edinburgh University Press, 2010).

26. Brian Boyd, *On the Origin of Stories: Evolution, Cognition, and Fiction* (Cambridge, MA: Belknap Press of Harvard University Press, 2009), 210. Boyd draws an analogy to Darwin, showing how fictional creativity "operates as a Darwin machine, through repeated cycles of variation and selection."

27. Deleuze, "Desert Islands," 11.

28. Ibid.

29. *Robinson Crusoe* fails because it reconstitutes ownership: nothing is invented, and everything is taken from the ship; *Suzanne and the Pacific* fails because the island provides her with a double of every object from the city (she does not need to create anything new and so is not separated from the world in that material sense).

30. Gilles Deleuze, *The Logic of Sense*, trans. Mark Lester with Charles Stivale (New York: Columbia University Press, 1990), 301–21.

31. Tournier, quoted in Ronald Bogue, "Speranza, the Wandering Island," *Deleuze Studies* 3, no. 1 (2009): 124–34, 128.

32. Deleuze, "Desert Islands," 13.

33. Ibid., 14.

34. John Rajchman, introduction to *Pure Immanence: Essays on Life*, by Gilles Deleuze, trans. Anne Boyman (New York: Zone Books, 2001), 15.

35. *Big Brother, Idols, Popstars, X-Factor, Looking for . . . (Evita, Mary Poppins, The New Michael Jackson,* etc.), *So You Think You Can . . . (Dance, Sing), Britain* (or *Holland, America, Germany . . .)'s Got Talent,* all follow the same competitive logic. This is not to downplay the real talents many of the participants do have or the addictive "democratic" potentials that such series promise in their combination of accessibility (anybody can sign up for the auditions, audiences can vote) and spectacle. But their standard format does not enable us to reach to the originary depths of universal mythology (rather, such formats become part of the infernal repetitions without differences of the contemporary media machine).

36. The film was shot on Monuriki, an island in the Mamanuca archipelago that became a tourist attraction following the film's release. Originary stories can be captured in the capitalist machine, but that does not forbid the recognition of the mythological powers of the film as such. See the film's wiki page (http://en.wikipedia.org/wiki/Cast_Away). *Lost*'s relations to capitalism are similar: the show is costly and must profit. However, that does not prevent the recognition of the creativity of the writers and production team.

37. For an overview of the characters see http://en.wikipedia.org/wiki/Characters_of_Lost.

38. I will return to the transmedial dissemination of the show. Here I will just mention the volume on philosophical interpretations of *Lost*: Sharon M. Kaye, ed. *"Lost" and Philosophy: The Island Has its Reason* (Malden, MA: Blackwell, 2008).

39. See http://en.wikipedia.org/wiki/Lost_tv_series.

40. As some critics have noted, among the themes that run through the series are "serious mum and dad issues." See Michael W. Austin, "What Do Jack and Locke Owe Their Fathers?" in Kaye, *"Lost" and Philosophy,* 9–18; and Charles Girard and David Meulemans, "The Island as a Test of Free Will: Freedom of Reinvention and Internal Determinism in *Lost*," in ibid., 89–110, 96.

41. Girard and Meulemans, "The Island as a Test of Free Will," 90.

42. See the Lostpedia: http://lostpedia.wikia.com/wiki/Philosophy; http://lostpedia.wikia.com/wiki/Science; and http://lostpedia.wikia.com/wiki/Literary_works.

43. Googling "John Locke" will bring up references to both the fictional character and the philosopher. For a more elaborate analysis of character developments in relation to specific philosophical points of view, see Sander Lee, "Meaning and Freedom on the Island," in Kaye, *"Lost" and Philosophy,* 63–77; and Shai Biderman and William J. Devlin, "The Tao of John Locke," in ibid., 193–204.

44. For a description of the episode on Hurley and numbers see http://en.wikipedia.org/wiki/Numbers_%28Lost%29; for fan theories about the numbers in *Lost* see http://thelostnumbers.blogspot.com/.

45. "*Lost*: On Location," *Lost*, season 2 (2005; ABC Studios, 2006 Buena Vista Home Entertainment), DVD Bonus. Of course, the name *Sarah* also has biblical connotations of miracles and birth.

46. David Hume, *Dialogues Concerning Natural Religion*, www.gutenberg.org/files/4583/4583.txt.

47. David Hume, "Of Miracles," in *An Enquiry Concerning Human Understanding* (Oxford: Clarendon Press, 2000), 84. A downloadable version of the book resides at http://18th.eserver.org/hume-enquiry.html.

48. Bell's references to Latour's Humianism suggest another account of evidence of reality (and in a scientific rather than religious discourse) that corresponds nevertheless to a Humian conception of "knowledge" that can be gained from testimonies. Specifically in Latour, "An entity gains in reality if it is associated with many others that are viewed as collaborating with it. It loses in reality if, on the contrary, it has to shed associates or collaborators (humans and nonhumans)" (Bell, *Deleuze's Hume*, 70).

49. Ibid., 99.

50. Rajchman, introduction to *Pure Immanence*, 17.

51. Bergson, *Mind-Energy*, 155.

52. Gregg Lambert, *The Non-Philosophy of Gilles Deleuze* (New York: Continuum, 2002), 130. Lambert also mentions ideology as a source of the transformation of the world into an object of belief.

53. Ibid., 131.

54. See http://en.wikipedia.org/wiki/Lost_tv_series.

55. Sebastian Charles on Lipovetsky's hypermodern times in the introduction to Lipovetsky, *Hypermodern Times*, 26.

56. Amy Herzog suggests that "looking even at the most hackneyed, clichéd films, the attentive thinker might see within their stuttering and pauses waves of affect that move against the prevailing current. This affectivity may take an infinite number of forms: a strain of music that overwhelms the narrative flow, a glance between characters that gestures toward a whole world of non-actualized becomings. It might even be mapped through the work's mode of presentation, the life which it takes on in the popular imagination, . . . beyond the will or control of their creators" (Herzog, "Affectivity, Becoming, and the Cinematic Event," 87).

57. Ibid.

58. Jenkins, *Convergence Culture*, 2.

59. Ibid., 16.

60. Bell, *Deleuze's Hume*, 150. Bell quotes here from *Anti-Oedipus*.

61. Apart from references to Homer's book and also Joyce's *Ulysses*, it is Desmond (Hume) himself who is compared to Odysseus. He sails around the world before being shipwrecked on the island; his wife Penelope faithfully waits for his return and (more actively) seeks to rescue him.

62. Arthur C. Clarke in "2001: The Making of a Myth," dir. Paul Joyce, on the *2001: A Space Odyssey* special edition DVD (Atlantic Celtic Films, 2007).

63. Similarities with the legend of Pocahontas are notable. Like Pocahontas (and many fictional representations of the seventeenth-century historical figure), Neytiri is a native princess who teaches a colonizer respect for nature and saves him from tribal imprisonment. However, unlike Pocahontas, Neytiri will not convert to Christianity and move to England. Quite the contrary, Jack will convert into a Na'vi, and malevolent settlers are sent back to Earth.

64. Sean Cubitt shows how LED technology (invented in the 1920s) is the dominant technology used in (commercial) urban screens around the world. See Sean Cubitt, "LED Technology and the Shaping of Culture," in McQuire, Martin, and Niederer, *Urban Screens Reader*, 97–118.

65. Deleuze, "Desert Islands," 13.

66. Ibid.

67. Genevieve Lloyd, *Providence Lost* (Cambridge, MA: Harvard University Press, 2008), 309.

68. Deleuze, *Difference and Repetition*, 83.

69. Williams, *Deleuze's Philosophy of Time*, 71-72.

70. Lloyd, *Providence Lost*, 267–68.

71. In *Bewustzijn: Van filosofie naar hersenwetenschap* [Consciousness: From Philosophy to Neuroscience] (Amsterdam: Boom, 2008), Herman Kolk discusses this problem extensively, arguing that the fact that we do not know our motives consciously (the body knows before we do) does not mean that free will has become a meaningless concept. In terms of the discussions in this chapter "free will" needs only to be revised in terms of selection within destiny's manifold path.

72. Resnais's intriguing film *Providence* (1977) raises these issues as well. *Providence* is the story of Clive Langham (John Gielgud), an old writer suffering from bowel cancer, who douses his pain in gallons of white wine and is constantly in a state of delirium. The film shows surreal interweavings and fantasmatic transformations of his personal memories (his children and his deceased wife play an important role) with world historical memories (such as the trauma of the deportation of Jews, a football stadium, but also cliché images of a man with a gun). Resnais's suggestion, too, is that destiny is related to (artistic) creativity.

CHAPTER 6

1. A shorter version of this chapter has been published as "Numbers and Fractals: Neuroaesthetics and the Scientific Subject," in *The Force of the Virtual: Deleuze, Science, and Philosophy*, ed. Peter Gaffney (Minneapolis: University of Minnesota Press, 2010), 229–54.

2. Gilles Deleuze, *The Fold: Leibniz and the Baroque*, trans. Tom Conley (Minneapolis: University of Minnesota Press, 1993).

3. For an analysis of the connections between Leibniz's baroque philosophy and mathematics see James Luchte, "Mathesis and Analysis: Finitude and the Infinite in the *Monadology* of Leibniz," *Heythrop Journal* 47 (2006): 519–43.

4. *Pi*, dir. Darren Aronofsky (1997; Santa Monica, CA: Artisan Entertainment, 1998), DVD; *The Fountain*, dir. Darren Aronofsky (2005; Burbank, CA: Warner Bros. Home Video, 2006), DVD.

5. Deleuze, *The Time-Image*, 265.

6. Ibid., 267.

7. Ibid., 266.

8. See Sean Cubitt, "Perspective as Special Effect," in *Digital Aesthetics* (London: Sage, 1998), 74–80; Sean Cubitt, "Neo-Baroque Film," in *The Cinema Effect* (Cambridge, MA: MIT Press, 2004), 217–44; and Sean Cubitt, "The Relevance of the Baroque," www.ucl.ac.uk/slade/digita/baroque.html. See also Angela Ndalianis, *Neo-Baroque Aesthetics and Contemporary Entertainment* (Cambridge, MA: MIT Press, 2005); and Timothy Murray, *Digital Baroque: New Media Art and Cinematic Folds* (Minneapolis: University of Minnesota Press, 2008). For an extended analysis of the New Baroque in music, painting, architecture, philosophy, and literature see Gregg Lambert, *On the (New) Baroque* (Aurora, CO: Davis Group, 2008).

9. Laura U. Marks, *Enfoldment and Infinity: An Islamic Genealogy of New Media Art* (Cambridge, MA: MIT Press, 2010), 153.

10. Ibid., 159. Art is *aniconic*, Marks explains, "when the image shows us that what we do not see is more significant than what we do. In both Islamic art and new media art, the most important activity takes place at a level prior to the perceptible level" (5).

11. Ibid., 162. Marks quotes here from Necipoglu, *The Topkapi Scroll*, which discusses Euclid's *Elements*.

12. Marks, *Enfoldment and Infinity*, 185–86.

13. Luchte, "Mathesis and Analysis," 520.

14. Deleuze, *The Fold*, 19.

15. In her book *Vibrant Matter* Jane Bennett explains this "unity" of "material-forces" by referring to the Spinozan notion of the impersonal forces of affect (also discussed in Chapter 3), equating "affect with materiality, rather than posit[ing]

a separate force that can enter and animate a physical body" (Jane Bennett, *Vibrant Matter: A Political Ecology of Things* [Durham, NC: Duke University Press, 2010], xiii).

16. Ibid., 26.

17. Marks proposes more concretely a baroque aesthetics of folding on three levels: image, information, and the infinite. She refers to the quantum physics theory of the implicate order that describes an underlying order of the universe that cannot be seen: "it can only be known through its perceptible effects. For example, the action of electrons can be understood in terms of a wave equation. The wave is enfolded in matter, in the electron's behavior; the electrons are unfolded from the wave" (Marks, *Enfoldment and Infinity*, 6).

18. In *What Is Philosophy?* Deleuze and Guattari also refer to the fractal nature of the plane of immanence; see Deleuze and Guattari, *What Is Philosophy?* 36.

19. G. N. Elston and B. Zietsch, "Fractal Analysis as a Tool for Studying Specialization in Neuronal Structure: The Study of the Evolution of the Primate Cerebral Cortex and Human Intellect," *Advances in Complex Systems* 8 (2005): 217–27; Paulus and Braff, "Chaos and Schizophrenia" (see above, Chap. 1n48); Hidekatsu Yoloyama, Shin-ici Niwa, Kenji Itoh, and Reiko Mazuka, "Fractal Properties of Eye Movements in Schizophrenia," *Biological Cybernetics* 75, no. 2 (1996): 137–40.

20. Leibniz, quoted in Sjoerd van Tuinen, "Leibniz und das psychophysische Gehirn," in *Gilles Deleuze: Philosophie und Nicht-Philosophie, aktuelle Diskussionen*, ed. Friedrich Balke and Marc Rölli (Bielefeld: Transcript Verlag, 2011), 293–94.

21. Giuliana Bruno has described how Wong Kar Wai's film *In the Mood for Love* (2000) weaves together fashion, film, and architecture to express mental (spiritual) life. See Giuliana Bruno, "Pleats of Matter, Folds of the Soul," in *Afterimages of Gilles Deleuze's Film Philosophy*, ed. D. N. Rodowick (Minneapolis: University of Minnesota Press, 2010), 213–33.

22. Deleuze, *The Time-Image*, 156 (Deleuze's emphasis).

23. Ibid., 167.

24. Ibid., 170.

25. Ibid., 173.

26. Ibid., 174–75.

27. Ibid., 179–80.

28. Anna Powell, *Deleuze, Altered States and Film* (Edinburgh: Edinburgh University Press, 2007).

29. The reference here is to Leibniz's famous expression: "Having decided these things, I thought I had reached the port, but when I set myself to think about the union of the soul with the body I was as it were carried back into the open sea" (quoted in Deleuze, *Negotiations*, 94).

30. "An Interview with Darren Aronofsky and Sean Gullette of *Pi*," interview by Anthony Kaufman (1998), *Darren Aronofsky Online*, http://aronofksy.tripod.com/interview2.html.

31. Ibid.; see also "Feature Interview with Darren Aronofsky," interview by Stephen Applebaum (2001), *Darren Aronofsky Online*, http://aronofksy.tripod.com/interview12.html.

32. "The Writer/Director of *Pi* Discusses the Limits of Filmmaking and Human Knowledge," interview by Andrea Chase (1998), *Darren Aronofsky Online*, http://aronofksy.tripod.com/interview21.html. Again, Laura Marks's *Enfoldment and Infinity* gives many beautiful examples of the relationship between mathematics, infinity, and the divine.

33. "The Whiz Kid—Darren Aronofsky, Writer/Director of *Pi*," interview by Anthony Kaufman (1998), *Darren Aronofsky Online*, http://aronofksy.tripod.com/interview3.html.

34. "An Interview with Darren Aronofsky and Sean Gullette of *Pi*," 5.

35. For a discussion of Kubrick's brain cinema see Gregg Lambert, "Schizoanalysis and the Cinema of the Brain," in Buchanan and MacCormack, *Deleuze and the Schizoanalysis of Cinema*, 27–38.

36. See, e.g., Teun Koetsie and Luc Bergmans, *Mathematics and the Divine: A Historical Study* (Amsterdam: Elsevier, 2005).

37. Deleuze, *Difference and Repetition*, 277.

38. Ibid., 293.

39. Ibid., 297.

40. Deleuze, *The Fold*, 17.

41. "Darren Aronofsky: *The Fountain*," interview by Daniel Robert Epstein (2005), Suicidegirls.com, http://suicidegirls.com/interviews/Darren+Aronofsky+The+Fountain, 2.

42. Peter Parks, quoted on the wiki page of *The Fountain*, http://en.wikipedia.org/wiki/The_Fountain_(film).

43. Deleuze, *The Fold*, 4.

44. Claire Colebrook, "Mathematics, Vitalism, Genesis," *A/V Actual/Virtual Journal*, no. 7 (2007), www.hssr.mmu.ac.uk/deleuze-studies/journal/av-7/.

45. See Patricia Pisters, "Touched by a Cardboard Sword: Aesthetic Creation and Non-Personal Subjectivity in *Dancer in the Dark* and *Moulin Rouge*," in *Discernments: Deleuzian Aesthetics*, ed. Joost de Bloois, Sjef Houpermans, and Frans-Willem Korsten (Amsterdam: Rodopi, 2004), 151–69.

46. Deleuze, *Difference and Repetition*, 222.

47. Ibid.

48. Ibid. Deleuze explains: "In so far as a system is constituted or bounded by at least two heterogeneous series, two disparate orders capable of entering into communication, we call it a signal. The phenomenon that flashes across this

system, bringing about the communication between disparate series, is a sign. 'The emerald hides in its facets a bright-eyed water-sprite.'" For a (popular) scientific description of what Deleuze describes see Robert M. Hazen, "Evolution of Minerals," *Scientific American*, March 2010, 42–49.

49. It is interesting to compare *The Fountain* to Terrence Malick's *The Tree of Life* (2011). Malick's view on the tree of life is much more Heideggerian in the sense that it questions "being in the world" of humans in relation to transcendental "Being" of God. In *The Fountain* the human and nonhuman are more immanently related and keep on returning in different assemblages (tree, human, celestial dust).

50. "Darren Aronofsky: *The Fountain*," 4.

51. In Terry Gilliam's *The Imaginarium of Doctor Parnassus* one scene literally depicts the story as debris flying around, containing the elements of the story.

52. See also Steven Shaviro, *Post-Cinematic Affect* (Winchester, UK: O-Books, 2010), 64–92.

CHAPTER 7

1. See also Deleuze (with Claire Parnet) on politics in Gilles Deleuze and Claire Parnet, eds., *Dialogues*, trans. Hugh Tomlinson and Barbara Habberjam (London: Athlone Press, 1987); Paul Patton, *Deleuze and the Political* (London: Routledge, 2000); and Patricia Pisters, "Micropolitiek," in *Deleuze Compendium*, ed. Ed Romein, Marc Schuilenburg, and Sjoerd van Tuinen (Amsterdam: Boom, 2009), 224–36.

2. Catherine Malabou argues in her book *What Should We Do with Our Brain?* that brain plasticity has led to a dominant (and licentious) neurological ideology that dialogues too well with an economy of neoliberal flexibility, normalizing us all as supple, docile, and uncreative beings. Malabou gives a normative answer to her question in the title of her book, arguing that we should "refuse to be flexible individuals who combine a permanent control of the self with a capacity to self-modify at the whim of fluxes, transfers, and exchanges, for fear of explosion. . . . To ask what should we do with our brain? is above all to visualize the possibility of saying no to an afflicting economy, political, and mediatic culture that celebrates only the triumph of flexibility, blessing obedient individuals who have no greater merit than of knowing how to bow their heads with a smile" (78–79). Malabou is right in arguing for a more profound understanding of neuroplasticity on the one hand (contra the neoliberal ideas of flexibility) and the need for a "reasonable materialism" (82) that acknowledges the difference between brain and mind (contra neurological determinism). However, her argument collapses a very complex set of phenomena (contemporary neoliberal society and neuroscientific discourse) into a narrow problem requiring a solution (the

power to resist both). Nevertheless, her call for a dialectical thinking that can understand the contradictory effects of brain plasticity (both forming and deforming) and the differences between brain and mind seems to have resonances with schizoanalysis and the investigation into micropolitics that I try to develop in this book. See Catherine Malabou, *What Should We Do with Our Brain?* trans. Sebastian Rand (New York: Fordham University Press, 2008).

3. Connolly, *Neuropolitics*, 129.

4. Ibid., 154.

5. Ibid. Connolly gives a list of eight Nietzschean thoughts of importance, such as antihierarchical forms of connection, an ethics that recognizes corporeal levels of "judgment," and an ethics that is nonjuridical. Coming to terms with a "rift of time and exploring the effects that changes in pace and tempo have on the shape and weight of culture" is the first moment of Nietzschean recognition.

6. Ibid., 145.

7. Derrida, *Archive Fever*, 4.

8. Ibid., 68. See also Jacques Derrida and Bernhard Stiegler, *Echographies of Television: Filmed Interviews*, trans. Jennifer Bajorek (Cambridge: Polity, 2002), in which regular reference is made to acts of memory and the archive in relation to television and other media technologies.

9. See Geoffrey Bowker, *Memory Practices in the Sciences* (Cambridge, MA: MIT Press, 2005). Bowker understands "memory practices" as the range of practices (technical, formal, social) in which acts of committing to record (archiving) are embedded (7).

10. Ibid., 230.

11. Ibid., 190.

12. Eric Ketelaar, "Tacit Narratives," *Archival Science* 1 (2001): 131–41, 141.

13. Eric Ketelaar, "A Living Archive, Shared by Communities of Records," in *Community Archives: The Shaping of Memory*, ed. Jeannette Bastian and Ben Alexander (London: Facet, 2009), 109–32. I am referring to an earlier lecture version of this essay, "Truths, Memories, and Histories in the Archives of the ICTR and the ICTY," presented at the conference "Sixty Years Genocide Convention," organized by the Amsterdam Centre for Holocaust and Genocide Studies (CHGS), the Amsterdam Centre for International Law (ACIL), and the Peace Library, The Hague, 8 December 2008, 13.

14. Ketelaar, "Truths, Memories, and Histories in the Archives of the ICTR and the ICTY," 14.

15. Ibid., 15.

16. Eric Ketelaar, *The Archival Image: Collected Essays* (Hilversum: Verloren, 1997), 77 (the original text is from 1988). In another essay in this volume, "Archives of the People, by the People, for the People," Ketelaar emphasizes the

political importance of archival heritages and the diversity of perspectives they hold: "People in changing societies, in Europe and elsewhere in the world, are witnessing the opening of depositories. We are discovering now the reality of control of all records and all memories by the Party, by every party. Be it KGB or CIA, be it covering up or uncovering by British, French, Argentinian, Greek or Dutch" (16).

17. Mary Ann Doane, *The Emergence of Cinematic Time: Modernity, Contingency, the Archive* (Cambridge, MA: Harvard University Press, 2002), 223.

18. For a radical analysis of the archive as pure practice of data storage see Wolfgang Ernst, "The Archive as Metaphor: From Archival Space to Archival Time," in *Open 7: (No) Memory: Storing and Recalling in Contemporary Art and Culture*, ed. Jorinde Seijdel and Liesbeth Melis (Rotterdam: NAi, 2004), 46–52; and Wolfgang Ernst, "Underway to the Dual System: Classical Archives and/or Digital Memory," in *Netpioneers 1.0*, ed. Dieter Daniels and Gunther Reisinger (Berlin: Sternberg Press, 2010). Ernst speaks of the "dynarchive," arguing that in digital archives content becomes less important than "logistical interlinking" in a permanent dynamic rewriting. See also Julia Noordegraaf, "Who Knows Television? Online Access and the Gatekeepers of Knowledge," in "Television Archives: Accessing TV History," ed. Lez Cooke and Robin Nelson, special issue, *Critical Studies in Television: Scholarly Studies in Small Screen Fictions* 5, no. 2 (2010): 1-19.

19. Doane, *The Emergence of Cinematic Time*, 207.

20. Ibid., 208.

21. This is perhaps why images used in court are still such powerful and difficult pieces of evidence, as Derrida and Stiegler argue about the famous Rodney King tapes: "the videographic recording may have served as an archive, perhaps as an exhibit, perhaps as evidence, but it did not replace testimony. Proof or evidence—evidence!—of this fact is that the young man who shot the footage was asked to come himself and attest, swearing before the living persons who constituted the jury and who were legitimate as such, swearing that it was really he who held the camera, that he was present at the scene, that he saw what he shot, etc." (Derrida and Stiegler, *Echographies of Television*, 94). See also Lawrence Douglas's interesting article on the first film used as evidence in court, "Film as Witness: Screening *Nazi Concentration Camps* Before the Nuremberg Tribunal," *Yale Law Journal* (November 1995): 11–37. Douglas emphasizes that to authenticate the images, the film includes many eyewitnesses (such as the inhabitants of Weimar who are "invited" by the Americans to come to Buchenwald).

22. Giovanna Fossati, *From Grain to Pixel: The Archival Life of Film in Transition* (Amsterdam: Amsterdam University Press, 2009), 144.

23. Fredric Jameson, *Postmodernism, or, The Cultural Logic of Late Capitalism* (Durham, NC: Duke University Press, 1991). See also Anne Friedberg, *Window*

Shopping: Cinema and the Postmodern (Berkeley: University of California Press, 1994).

24. Lipovetsky and Serroy, *L'écran global*, 174 (my trans.).

25. Ibid., 178 (my trans.).

26. See also Thomas Elsaesser, "Subject Positions, Speaking Positions: From Holocaust, Our Hitler, and Heimat to *Shoah* and *Schindler's List*," in *The Persistence of History: Cinema, Television, and the Modern Event*, ed. Vivian Sobchack (London: Routledge, 1996), 145–86; and Frank van Vree, "The Echo Chamber of History," in Kooijman, Pisters, and Strauven, *Mind the Screen*, 310–21.

27. In a comparable way one can consider the television series *Mad Men* (AMC, since 2007) also as an example of "hypercinema" that gives a past to our present. One of the most shocking moments in season 1 occurs when Don Draper and his lovely 1950s family go on a Sunday outing and have a picnic on a grass field. When they finish the food, they pack their stuff and leave all the waste in the grass, a collective gesture emphasized by Don, who before entering his car throws away an empty can of beer. In a 1950s film (think of the melodramas of Douglas Sirk) this throwing of litter would never have been shown. For all its deep drama and vivid aesthetics, classical melodramas are clean. *Mad Men* shows us aspects of the past that we need to see as our past in order to get a grasp of the present and the future (such as ecological issues; gender relations also receive this revisionary treatment in the series). Remakes of classical movies provide other interesting cases that take the present into the past. Todd Haynes's *Far from Heaven* (2002), for instance, is a remake of Sirk's *All That Heaven Allows* (1955). The difference between them is that in the new version hidden stories of the past unfold: the lonely housewife's husband is now struggling with his homosexuality and the gardener who becomes her lover is a black man.

28. Gilles Deleuze, *The Time-Image*, p. 117.

29. Fernando Solanas and Ottavio Gettino, "Towards a Third Cinema: Notes and Experiences for the Development of a Cinema of Liberation in the Third World," in *Film and Theory: An Anthology*, ed. Robert Stam and Toby Miller (Malden, MA: Blackwell, 2000), 278.

30. See Deleuze, *The Movement-Image*, 141–77.

31. See Mike Wayne, *Political Film: The Dialectics of Third Cinema* (London: Pluto, 2001).

32. See the film's wiki page, http://en.wikipedia.org/wiki/The_Battle_of_Algiers.

33. Murray Smith has given an extended analysis of the ways in which the film text itself distributes its allegiances. See Murray Smith, "*The Battle of Algiers*: Colonial Struggle and Collective Allegiance," in *Terrorism, Media, Liberation*, ed. David Slocum (New Brunswick, NJ: Rutgers University Press, 2005), 94–110.

34. *The Battle of Algiers*, dir. Gillo Pontecorvo (1966; Criterion Collection, 2004), DVD. Kael's review is referenced in the bonus materials. This three-disc edition includes a new high-definition digital transfer; original and rerelease trailer; improved English subtitles; a documentary on Pontecorvo from 1992, narrated by Edward Said; a documentary on *The Battle of Algiers*; commentaries by five directors on the film's influence; and a whole disc on the film in history (including the film's lessons for counterterrorism after 9/11).

35. Wayne, *Political Film*, 5–24; and Smith, "*The Battle of Algiers.*"

36. Elsewhere I have argued (agreeing with Mike Wayne) that all political cinema is a mixture of First, Second, and Third Cinema as dimensions of one another. See Patricia Pisters, "Arresting the Flux of Images and Sounds: Free Indirect Discourse and the Dialectics of Political Cinema," in *Deleuze and the Contemporary World*, ed. Ian Buchanan and Adrian Parr (Edinburgh: Edinburgh University Press, 2006), 175–93.

37. *The Battle of Algiers*, http://en.wikipedia.org/wiki/The_Battle_of_Algiers.

38. Charles Paul Freund, "The Pentagon's Film Festival: A Primer for *The Battle of Algiers*," *Slate*, 27 August 2003, http://slate.msn.com/id/2087628.

39. Stephen Hunt, "The Pentagon's Lessons from Reel Life: *Battle of Algiers* Resonates in Bagdad," *Washington Post*, 31 October 2003.

40. Freund, "The Pentagon's Film Festival," 2.

41. *The Battle of Algiers* is also a recurrent reference in media theory. Robert Stam, for instance, relates *The Battle of Algiers* by emphasizing the legacy of Frantz Fanon in the film and its importance for postcolonial studies. In respect to *The Battle of Algiers*, Stam argues that at times it is as if Fanon had written the script for this film. The scenes that involve Algerian women seem like a passage from "Algeria Unveiled" in Fanon's *A Dying Colonialism*: "The soldiers, the French patrols, smile to her as she passes, compliments on her looks are heard here and there, but no one suspects that her suitcases contain the automatic pistol which will presently mow down four or five members of one of the patrols" (quoted in Robert Stam, "Fanon, Algeria, and the Cinema: The Politics of Identification," in *Multiculturalism, Postcoloniality, and Transnational Media*, ed. Ella Shoat and Robert Stam [New Brunswick, NJ: Rutgers University Press, 2003], 30). David Slocum discusses the repeated references to the film in the broader conception of audiovisual media related to terrorism. See Slocum, "Introduction: The Recurrent Return to Algiers," in Slocum, *Terrorism, Media, Liberation*, 1–36. In Chapter 8 I will return to postcolonial theory and violence.

42. Wayne, *Political Film*, 17.

43. In his poignant documentary *Guerre sans images* (2002), Mohammed Soudani returns to Algeria with photographer Michael von Graffenried to find people he photographed (as one of the very few) during the 1990s. One of the last fiction films shot secretly in Algiers at the beginning of the civil war was Merzak

Allouache's *Bab El-Oued City* (1994). *L'autre monde* (2001) traces the devastating trajectory of a return to Algeria of migrant children. In *Babel Web* (2005) Allouache returns to his neighborhood in Algiers, Babel Oued, to show in a much lighter way how the Internet makes transnational encounters possible, while still being an unavailable option for many.

44. See Sonia Combe, *Archives interdites: L'histoire confisquée* (1994; Paris: La Decouverte, 2001) for an important and critical study on the difficulty of accessing historical archives and other documents related to the French-Algerian war and political assassinations. Still today not all documents are accessible. The work of many historians has to be mentioned here as a basis for the various cinematographic historic perspectives. See, e.g., Benjamin Stora, *Histoire de la guerre d'Algerie, 1954–1962* (Paris: La Decouverte, 1993). See also the extended French wiki page, http://fr.wikipedia.org/wiki/Guerre_d'Algerie.

45. Digital tools allow films to be cut according to different styles more easily than ever before. Dutch filmmaker Jean van de Velde made the political film *Wit Licht* (2008), about child soldiers in East Africa, in accordance with First Cinema aesthetics. For screening in Cannes it was reedited as an art house version: *The Silent Army* (2009). This version is narratively less explicative, without music, and with fewer dramatic effects. For many filmmakers, any reediting of their finished film would be inconceivable; Van de Velde was compelled by the interest of French critic Pierre Rissient, who saw in the film another film for a politically interested art house and festival public. The director explained at a public screening and debate about the film at the Dutch Film Academy in 2009 that with digital technologies it took them only two days to make a completely new version. This is an interesting indication of the database logic of contemporary culture, which, although always already a part of cinema, now becomes more evident. See http://en.wikipedia.org/wiki/The_Silent_Army.

46. Daniel Coffeen, "Film, Play, Power and the Computational, or Byting Celluloid," Tate Intermediate Art program, 2006, www.tate.org.uk/intermedia art/entry15539.shtm.

47. See www.tate.org.uk/intermediaart/battle_of_algiers.shtm.

48. Coffeen, "Film, Play, Power and the Computational, or Byting Celluloid."

49. Ibid.

50. The hugely popular online participatory YouTube film *Where the Hell Is Matt?* (www.wherethehellismatt.com/) takes up with this database logic quite literally, creating a transnational world-memory of "unconnected places."

51. Julia Noordegraaf, for instance, shows how the reuse of colonial and ethnographic footage of the Dutch Indies in the films and videos of Fiona Tan questions the historic colonial subject position by introducing an "affect of concern" both in the altered aesthetics of the images (which are repeated, slowed down, emphasized) and in the effects it has on the viewers. See Julia Noordegraaf,

"Displacing the Colonial Archive: How Fiona Tan Shows Us Things We Don't Know We Know," in Kooijman, Pisters, and Strauven, *Mind the Screen*, 322–32.

52. Freund, "The Pentagon's Film Festival."

53. Eyal Weizman, "The Art of War," *Frieze*, no. 99 (May 2006): www.frieze .com/issue/article/the_art_of_war.

54. Ibid.

55. See Deleuze and Guattari, "The Smooth and the Striated," in *A Thousand Plateaus*, 474–500.

56. Weizman, "The Art of War."

57. Ibid.

58. Ibid.

59. Ibid.

60. Connolly, *Neuropolitics*, 137.

CHAPTER 8

1. An earlier and shorter version of this chapter has been published as "Violence and Laughter: Paradoxes of Nomadic Thought in Postcolonial Cinema," in *Deleuze and the Postcolonial*, ed. Simone Bignall and Paul Patton (Edinburgh: Edinburgh University Press, 2010), 201–20.

2. Stephan Sanders, "Meedogenloze filosofische acrobatiek," *de Volks-krant*, 14 August 2009, www.volkskrant.nl/archief_gratis/article1276678.ece/ Meedogenloze_filosofische_acrobatiek.

3. See also Luuk van Middelaar, *Politicide: De Moord op de Politiek in de Franse Filosofie* (Amsterdam: Van Gennep, 1999), who sees this "escape from politics" as a fundamental problem of Deleuzian philosophy (and of twentieth-century French philosophy in general).

4. Sanders, "Meedogenloze filosofisch acrobatiek" (my trans.).

5. Cass R. Sunstein, *Republic.com 2.0* (Princeton, NJ: Princeton University Press, 2007).

6. Deleuze prefaces *Negotiations* with this comment: "Philosophy isn't a Power. . . . Not being a power, philosophy can't battle with the powers that be, but it fights a war without battles, a guerrilla campaign against them. . . . [Philosophy] can only negotiate. Since the powers aren't just external things, but permeate each of us, philosophy throws us all into constant negotiations with, and a guerrilla campaign against, ourselves" (vii). In the same volume Deleuze discusses art as "war-machines" in this philosophical sense (172).

7. Joshua Delpech-Ramey, "Without Art: Peter Hallward's *Out of This World: Deleuze and the Philosophy of Creation*," *Journal for Cultural and Religious Theory* 8, no. 3 (2007): 136–45, 143.

8. I would like to thank Cineart (Amsterdam) for allowing me to see a copy of *The Time That Remains*.

9. On the power of philosophy to invent concepts and thus redescribe the world see Paul Patton, "Redescriptive Philosophy: Deleuze and Guattari's Critical Pragmatism," in *Micropolitics of Media Culture: Reading the Rhizomes of Deleuze and Guattari*, ed. Patricia Pisters (Amsterdam: Amsterdam University Press, 2001), 29–42.

10. Gayatri Spivak, "Can the Subaltern Speak?" in *Colonial Discourse and Post-Colonial Theory: A Reader*, ed. Patrick Williams and Laura Chrisman (New York: Columbia University Press, 1994), 66–111. For a reevaluation of Deleuze in respect to postcolonial theory see Simone Bignall and Paul Patton, eds., *Deleuze and the Postcolonial* (Edinburgh: Edinburgh University Press, 2010). See also Paul Patton, *Deleuze and the Political* (London: Routledge, 2000).

11. See Deleuze, *Difference and Repetition*, 138.

12. Spivak, "Can the Subaltern Speak?" 74.

13. Ibid., 68.

14. Christopher Miller, "We Shouldn't Judge Deleuze and Guattari: A Response to Eugene Holland," *Research in African Literature* 34, no. 3 (2003), 129–41. See also Christopher Miller, "The Postidentitarian Predicament in the Footnotes of *A Thousand Plateaus*: Nomadology, Anthropology, and Authority," *Diacritics* 23, no. 3 (1993), 6–35.

15. Spivak, "Can the Subaltern Speak?" 76.

16. Miller, "We Shouldn't Judge Deleuze and Guattari," 134.

17. Julie Wuthnow, "Deleuze in the Postcolonial: On Nomads and Indigenous Politics," *Feminist Theory* 3, no. 2 (2002): 183–200, 184.

18. Ibid., 189.

19. Peter Hallward, *Out of This World: Deleuze and the Philosophy of Creation* (London: Verso, 2006), 161.

20. Hallward explains Deleuze's creation as "primordially and essentially self-differing, and its 'self-differentiation is the movement of a virtuality which actualizes itself'" (ibid., 27).

21. Ibid., 164.

22. See, e.g., Delpech-Ramey, "Without Art"; Stephen Shaviro, "Hallward on Deleuze," www.shaviro.com/Blog/?p=567 (2007); and Gregory J. Seigworth, "Little Affect: Hallward's Deleuze," http://rime.tees.ac.uk/cmach/Reviews/rev65.htm (2007).

23. Marks, *The Skin of Film*, 60.

24. Janet Harbord, *The Evolution of Film: Rethinking Film Studies* (Cambridge, UK: Polity, 2007), 157–58.

25. Gilles Deleuze, *Pure Immanence: Essays on a Life*, trans. A. Boyman (New York: Zone Books, 2001), 28.

26. Deleuze, *The Movement-Image*, 160–77.

27. Ibid., 171.

28. After seeing *Lebanon* (Samuel Maoz, 2009), which depicts the Israeli invasion of Lebanon in 1982 as seen through the eyes of young Israeli soldiers in a tank, the image of the tank also becomes less symbolic (infused with the suffocating and horrifying actuality of soldiers inside the tank). *Lebanon*, for all its emphasis on the subjective traumatic experience of war situations, is a contemporary neuro-image as well. It presents a brain-screen from an Israeli point of view that is underneath the official ideology. This does not make state politics less important or influential. But it is significant that in contemporary media culture the micropolitical dimension, underneath the macropolitical, is addressed and expressed from all points of view (this is where we become "impersonal" and can connect before returning to the macropolitical dimensions). I will return to this point in the next chapter. Here I want to remark that it is significant that recent Israeli cinema critically and micropolitically investigates official political history.

29. In "The Actual and the Virtual" Deleuze argues, "There is no pure actual object. Every actual is surrounded by a mist of virtual images . . . Virtual images react to the actual" (Gilles Deleuze and Claire Parnet, "L'actuel et le virtuel," in *Dialogues* [Paris: Edition Flammarion, 1996], 183–84 [my trans.]).

30. Deleuze and Guattari, *A Thousand Plateaus*, 187.

31. Deleuze, *The Time-Image*, 215–24.

32. For a more elaborate account of this problem see Patricia Pisters, "Arresting the Flux of Images and Sounds: Free Indirect Discourse and the Dialectics of Political Cinema," in *Deleuze and the Contemporary World*, ed. Ian Buchanan and Adrian Parr (Edinburgh: Edinburgh University Press, 2006), 175–93.

33. Stuart Hall, "New Ethnicities," in *Critical Dialogues in Cultural Studies*, ed. D. Morley and K. Chen (London: Routledge, 1996), 441–49.

34. Deleuze, *The Time-Image*, 222.

35. Ibid.

36. Suleiman interview, *Divine Intervention*, dir. Elia Suleiman (2002; Amsterdam: A-Film, 2003), DVD. See also "A Chat with Palestinian Filmmaker Elia Suleiman," www.youtube.com/watch?v=bSdme1UrpLk.

37. Deleuze, *The Time-Image*, 243.

38. Ibid., 215.

39. Deleuze, *Two Regimes of Madness*, 338.

40. A dialogue between Simone Bitton (director of the documentary *The Wall*, 2004) and Elia Suleiman begins with a remark by Bitton on the necessity of telling such stories differently, since none of the classic versions are doing sufficient justice to the madness of the situation and to the interplay between fictions and realities. While acknowledging the similarities in their approach to political reality, both directors also adhere to their respective traditions of documentary

and fiction film. See "Simone Bitton et Elia Suleiman: Paris, 7 May 2005," www
.youtube.com/watch?v=Q3uNompSM_U&feature=related.

41. Wuthnow, "Deleuze in the Postcolonial," 184.

42. For rigorous analyses of the concept of the "nomad" see Rosi Braidotti,
*Nomadic Subjects: Embodiment and Sexual Difference in Contemporary Feminist
Theory*, 2nd ed. (New York: Columbia University Press, 2011); Ronald Bogue,
"Apology for Nomadology," *Interventions* 6, no. 2 (2004): 169–79; and Eugene
Holland, *Nomad Citizenship and Global Democracy* (London: Continuum, 2009).

43. Gilles Deleuze, "Nomadic Thought," in *Desert Islands and Other Texts,
1953–1974*, ed. David Lapoujade, trans. Michael Taormina (Los Angeles:
Semiotext(e), 2004), 252–61.

44. Suleiman interview, *Divine Intervention*, dir. Elia Suleiman (2002; Amsterdam: A-Film, 2003), DVD.

45. Harbord, *The Evolution of Film*, 159.

46. Deleuze, "Nomadic Thought," 255.

47. Ibid.

48. Ibid., 257.

49. See also Genevieve Lloyd, *Providence Lost* (Cambridge, MA: Harvard
University Press, 2008), 267–68.

50. Delpech-Ramey, "Without Art," 139.

51. Deleuze, "Nomadic Thought," 258.

52. René Schérer, "*Homo tantum*—L'impersonnel: une politique," in *Gilles
Deleuze, une vie philosophique*, ed. Eric Alliez (Paris: Institut Synthelabo, 1998),
25–42, 33.

53. Deleuze, *Pure Immanence*, 28.

54. Schérer "*Homo tantum*," 36.

55. Frantz Fanon, *The Wretched of the Earth*, trans. C. Farrington (New York:
Grove, 1963), 3.

56. Ibid., 106.

57. Paola Marrati, "Against the Doxa: Politics of Immanence and Becoming-
Minoritarian," in *Micropolitics of Media Culture*, ed. Patricia Pisters, 205–220,
214.

58. Kay Dickinson, "The Palestinian Road (Block) Movie: Everyday Geog-
raphies of Second Intifada Cinema," in *Cinema at the Periphery*, ed. Dina Iordonova, David Martin-Jones, and Belén Vidal (Detroit: Wayne State University
Press, 2010), 137–55, 148.

59. Elia Suleiman, *The Time That Remains*, interview, Cannes Film Festival,
2009, www.youtube.com/watch?v=qaLAZvXbqBo.

60. Marks, *The Skin of Film*, 42.

61. For the complete translated text see www.arabicmusictranslation.com
/2007/04/natacha-atlas-why-are-we-fighting-leysh.html. Addressing explicitly

many periods of history and the long conflict between Israel and Palestine ("between us there is a long history"), this song of Natacha Atlas's is bringing back "the whole of the past" as much as it is opening "the whole of the future," as is characteristic for the third synthesis of time.

62. Also significant is the beginning of the film, where Suleiman is in the back of a taxi. It is night, and heavy rainstorms block the view. The Israeli driver stops the car. Unable to see anything or to move any further, he asks himself, "Where am I?" Of course this is a rhetorical and allegorical scene that refers to the disorienting madness of the political situation, just like the scene where Israeli soldiers in a patrol car announce curfew to dancing youngsters and Suleiman frames the soldiers as imprisoned behind the iron bars of the car window in close-up. In a long shot he then shows how they actually also move to the rhythm of the music that the young Palestinians in the club continue to play and dance to. Their bodies speak of an intensity that is quite different from the order of words that come out of their mouths.

63. "Simone Bitton et Elia Suleiman: Paris, 7 May 2005."

64. Bitton's more recent film *Rachel* (2009) is about the death of Rachel Corrie, an American who came to Palestine to help protect Palestinians displaced from their homes. An IDF bulldozer crushed her in front of a Palestinian house in 2003.

65. Another interesting discussion is about the difference between documentary and fiction films. Bitton argues that in a fiction film when a person dies, you can be moved while knowing the person will get up and live on, which makes it different from the death of a person in a documentary. Differently, Suleiman insists that when a person dies in a fiction film, this is a sign of real death and thus can be just as powerful. To Bitton's "It's only cinema" he suggests that documentary "is only reality, and it can be false." Nevertheless, they both agree that their films have a lot in common in the mixture of fiction and documentary.

66. As I indicated earlier in this chapter, both filmmakers stand for a much larger group of Palestinian and Israeli filmmakers that address the present conditions explicitly in their films. I would like to insist that with all the emphasis I have put here on the Palestinian experience of the problem, I do not at all imply that the history of the Jewish side, and the importance of Israel for the Jewish people, could ever be forgotten. Writing most of this book in Weimar and having visited the memorial sites of Buchenwald, I cannot emphasize enough the importance of remembering the Holocaust. But it seems therefore all the more painful that new walls, new ghettos are now being made in both Palestine and Israel.

CHAPTER 9

1. An earlier and shorter version of this chapter has been published as "Logistics of Perception 2.0: Multiple Screen Aesthetics in Iraq War Films," *Film-Philosophy Journal* 14, no.1 (2010): www.film-philosophy.com/index.php/f-p/article/view/221/179.

2. Nicholas Mirzoeff, *Watching Babylon: The War in Iraq and Global Visual Culture* (New York: Routledge, 2005), 178.

3. Ibid., 67.

4. Other films include *The Mark of Cain* (Marc Munden, 2007), about the British troops in Iraq; *Grace Is Gone* (James Strouse, 2007), about a father of two daughters who receives the message of his wife having been killed in Iraq; and *Rendition* (Gavin Hood, 2007), which deals with secret detention facilities outside the United States used to interrogate suspects in the War on Terror.

5. See also http://en.wikipedia.org/wiki/Category:Iraq_War_documentaries.

6. Paul Virilio, *War and Cinema: The Logistics of Perception*, trans. Patrick Miller (London: Verso, 1989), 7.

7. Ibid., 6.

8. Ibid., 8.

9. Ibid., 17.

10. Jean Baudrillard, *Simulacra and Simulations*, trans. Paul Foss, Paul Patton, and Philip Beitchman (New York: Semiotext(e), 1983), 5–6.

11. Jean Baudrillard, "The Gulf War Did Not Take Place," in *Jean Baudrillard Selected Writings*, ed. Mark Poster (Cambridge, UK: Polity, 2001), 231–53, 242.

12. Based on the experiences of Anthony Swofford, a former marine who served during Operations Desert Shield and Desert Storm, Sam Mendes's film *Jarhead* (2005) shows how even for the soldiers on the ground, waiting in the desert, this was a nonwar.

13. Baudrillard, "The Gulf War Did Not Take Place," 232.

14. Ibid., 236.

15. Paul Virilio, *The Desert Screen: War at the Speed of Light*, trans. Michael Degener (London: Athlone Press, 2001), 41.

16. Paul Virilio, *The Vision Machine*, trans. Julie Rose (London: BFI, 1994), 47, 49.

17. Paul Virilio, *Art as Far as the Eye Can See*, trans. Julie Rose (Oxford: Berg, 2007), 20.

18. Ibid., 21.

19. Mirzoeff, *Watching Babylon*, 97.

20. Ibid., 87.

21. Ibid., 74.

22. Ibid., 77.

23. Deepa Kumar, "Media, War, and Propaganda: Strategies of Information Management During the 2003 Iraq War," in *Key Readings in Media Today*, ed. B. E. Duffy and J. Turow (London: Routledge, 2009), 441–61, 450.

24. Mirzoeff, *Watching Babylon*, 14.

25. In this respect the Israeli animated film *Waltz with Bashir* (Ari Folman, 2008) could be mentioned as well.

26. Brian De Palma, "Reasons for Making *Redacted*," http://nl.youtube.com/watch?v=52dC14Od5Ks (and follow-up links of this press conference at the New York Film Festival).

27. Anne Friedberg, "Virilio's Screen: The Work of Metaphor in the Age of Technological Convergence." *Journal of Visual Culture* 3, no. 2 (2004): 183–93, 183.

28. Jay Bolter and Richard Grusin, *Remediation: Understanding New Media* (Cambridge, MA: MIT Press, 1999).

29. Bill Nichols has introduced the genre of reflexive documentary. Although initially meant to indicate documentaries reflecting on their own process, it also has come to designate films that reflect on more general questions of the events portrayed. See Bill Nichols, *Representing Reality: Issues and Concepts in Documentary* (Bloomington: Indiana University Press, 1991).

30. Walid el Houri and Dima Saber, "Filming Resistance: A Hezbollah Strategy," *Radical History Review* 106 (2010): 70–85.

31. Ibid., 81.

32. Andrew Exum, "The Spectacle of War: Insurgent Video Propaganda and Western Response," *Arab Media and Society* (2008): www.arabmediasociety.com /index.php?article=672; quoted in El Houri and Saber, "Filming Resistance," 79.

33. Deleuze and Guattari, *A Thousand Plateaus*, 400.

34. Felicity Colman, "Affective Imagery: Screen Militarism," in *Gilles Deleuze: Image and Text 8*, ed. Eugene Holland, Daniel Smith, and Charles Stivale (London: Continuum, 2009), 143–59.

35. See "Blackwater in Iraq," www.youtube.com/watch?v=EwjBSwvidvY.

36. Colman, "Affective Imagery," 148–49.

37. Ibid., 144.

38. Colman, "Affective Imagery," 151–52.

39. John Protevi, "Affect, Agency and Responsibility: The Act of Killing in the Age of Cyborgs," *Phenomenology and the Cognitive Sciences* 7, no. 3 (2008), 405–13. Quotes here are from the draft version at www.protevi.com/john /Cyborg_Killing_final_draft.pdf (1–15).

40. For extended and insightful analyses of *America's Army* see David Nieborg, "*America's Army*: More Than a Game?" in *Transforming Knowledge into Action Through Gaming and Simulation*, ed. Thomas Eberle and Wille Christian Kriz (Munchen: Sagsaga, 2004), CD-ROM (downloadable at www.GameSpace .nl); and David Nieborg, "Changing the Rules of Engagement. Tapping into the Popular Culture of America's Army, the Official U.S. Army Computer Game," master's thesis, 2005 (downloadable at www.GameSpace.nl).

41. See http://nl.youtube.com/watch?v=-8zJTwJ_rGU.

42. Protevi explains this guilt as "proto-empathic identification which produces psychological trauma at the sight of blood and guts of the killed enemy, despite the common practice of dehumanisation of the enemy" (Protevi, "Affect, Agency and Responsibility," 1).

43. Later in the film Brandon visits the wounded soldier, Rico, in military hospital. Rico is of Latin American descent and argues that if he had been

stop-lossed and killed, it would at least make sense because his family would then have obtained a green card.

44. In *The War Tapes* the soldiers' most traumatic moment is a very similar accident, when the soldiers hit an innocent girl, who, while selling cookies, is completely crushed by the military vehicle. Although the soldiers admit that this image will be forever in their heads, they manage to keep themselves together, unlike the soldiers in *In the Valley of Elah*.

45. Nicholas Mirzoeff, "Invisible Empire: Visual Culture, Embodied Spectacle, and Abu Ghraib," *Radical History Review* 95 (2006): 21–44.

46. Ibid., 23.

47. Ibid., 36.

48. Rodowick, *The Virtual Life of Film*, 146.

49. Ibid., 147.

50. The documentary *Heart of Jenin* (Leon Geller and Marcus Vetter, 2009) is much more interesting and politically sharp in this respect. The filmmakers follow Ismael Khatib, who in 2005 lost his twelve-year-old son when he was killed by Israeli soldiers. After the son's death the family decided to donate his organs to six Israeli people. In the film the father visits three of the organ recipients, one of whom is an Orthodox Jewish girl, the others a Bedouin boy and a Druze girl. Refusing to fight, enabling life, is an act of resistance for this father, who has set up a center for children and reopened a cinema in Jenin. The film of Khatib's journey through Israel shows the complexities of the conflict: "deep-seated animosity, hardened judgments, and heartfelt generosity" are felt in the encounters of the different groups. The encounter between the Orthodox Jewish family and Khatib and his brother is especially moving in the courage that both parties have in agreeing on a filmed meeting. The film can also be seen online at *Wideangle*, www.pbs.org/wnet/wideangle/episodes/heart-of-jenin/video-full-episode/5120/.

51. The documentary *Iraq in Fragments* (James Longley, 2006) presents the war from three different Iraqi perspectives.

52. Adrian Parr, *Deleuze and Memorial Culture: Desire, Singular Memory and the Politics of Trauma* (Edinburgh: Edinburgh University Press, 2008).

53. Ibid., 98.

54. Foucault, quoted in ibid., 101.

55. Mirzoeff, "Invisible Empire," 33.

56. Ibid., 37–38.

57. Ibid., 36–37.

58. Parr, *Deleuze and Memorial Culture*, 101.

59. Ibid., 107–8.

60. John Mullarkey, "Forget the Virtual: Bergson, Actualism, and the Refraction of Reality," *Continental Philosophy Review* 37 (2004), 469–93.

61. Ibid., 471.

CONCLUSION

1. Deleuze, *The Time-Image*, 264. Deleuze is here obviously referring to Benjamin.

2. Deleuze, *The Movement-Image*, 206.

3. Ibid.

4. Michael Hardt and Antonio Negri, *Empire* (Cambridge, MA: Harvard University Press, 2000).

5. See Dave Crocker, "E-mail History," www.livinginternet.com/e/ei.htm.

6. See Lipovetsky and Serroy, *L'écran global*, 71. Lipovetsky and Serroy situate the emergence of hyper- or ultramodern cinema in the 1980s.

7. Jean Baudrillard, *The Spirit of Terrorism*, trans. Chris Turner (London: Verso, 2002), 28.

8. Ibid.

9. See, e.g., Dominic Pettman, "From September 11 to 7-11: Popular Propaganda and the Internet's War on Terrorism," Largeur.com, 5 January 2002; and Alison Young, "Images in the Aftermath of Trauma: Responding to September 11th," *Crime, Media, and Culture* 30, no. 3 (2007): 30–48. See also Jenkins, *Convergence Culture*.

10. Gazzaniga, *The Mind's Past*, xi–xii.

11. Warren Neidich, "Neuropower," *Atlantica Magazine of Art and Thought* 48/49 (2009): 119–65, 123.

12. See, e.g., Dana Rosenblatt, "Behavioral Screening: The Future of Airport Security?" 17 December 2008, http://edition.cnn.com/2008/TECH/12/02/airport.security/index.html?eref=rss_topstories; and Gareth Beavis, "Don't Think About Bombs, Don't Think About Bombs," *TechRadar.com*, 11 May 2009, www.techradar.com/news/world-of-tech/eu-tests-brain-scanning-to-catch-terrorists-597786.

13. James Canton, *The Extreme Future: The Top Trends That Will Reshape the World in the Next 20 Years* (New York: Plume, 2007), x.

14. Richard Grusin refers to contemporary media culture as a culture of premediation and anticipation that describes in another way a context of the neuro-image. See Richard Grusin, *Premediation: Affect and Mediality After 9/11* (Houndmills, Basingstoke: Palgrave, Macmillan, 2010). See also his blog, http://premediation.blogspot.com/.

15. Kolkman and Vaughan, "Henri Bergson's *Creative Evolution* 100 Years Later" (see above, Chapter 4n20).

Index

Freddie Rokem, *Philosophers and Thespians: Thinking Performance*

Roberto Esposito, *Communitas: The Origin and Destiny of Community*

Vilashini Cooppan, *Worlds Within: National Narratives and Global Connections in Postcolonial Writing*

Josef Früchtl, *The Impertinent Self: A Heroic History of Modernity*

Frank Ankersmit, Ewa Domanska, and Hans Kellner, eds., *Re-Figuring Hayden White*

Michael Rothberg, *Multidirectional Memory: Remembering the Holocaust in the Age of Decolonization*

Jean-François Lyotard, *Enthusiasm: The Kantian Critique of History*

Ernst van Alphen, Mieke Bal, and Carel Smith, eds., *The Rhetoric of Sincerity*

Stéphane Mosès, *The Angel of History: Rosenzweig, Benjamin, Scholem*

Pierre Hadot, *The Present Alone Is Our Happiness: Conversations with Jeannie Carlier and Arnold I. Davidson*

Alexandre Lefebvre, *The Image of the Law: Deleuze, Bergson, Spinoza*

Samira Haj, *Reconfiguring Islamic Tradition: Reform, Rationality, and Modernity*

Diane Perpich, *The Ethics of Emmanuel Levinas*

Marcel Detienne, *Comparing the Incomparable*

François Delaporte, *Anatomy of the Passions*

René Girard, *Mimesis and Theory: Essays on Literature and Criticism, 1959-2005*

Richard Baxstrom, *Houses in Motion: The Experience of Place and the Problem of Belief in Urban Malaysia*

Jennifer L. Culbert, *Dead Certainty: The Death Penalty and the Problem of Judgment*

Samantha Frost, *Lessons from a Materialist Thinker: Hobbesian Reflections on Ethics and Politics*

Regina Mara Schwartz, *Sacramental Poetics at the Dawn of Secularism: When God Left the World*

Gil Anidjar, *Semites: Race, Religion, Literature*

Ranjana Khanna, *Algeria Cuts: Women and Representation, 1830 to the Present*

Esther Peeren, *Intersubjectivities and Popular Culture: Bakhtin and Beyond*

Eyal Peretz, *Becoming Visionary: Brian De Palma's Cinematic Education of the Senses*

Diana Sorensen, *A Turbulent Decade Remembered: Scenes from the Latin American Sixties*

Hubert Damisch, *A Childhood Memory by Piero della Francesca*

José van Dijck, *Mediated Memories in the Digital Age*

Dorothea von Mücke, *The Rise of the Fantastic Tale*

Marc Redfield, *The Politics of Aesthetics: Nationalism, Gender, Romanticism*

Emmanuel Levinas, *On Escape*

Dan Zahavi, *Husserl's Phenomenology*

Rodolphe Gasché, *The Idea of Form: Rethinking Kant's Aesthetics*

Michael Naas, *Taking on the Tradition: Jacques Derrida and the Legacies of Deconstruction*

Herlinde Pauer-Studer, ed., *Constructions of Practical Reason: Interviews on Moral and Political Philosophy*

Jean-Luc Marion, *Being Given That: Toward a Phenomenology of Givenness*

Theodor W. Adorno and Max Horkheimer, *Dialectic of Enlightenment*

Ian Balfour, *The Rhetoric of Romantic Prophecy*

Martin Stokhof, *World and Life as One: Ethics and Ontology in Wittgenstein's Early Thought*

Gianni Vattimo, *Nietzsche: An Introduction*

Jacques Derrida, *Negotiations: Interventions and Interviews, 1971–1998*, ed. Elizabeth Rottenberg

Brett Levinson, *The Ends of Literature: The Latin American "Boom" in the Neoliberal Marketplace*

Timothy J. Reiss, *Against Autonomy: Cultural Instruments, Mutualities, and the Fictive Imagination*

Hent de Vries and Samuel Weber, eds., *Religion and Media*

Niklas Luhmann, *Theories of Distinction: Re-Describing the Descriptions of Modernity*, ed. and introd. William Rasch

Johannes Fabian, *Anthropology with an Attitude: Critical Essays*

Michel Henry, *I Am the Truth: Toward a Philosophy of Christianity*

Gil Anidjar, *"Our Place in Al-Andalus": Kabbalah, Philosophy, Literature in Arab-Jewish Letters*

Hélène Cixous and Jacques Derrida, *Veils*

F. R. Ankersmit, *Historical Representation*

F. R. Ankersmit, *Political Representation*

Elissa Marder, *Dead Time: Temporal Disorders in the Wake of Modernity (Baudelaire and Flaubert)*

Reinhart Koselleck, *The Practice of Conceptual History: Timing History, Spacing Concepts*

Niklas Luhmann, *The Reality of the Mass Media*

Hubert Damisch, *A Theory of /Cloud/: Toward a History of Painting*